Business Law

Made Simple

The Made Simple series
has been created
especially for self-education
but can equally well
be used as
an aid to group study.
However complex the subject,
the reader is taken
step by step,
clearly and methodically,
through the course. Each volume
has been prepared by experts,
taking account of
modern educational requirements,
to ensure the most
effective way of
acquiring knowledge.

In the same series

Accounting
Acting and Stagecraft
Administration in Business
Advertising
Basic
Biology
Book-keeping
British Constitution
Business Calculations
Business Communication
Business Law
Calculus
Chemistry
Child Development
Commerce
Computer Electronics
Computer Programming
Computer Programming Languages in Practice
Computer Typing
Cost and Management Accounting
Data Processing
Economic and Social Geography
Economics
Education
Electricity
Electronics
Elements of Banking
English
First Aid
French
Geology
German
Graphic Communication
Italian
Journalism
Latin
Law
Management
Marketing
Marketing Analysis and Forecasting
Mathematics
Modelling and Beauty Care
Modern European History
Money and Banking
MSX
Music
Office Practice
Personnel Management
Philosophy
Photography
Physical Geography
Physics
Politics
Practical Typewriting
Psychiatry
Psychology
Russian
Salesmanship
Secretarial Practice
Social Services
Sociology
Spanish
Statistics
Taxation
Teeline Shorthand
Typing

Business Law

Made Simple

Abdul Kadar, LLM, BA(Hons) in Law, FBSC, Cert Ed
Ken Hoyle, BSc(Econ)
Geoffrey Whitehead, BSc(Econ)

MADE SIMPLE
BOOKS

HEINEMANN PROFESSIONAL PUBLISHING

Made Simple Books
An imprint of Heinemann Professional Publishing Ltd
Halley Court, Jordan Hill, Oxford OX2 8EJ

OXFORD LONDON MELBOURNE AUCKLAND

First published 1984
Reprinted 1985
Second edition 1987
Reprinted 1988

British Library Cataloguing in Publication Data
Kadar, Abdul
Business law made simple. – (Made simple books, ISSN 0265–0541)
1. Corporation law – England
I. Title II. Hoyle, Ken
III. Whitehead, Geoffrey IV. Series
344.206′65 KD2057

ISBN 0 434 98564 3

Made and printed in Great Britain by
Richard Clay Ltd, Bungay, Suffolk

Foreword

Business people today face an extensive range of legal restrictions on their activities, and a climate of business law much less favourable to them than at any time in the past. As one commentator said, the traditional rule of *caveat emptor* (let the buyer beware) has almost been changed into *caveat venditor* (let the seller beware). Not only have the suppliers of goods and services come under enormous pressure in their actual business arrangements, but the climate of legal restraints surrounding these activities, administrative and ecological controls, have become steadily more burdensome.

This book seeks to set out the chief features of all the major branches of law affecting businesses. It covers contract law, the sale of goods, the supply of services, business organisation, transport, banking, insurance, administrative law, the law of tort and the law of property.

It will be helpful for students of business law and commercial law studying for all the major examinations of professional bodies, such as the Association of Certified Accountants, the Institute of Chartered Secretaries, the Institute of Commercial Management, the Institute of Freight Forwarders, etc. It will also be helpful for BTEC students taking options in business law, for students of the Chartered Institute of Bankers and for degree students taking commercial law.

In writing this book we have been greatly assisted by certain firms who have sanctioned the use of copyright material. Their courtesy is acknowledged overleaf. We should particularly like to thank Mr T. G. Reeday for his painstaking reading of the text, Mr A. F. Somerville Ford of the Bournemouth Business Studies Centre for his helpful comments, and Robert Postema, publisher of the Made Simple series, for his encouragement during the preparation of the book.

ABDUL KADAR
KEN HOYLE
GEOFFREY WHITEHEAD

Acknowledgements

In preparing this book the following firms and organisations have been very helpful; their courtesy is gratefully acknowledged:

Clearway Publishing Co. and The Law Society, for permission to reproduce three diagrams of the courts.
Butterworth and Co., for permission to reproduce cases from *Cracknell's Law Students' Companion* (Contract) and (Tort).
Witherby and Co. Ltd, for permission to reproduce the 1.1.82 Clauses (A).
Woodhead Faulkner & Co., for permission to reproduce extracts from their publication *Elements of Export Law*.
Formecon Services Ltd, for permission to reproduce a bill of exchange.

Contents

Part 1: The Framework of Business Law

1
Elements of English Law

1.1 A Definition of Law

Law has been defined as follows:

Law is a body of rules for the guidance of human conduct which are imposed upon, and enforced among, the citizens of a given state.

This enduring definition includes three very important features. First, laws are **imposed upon** the citizens of a given state. This implies that there is some sovereign body, which promulgates laws and imposes them from above upon the general body of citizens. There have been many kinds of sovereign bodies in the past, ranging from tyrants on the one hand to democracies (rule by the people) on the other. In the UK the sovereign body is the 'Queen in Parliament', which makes law by enacting 'Acts' of Parliament.

Second, laws must be **enforced among** the citizens of a given state; without enforcement of the law there is no law. There are several elements in enforcement. First, the criminal laws must be policed by a body of police officers with powers of arrest, so that those in breach of the law may be brought before the courts. The courts, whether at low or high levels, decide if a breach of the law has occurred and if appropriate penalties have to be imposed. These can include fines, imprisonment or death on the criminal side, and damages or equitable remedies on the civil side. The penalties imposed by the courts are enforced through the court administration and prison services, who collect fines, or ensure that probation or prison sentences are served in a proper manner.

Finally, laws apply **only within the boundaries of nation states**. The laws apply within the territory of the state to all citizens and non-citizens alike who are resident there, for however short a period. If a breach of the law has occurred, and we can bring the person concerned before the courts, justice can be obtained. It is much more difficult if they are outside the jurisdiction of the courts, for the foreign court may not be prepared to hear the case, or may consider that no breach of the law has occurred. At best we shall be put to extra cost in bringing the case, and finding a lawyer who will represent us. At worst it may be quite impossible to secure justice.

1.2 A Definition of Business Law

The term 'business law' as used in the title of this book, *Business Law Made*

Simple, is much wider than the terms more generally used about laws to do with business. In the past the terms 'commercial law' and 'mercantile law' have been used to describe the laws which control the commercial activities of merchants. Today these terms are too restrictive, although the bodies of law which they describe are of enormous importance to businessmen and businesswomen.

(At this point the authors would like to make a statement about the use of 'sexist' words in this book. It is unfortunate that to date no sovereign body has pronounced on the use of suitable words for describing persons carrying on institutions like businesses who may be both male and female. Long before the present nationwide discussion began, and the Equal Opportunities Commission was appointed, the *Interpretation Act, 1889*, laid it down that 'the male includes the female gender' or, as one wag put it, 'Ever since time immemorial male has embraced female.' The *Interpretation Act, 1978*, re-enacted this same rule. To avoid endless repetitions of the phrases 'business men and business women' and his/her, we have elected to follow the statute. The term 'businessman' should therefore be read as 'businessman/woman' and no slur is intended whatsoever to the female sex.)

Today a businessman is concerned with the whole environment within which he must operate and the laws which govern the various institutions and situations to be found in this environment. The traditional commercial law – of contracts, the sale of goods, the carriage of goods by land, sea and air, payments, etc. – is still a large part of this environment, but there are several other fields to be considered.

Businesses operate within a framework of **administrative law**, which influences many of the things they do. Businesses must observe planning regulations, comply with rules about health and safety at work, and with employment legislation. Another area is that known as the **law of tort**. Torts are civil wrongs. It is a very simple matter for businesses to harm other institutions or individuals, and find themselves facing actions for damages for negligence, nuisance, trespass, defamation and other torts. Another area which has come into prominence in the last half century is the area of **economic law**, which attempts to influence and control the financial and trading practices of firms. Thus the monitoring of restrictive practices, monopoly legislation, the control of prices and incomes, and consumer protection legislation may be considered parts of economic law.

Within the limits imposed by space and cost we shall endeavour to deal with all these topics adequately.

We may therefore define business law as being those areas of law which form the legal environment within which business entities come into existence, enter into business relationships, pursue their activities and achieve their aims.

1.3 About This Book

This book attempts to cover the business law requirements of several bodies of students, particularly those studying for examinations run by professional bodies such as the various accountancy institutions, the Institute of Bankers, the Institute of Commercial Management and the various institutes in the transport and freight-forwarding fields. Another large group are those students preparing for examinations controlled by the Business and Technician Education Council, particularly the BTEC National and Higher National courses. Many students reading business law as a background subject for degrees in economics, accountancy, business administration, etc., will find this book helpful.

The study of law usually proceeds in the following way. The student first reads elements of English law, an introductory subject, and then proceeds to specialise; in this case in business law. We should therefore assume that the student already has some background in the study of law, and that the present volume can develop this background at once to cover the specialist subject of business law. Unfortunately, there will be many readers who do not already have such a background, and some compromise is necessary. We therefore have some introductory chapters which cover the framework of English law – its development and the system of courts. In addition, wherever necessary throughout what is inevitably a complex book, we begin each part with a re-statement of basic principles to assist those who have not pursued a course in elements of law. Such readers are recommended to read *Law Made Simple*, a companion volume to this book.

Cases. The study of cases is an important element in English law. In this volume we have kindly been permitted to quote cases from the series *Cracknell's Law Students' Companion.* This series consists of several volumes, of which the most useful to students of business law are:

(*a*) *Commercial Law*, by G. H. H. Glasgow and D. Grace
(*b*) *Contract*, by Vincent Powell-Smith
(*c*) *Torts*, by M. G. Lloyd
(*d*) *Company Law*, by F. E. Smith
(*e*) *Conflict of Laws*, by M. R. Chesterman
(*f*) *Constitutional Law & English Legal System*, by W. H. Holland

The student is strongly recommended to obtain at least some of these titles, which will be of enduring interest.

Students are often perplexed to know how they are expected to use their knowledge of cases in examinations. Ideally one should be able to name any case that is relevant to the discussion in hand, and quote the year in which it was decided. It is then helpful to be able to give the facts of the case and the ***ratio decidendi***. A decision has three basic elements: findings of material facts, direct or inferential; the statement of the principle of law applied to these facts; and the judgement based on the combined effects of the two. It is the statement of the principle of law contained in the decision that is the vital element and which is termed the *ratio decidendi* (the reason for the decision). This is the binding element and in a subsequent case the judge is bound to apply it if the facts are similar. The actual rules about following precedent are explained later (see Chapter 2), because higher courts are not bound to follow decisions made in lower courts so that the hierarchy of courts enters into the picture. The student should therefore be able to show that the facts are similar, and recommend that the precedent is followed. If the facts are not exactly similar the case under discussion may be 'distinguished' from the precedent, but it may still be 'persuasive' even if it is not binding. The student will recommend a decision which is appropriate for the set of facts under consideration in the question he is attempting to answer.

In order to assist students to recall the names of cases, the facts, etc., these have usually been featured in the revision pages at the end of each chapter. They should be learned by heart, using the self-testing pages. Even so, it is possible that in the heat of an examination some detail will not be recalled. In that case, give what you can remember. For example, it is better to say:

'In one case in 1908 a tailor who had supplied eleven fancy waistcoats to a student failed in his action to secure payment because he could not establish that the waistcoats were necessaries, since the parents of the student proved that their son was already adequately supplied with clothing.'

This does not tell us the name of the case (*Nash v. Inman*) but it does tell us a great deal, and is clearly worth a few marks.

1.4 The Divisions of the Law

Law is an enormous subject and some specialisation is essential. A complete classification would require a very detailed chart, but the more important branches of the law are displayed in Fig. 1.1. This is largely self-explanatory, but a few points require further explanation. These are:

(*a*) **International law** may be divided into two parts. One is the law about the mutual relationship between states. This may be described as public international law. It is also concerned with international organisations, e.g. the United Nations Organisation and its associated bodies. International law consists of the general principles of law recognised by civilised nations, and internationally recognised customs, international conventions or treaties, decisions of the World Court and the teachings of the most highly qualified publicists of the various nations.

The other branch of international law, private international law, is sometimes called the 'conflict of laws'. It concerns the difficulties which arise when legal disputes occur between parties from different nations. Thus if an Englishman does business with Japan, which body of laws shall be used to decide any dispute, which courts shall have jurisdiction, to whom should appeals lie, how should damages be decided, in what currency, and how shall payment be compelled? These are difficult problems.

(*b*) **Municipal Law.** The term 'municipal' in common use refers to the administration of a city or town. Its use in law is wider – it refers to a nation state. It is thus the opposite of international law. Municipal law is the sum total of law that applies in a particular realm, whether constitutional, administrative, criminal or private. Hence all the branches of law mentioned in Fig. 1.1 (except international law) are part of municipal law.

(*c*) **Public Law and Private Law.** Public law is primarily concerned with those cases in which the state is involved, as representing the public in

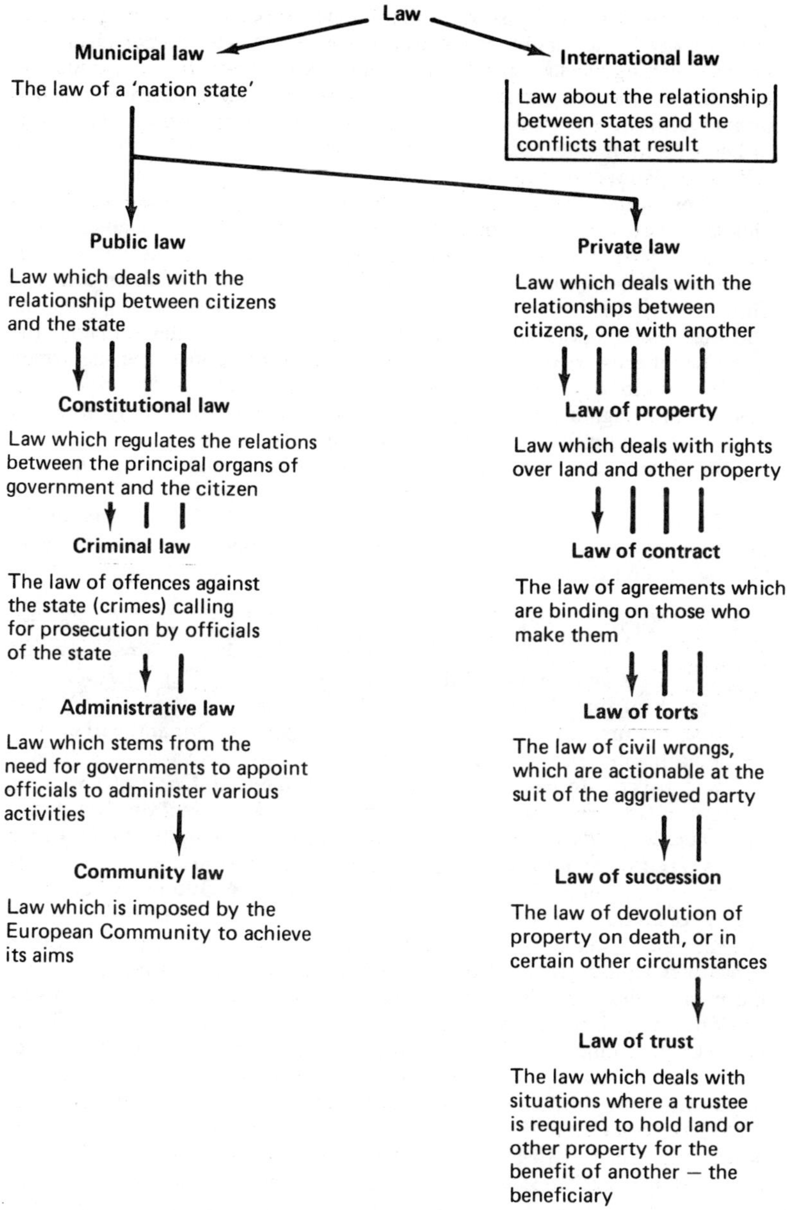

Fig. 1.1. The branches of the law

general. Thus the public is interested in the prevention of crime, so that criminal law is actionable officially by the **prosecution** of **offenders**. The branches of public law are shown in the chart. Private law includes all branches of the law which involve disputes between citizens, where one individual has a complaint against the other. The various matters are said to be 'actionable at the suit of the aggrieved party'. The aggrieved party is called the **plaintiff** who **sues** the **defendant**.

(*d*) **Constitutional and Administrative Law.** Constitutional law is that law which regulates the relations between the principal organs of government and the citizen. It deals with such topics as the monarch and the royal prerogative; the executive in the form of the Prime Minister and the Government; the relationship and functions of the House of Commons and the House of Lords; the position of the courts and the judiciary; the structure of local government; and the status of the police and the armed forces. An understanding of constitutional law enables citizens to appreciate their rights, e.g. freedom of person, freedom of property, freedom of expression and freedom to hold meetings, processions, etc.

There is no exact demarcation between constitutional law and administrative law, as both are concerned with the exercise and control of governmental powers. While the former is concerned with the structure of the primary organs of government, the latter is concerned with the functioning of official agencies providing various services.

Since most branches of public law involve penalties at one stage or another, which thus involve the prosecution of offenders, we may say that criminal law is an extensive body of law brought into effect wherever there is a breach of public law. By contrast, private law is often spoken of as civil law, because it is available to the general public, civilians, rather than to the authorities.

There are certain basic differences between the two. **Criminal law** is the concern of the state, and a criminal case is normally brought by the state – or rather the police as the agents of the state – against an individual. The case is reported as *R. v. Bloggs* (the surname of the accused). *R.* stands for *Rex* or *Regina*, in Latin, meaning 'the King' or 'the Queen'. However, in respect of certain crimes, e.g. malicious prosecution or false imprisonment, any member of the public can commence criminal proceedings. **Civil law** is concerned with regulating the relationships of an individual with other individuals and comprises contract law, tort, the law of property and succession, family law, etc. The cases are reported as *Smith v. Bloggs*, Smith being the surname of the plaintiff and Bloggs the surname of the defendant.

It is wrong to confuse criminal and civil terms. One individual does not prosecute another for breach of contract or some other civil matter. 'Prosecution' is a term used in criminal law. The most famous example of confusion is the 'wooden lie' – a notice reading 'Trespassers will be prosecuted'. Since trespass where no damage is done is nearly always a civil matter between private citizens, it is incorrect to say 'prosecuted'. The good law student feels an uncontrollable impulse to amend such a notice to read 'Trespassers will *not* be prosecuted – but they will be sued'.

Lastly, a successful party in a civil case is awarded monetary compensation called **damages**. Other remedies in the form of **injunctions** or an order of **specific performance** are also available. In a criminal case the **accused**, if found guilty, is fined, or imprisoned according to the penalties laid down for the offence in question.

1.5 The Sources of English Law

Every legal system has its roots, the original sources from which authority is drawn. Sometimes these will only go back as far as some revolutionary overthrow of a previous social order. For example, there cannot be much of Tsarist law which is of influence in Soviet society today. Other revolutions have been less complete. American law still has its roots in English law despite the Declaration of Independence, and the law of England was not greatly changed by the Civil War of 1649 except in the field of constitutional law.

The sources of English business law may be listed as follows:

(*a*) The ancient custom of the realm
(*b*) Common law
(*c*) Equity
(*d*) The law merchant
(*e*) Statute law
(*f*) European Community law
(*g*) Books of authority
(*h*) Other sources

A short account of each of these is desirable.

(*a*) **Ancient Custom of the Realm.** Before the Norman Conquest in 1066 Saxon England was ruled by kings whose power was based on their acceptability to the broad democratic assembly of a tribal society. Every man could speak at the tribal gathering, though in practice a *witenagemot* (meeting of wise men) acted as a parliament. England at that time was divided into various tribal areas such as Mercia, Kent, Wessex and so on. Each tribal area had its own laws based on the original customs of the settlers in question. There were three distinct legal systems applying to different areas of England: the 'Dane law' applied in the coastal areas of northern and north-eastern England; 'Mercian law' applied around the Midlands; and the 'Wessex law' applied in the south and west of England.

The influence of 'ancient custom of the realm' is not great today, but it is still important in one or two areas of law. In particular, in the law of carriage the concept of the 'common carrier of goods' is still important. Carriage is a very ancient activity and inevitably takes the carrier over the hills and far away with our property. In such circumstances we cannot possibly know what is happening to our goods, and the ancient custom held that the carrier was liable for every loss that occurred, whether it was his fault or not. He is said to be like 'an insurer of the goods'. It is true that later the common law developed certain exceptions to this rule, called the 'common law exceptions'. These included Act of God, Act of the King's (or Queen's) enemies, fault of the consignor, fraud of the consignor and inherent vice. If a carrier proved that the loss was due to one of these causes he could escape liability. See Chapter 16.

The Norman kings gradually displaced ancient custom of the realm by a system known as 'common law'. The trouble with ancient custom was that it was not a national system of law, since it depended on the traditions and customs of tribal peoples with different ethnic backgrounds, who were now to be welded into one nation by the Norman nobility who had seized control. The process, which is explained under (*b*) below, was virtually completed by AD 1189. This year became known as the 'limit of legal memory'. After that date all was clear, recorded and remembered; before that date all was vague and uncertain, because no national system of law prevailed. This period is known as 'time immemorial', a time so ancient that it is beyond memory or record. If you wish to establish that you do something by ancient custom of the realm (for example, walk along a footpath from A to B) you should really prove that your great, great, grandfathers did it before AD 1189. In practice you only need to prove that people have been doing it for as long as anyone can remember. This establishes a 'presumption of antiquity' which shifts the 'burden of proof' to the person who seeks to deny you this ancient right. It is up to this person to prove that the right was *not* exercised before AD 1189. The case of *Mercer v. Denne* (*1905*) illustrates the point.

Mercer v. Denne (*1905*). D owned part of a beach where local fishermen had for at least 70 years dried their nets. D wished to build houses on the land, but was prevented, since the presumption of antiquity could not be rebutted by proof that the right was not exercised before AD 1189.

To conclude, we may say that custom is in one sense the principal source of English law since it was the original source of common law, and gave it its broad democratic basis which is rather different from foreign, authoritarian, codes of law.

(*b*) **Common Law.** The mechanism used by the Norman kings to replace ancient custom of the realm by a system of law common to the whole country was the system of assizes, which was only finally abandoned in 1971. The king would appoint judges (originally called 'itinerant justices in Eyre') who travelled round the country, holding sittings (*assises*) whose function was to hear and settle any cases waiting to be tried in the county towns. In so doing they were made aware of many local customs, some of which were better than others. By a process of supporting good customs and rejecting bad customs the general level of law was improved. By making the decisions of judges binding upon other judges a good custom supported in one assizes was bound to be followed if a similar case arose in another area. As a result a 'common law' was formulated and established throughout the country, and inconsistencies between the law in one locality and the law in another locality were overcome. Common law therefore means the law common to all areas of England and Wales. Later it was also applied in Northern Ireland to a very considerable extent, but Scotland has its own, largely distinct, law. The common law is still a vital element in English law today, but it soon became clear that it was not entirely satisfactory. The chief difficulties were as follows:

(i) Action was commenced by the issue of a royal writ – a paper on which one of the more common complaints was written. The claim was required to be stated in an acceptable manner, called the 'form of action'. The writ called on the sheriff to summon a jury to hear the case. The variety of complaints for which an action could be commenced was not large and many cases could not be brought to trial at all because a writ of the type required was not available. For example, there were no writs about negligence in the early days.

(ii) Another defect in the common law was its view that money satisfies all wrongs. The only remedy at common law was, and is, money damages. Although compensation is often all that is required it does not answer every case. Thus if my neighbour's workshop produces unpleasant smells which ruin my enjoyment of my property, it is of no help to me to receive money as compensation. I want him to stop making the unpleasant smells. This requires some sort of court order, an **injunction** to restrain him from continuing the process that is a nuisance.

(iii) The third defect of common law was the pressure that could be exerted by high officials on the legal system. At a time when some barons and earls were as powerful as the king it was often difficult to secure justice against people in high places. Equality before the law is a basic principle of justice, but some people proved to be 'more equal than others' (to use George Orwell's phrase).

The solution was found to lie in bringing such cases before a special court, the Court of Chancery, where equity (Latin *aequitas* = fair) could be achieved.

(*c*) **Equity.** If law is to be respected, and trusted, it must be fair. Complaints about the defects in the common law were made to the king, who appointed the Lord Chancellor to deal with them. The word 'chancel' refers to a place in a church closest to the altar. The chancellor was not only the king's legal adviser and right-hand man, but also his spiritual adviser. The link between justice and religion was closer in those days, and since all were equal in the eyes of God, equity in law was also deemed to be a religious affair. Equity (principles of fairness, or natural justice) guided successive chancellors in their decisions, and the sum total of their legal decisions over the years is spoken of in law as 'equity'. The problems of the common law referred to above were solved by the removal of cases where common law was inadequate to a special, powerful court in London, called the Court of Chancery. How did the Court of Chancery solve the three problems outlined above?

First, the chancellor was second only to the king, and could command the appearance in court of even the highest nobles. They could not influence his decisions or avoid the damages or fines he imposed.

Second, the problem of a shortage of writs was overcome by the chancellor ordering new types of writ as required. It is true that this process eventually caused trouble, because litigants soon found that justice could be obtained more easily in London than at their local courts. The nobles therefore lost the lucrative business carried on in their own courts and forced the king to stop the creation of further writs in an enactment called the Provisions of Oxford (1258). This was later modified in the Statute of Westminster II, 1285, which declared that new writs could be developed if they were similar to writs in existence already. This led to a slow growth in the type of writs, since new writs were acceptable only if they could be proved to be similar to writs already in existence.

Finally, the Court of Chancery solved the problem of the inadequacy of money damages by introducing new 'equity' remedies. The chief of these were the **injunction**, to restrain a defendant from continuing the action complained of by the plaintiff, and **specific performance**. This required the defendant to do what he had promised to do.

Other important contributions made by equity to English law involved the creation of new rights where none had existed before. For example, the whole law of trusts owes its existence to the willingness of equity to recognise and enforce the rights of a beneficiary under a trust. Equity also introduced new procedures which enabled witnesses to be subpoenaed, to compel their attendance at court. Another important development was the process known as 'discovery of documents' which enables a party to a case to inspect the relevant documents in the possession of the other party.

Hence there was a time during the development of English law when there were two parallel sets of laws, one under equity and the other under common law. The Court of Chancery administered equity while the other courts, called the Common Law Courts, administered common law. Where two systems of law exist there is bound to be a conflict sooner or later. These conflicts caused delays, particularly in the Court of Chancery – which was overloaded with work anyway – and eventually it became a byword for slowness and procrastination. The major conflict between common law and equity was resolved in 1616, in the Earl of Oxford's case, with the decision that where there was a conflict between the two, equity should prevail. This rule was given a formal, statutory basis in the *Judicature Acts, 1873–5*. These acts also empowered all courts to give both common law and equity decisions in cases coming before them. The separation between the courts, which had lasted more than five hundred years, was ended. All courts now give appropriate remedies: the common law remedy of money damages if this is adequate for the case in hand; if not, the equitable remedies of injunctions, specific performance, etc. The system of courts established in 1873–5 progressively developed into the present system of courts (see Chapter 2) and the availability of both types of remedy in all courts continues unchanged.

(*d*) **The Law Merchant.** Trade is older than nationality. For thousands of years ships have plied the oceans and kings have welcomed merchants, and accorded them rights of passage and exemption from local taxes. From the earliest times a sophisticated cosmopolitan crowd of merchants moved around the known world, dealing with one another in ways which were not fettered by legal concepts imposed upon them. Their commercial principles such as 'my word is my bond', 'bethink you of my poor honesty' and 'goodwill' had evolved commercial practices of the greatest importance today: freedom of contract; freedom to transfer property; assignability and negotiability; the seal; stoppage in transit; the bill of exchange; the charter-party; general average – these are almost as old as time.

The law's delay was anathema to the early merchants, who settled cases in their own courts quickly. These were often based in ports, like Lubeck in the Baltic –

'What can you want more
Than the old Lubeck law'

goes an old German saying. In ports cases were often settled 'between the tides', while in the 'Piepowder courts' at the inland fairs disputes were settled on the last day of the fair. The origin of this name has been suggested as 'dusty feet – *pieds poudreux*'. The judges were senior members of the merchant community, and since disputes were frequently between local people and the foreign merchants it was usual to have equal numbers of each in the panel who settled cases.

Merchant law was cosmopolitan and uniform wherever trade was conducted. Its privileged system was bound to conflict with the newer concept of a 'nation state' ruled by an autocratic king imposing law from above upon the citizens of his state. The problem was to reconcile the 'law merchant' with the 'common law' of the country, and thus bring the merchants under control without killing the goose that laid the golden eggs.

In England the solution was found in the principle that 'the courts will always uphold the reasonable expectations of businessmen'. This principle is sound because it not only supports the existing practices of merchants, but also covers any sensible developments which may be devised. Thus in the City of London, over the years, new markets have been established in all sorts of commodities and monetary instruments, without any legislative activity. If a market is needed in Sterling Certificates of Deposit, or palm oil, or crude oil, etc., it is only necessary for a body of interested persons to come together, lay down agreed guidelines and start to quote prices, for the market to be established and have the full backing of the law. To the extent that it is reasonable the law will uphold the commercial practices of the merchants.

The law merchant, which during the Middle Ages had become the basis for an expanding commerce throughout the Mediterranean, the Atlantic seaboard and the Baltic, became in the next three hundred years an integral part of the law of the separate great trading nations – the English, the French, the Dutch, the Spanish and the Portuguese. In England, for example, by the mid-eighteenth century the Common Law Courts had absorbed almost all the jurisdiction of the local courts merchant, with the exception of maritime law and prize law which was applied in the Maritime Courts. Eventually the whole area of law relating to merchants and traders was absorbed into the common law of England. In the process of absorption by national laws the law merchant lost to some extent its cosmopolitan nature, but in the fields where a conflict of laws between national legal systems was inevitable – in carriage by sea, in international trade, in marine insurance, etc. – there were sufficient threads remaining to settle disputes in peace time, and preserve reasonable behaviour in times of war. Nations had still to behave reasonably if trade was to prosper.

(*e*) **Statute Law.** In a sovereign state the fountain of law is the sovereign body which promulgates laws which it imposes upon and enforces among the citizens. In the UK this sovereign body is 'the Queen in Parliament', its promulgations are called Acts of Parliament, or Statutes, and they are the major source of all new law today. Acts of Parliament alone can overthrow custom, the decisions of judges, the rules of merchants, earlier Acts of

Parliament, etc. One of their most common uses today is to tidy up, or codify, the law when it has become excessively complicated and beset by contradictory decisions over the years or abused by clever businessmen and their legal advisers.

Some celebrated statutes, such as the *Partnership Act, 1890*, the *Bills of Exchange Act, 1882*, and the *Sale of Goods Act, 1893* (now re-enacted as the *Sale of Goods Act, 1979*), are models of what a statute should be – carefully worded to eliminate ambiguity. Students should read the proceedings of the parliamentary committees on legislation to see the quality of the discussion and the detailed consideration given to a bill in its 'committee stage'. We certainly owe much to Members of Parliament who devote months of their time to closing loopholes. One Member of Parliament recently said: 'The Right Honourable Member shares with me the privilege of having debated three major companies bills in five years. It is the sort of exercise for which campaign medals are given in other fields.'

Legislation is the major source of new law. Legislation takes the form of an Act of Parliament, which is a printed document. It represents the will of the sovereign Parliament. Sovereignty of Parliament implies that Parliament can make or unmake any laws, and no person or body has a right to override or set aside an Act of Parliament. The courts must give effect to, and the law enforcement agencies must enforce, legislation. The term 'Parliament' comprises the Queen, the House of Lords and the House of Commons. For a measure that has been drafted (normally called a 'bill') to become an Act of Parliament it must have the approval of the three distinct elements that make up Parliament. Within the legislative process, the House of Commons is the dominant House while the powers of the House of Lords have been severely curtailed as a result of the *Parliament Acts, 1911* and *1949*. The monarch's position in Parliament has long been a formality and Royal Assent has not been refused since the reign of Queen Anne in 1707.

A statute can displace any previous piece of law, repeal former statutes or parts of statutes, impose new rules and lay down principles which will guide judges in the future. It comes into effect on a particular date, after which time businessmen must comply with its rules. Many Acts empower officials at a variety of levels to make **'Orders'** which have statutory effect since their authority is drawn from the Act of Parliament. Some of these are designed to deal with emergencies – like the prohibition of cattle movements in an outbreak of foot-and-mouth disease. Others are not emergency measures, and have time to 'lie upon the table' at the House of Commons for MPs to consider them, and object to them if necessary. This vast body of rules created by subordinate bodies under specific powers delegated to them by the sovereign Parliament are described as **delegated legislation**. Delegated legislation can take the form of:

(i) **Orders in Council.** Under the *Emergency Powers Act, 1920*, the state can in specified circumstances proclaim a state of emergency and by Order in Council issue rules and regulations to counter the emergency.

(ii) **Statutory Instruments.** Most delegated legislation is made in the form of statutory instruments. For example, power is delegated to Ministers of the Crown to make regulations for specific purposes. The paper containing this law is called a statutory instrument and about 2000 of the more important ones are published every year.

(iii) **Bye-laws.** Parliament delegates authority to local authorities and other public bodies to make bye-laws over their respective areas.

(*f*) **European Community Law.** By the Treaty of Accession dated January 22, 1972, the UK became a member of the European Community with effect from January 1, 1973. To give legal effect to community law in the UK, the *European Communities Act, 1972*, was passed. By accession to thc Treaty of Rome and other specialist treaties, member states have limited their sovereign rights and created a body of law which binds their nationals and themselves. European community law consists of:

(i) **The Treaties.** The principal sources of community law are the treaties which established the three communities, i.e. the European Coal and Steel Community (1951), the European Economic Community (1957) (the treaty known as the Treaty of Rome) and the European Atomic Energy Community (1957). These treaties are binding on member states and Community institutions and in certain circumstances they may create rights for individuals which may be enforced in national courts.

(ii) **Regulations.** These are binding in all member states without requiring any implementation or adoption by the national parliament. They apply directly, and prevail over national law. They can create rights enforceable by individuals in national courts.

(iii) **Directives.** Although a directive is binding, it leaves member states a choice of the method by which the result required by the directive must be achieved. This can be done by an Act of Parliament or delegated legislation. In certain circumstances a directive can create rights for individuals enforceable in national courts.

(iv) **Decision.** A decision is binding in its entirety upon those to whom it is addressed whether it be member states, individuals or companies.

Decisions of the Court of Justice of the Communities are binding on the highest courts in member nations, so that the House of Lords must accept a European Court decision as binding – for example, as to the meaning of a clause in the Treaty of Rome.

(*g*) **Books of Authority.** In general, books of authority are not very influential in English law, but some celebrated ones in the past, written by eminent judges, have been widely quoted in the courts. More recently the development of university departments of law has raised the standing of books of authority and some major textbooks are quoted in the courts, or counsel may ask the judge's permission to adopt the arguments in the presentation of their client's case.

(*h*) **Other Sources.** English law differs greatly from **Roman law**, which is very influential on the Continent of Europe though now largely replaced by modern codes of law developed from the Napoleonic Code. The need to harmonise law under the EEC is likely to bring some further Roman influences. **Canon law** is largely ecclesiastical law, but the close link between the Church (in those days a Roman Catholic Church) and the Court of Chancery meant that canon law influenced equity decisions (since equity was to do with morality as much as legality). **Foreign law** can also be an important influence, especially if it comes from a country which has a system of laws developed from English common law. Thus decisions of the US Courts might be influential – persuasive precedents – though they cannot be binding. In certain conventions – for example, the Hamburg Rules developed by the United Nations Convention – judges are required to take account of decisions elsewhere. Article 3 of the Hamburg Rules of 1978 reads:

> 'In the interpretation and application of the provisions of this Convention regard shall be had to its international character and to the need to promote uniformity.'

Clearly this requires judges to consider decisions of foreign courts in similar cases as persuasive precedents.

1.6 Revision Test

In this book each chapter ends with a test-yourself section, which acts both as a chapter summary and a revision test. Cover the page with a sheet of plain paper and uncover the first question. Try to answer it from your knowledge of the chapter. Lower the paper and read the answer to question 1. Then read question 2 and try to answer it, and so on.

Answers	*Questions*
–	**1.** Define law.
1. Law is a body of rules for the guidance of human conduct which is imposed upon, and enforced among, the citizens of a given state.	**2.** What legal concept is implicit in the term 'imposed upon'?
2. The concept of a sovereign body which alone can promulgate and enforce laws.	**3.** What body is 'sovereign' in the UK?
3. The Queen in Parliament.	**4.** Who enforces the law in the UK?
4. In criminal matters the police have power of arrest, and bring offenders before the judiciary. In civil matters plaintiffs sue the defendants and hearings are held at which defendants may appear to answer the plaintiff's complaint, before a judge.	**5.** What are the chief branches of public law?
5. Constitutional law, criminal law, administrative law and community law.	**6.** What are the chief branches of civil law?
6. Property law, contract law, tort, succession and trust.	**7.** What are the sources of English law?

Answers	*Questions*
7. (*a*) Ancient custom of the realm; (*b*) Common law; (*c*) equity; (*d*) the law merchant; (*e*) statute law; (*f*) 'European Community' law; (*g*) books of authority; (*h*) other sources, such as Roman law and canon law.	**8.** What is meant by 'time immemorial'?
8. A time so ancient that it is beyond memory and record. The year AD 1189 is set as the limit of legal memory.	**9.** What was *Mercer v. Denne* about?
9. It was a 1905 case in which Denne, who owned a beach on which he wished to build two houses was prevented from doing so because local fishermen proved that since time immemorial they had dried their nets on this piece of beach.	**10.** How was common law established?
10. By a system of assizes in which judges travelled round the country trying cases according to local law, but over-riding bad customs and supporting good ones. Since judges had to follow precedents from other courts a national 'common law' quickly developed.	**11.** What were the defects of common law?
11. (*a*) Money damages were the only remedy; (*b*) actions could only be commenced if a suitable writ was available; (*c*) privileged people could secure favourable treatment.	**12.** How did equity improve on the common law?
12. (*a*) By expanding the range of writs available; (*b*) by giving other remedies, especially injunctions and specific performance; (*c*) by the power of the chancellor, who could call even the highest people before the Court of Chancery.	**13.** Go over the questions until you are sure of the answers. Then try some of the written questions in Appendix 1.

2
The Courts of Law

2.1 The Structure of Courts in the UK

A civilisation depends on law and order for its existence. Justice does not depend solely on having a comprehensive set of laws; it also requires machinery for the administration and enforcement of the laws of the land. While the task of enforcing the laws falls primarily on the police, the question of interpreting and applying the laws is the concern of the courts. Hence the courts exist to uphold and interpret the law and undoubtedly occupy a central role in the legal system.

The present-day court system in England consists of a hierarchy of courts each having its own functions, and connected to the courts above and below it by a chain of responsibilities, duties and powers. The structure of the courts today is shown in Fig. 2.1, and dates from two fairly recent Acts, the *Administration of Justice Act, 1970*, and the *Courts Act, 1971*. A more recent, major Act is the *Supreme Court Act, 1981*.

The court structure, which is one of the most complete systems in the world for the administration of justice, has developed into its present form as a result of many important changes in the past. These changes were the result of experience. Each of the courts in the hierarchy will be looked at individually from the point of view of such matters as the court's origin and history, its jurisdiction and internal organisation.

2.2 The House of Lords

The House of Lords developed from the **Curia Regis** or King's Council, which was the effective governing body of the Norman and Plantagenet kings. As such it had legislative, administrative and judicial powers. These judicial powers were the highest in the land and persist today. The House of Lords is the superior court (except on certain European Community matters). It is the ultimate court of appeal for civil and criminal cases. Until the nineteenth century, an appeal to the House was considered as an appeal to the whole House but today there is a convention whereby lay peers may not participate in the judicial sittings of the House. Today the House of Lords sitting as the final court of appeal is distinct from the House of Lords in its legislative capacity. Because of a shortage of peers who had held high judicial office, the *Appellate Jurisdiction Act, 1876*,

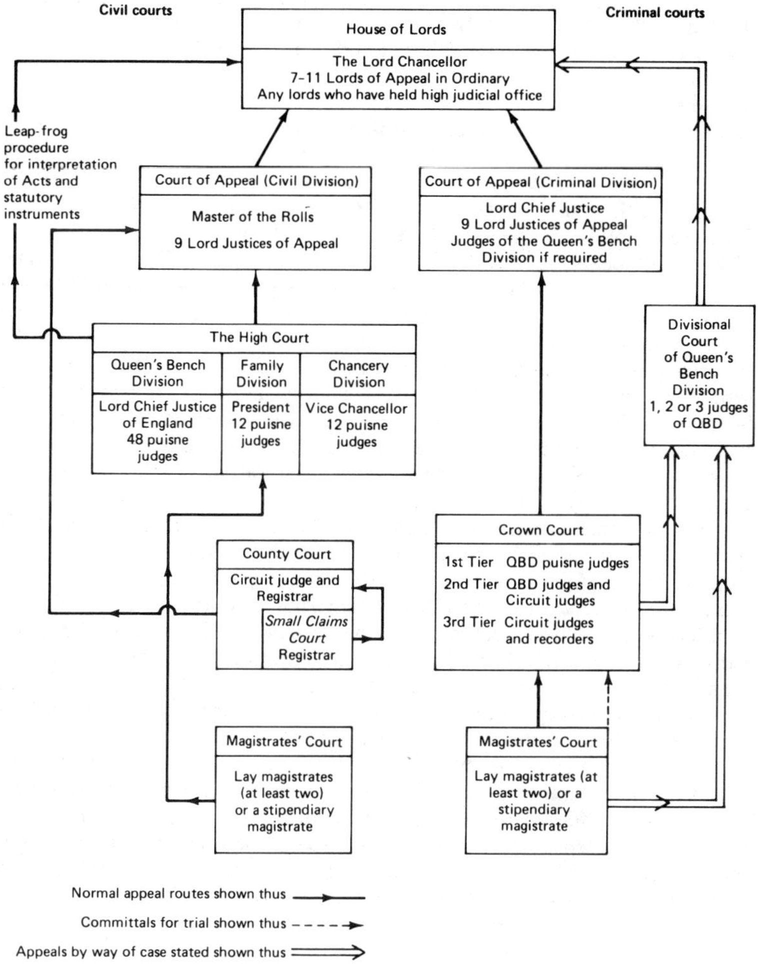

Fig. 2.1. The court system

provided for the appointment of salaried life peers to hear appeals. The features of this Act were as follows:

(*a*) It provided for the appointment of two Lords of Appeal in Ordinary (Law Lords) who had held high judicial office in the UK, or had been practising barristers (or advocates in Scotland) for a period of 15 years.

(*b*) The Act declared that appeals should only be heard when at least three of the following were present: the Lord Chancellor, the Lords of Appeal in Ordinary and such peers as have held high judicial office in the UK. A quorum is therefore three.

The Lords of Appeal in Ordinary are the senior members of the judiciary and are generally appointed from the ranks of the Court of Appeal. Their number, originally fixed at two, is now usually nine (not less than seven nor more than 11). They are salaried staff and are under an obligation to sit for appellate work. There is also a convention that an ex-Lord Chancellor should serve when requested to do so by the Lord Chancellor. Usually appeals are heard by five judges but in exceptional cases seven judges may sit. By custom, one or two of the law lords are Scots and the Scottish judges generally sit when the House hears appeals from the Court of Session, the Scottish equivalent of the Court of Appeal.

The jurisdiction of the House of Lords is almost entirely appellate. In civil cases it hears appeals from the Court of Appeal (Civil Division) in England, the Court of Appeal in Northern Ireland and the Court of Session in Scotland. The grounds for an appeal are normally that a point of law of public importance is involved, but this does not necessarily have to be the case. A 'leap-frog' procedure was introduced by the *Administration of Justice Act, 1969*, whereby in certain cases an appeal can now be made direct from the trial court to the House of Lords without the need for a prior appeal to the Court of Appeal. It is used when a ruling is required on the construction (interpretation) of an Act of Parliament, or a statutory instrument.

In criminal cases appeal lies from the Court of Appeal (Criminal Division), the Court of Criminal Appeal in Northern Ireland and from the Courts-Martial Appeal Court. The House of Lords has, however, no jurisdiction in Scottish criminal cases. Hearings result in decisions known as 'opinions', which are delivered to the parties in printed form. The case is then remitted to the Appeal Court which translates the 'opinion' into a judgement.

Being at the peak of the hierarchy of courts in the UK, the House of Lords enjoys great authority and exerts a powerful influence on the development of the law. Decisions of the House of Lords are binding upon all other courts trying civil or criminal cases. Previously the House regarded itself as strictly bound by its own earlier decisions. However, since 1966 the House will depart from its own earlier decisions when it appears right to do so. For example, the earlier decision may have been made *per incuriam*. (*Per incuriam* means that the court which made the earlier decision was not in possession of the full facts at the time, or its decision was arrived at through carelessness or oversight.)

In one respect only the House of Lords is no longer the supreme legal authority in the UK. This is in matters regarding the interpretation of the Treaty of Rome, the treaty which is the basis of the European Economic Community. The **Court of Justice of the European Communities (the European Court)** is the final court of authority on the meaning of the Treaty. English courts are bound by the decisions of the European Court on any matters relating to the treaty, and the interpretation of Community legislation.

2.3 The Court of Appeal

The *Judicature Acts, 1873–5*, created a new Supreme Court of Judicature divided into two parts: the High Court and the Court of Appeal. The jurisdiction of the Court of Appeal was gradually extended and by the *Criminal Appeal Act, 1966*, it was divided into two divisions: a Civil Division and a Criminal Division. The Civil Division's jurisdiction is entirely civil and almost entirely appellate. It hears appeals from the High Court, the County Courts, the Restrictive Practices Court and various tribunals – for example, the Lands Tribunal.

The Civil Division hears appeals on questions of law and of fact, rehearing the whole of the evidence presented to the court below relying on the notes made at the trial. If the appeal is allowed the court may reverse the decision of the lower court, or amend it, or order a retrial. It can hear appeals about the exercise of discretion – for example, discretion as to costs.

The Criminal Division of the Court of Appeal has no civil jurisdiction and its criminal jurisdiction is solely appellate. It hears appeals from persons convicted on indictment at the Crown Court. It considers references made to the Division by the Home Secretary of cases under section 17 of the *Criminal Appeal Act, 1968*, and it can hear an appeal against a verdict of 'not guilty by reason of insanity' or against findings of fitness and unfitness to plead. It has powers to dismiss appeals, or to quash convictions and order a new trial. It can substitute an alternative verdict, reduce the sentence or vary it, receive fresh evidence and order a proper trial.

The Court of Appeal is partly composed of the following *ex officio* judges; the Lord Chancellor, the Master of the Rolls (who heads the Civil Division), the Lord Chief Justice (who heads the Criminal Division), the President of the Family Division of the High Court, former Lord Chancellors and the Lords of Appeal in Ordinary. The rest of the judges are Lords Justices of Appeal, who are appointed by the Queen from judges of the High Court or barristers of at least 15 years standing. There are not less than eight or more than 16 Lords Justices of Appeal, the maximum number being capable of increase by Order in Council. Judges of the Queen's Bench Division may also serve on the Criminal Division.

Normally an appeal is heard by three judges. However, interlocutory appeals (heard during the course of a legal action) may be heard by two judges, while a single judge may hear an appeal in the Criminal Division in regard to certain legal matters. Occasionally five or more judges can sit to hear appeals involving matters of exceptional importance in both the Civil and Criminal Divisions.

Decisions of the Court of Appeal bind all inferior courts trying civil or criminal cases, including the Divisional Courts. It will be seen later that a Divisional Court is a hearing at which two or three judges from a division of the High Court hear an appeal sitting together.

In civil matters the Court of Appeal is bound by decisions of the House of Lords and by its own earlier decisions except where:

(*a*) There are two earlier conflicting decisions.

(*b*) The Court's earlier decision cannot stand with a subsequent House of Lords decision.

(*c*) The Court's earlier decision was given *per incuriam* (through carelessness or oversight).

These principles were laid down by Lord Greene, M.R., in *Young v. Bristol Aeroplane Co. Ltd (1944)*.

In criminal matters the Court would depart from its earlier decision in the interests of justice. This principle was laid down by Lord Goddard, C.J., in *R. v. Taylor (1950)*.

2.4 Divisional Courts of the High Court

Many appeal matters are not of sufficient importance to merit the attention of the Court of Appeal, and are dealt with by Divisional Courts of the High Court. Thus a Divisional Court of the Queen's Bench Division hears appeals on criminal matters from the Magistrates' Courts and the Crown Court. It also hears appeals from certain tribunals, and Solicitors' Disciplinary Tribunals. A Divisional Court of the Family Division hears appeals from the Magistrates' Courts on matrimonial issues, and a Divisional Court of the Chancery Division hears appeals from the County Court on bankruptcies, and from the Commissioners of Taxes on tax matters.

A Divisional Court usually consists of two or three judges of the appropriate division, sitting together. An important aspect of such appeals is that the decisions act as precedents for future cases, whereas decisions at a Magistrates' Court do not. Thus it is quite common for the prosecution to appeal against an acquittal at a Magistrates' Court, not as a matter of vindictiveness against the acquitted person, but in order to get a clear legal precedent. There may be hundreds of other cases of a similar nature in the pipeline. If the Divisional Court upholds the magistrates' view and gives a clear legal precedent for all the rest, the backlog of cases can be dropped to the very great benefit not only of the many accused but of the courts too.

Divisional Courts in civil matters are bound by decisions of the House of Lords, the Court of Appeal (Civil Division) and their own previous decisions. In turn, they bind the High Court in their own Divisions, and all lower courts. In criminal matters the Divisional Courts have a right of appeal to the House of Lords under the *Criminal Justice Act, 1960*, and are not strictly bound by decisions of the Criminal Division of the Court of Appeal.

2.5 The High Court

The lower half of the Supreme Court of Judicature set up in 1873–5 is the High Court. Today its three divisions have been renamed: they are the Queen's Bench Division, the Chancery Division and the Family Division.

All divisions of the High Court have equal competence to try any actions although certain specific matters are reserved for each of them. Details about the divisions are as follows:

(*a*) **The Queen's Bench Division.** This is the busiest division, trying the very large numbers of cases about contracts and torts. The division is headed by the Lord Chief Justice and there are about 40–50 puisne (pronounced 'puny' and meaning 'lesser') judges. There is also within the division an 'Admiralty Court' which deals with actions to enforce claims for damages, loss of life or personal injury arising out of accidents at sea, collision between ships, and loss of or damage to goods carried in a ship. There is also a Commercial Court, set up by the *Administration of Justice Act, 1970*. It deals with cases brought by traders and merchants such as insurance claims, etc. There are three judges nominated by the Lord Chancellor as commercial judges. The aim is to have such cases tried by judges experienced in the general areas of business law. Generally speaking, a quorum in the Queen's Bench Division is one; a judge sits alone and decides both questions of fact and questions of law. A jury may be empanelled to decide matters of fact, the judge then applies the law to the facts as found. There is no limit to the jurisdiction (i.e. damages may be for any amount).

Although contract and tort cases predominate, the Queen's Bench Division has residual jurisdiction over all cases not naturally falling to the Family and Chancery Divisions. The Division also provides all the puisne judges trying criminal cases in the Crown Courts. This forms much of the work of the very large body of puisne judges available to the Division. The Division also has the appellate function referred to in Section 2.4 above, and a supervisory function over all lower courts and tribunals to ensure proper conduct of such bodies.

(*b*) **The Chancery Division.** This division has important functions inherited from earlier times, when the old Chancery Court was concerned with all the more difficult and involved branches of law. The administration of estates of deceased persons; trusts; mortgages; sale of property subject to liens and charges; company, partnership and bankruptcy matters; taxation, etc. – are typical subjects for its original jurisdiction. It also hears certain appeal matters from County Courts. The division, while nominally headed by the Lord Chancellor and the Master of the Rolls, is actually run by a Vice Chancellor, with the help of about 10–12 puisne judges. Numbers vary, but the names of all serving judges may be found in publications such as the quarterly *Vacher's Parliamentary Companion*.

(*c*) **The Family Division.** This consists of the President and not less than three puisne judges. It has jurisdiction over matrimonial cases, dissolution of marriage, validity of marriage, wardship, adoption and the guardianship of minors. It has exclusive jurisdiction over matrimonial disputes and the rights of children.

The High Court normally sits at the Strand in London but there are 15 other towns to which judges of the High Court travel to hear common law claims and divorce cases. All other matters are dealt with in London. In civil matters, the High Court is bound by decisions of the House of Lords, the Court of Appeal and also by decisions of the Divisional Courts of the same Division. The decisions of High Court judges sitting alone at first instance are not binding on other High Court judges, although these decisions do bind inferior courts.

In criminal matters, the position of the High Court is similar to the Court of Appeal – namely, it will depart from its own earlier decisions in the interests of justice.

2.6 The Crown Court

The Crown Court came into existence as a result of the *Courts Act, 1971*, which abolished the ancient system of quarter sessions and assizes. The new Crown Court was expressly stated to be a part of the Supreme Court of Judicature, and Section 1 of the *Supreme Court Act, 1981*, defines the Supreme Court as the Court of Appeal, the High Court of Justice and the Crown Court. Unlike the assizes and quarter sessions, the jurisdiction of the Crown Court is not local, and Section 4(4) of the 1971 Act provides that its sittings may be held anywhere at any time. There are three levels, called tiers, the first tier being served by puisne judges from the Queen's Bench Division and trying the most important cases. The second tier may be served by circuit judges as well as High Court judges, and the lowest tier by circuit judges or recorders. Circuit judges and recorders are appointed by the Queen on the recommendation of the Lord Chancellor. Unlike circuit judges, who have full-time permanent appointments, recorders are part-time judges appointed on a temporary basis. In addition to the judges the Court also consists of 12 members of the jury. Between two and four lay Justices of the Peace may also be present, especially when the Court is hearing an appeal or a committal for sentence from the Magistrates' Court, and triable before a judge and jury.

The three tiers in the Crown Court deal with cases of increasing seriousness. Class 1 offences (murder, treason, etc.) must be tried by a High Court judge. Class 2 offences, which include manslaughter, rape and infanticide, must be tried by a High Court judge unless released by a High Court judge to be tried by a circuit judge or a recorder. This also applies to Class 3 offences, of a less serious nature. Class 4 offences, which include all offences triable summarily if preferred, are usually heard by circuit judges or recorders in the lowest tier of the Crown Court.

The Crown Court has jurisdiction over cases involving indictable offences, i.e. those offences punishable with three months' imprisonment or more. It hears appeals from the Magistrates' Courts and the Juvenile Courts. The Court also sentences offenders committed from the Magistrates' Courts where the lower court has insufficient powers to deal with the offender. Finally, the Court has a limited civil jurisdiction, mainly concerned with licensing appeals.

Some idea of the personalities and layout of the Crown Court is given in Fig. 2.2.

2.7 The County Court

This court has exclusively civil jurisdiction. County Courts were initially established by the *County Courts Act, 1846*, and their composition and jurisdiction is governed by the *County Courts Act, 1959*. The Court is usually presided over by a circuit judge appointed by the Crown on the advice of the Lord Chancellor. The judge normally sits alone, but on rare occasions a jury of eight persons may be empanelled. There are some 300 County Courts in England and Wales, administered by **registrars** who keep the records and carry out the administrative work associated with the Court.

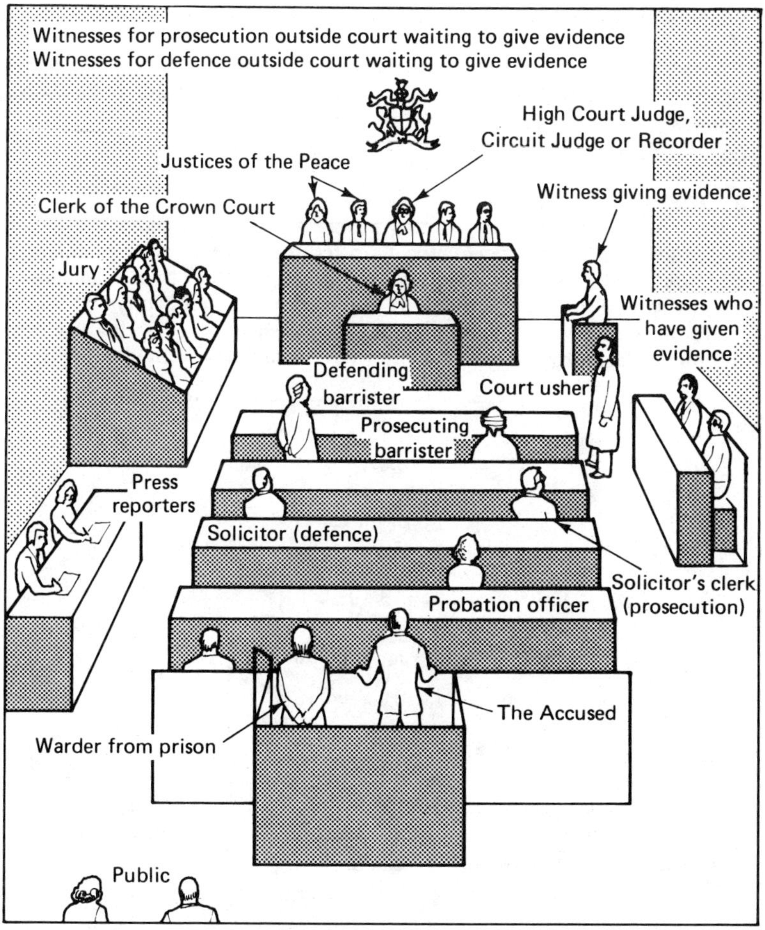

Fig. 2.2. The Crown Court
(By courtesy of Clearway Publishing Co. and The Law Society)

The Court's jurisdiction is to deal with all minor civil cases up to certain limits of action, beyond which the case must be tried at the High Court. Actions founded in contract and tort (except defamation) are dealt with up to a limit of £5000; trusts and mortgages up to £30,000; land matters up to a rateable value of £1000; probate matters for estates up to £30,000; winding up of companies with a paid-up capital up to £120,000; and a variety of other matters such as hire purchase, bankruptcy, landlord and tenant and other cases brought into the County Court by a variety of statutes. Certain County Courts are designated as Divorce County Courts and may hear *undefended* matrimonial causes.

Appeal against decisions in the County Court lies to the Court of Appeal.

Some idea of the personalities and layout of the County Court is given in Fig. 2.3.

To reduce the litigation coming before the County Court, and enable those with very small claims to bring an action without fear of excessive court costs, a 'small claims' procedure is now available.

2.8 The Small Claims Court

The County Court has been able to offer, since 1974, a 'small claims' procedure which enables plaintiffs who have claims of less than £500 arising from the sale of goods, the provision of services, the repayment of loans, arrears of rent, possession of property, negligence, etc., to claim with a minimum of legal formality. The majority of small claims are dealt with by

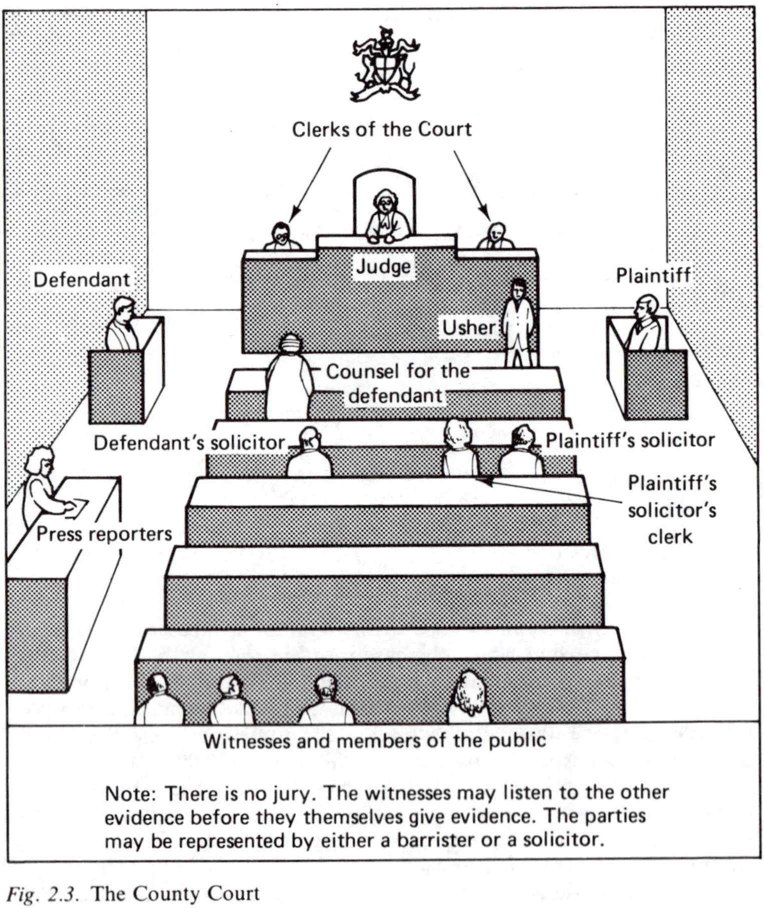

Fig. 2.3. The County Court

(By courtesy of Clearway Publishing Co. and The Law Society)

the registrar, but the circuit judge may hear some cases. Others may be settled by arbitration, usually with the registrar acting as arbitrator.

Many claims do not come to trial and of those that do it is the facts which are usually in dispute rather than a question of law. The registrar, or the judge, hears both sides and decides which version he thinks is right. A booklet *Small Claims in the County Court* is available from Courts, and gives sound advice to both plaintiffs and defendants. Appeal from the decisions of a registrar goes to the circuit judge, at the County Court.

2.9 The Magistrates' Court

These courts deal with more cases than any other courts under the English legal system. A vast amount of criminal work is handled by the Magistrates' Courts since the Crown Court tries only the more serious criminal cases, i.e. cases on indictment with juries. Magistrates' Courts also deal with a variety of civil cases too trivial to be heard in the High Court. Examples are matrimonial matters, affiliation orders, consent of minors to marry, children in care, etc.

A Magistrates' Court consists of between two and seven **justices of the peace**. The justices of the peace are local people with intimate experience of the surrounding area. These people give their time to discharge judicial functions. They are laymen who do not receive a salary but only expenses incurred in the performance of their judicial duties.

Apart from the justices of the peace, whose office is ancient and originated in the thirteenth century, in big cities and towns one also finds **stipendiary magistrates**. Unlike the lay justices, stipendiary magistrates are full-time members of the court appointed by the Queen on the advice of the Lord Chancellor. A stipendiary magistrate is normally a barrister or a solicitor of at least seven years' standing. Unlike the lay Magistrates' Court, where a quorum of two magistrates is required, a stipendiary magistrate may sit alone.

A Magistrates' Court has a **clerk to the justices**, normally a solicitor or a barrister of at least five years' standing, appointed by the Magistrates' Court Committee (*Justices of the Peace Act, 1949*). Apart from performing the administrative work of the court, the main function of the clerk is to advise the justices on points of law and procedure.

The personalities and layout of the Magistrates' Court are shown in Fig. 2.4.

The criminal jurisdiction of the Magistrates' Court is mainly concerned with summary offences, i.e. offences tried without a jury. These are comparatively minor offences and carry a maximum penalty of £1000 fine and/or six months' imprisonment. Such offences would include minor motoring offences such as speeding, unauthorised parking, driving without a licence and/or insurance, failing to obey traffic signals, etc. Other offences would include petty theft, drunkenness, common assault, wilful damage, begging in a public place, etc.

A Magistrates' Court has jurisdiction to try an indictable offence summarily with the consent of the accused. Where a defendant deserves a greater sentence than the maximum permitted in the Magistrates' Court,

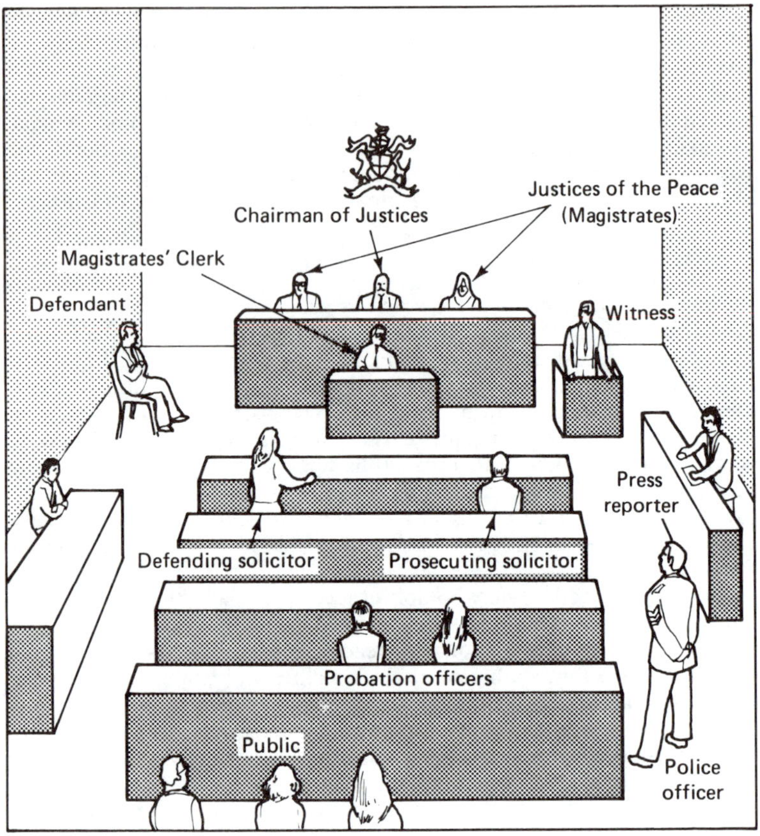

Fig. 2.4. The Magistrates' Court
(By courtesy of Clearway Publishing Co. and The Law Society)

the defendant is committed to the Crown Court for sentence.

As a court of preliminary investigation, a Magistrates' Court holds committal proceedings to examine an accused who has committed an indictable offence (offences punishable with a minimum of three months' imprisonment), to establish whether or not a *prima facie* case exists for committal to a Crown Court. The Court's civil jurisdiction includes making affiliation orders, separation and maintenance orders, orders under the *Mental Health Act, 1959*, questions about the adoption and custody of children, matters relating to invoking and granting of licences for alcoholic drinks and betting, enforcement of rates and recovery of debts, e.g. income tax, rates, electricity bills, etc.

Appeals from a Magistrates' Court lie to the Crown Court for both conviction and/or sentence, to the Divisional Court of the Queen's Bench by way of 'case stated' and, lastly, to the Divisional Court of the Family Division concerning matrimonial orders. Further appeal lies to the Court of Appeal and the House of Lords – in each case with permission only.

Appeals by way of case stated are made on matters of law only (not on matters of fact). A prosecutor or defence lawyer who is dissatisfied on a point of law with the decision of a Magistrates' Court or a Crown Court may require the lower court concerned to 'state a case' for the opinion of the Divisional Court. This is a panel of judges from the Queen's Bench Division of the High Court. They will consider the case as stated, and send the matter back to the lower court instructing it how to proceed. This is advantageous in that it creates a precedent for all future cases (whereas decisions of a Magistrates' Court do not create precedents).

2.10 Special Courts

The Judicial Committee of the Privy Council. The Judicial Committee of the Privy Council has appellate jurisdiction in a number of areas not covered by the appellate powers of the ordinary courts. It has its origins in the Curia Regis (King's Council) of Norman times. The Curia Regis under the Norman kings was an inner cabinet which performed governmental functions, i.e. legislative, executive and judicial functions, all together. Today, after a series of revisionary Acts of Parliament, it consists of The Lord President of the Council, the Lord Chancellor, ex-Lord Chancellors, the Lords of Appeal in Ordinary (the Law Lords) and Privy Councillors who have held high judicial office in the UK and the Commonwealth countries.

The Privy Council is not part of the Supreme Court and its decisions have persuasive authority only and hence are not binding on English courts. It does not pass a judgement but merely tenders advice to the Sovereign in person. This is followed and implemented by an Order in Council. Matters coming before the Judicial Committee concern appeals from:

(i) The Isle of Man, the Channel Islands, British Colonies and Protectorates and those independent Commonwealth countries whose domestic laws allow this right of appeal.

(ii) The ecclesiastical courts, i.e. the Canterbury Court of Arches and the Chancery Court of York.

(iii) The prize court, whose jurisdiction is now exercised by the Admiralty Court of the Queen's Bench Division and extends over matters concerning the ownership of ships and cargoes and their capture during time of war.

(iv) Medical tribunals appertaining to doctors, dentists and opticians as when a person's name has been erased from the Medical Register by the Professional Conduct Committee of the General Medical Council under the *Medical Act, 1978*. Similar provisions exist under the *Dentists Act, 1957*, and the *Opticians Act, 1958*.

Lastly, apart from the appellate jurisdiction outlined above, the Privy Council can sometimes be called upon by the Sovereign for advice on matters of law. Exercising this jurisdiction, the Privy Council has tendered advice on diverse matters such as the powers of colonial judges, legislation in Jersey and eligibility of a person for membership of the House of Commons.

The Restrictive Practices Court. This is a court of record created by the *Restrictive Trade Practices Act, 1956*, and reconstituted by the *Restrictive Practices Court Act, 1976*. The Court is concerned with restrictive trade agreements (agreements where restrictions are placed on price, quantity, quality or method of distribution of goods) referred to it by the **Director General of Fair Trading**, whose office was set up under the *Fair Trading Act, 1973*.

Matters concerned with restrictive trade practices are covered by the *Restrictive Practices Court Act, 1976*, the *Restrictive Trade Practices Act, 1976*, the *Resale Prices Act, 1976*, and certain provisions of the Treaty of Rome, especially articles 85 and 86 which deal with rules on competition.

The Court, which has equal status to the High Court, consists of three judges of the High Court appointed by the Lord Chancellor, a judge from the Court of Session (Scotland) nominated by the President of that court, a judge from the Supreme Court of Northern Ireland nominated by the Lord Chief Justice of Northern Ireland and 10 lay members appointed by the Crown from industry, commerce or public office. A duly constituted court consists of a judge and two lay members. Appeals on questions of law only lie to the Court of Appeal and its counterparts in Scotland and Northern Ireland.

Over the years very few of the restrictive practices which firms have sought to register under the Acts have been found by the Court to be in the public interest, and the vast majority of such practices have been swept away since 1956. The dire consequences which were envisaged as a result of the ending of such practices have in general not followed the Court's rulings, and the general public have largely benefited from the greater freedom in the availability of goods and the increased competition in resale prices.

The European Court of Justice. The UK became a member of the European Community from January 1973 and to give legal effect to the Community law in the UK the *European Communities Act, 1972*, was passed. While Section 2 of the Act makes the Community law directly effective in the UK, Section 3 requires local courts to take judicial notice of any decision of the Court of Justice on Community law.

Article 164 of the Treaty of Rome 1957 gives the Court authority to ensure that the interpretation and application of the Treaty is observed. The Court consists of at least one judge from each member state appointed by the governments of the member states. Judges are appointed for a renewable term of six years. They are assisted by four Advocates General whose prime function is to consider the issues of each case independently of the judges and make reasoned submissions in open court after the parties to the case have completed their submissions. The Advocate General does not participate in the formulation of the judgement and his submissions are not binding on the Court. However, the Court frequently accepts his conclusions and refers to them in its judgement. A single judgement is given and no dissenting views are given. These judgements are then enforced through the national Courts of member states.

Jurisdiction of the Court of Justice. The types of action brought in the Court of Justice are as follows:

(*a*) *Action against member states.* Under Articles 169 and 170 of the Treaty of Rome an action may be brought in the Court of Justice against any member state, by another member state, or by the Commission. In fact such actions are not common, because the emphasis is on cooperation, not confrontation, between member states. Where a member state has failed to honour a particular provision of the Treaty, other member states have tended to leave the Commission to bring any action that is required.

(*b*) *Action against Community institutions.* If Community legislation adopted by either the Council of Ministers or the Commission is believed to be unlawful for any reason, an action may be brought by a member state, or by the Council, the Commission or even a natural or legal person. The grounds are four:

(i) That the institution is not competent to take the action objected to;
(ii) That procedural rules were not followed;
(iii) That a provision of the Treaty was infringed;
(iv) That a lawful power was misused for an improper purpose.

A successful action leads to a declaration that the legislation is void, in whole or in part.

It is also possible to bring an action against an institution for failure to act where the Treaty imposes a duty to act (Article 175).

(*c*) *Preliminary rulings.* Under Article 177 of the Treaty, national courts or tribunals are required to bring certain questions about the interpretation of the Treaty, or the interpretation of acts of Community institutions, before the Court for a preliminary ruling. Since the Court is the final arbiter on all matters relating to the interpretation of the Treaty, it may sometimes be necessary for a national court to have the Treaty interpreted before they can come to a decision about a particular matter. They usually have discretion in deciding whether to bring the matter before the European Court, but it is mandatory if:

(i) The national court is the highest in the land, against whose decisions there is no national judicial remedy, and

(ii) Where a decision on the point of Community law is essential if the Court is to be able to give judgement.

The point of law is settled by the ruling of the European Court, and referred back to the national court for implementation in its judgement.

UK Courts and Community Law. Community law is developed by the Court of Justice, either under Article 177 (preliminary rulings) or cases brought by member states, etc. The decision is then passed back to the national court, which must apply the decision in its national legal system. We thus have a harmonising influence at work to achieve uniformity in the application of Community law. However, the natural conservatism of English law has not favoured references from lesser courts to the European Court. In the interesting case of *H. P. Bulmer v. J. Bollinger SA (1974)*, two English companies sought declarations that they were entitled to manufacture drinks described as 'champagne cider' and 'champagne perry'. The French company disputed this claiming that it was contrary to Community law, and asked the Court of first instance to refer the matter under Article 177. This was refused. On appeal Lord Denning, M.R., suggested certain guidelines for such references. These were:

(i) *Is the point conclusive?* The English court must consider whether the point is so important that a decision cannot be made on the matter before the court unless the point is resolved. If a judgement can be given without resolving the point then it is not necessary to seek a preliminary ruling.

(ii) *Is there already a precedent?* If the European Court has already decided substantially the same point, the English court need only follow the precedent.

(iii) *Is it an 'acte claire'.* If the point is reasonably clear, we do not need to interpret the Treaty, only to apply it.

(iv) *Decide the facts first.* Before any reference on the law it is best to decide the facts first.

(v) *Consider the circumstances at the time.* An appeal to the European Court should not be made against the wishes of the litigants, or if the expense or delay was likely to cause hardship, or if it was likely to overburden the European Court.

(vi) *Article 177(3).* Section 3 of Article 173 makes an application for a preliminary ruling mandatory only if the highest national court is involved, 'against whose decisions there is no judicial remedy under national law'. Lord Denning held that this applied only to the House of Lords in the UK. Other courts therefore had no duty to apply for a ruling, only a discretion which they could exercise if they wished.

All these guidelines are only *'obiter dicta'* (sayings by the way), not *'ratio decidendi'*. They are therefore not binding precedents, but they have proved very persuasive. However sound this advice may be, the guidelines cannot relieve a court or a tribunal from exercising its own discretion under Article 177, and it is possible that the Article may apply to other English courts and tribunals (see *Miliangos v. Frank (Textiles) Ltd (1976)*).

2.11 The Doctrine of Binding Precedent and its Effect on Litigation

To recapitulate what was said in Chapter 1 about binding precedent a judicial decision may be divided into three elements: findings of material facts; a statement of the principles of law concerning these facts; and the judgement based upon the principles stated. It is the statement of the principles of law which is the *ratio decidendi* (the reason for the decision), and forms the binding precedent for the future. Judges follow earlier decisions for guidance and apply the law enunciated in those decisions. The *ratio decidendi* always refers specifically to the facts as found in the particular case being tried. Any other statement of law which is not strictly relevant to the facts of the case is termed an ***obiter dictum*** (something said by the way). An *obiter dictum* is not a *binding* element of a decision but it does have persuasive authority, especially if the statement of law concerned emanates from a court of high authority. A case which illustrates a distinction between a *ratio decidendi* and an *obiter dictum* is:

Rondell v. Worsley (1967). The House of Lords had to decide on the question whether a barrister could successfully sued for negligence when conducting a case in court in the performance of his duties towards his client. The House held that no action could lie against a barrister for negligence in the conduct of his duty towards a client. This was the *ratio decidendi* of the case. However, the court went further and expressed opinions not quite relevant to the case in hand and these were that a barrister might be held liable in tort when acting outside the sphere of litigation and that a solicitor acting as an advocate might enjoy immunity. These opinions are *obiter dicta.* They are not binding on any court, but they could be persuasive in any future case where a barrister was sued for negligence on some matter outside his advocacy of a client's case, or where a solicitor acting as an advocate was sued for negligence in his pleading on behalf of his client.

We have seen that there is a hierarchy of courts with a chain of binding precedents imposed from higher upon lower courts. What is the advantage of this system? The answer is that it gives greater certainty in law, and thus reduces litigation. For example, if A has sold goods to B in certain circumstances, and sues for payment of the price, the decision of the court in that case, based on that exact set of facts, will act as a precedent for all similar cases. Suppose that B was a minor and the court held that the contract between A and B was void under the *Infants' Relief Act, 1874.* When C sells goods to D in a similar way, and approaches a solicitor to commence an action for payment of the price his solicitor will explain that the case of *A v. B* has already decided the point, and an action against D would not succeed. The litigation will not proceed, and C has no redress for his grievance – which was his own fault. He failed to enquire whether D had the capacity to contract.

Even when litigation is commenced, it is frequently only a method of putting pressure on the other party, and forcing him to act sensibly. Thus in a typical recent year more than a million cases were commenced in the County Court, but only about 100,000 actually reached a hearing; the rest were settled out of court. This happens because the party in the wrong, when he takes legal advice, is advised to settle out of court, and thus avoid the costs which will follow from losing the case.

There is the disadvantage about certainty in the law, that bad law becomes just as entrenched as good law. Since a legal precedent can be disturbed only by appeal to a higher court, a case may appear to be good law until someone affluent enough to risk the costs involved appeals against the decision of a judge who followed the precedent. It is true that judges may refuse to follow a particular precedent by 'distinguishing' the case from the one they are trying. This means they hold that the facts of the earlier case were not quite the same as the facts of the case they are trying at present. This gives them an excuse to avoid following the precedent. When a case has been decided wrongly most of the judges 'distinguish' it. As one wag put it, 'Some cases become "very distinguished".'

To conclude, the benefit of precedent is that it increases certainty in law, and thus reduces litigation. In the process we may find that an occasional 'hard case' results – justice is not quite done to everybody. Is it worth destroying the certainty in the law for the sake of easing the odd injustice? In former times the general opinion was that it was undesirable to reduce certainty in the law – 'Hard cases make good law' is an old saying. Today there is usually some sort of review process which leads to a change in the law in these situations, though the change may come too late for the individual whose unjust treatment led to the review.

The other adverse aspect of the system is that case law can be excessively complex, with a vast body of cases to be considered by the court. This complexity is frequently reduced by codifying the law – enacting the present state of the law as a statute which supersedes case law for the present. A further body of case law may then be built up from the interpretation of the statute, over the years.

2.12 Revision Test

Answers	*Questions*
–	**1.** What is the hierarchy of courts for civil matters of a commercial nature? Start from the bottom.
1. (*a*) County Court; (*b*) the High Court (Queen's Bench Division); (*c*) Court of Appeal (Civil Division); (*d*) House of Lords.	**2.** What is the hierarchy of courts for criminal matters? Start from the bottom.
2. (*a*) The Magistrates' Court; (*b*) the Crown Court (three tiers); (*c*) the Court of Appeal (Criminal Division); (*d*) the House of Lords.	**3.** What is the chain of binding precedents?
3. (*a*) Decisions of the House of Lords bind both divisions of the Court of Appeal and all lower courts. It reserves the right not to be bound by its own earlier decisions. (*b*) Decisions of the Court of Appeal bind the Court of Appeal itself (except in a few circumstances) and all lower courts. In certain criminal matters decisions of the Court of Appeal do not bind a Divisional Court because appeal lies direct to the House of Lords. (*c*) Decisions of Divisional Courts bind the Divisional Court itself, and all lower courts. (*d*) Decisions of High Court judges sitting alone do not bind other High Court judges. They do bind all lower courts.	**4.** What is the chain for appeals to a High Court, on the civil side?

Answers	*Questions*
4. (*a*) Appeals from the Small Claims Court lie to the circuit judge at the County Court. (*b*) Appeals from the County Court lie to the Court of Appeal (Civil Division). (*c*) Appeals from the Court of Appeal lie to the House of Lords.	**5.** What is the chain of appeal on the criminal side?
5. (*a*) For full appeals we have: (i) From the Magistrates' Court appeal lies to the Crown Court; (ii) from the Crown Court appeal lies to the Court of Appeal (Criminal Division); (iii) from the Court of Appeal (Criminal Division) appeal lies to the House of Lords. (*b*) For appeals by way of case stated we have: (i) from the Magistrates' Court appeal lies to the Divisional Court of the Queen's Bench Division; (ii) from the Divisional Court appeal lies to the House of Lords.	**6.** What are the functions of the European Court?
6. (*a*) It is the final arbiter on all matters concerning the interpretation of the Treaty of Rome. (*b*) It is the final authority on the validity of the acts of Community institutions and the interpretation of Community legislation.	**7.** What sort of actions may be brought in the European Court?
7. (*a*) Actions against member states. (*b*) Actions against Community institutions, i.e. the Council, the Commission, etc. (*c*) Actions asking for a 'preliminary ruling' under Article 177 of the Treaty.	**8.** Now try some of the questions in Appendix 1.

Part 2: The Law and Business Entities

3
The Legal Environment for Business Entities

3.1 The Concept of Business Entity

Every business exists as a distinct unit separate from all other units, and sometimes even distinct from its owners. This is recognised by law, which accords different rights and duties to those in business as sole traders, partnerships, etc. In the UK a limited-liability company has a separate legal status independent of its shareholders: it is an incorporation, which means it has been given authority to act in a business capacity. Partnerships, sole traders, trade unions and clubs are not corporations and do not have a separate legal status distinct from their owners or members.

A **sole trader** is a person who enters business on his own account; selects a site appropriate to the activities he has in mind; labours in the business with or without the assistance of employees; contributes the original capital by personal saving or borrowing on his own responsibility; and finally receives as his reward the proceeds (if any) of the venture.

A **partnership** is formed when two or more persons (the partners) agree to join together to pursue a particular type of activity. There need not be any formal arrangements, but it is best if a deed of partnership is drawn up at the start. A good lawyer will often suggest many points that the partners should agree on from the start, and if these are put in writing, and witnessed, many later difficulties may be avoided. There is no limit to the arrangements that may be made, but bodies of rules have grown up over the years about partnership behaviour, and these were embodied in an important act, the ***Partnership Act, 1890***.

Sole traders and partners are natural, legal persons, and operate as separate entities, with their own rights and obligations. They do *not* have a separate legal existence from their businesses, as is the case with a company.

Trade unions, social and sports clubs, literary societies or arts groups are termed 'unincorporated associations'. The law regards them as a group of persons bearing individual responsibility for their association's actions.

Other legal persons are not natural, but are artificial persons – or corporations. The term means 'formed into a body'. The commonest types of corporations are companies registered under the *Companies Act, 1985*. There are also statutory companies set up by private Act of Parliament, and chartered companies. The legal basis of a chartered company is a Royal Charter.

Although this chapter is basically concerned with types of business units in the private sector, there are large areas of British industry that have been progressively nationalised since 1939 and a brief mention of **public corporations** is not out of place. Public corporations have been formed to run various public utilities like the public transport, electricity, gas, coal and steel industries. The Bank of England, British Airways, the Independent Broadcasting Authority and the Post Office are under public ownership and run as independent public corporations. Public corporations are created as a result of an Act of Parliament or by a Royal Charter as in the case of the BBC. For example, the National Coal Board was created by the *Coal Industry Nationalisation Act, 1946*, the British Railways Board by the *Transport Act, 1947*, and the Independent Broadcasting Authority by the *Television Act, 1954*.

The organisational structure for each nationalised corporation may vary from one corporation to another. However, each is headed by a Minister of the Crown who is answerable to Parliament for the corporation's general policy. Day-to-day management is in the hands of a board headed by a chairman appointed for fixed periods by the appropriate minister. Like any other corporation, a public corporation has the independence of a company but it does not have shares or shareholders. It can enter into contracts, own land, buy property, engage staff, be vicariously liable for the torts of its servants, and can sue and be sued. Although ultimate control of a public corporation rests with Parliament, day-to-day management is in the hands of the board and Parliament cannot interfere. Unlike business enterprises in the private sector, public corporations do not exist solely for making profit. Although they are required to be self-sufficient financially, public ownership implies that they strive to provide an efficient public service and operate in the national interest. Some attempt is being made at present (1987) to privatise many public corporations.

In the next few chapters we shall consider the legal positions of the various types of business unit and demonstrate the chief features of the legal environment in which they operate.

3.2 Sole Trader Enterprises

A sole trader enterprise is inseparable in law from the individual who set it up and labours in it. Usually the business name is the same as the name of the sole trader. If it is not then certain rules, which are explained below, have to be observed. They are laid down in the *Business Names Act 1985*. This Act replaces an earlier (1916) Act of the same name which set up A Register of Business Names – to prevent any possibility of confuson between businesses using the same name. This register was discontinued, largely to save administrative expense. However, in order to enable those dealing with such businesses to know the identity of the owners, from that date businesses covered by the new Act must display their owners' names and addresses at business premises and on business stationery, and supply this information on request to any customer or supplier. A leaflet about this, and a specimen notice like the one reproduced in Fig. 3.1, are available from the Companies Registration Office, Department of Trade, Guidance Notes Section, 55 City Road, London, EC1Y 1BB.

A sole trader's legal personality is not separate or distinct from the business he runs. Just like any other legal individual a sole trader is bound by the ordinary civil and criminal law of the land. It is this law that gives him certain rights and imposes certain obligations on him. These legal rights and duties are adequately explained in the various chapters of this book on contract, tort administrative law, agency, sale of goods, carriage of goods by land, sea and air, etc.

Anyone can set up in business as a sole trader and no formal procedures are required for setting up. A licence is required for certain types of businesses. With the repeal of the *Registration of Business Names Act, 1916*, the onus is now on the sole trader to ensure that the name of his business conforms with the laws of the land. For example, he cannot use an offensive name or the name of an existing business. He leaves himself

PARTICULARS OF OWNERSHIP
OF

-- *

as required by section 4 of the Business Names Act 1985

Full name(s) of Proprietor(s)	Address within Great Britain at which documents may be effectively served on the business

* Insert Name of Business

Fig. 3.1. A specimen notice of ownership

open to a civil or criminal action if he does so. If the business name is not the true name or names of the proprietor then, as explained above, his full name and address must be displayed at business premises, on business stationery and be readily available to a customer or supplier on request.

This type of business unit was common before the beginning of the nineteenth century, when a large number of manufacturing businesses operated as sole traders. However, rapid industrialisation, specialisation and large-scale production with the consequent need for large capital, meant that large businesses could no longer be run as sole traders. (The only noticeable area where this form of business unit survives today is in the retail trade.)

In this form of business unit it is normally one person who provides all the capital and assumes all the risks associated with a business, e.g. business losses, losses resulting from theft, burglary, fire and other calamities such as public disorder, natural disaster, etc. With the advent of insurance, many of the risks can be minimised although a fully comprehensive insurance policy may be too costly for the proprietor to afford. He may run the business by himself or employ others to work for him. He may call on the services of members of his family. Success or failure of the business depends entirely on his efforts. He is primarily responsible for the following business activities, although he may delegate these to others:

(*a*) He is the sole manager.
(*b*) He keeps in touch with market trends and customer preferences.
(*c*) He is the general clerk and secretary.
(*d*) He displays, stocks and orders goods.
(*e*) He keeps business records and accounts, though he may require the services of an accountant from time to time for auditing accounts.
(*f*) He is responsible for publicity and advertising, often on a small scale only through local newspapers and magazines.

In large businesses these activities are undertaken by different persons and this ensures specialisation and increased efficiency. A sole trader is necessarily a 'Jack of all trades and a master of none'.

The advantages of operating as a sole trader may be listed as follows:

(*a*) He is the master of his own destiny. He does not have to consult others or receive their approval in making business decisions and implementing them. Being the sole provider of capital, he is entitled to all the profits. There is consequently a greater incentive for him to work hard.

(*b*) There is no delay in the making and implementing of decisions. Prompt attention can be given to the needs of customers. In big businesses, decision-making and the implementation of management policies are subject to delay.

(*c*) Smallness of the business ensures that he can keep in close touch with his customers and provide a personal service. The impersonal nature of the services provided by large businesses is a constant source of irritation and inconvenience for many customers.

(*d*) Personal supervision can ensure business efficiency and this is easier for a small business unit.

(*e*) He is not required to disclose, or make public, details of his profits or losses to anyone other than the Inland Revenue.

The disadvantages of operating as a sole trader are:

(*a*) The sole trader has to put in long hours of work and there is little time for vacations. Many have to work at non-business hours, at evenings and weekends. All this may have a detrimental effect on his health. The sole trader cannot afford to be sick as the business might have to be closed or run with difficulty.

(*b*) The proprietor carries personal responsibility for all the debts and obligations of the business. In the event of bankruptcy, creditors can call on the personal assets of the proprietor to satisfy their demands.

(*c*) Limitation on capital means that the business cannot be expanded and in many cases modernised. Almost all the capital has to be provided from his personal resources and the facilities for borrowing are limited when compared to a company or a partnership.

(*d*) The business can only be run as a high-cost enterprise because of limited specialisation. It cannot compete with the prices offered by large enterprises since it buys on a small scale, probably from a middleman who adds his commission to the price of the product.

(*e*) He is personally responsible for the business. On his death the business is normally inherited by members of his family, but there is no guarantee that the successor will be interested in or able to manage the business.

For the reasons listed many sole traders take a partner and operate as a partnership.

3.3 Partnerships

Definition and nature of partnership. The *Partnership Act, 1890*, is the principal statute that governs all partnerships and S.1(1) of this Act defines a partnership as 'the relation which subsists between persons carrying on business in common with a view of profit.' The business entity that is created as a result of persons entering into partnership with one another is called a **firm** (S.4). A key phrase in the definition distinguishes a partnership from other entities which appear similar, e.g. a social or a cricket club, a debating society or a co-ownership. A club or a society is not formed to make a profit and is not therefore organised on business principles: all partners are jointly liable for the debts of a firm whereas members of a club or a society are liable for any losses only up to the extent of their individual subscription that is outstanding. Similarly, a partnership exists to make a profit and this may not be the case with a co-ownership. In deciding whether or not a partnership exists it depends entirely on the intention of the parties to the arrangement. Intention is something that is expressly stated in the contract or it can be implied from the conduct of the parties to the contract. Examples of arrangements that do not necessarily constitute evidence of a partnership since they may not be 'carrying on a business in common with a view of profit' (S.2, 1890 Act) are:

(*a*) Joint tenancies.
(*b*) Tenancies in common.
(*c*) An arrangement where gross returns are shared.
(*d*) Receipt of a share of profits.
(*e*) Payment of a debt through instalments out of accruing profits.
(*f*) Payment of servants or agents through a share of the profits.
(*g*) Payment to money lenders through a share of the profits.
(*h*) Annuity payments to a widow or a child of a deceased partner out of profits.
(*i*) Payment of a portion of the profits as goodwill.
(*j*) Charitable or religious organisations.

In order to safeguard those involved in any arrangement that does not fall into the category of a partnership, documents called 'Heads of Agreement' are usually drawn up. The documents detail the nature of the particular arrangement, state that no partnership exists but give details of the duties, rights and obligations of the parties to the particular arrangement.

Partnerships are often described as 'ships that sink in rough seas' and unless the partners know and trust each other implicitly, with the exception of professional firms, this type of business entity usually fails when partners fall out.

3.4. Formation of a Partnership

A partnership is created as a result of a contract between two or more persons. This contract may be either in writing or oral or both. The contract may be signed and sealed, i.e. a deed. A contract in writing creating a partnership is known as the 'Articles of Partnership' and a signed and sealed contract is termed a 'Deed of Partnership'. All partners are bound by the terms mentioned in the Articles or Deed of Partnership and the *Partnership Act, 1890*, will only apply in so far as particular points are not covered by the Articles or Deed of Partnership. The terms of the Act can be varied by the Articles or the Deed.

The Articles or Deed of Partnership will normally include the following matters:

(*a*) The business's trading name.
(*b*) The nature or purpose of the business.
(*c*) Details of the individual capital contributions of the partners.
(*d*) The method for sharing profits or losses.
(*e*) The powers of the partners.
(*f*) Rules about the admission of new partners.
(*g*) Rules about the expulsion of a partner.
(*h*) Rules about the dissolution of the partnership.
(*i*) Rules about the accounts and audit of the books.
(*j*) How goodwill is to be determined.

(*k*) How the amounts payable to outgoing partners or deceased partners' estates shall be calculated.

(*l*) Rules about the use of arbitration in case of disputes between partners.

Goodwill, mentioned in (*j*) above, is important in partnerships because at any time when a change in the relationships between partners occurs – such as the admission of a new partner, the departure or death of an existing partner, a rearrangement of work-loads, etc. – it is necessary to value the goodwill, so that the net worth of the business can be accurately assessed.

A partnership contract may be express or it may be implied by a court from the conduct of the parties – for example, if a person holds himself out as a partner or allows himself to be held out as such, he may incur the liabilities of a partner (*Bevan v. The National Bank Ltd* (*1906*)). Being a contractual arrangement, a partnership agreement is subject to the same principles and rules of contract law that are applicable to any other contract (see Section 3). Some of the consequences that arise are as follows:

(*a*) A minor may become a partner. During his minority the contract of partnership cannot be enforced against him. On attaining his majority the contract becomes voidable, i.e. it can be avoided by him within a reasonable period. If no steps are taken to avoid the contract within a reasonable time, it becomes binding on him (*Goode v. Harrison* (*1821*)). A minor is liable for such debts of the firm as are incurred subsequent to his attaining his majority if he does not take steps to avoid the partnership.

(*b*) Although an alien may become a partner, upon the outbreak of war the partnership dissolves since he becomes an enemy alien and the partnership contract becomes illegal.

(*c*) Mental incapacity of a partner is a ground for dissolution. However, a mentally incapacitated person may become a partner with the consent of existing partners.

(*d*) Death or bankruptcy of a partner, unless otherwise agreed, results in the dissolution of a partnership (S.33(1), 1890 Act).

(*e*) A partnership can be terminated by mutual agreement of all the parties.

(*f*) The maximum number of partners should not exceed 20 (*Companies Act, 1985*, S.716), with the exception of professional partnerships – e.g. solicitors, accountants, stock exchange firms – where the maximum number of 20 can be exceeded (see the same section). Under the *Companies Act, 1948*, the maximum numbers for a banking partnership was 10; the 1967 Act allowed this number to be exceeded up to a maximum of 20 provided the Board of Trade's approval was obtained. The *Banking Act, 1979*, removes the limit on maximum numbers.

The duration of a partnership depends on whether it is formed for a specified time, for a particular business venture, or for an indefinite time (partnership at will, which can be terminated at any time at the discretion of a partner, by giving notice to the other, or others, of his intention to dissolve the partnership (S.32, 1890 Act)).

The Firm's Name. The *Registration of Business Names Act, 1916*, has been replaced by the *Registration of Business Names Act, 1985*. Firms that do not operate under their owners' true names do not have to register at a central registry which has now been abolished. In order to enable those dealing with such businesses to know the identity of the owners, the owners' names and addresses must be displayed at business premises, on business stationery and this information must be freely available on request to any customer or supplier. A partnership can use the word '& Company' after its name but it cannot also use the word 'Limited' as a last word.

3.5 Relationship of Partners with Third Parties

According to S.5 of the 1890 Act every partner (except a limited partner) is considered an agent of the firm and will therefore bind other partners on any transaction within the ordinary course of the firm's business with an outsider. This will not apply if the partner has no authority to act on behalf of the firm and the outsider is aware of this lack of authority or does not know or believe the other party to be a partner. Apart from this limitation, a partner has implied authority to bind the firm in relation to the following transactions:

(*a*) Buying and selling of goods that are normally associated with the firm's business.

(*b*) Receiving payments from debtors and issuing receipts against them.

(*c*) Engagement and dismissal of employees of the firm.

The implied powers just mentioned apply equally to a non-trading partnership as to a trading partnership. However, certain additional powers are imputed to a partner in a trading partnership, i.e. one that is involved in buying and selling of goods (*Higgins v. Beauchamp* (*1914*)), and these are:

(*a*) Accepting, drawing and issuing negotiable instruments on behalf of the firm.

(*b*) Borrowing money and pledging the firm's goods or chattels as security. If the credit of the firm is pledged for a purpose not connected with the ordinary course of business, the firm is not bound unless specific authority has been given to the partner and in such a case the partner is personally liable (S.7). His action can always be ratified by the firm.

(*c*) Hiring the services of a solicitor if an action is commenced against the firm (*Tomlinson v. Broadsmith* (*1896*)).

In a non-trading partnership the additional powers mentioned above can be expressly provided by the articles, or the Deed of Partnership.

S.9 of the 1890 Act makes every partner jointly liable for the firm's contracts. This means that a partner is liable along with all other partners and not by himself alone. A claim may be made against the private resources of each partner to satisfy a judgement. Joint liability meant that a plaintiff who sued one of the partners on a contract with the firm could not subsequently sue the other partners (*Kendall v. Hamilton* (*1879*)). However, this position has been changed by the *Civil Liability* (*Contribu-*

tion) Act, 1978, which provides that a judgement obtained against one partner does not preclude an action against the other partners.

A firm and its partners are jointly and severally liable for any torts or wrongs committed by a partner in the ordinary course of the firm's business or with the authority of other partners (S.12) (*Hamlyn v. Harston & Co.* (*1903*)).

It would follow that if a tort was committed by a partner outside his apparent or ostensible authority, the firm is not liable and the partner concerned will incur personal liability (*Arbuckle v. Taylor* (*1815*)). Joint and several liability of partners means that if an action were brought against one of them for a wrong committed by the firm and the third party obtains a judgement with which he is not satisfied, he can bring an action against the other partners since their liability is joint and several.

Liability of Incoming and Outgoing Partners. The estate of a deceased partner is liable only for such obligations and liabilities as are incurred by the firm prior to his death. The estate is not liable for any debts contracted subsequent to the death (S.14(2); *Bogel v. Miller* (*1903*)). Similarly, the estate of a bankrupt partner is liable only for debts acquired prior to the date of bankruptcy and not those resulting subsequent to the date of bankruptcy. A newly admitted partner is not liable for those debts of the firm that result from acts done prior to his entry as a partner (S.17(1)). The new partner may acquire this obligation through a contract called 'novation' with the consent of the creditor, the newly constituted firm and the new partner.

A retiring partner is liable for those debts and obligations incurred by the firm prior to his retirement. After retirement he is liable to those previously dealing with the firm who have not been given notice of the retirement (S.36). To those with no previous dealings with the firm, he is liable unless he has advertised his retirement in the *London Gazette* or given them notice of his retirement. To those with no previous dealings with the firm who are unaware that he was a partner of the firm, he is not liable (*Tower Cabinet Co. Ltd v. Ingram* (*1949*)).

3.6 Interrelationship of Partners

The relations between partners are governed by the provisions of the Articles or the Deed of Partnership. Because partners are *agents* of each other and can bind each other when making contracts on behalf of the firm, it is important for trust to exist between them. The law recognises this and deems them to be in a **fiduciary** relationship with each other (*fides* is the Latin for confidence or trust). Each partner is also a **principal** and under normal circumstances the relationship between partners will be governed by the provisions of the articles or Deed of Partnership. In the absence of a written partnership agreement, their relations with each other may be inferred from the course of dealings between them. The provisions of the *Partnership Act, 1890*, apply only in so far as the partnership agreement does not either expressly or impliedly provide for the relations of partners to each other. The rights and duties between partners as provided in the 1890 Act (SS.24–30) are as follows:

(*a*) All partners are to share equally in the capital, profits or losses of the firm.

(*b*) No partner is entitled to interest on his subscribed capital. Interest at the rate of 5 per cent per annum is payable on loans which exceed the subscribed capital.

(*c*) No partner is entitled to renumeration for acting on behalf of the firm.

(*d*) A partner is to be indemnified for any expenses incurred by him when acting properly on behalf of the firm in the ordinary course of business.

(*e*) All partners are entitled to participate in the management of the firm except a limited partner (see Section 3.9).

(*f*) To introduce a new person as a partner requires the consent of all the existing partners.

(*g*) Ordinary business matters are to be decided by a simple majority but no change to the nature of the partnership business may be made without the unanimous consent of all the partners.

(*h*) A partner cannot be expelled by a majority of the co-partners unless this power has been reserved in the partnership agreement.

(*i*) The partnership books must be available for inspection by any partner or his agent (*Bevan v. Webb* (*1901*)).

(*j*) Each partner is owed a duty of utmost good faith by his fellow partners in all partnership matters. This means all partners are required:

(i) To render true accounts.

(ii) To provide full information on all aspects of the partnership business.

(iii) To account for any benefit derived (*Featherstonhaugh v. Fenwick* (*1810*)).

(iv) To disclose any secret profit made (*Bentley v. Craven* (*1853*)).

(v) Not to carry on business that competes with that of the firm.

(vi) Not to use partnership documents and other confidential information elsewhere (*Floydd v. Cheney* (*1970*)).

3.7 Partnership Property

SS. 20 and 21 of the 1890 Act define partnership property to include property originally introduced into the partnership business, property subsequently acquired on behalf of the firm for the purposes and in the course of the partnership business and any property bought with the firm's money. The partnership property is required to be applied exclusively to the business of the firm and in accordance with the terms of the partnership agreement.

The partnership property is distinct and separate from the property belonging to the individual partners. If bankruptcy were to occur, the partnership property forms part of a joint estate whereas each partner's personal property forms a separate estate.

3.8 Assigning a Share in a Partnership

Under S.31 of the 1890 Act a partner may mortgage or assign his share in the partnership to an outsider if the partnership agreement does not prevent this. The newcomer (mortgagee or assignee) does not have the full rights of a partner. He is entitled to the share of the profits due to the assigning partner and also to his share of the partnership property on dissolution. He has no right to interfere in the management or administration of the firm or to inspect the books of the firm. The assignee is entitled to an account in the event of dissolution (*Watts v. Driscoll* (*1901*)).

Although an assignor will remain liable for the firm's debts, normally the assignee agrees to take over this liability. It follows, for example, that if the existing partners entered into a *bona fide* agreement to pay themselves salaries, such agreement would be binding on the assignee (*Re Garwood's Trust, Garwood v. Paynter* (*1903*)).

3.9 Limited Partnerships

Under the *Limited Partnership Act, 1907*, a limited partnership may be formed. The Act allows one or more limited partners with limited liability but there must be at least one general partner with unlimited liability. The maximum number of partners is the same as for ordinary partnerships. A limited partner contributes a certain amount of capital and his liability for the firm's debts is limited to the amount he has contributed. A limited partnership must be registered with the Registrar of Companies, who must be provided with particulars such as the firm's name, place of business, purpose of the business, full names of each partner, a statement that the partnership is limited and the sum contributed by each limited partner.

The following rights and duties are attributed to a limited partner (S.6):

(*a*) He cannot take part in the management of the firm. If he does, he is liable, just like a general partner, for all the debts and liabilities of the firm.

(*b*) He cannot bind the firm in dealings with outsiders.

(*c*) He can examine the firm's books and advise the other partners accordingly.

(*d*) His death or bankruptcy does not dissolve the partnership; mental disorder is a ground for dissolution if his share in the partnership cannot be ascertained or realised otherwise.

(*e*) To assign his share, he requires the consent of all the general partners.

(*f*) The partnership cannot be dissolved by him by notice.

(*g*) The limited partner's consent is not required if a new partner is introduced by the general partners.

Because of the ease with which a limited company may be registered with all participants enjoying limited liability, the popularity of the limited partnership has declined and very few of them are now registered.

3.10 Dissolution of a Partnership

Dissolution of a partnership would depend on the terms of the partnership agreement. Subject to this, if a partnership was entered into for a particular business venture, then the completion of this venture would bring the partnership to an end. If the partnership was entered into for a fixed period, the partnership ends at the expiry of this period. Where, however, the partnership is entered into for an indefinite time (partnership at will) then it can be ended by one partner giving notice (S.32). Apart from the grounds of dissolution just mentioned and subject to the provisions of the partnership agreement, a partnership may be dissolved on any of the following grounds:

(*a*) *By Court Order*. Under S.35 any partner may apply to the Court for dissolution if:

(i) One of the partners cannot manage or administer his affairs because of mental incapacity.
(ii) A partner, other than the applicant, becomes permanently incapable of carrying out his duties under the partnership contract.
(iii) A partner, other than the applicant, is found guilty of conduct prejudicial to the business. In *Carmichael v. Evans* (*1904*), dishonesty, i.e. travelling on the railway without a ticket, was considered an adequate ground for dissolution of the partnership.
(iv) A partner, other than the applicant, wilfully or persistently breaks the partnership agreement or conducts himself in such a way that it becomes impractical for the other partners to carry on in partnership with him.
(v) The business can only be carried on at a loss.
(vi) The court considers it just and equitable. In *Re Yenidje Tobacco Co. Ltd* (*1916*) a deadlock in the management of a private company was held to be adequate grounds for winding up the company. Although this was a case about a company the rule might well be applicable to a partnership in similar circumstances.

(*b*) *Without Reference to Court*. A partnership may be dissolved on the following other grounds, subject to the terms of the partnership agreement:

(i) On bankruptcy or death of a partner (S.33).
(ii) When a court orders a partner's share in the firm to be charged to a separate debt, the other partners have an option to dissolve the partnership (S.33).
(iii) On bankruptcy of the partnership (S.34).
(iv) On grounds of illegality (S.34), i.e. a partnership with an alien enemy at the outbreak of a war.
(v) Through mutual consent of all the partners.

On dissolution the partnership property including the goodwill is sold. The proceeds are then applied to pay outstanding debts and liabilities. If the amount realised is insufficient to discharge all the debts, each partner bears personal responsibility to pay for the deficiency in proportion to his entitlement to profits of the firm. If, however, a residual amount is left after discharge of all the debts, this will be divided amongst the partners in proportion to their normal entitlement to profits. In the event of bankruptcy of a partner when the partnership is dissolved, the partnership estate must be applied initially for the payment of partnership debts and it is the individual estate of each partner which must be applied in payment of their separate debts. Any surplus in the partnership estate becomes part of the separate estates of each partner in proportion to their respective entitlement to the partnership estate.

An important case arising from insolvency of a partner in the dissolution of a partnership is *Garner v. Murray (1903)*. The facts were that the partnership was dissolved, and all the creditors were paid, but there were insufficient funds to repay their capital to the partners. The actual figures were:

Assets to repay partners		*Liabilities (Capital)*	
	£		£
Cash	1916	Garner	$2288\frac{1}{3}$
		Murray	$102\frac{1}{3}$
			$2390\frac{2}{3}$
		Less	
		Wilkins (deficit)	$474\frac{2}{3}$
	£1916		£1916

Wilkins was insolvent and unable to bring in any money to repay his deficit on capital account, so that the other partners could not obtain the return of their funds. The question that arose was how this loss should be shared. It was held that such a loss was not an ordinary trading loss, but a capital loss. The deficit should not be shared in the usual proportions in which profits were shared, but in the ratios of their capitals at the start of the year. The loss therefore fell more heavily on Garner than on Murray, who had only a small amount of capital, although they shared ordinary profits equally.

3.11 Advantages and Disadvantages of Operating as a Partnership

Advantages

(*a*) A large amount of capital can be raised, although this cannot compete with the capital that can be raised by forming a company.

(*b*) Responsibilities, expertise and experience can be shared for the common good of the business.

(*c*) For some professional businesses (accountants, lawyers, doctors, etc.) partnerships are ideal business entities. There is no need for large capital; the environment is not cumbersome or impersonal as with large companies; everyone knows everyone else and so close contact and co-operation is maintained.

(*d*) Partnerships are suitable for small businesses with no need for a large injection of capital and those businesses that prefer operating on a family basis with no need for further expansion.

(*e*) Privacy of business affairs can be ensured, unlike a company whose business affairs become public knowledge in that various documents including accounts have to be filed with the Registrar of Companies and are open for inspection.

(*f*) All the partners are provided with equal incentives to work for the interests of the firm. They have all provided capital from their personal resources and can participate fully in the management of the firm.

(*g*) Less formality, publicity and expense are involved in forming a partnership as opposed to a company.

(*h*) Holidays, days off and sickness are easily covered by the partners.

Disadvantages

(*a*) Unlimited liability means that in the event of dissolution a partner may be called upon to make good outstanding debts of the firm from his personal assets.

(*b*) Business decisions require consultation and agreement of all the partners and this may not be always forthcoming.

(*c*) Death or bankruptcy may result in the dissolution of a partnership, unlike a company which enjoys perpetual succession.

(*d*) A partnership cannot raise capital by issuing shares or debentures and the facilities for raising capital are more restrictive when compared to a company.

3.12 Revision Test

Answers	*Questions*
–	**1.** What is the concept of 'business entity'?
1. The concept that holds each business to be a separate unit distinct not only from other businesses but also from its owner.	**2.** A sole trader does not trade under his own name but under an invented name. What rules must he observe?
2. He must display on a notice at his premises the 'Particulars of Ownership', and these must also appear on all letterheads, business documents, etc.	**3.** What is the sole trader's business position?
3. One of unlimited liability; he is the business and the business is him, and there is no separate business legal personality.	**4.** List the advantages of being a sole trader.

Answers	*Questions*
4. (*a*) Independence; (*b*) the full profits are available to the proprietor; (*c*) rapid implementation of decisions; (*d*) close credit control; (*e*) personal supervision of work done and therefore maximisation of goodwill.	**5.** List the disadvantages of being a sole trader.
5. (*a*) Long hours of work; (*b*) no holidays; (*c*) sickness seriously affects the business; (*d*) unlimited liability for debts and torts; (*e*) difficult to accumulate capital; (*f*) inadequate capital may mean high-cost activities.	**6.** What Act controls partnerships?
6. The *Partnership Act, 1890.*	**7.** Define a partnership.
7. A partnership is the relation which subsists between persons carrying on a business in common with a view of profit.	**8.** What matters should be included in a Partnership Deed?
8. (*a*) The trading name; (*b*) the nature of the business; (*c*) details of capital contributions, sharing of profits, and arrangements about drawings; (*d*) the powers of the partners; (*e*) details about admissions, retirement and dissolution of the business; (*f*) details about accounting and audit procedures; (*g*) how goodwill is to be revalued.	**9.** What is the relationship of the partners to one another?
9. Every partner is an agent of the other partners and binds them on all actions he takes which are within the ordinary business transactions of this type of partnership.	**10.** What liability has a partner for the debts of the business?
10. They are jointly liable for debts and jointly and severally liable for torts under the Act of 1890. However, under the *Civil Liability (Contribution) Act, 1978*, it is also possible now to hold partners jointly and severally liable for debts.	**11.** The *Partnership Act, 1890*, is often said to have a residual effect only on the relationships between partners. What does this mean?

Answers	*Questions*
11. It means that if the partners have agreed expressly or impliedly on a particular procedure this is the procedure to be followed. The Act only takes effect if no other agreement has been made, or a particular element of disagreement was not foreseen and covered by the Partnership Deed or Articles.	**12.** What does the Act say in this case about the relationship between the partners?
12. (*a*) All partners share equally in the capital, profits and losses of the firm. (*b*) No interest to be given on capital. (*c*) Interest on loans over and above capital to earn 5 per cent. (*d*) No partner is entitled to a salary. (*e*) Ordinary business matters to be decided on a simple majority but matters fundamental to the partnership require the consent of all the partners.	**13.** Go over the questions again until you are sure of all the facts. Then try some of the written questions in Appendix 1.

4
Business Entities: Unincorporated Associations

4.1 Introduction

An unincorporated association is one where members act together in pursuance of certain aims without taking on any formal separate legal structure. They may take the form of clubs, societies, cooperative societies, trade unions, employers' associations and partnerships. They may be profit-making or non-profit-making units. Their distinctive feature is that no separate legal body (corporation) is created when the association is formed.

The most common form of unincorporated association is the non-profit-making club, which does not exist solely to make a profit in the true sense of the word. In this category come clubs and societies which exist essentially to provide their members with certain benefits, e.g. club facilities, discount trading, etc. Usually membership of the club is obtained by paying a subscription which entitles the member to share in the facilities and services available. If profits are made by the club they are not profits in the usual sense of that word, but over-subscriptions (the members having jointly paid more for the services than was really necessary). The profits are therefore called surpluses. They may be used in improving or expanding existing facilities, buying new equipment, etc. Alternatively, they may be refunded to the membership. The income of the clubs and societies is drawn from the members' subscriptions, hiring of club facilities, and raising funds from activities like club trading, holding festivals or discos. Working men's clubs, social and sports clubs, cricket clubs and debating societies are examples of this type of unincorporated association.

4.2 Organisation of a Club

A club or society is managed by a committee headed by a chairman. Unlike a corporation, a club or society does not have a separate legal existence from its members. The *rules* of a club may be very important, and lay down not only the way the club is organised, but such legal matters as the responsibility of members for the acts of the committee, the powers of the officials and whether they act as agents of the committee, and their right to act as a tribunal in deciding disciplinary matters, the expulsion of members, etc. At meetings of the club it is common for points of order to be raised, which refer back to the rules of the club and question whether the matter under discussion is being properly considered.

The committee usually consists of a chairman, who conducts the meetings impartially to ensure all voices are heard and all opinions expressed; a secretary who takes a leading role in the organisation and deals with correspondence; and a treasurer who deals with the subscriptions and disbursements of funds, and prepares a suitable receipts and payments account for presentation to the members at the annual general meeting. Other members may be appointed to the committee for general purposes (a social secretary, for example). Subcommittees may be appointed to deal with particular matters: their authority comes from the committee, or possibly from the members themselves if the appointment was from a general meeting of a club. Any action taken by such a committee (for example, suspension of a member) is subject to the rules of natural justice and the constitution of the club.

The powers, duties and functions of the management committee are normally contained in the constitution of the club or society.

4.3 Legal Liability of Unincorporated Associations

The law regards these organisations as mere collections of individuals banded together to pursue certain aims, and bearing individual responsibility for the actions of the association. A member making contracts ostensibly on behalf of the club, but without actual authority to act as the club's agent will be personally liable on the contract. If he acts in an official capacity on behalf of the committee, the committee which authorised the agency will be jointly liable, or the members may be jointly liable if they collectively authorised the contract.

With regard to torts, where a tort is committed by an individual member that individual will be liable, as in *Prole v. Allen (1950)*.

Prole v. Allen (1950). Acting through the committee, all the members of an unincorporated members' club appointed a steward who, by his negligence, caused injury to the plaintiff, a club member. **Held:** the steward, but not the members of the committee, was liable to the plaintiff in respect of the injuries which she received. (Courtesy of *Cracknell's Law Students' Companion*)

However, where the committee have approved the employment of an incompetent person to do work they may be held jointly liable, as in *Brown v. Lewis (1896)*.

Brown v. Lewis (1896). The stand at the ground of the Blackburn Rovers Football Club collapsed and caused injury to the plaintiff. The accident occurred because the club committee had employed an incompetent person to repair the stand. **Held:** the members of the committee were personally liable and the plaintiff was entitled to recover damages from them. (Courtesy of *Cracknell's Law Students' Companion*)

The members are not usually liable, unless the rules make it quite clear that they are liable.

4.4 Unincorporated Associations and the Ownership of Land

Where many people own land jointly it becomes very difficult to transfer landed property, since the agreement of all must be secured. To overcome this type of difficulty the *Law of Property Act, 1925*, restricted the number of people who could own any piece of land to four. Consequently the members of a club may nominate up to four members to hold land as trustees. In any transfer of land the agreement of the trustees is all that is required, and the trustees are also entitled to sue or be sued on any matter affecting the property.

4.5 Legal Actions affecting Unincorporated Associations

When a club is involved in a legal action it is usual for one representative or more to sue, or be selected as a target to be sued, in the courts. The rules of the Supreme Court say that the proceedings may be begun, and continued, unless the court otherwise orders, against one or more representing all. The decision of the court will then be binding on the association.

Where an organisation is a trade union recognised as such by inclusion in a special register of trade unions, or is an employer's association included in a special register of employers' associations, it shall be capable of suing in its own name, and being sued in its own name, save that the law has recognised the immunity of such bodies (at present) from actions in tort for damage suffered, caused by action in furtherance of a trade dispute. Secondary action – defined in the *Employment Act, 1980*, as amended by the *Employment Act, 1982* – is not protected by this immunity in certain circumstances.

The Registrar of Friendly Societies is given the task of compiling lists of trade unions and employers' associations and ensuring that they comply with certain administrative and accounting requirements.

4.6 Revision Test

Answers	*Questions*
–	**1.** What is an unincorporated association?
1. It is a business unit whose members act together to achieve certain aims without assuming any separate corporate legal status.	**2.** Give examples of unincorporated associations.
2. Clubs, societies, certain types of cooperatives, trade unions, employers' organisations and partnerships.	**3.** How may such bodies bring legal actions, or be sued?

Answers	*Questions*
3. Representatively, by choosing one or more individuals to bring the action, or be the target for the action.	**4.** Where does the legal responsibility lie for contracts made by unincorporated associations?
4. If the contract is made by a particular individual it lies with that individual. If the individual can show he was authorised by a committee the committee will be collectively liable.	**5.** Are the members personally liable?
5. Not usually, unless the rules clearly state that this is so.	**6.** Who is liable for torts performed by a member acting for the club?
6. Usually the member will be liable, but if the loss suffered arose from the acts of a committee the whole committee may be jointly liable.	**7.** How is landed property owned by an unincorporated association?
7. Up to four members may be nominated as trustees to hold the land for the benefit of the club.	**8.** What is special about the situation of trade unions and employers' organisations?
8. (*a*) They can sue and be sued in their organisation's name, provided they are registered. (*b*) They cannot be sued in tort for losses suffered in consequence of a trade dispute, except for certain cases of secondary action, i.e. action against an individual not directly engaged in the dispute.	**9.** Go over the page again if necessary. Then try some of the questions in Appendix 1.

5
Business Entities: Limited Companies

5.1 The Nature of a Limited Company

As industry developed the demand for capital could not be satisfied from profits created in business, and it became necessary to ask other people – not directly involved in the business – to contribute capital. In the early days of the Industrial Revolution those who contributed capital in this way were held to be full partners, with unlimited liability. Since many projects were highly speculative, and collapsed leaving enormous debts, many unsophisticated investors were ruined. Thousands lost their homes when speculative projects collapsed and the partners were required to contribute to pay the debts of the firms concerned. Only in 1855, when the increasing demands for capital met resistance from savers who had already seen others suffer hardship through no fault of their own, did Parliament sanction limited liability for shareholders. Parliament took the view that where a person has funds to contribute which can be used by others for the promotion of business activity, but does not wish himself to take any part in the conduct of the business or the management of the firm, it seems unfair to require him to carry the burden of unlimited liability which attaches to sole traders or partners. The principle of limited liability holds that such a person should be liable to the extent of the capital he has contributed, or agreed to contribute, but no further than this. The limitation of liability in this way unlocks savings which would otherwise merely be hoarded by their owners, and releases them to play a productive part in the industrial and commercial fields.

Companies are also called corporations and are of three types, depending on their mode of creation: chartered companies, statutory companies and registered companies. **Chartered companies** are set up by the granting of a Royal Charter, and the classic examples were the East India Company, the Hudson Bay Company, and certain universities. Today charters are usually reserved for professional organisations like the Chartered Institute of Transport. **Statutory companies** were set up by the passage of an Act of Parliament. This method was used for most of the early companies, such as canal and railway companies. The Act embodied the safeguards Parliament deemed necessary, and accorded the powers to purchase land compulsorily, etc. As the number of such enterprises grew a simpler system was required. The **registered company** system enabled companies to be set up by a simple procedure of registration with the Registrar of Companies.

The first Companies Act also accorded limited liability to the shareholders: today the effective Act is the *1985 Companies Act*, which consolidated all the earlier Acts of 1948, 1967, 1976, 1980 and 1981 into a single comprehensive statute. It is an essential study for any student of Business Law.

However the law on insolvency both for individuals and companies required serious revision and it was decided to consolidate insolvency law into a single Act, the Insolvency Act 1986. Accordingly, in this chapter such matters have been given the references of this 1986 Act, e.g. I.A.:S.120.

Types of Registered Companies. Registered companies are of two kinds: **public companies** and **private companies**. Public companies tend to be larger than private companies, and are required to have a name which ends with the words 'Public Limited Company' (abbreviated to PLC). It must have a capital of at least £50,000 and one quarter at least of each share shall actually have been paid. The figure of £50,000 may be modified to such sum as the Secretary of State may determine at some future time (to take account of inflation) (S.118, *Companies Act, 1985*). Public companies may offer their shares to the public, but private companies, whose names must end in the word 'Limited', are not allowed to offer their shares to the public. Provisions exist for a company to convert from one type to the other; for example, for a private company to register as a public company a special resolution must be passed to authorise the company to conform with the requirements mentioned above (S.43 and 45, 1985 Act).

5.2 Basic Characteristics of a Public Company

(*a*) It must be incorporated or formed by registration in accordance with the *Companies Acts, 1985*.

(*b*) It must display the letters 'PLC' (public limited company) after its name – for example, on its memorandum of association, in notices on public display at its place of business and on its company stationery.

(*c*) It must have a minimum capital of £50,000 of which at least one quarter must be paid before trading commences.

(*d*) Where its articles do not provide otherwise, the company may apply for a stock exchange quotation and offer its shares to the public.

(*e*) It may transfer its shares freely.

(*f*) The minimum membership is two, and there is no maximum, except that the limit is set by the number of shares issued.

(*g*) It must have at least two directors.

(*h*) Before issuing shares, the promoter of the company must issue a prospectus, or a statement in lieu of prospectus must be filed with the Registrar of Companies at least three days before any shares or debentures are allotted.

5.3 The Formation of a Company

To form a company certain formalities are required to be followed. The law requires that the following documents must be forwarded to the

Registrar of Companies for England and Wales along with the requisite fees and stamp duties:

(*a*) A memorandum of association.
(*b*) A set of articles of association.
(*c*) A statutory declaration that the requirements of the Companies Act in respect of registration have been complied with.
(*d*) The names of the intended first director or directors and first secretary or joint secretaries with their written consents to take up shares.
(*e*) A statement of capital.

When the Registrar receives the documents he examines them to see that they have been completed satisfactorily and that the statutory requirements have been complied with. These are that the memorandum has been signed by at least two persons; that the company is being formed for a lawful purpose; that the proposed name is acceptable; and that the memorandum and articles are in the statutory form. When satisfied, the Registrar issues a **Certificate of Incorporation**, which can be described as the company's birth certificate. A private company may commence trading at this point while a public company has to wait until the Registrar issues a **trading certificate** under S.117 of the 1985 Act. S.117(6) of the 1985 Act provides that a Certificate of Incorporation is conclusive evidence that all the requirements of the Act in respect of registration have been complied with. The effect of registration is that from the date in the certificate the original subscribers and any others who later become members are a body corporate with the name given in the Memorandum.

Before a company begins trading it must secure the capital it needs. With a private company this will be contributed largely by the founders so there is no difficulty. With a public company it must be obtained from the public either directly or indirectly through the institutional investors. In order to do this the company issues a prospectus which tells members of the public about the company and invites them to subscribe for shares in the enterprise. Two of the most important documents connected with registration of a company – namely, the memorandum and the articles of association – will now be considered individually.

The Memorandum of Association

This document is a deed signed by at least two persons, called 'subscribers' or 'promoters', which states and defines the constitution and powers of the company. The format of a memorandum for each type of company is issued in a statutory instrument under S.3 of the 1985 Act. The Act requires that a memorandum contains the following pieces of information.

(*a*) *The name of the company, with 'Limited' as the last word for a private limited company*. A public company's name must end with the words 'public limited company' which is abbreviated to PLC. The word 'limited' tells anyone who does business with the company that the shareholders have limited liability. It is a warning to them not to deal with the company unless they are quite sure they can afford the risk. Many people think a company is more reliable to deal with than a sole trader or partnership, but this is not necessarily so, since creditors can only claim against the capital contributed. This may be as low as the members like, and in practice £100 companies are often formed to be available at any time they are required. If the reader consults any newspaper which has a business section he will see companies offered for sale. At the time of writing the cost is about £120 and the companies are usually £100 companies. A businessman wishing to set up a company saves time and trouble by purchasing one ready-made. The objects of a company can be varied by a simple procedure, and so can the authorised capital, and the name. So a company which has been set up by a specialist company promoter can be taken over for a nominal sum and altered to suit the needs of any businessman. Whether a company is taken over in this way or set up in the way being described, the word 'limited' at the end of the name tells everyone dealing with the company that they can only look to that £100, or any authorised increased sum, for satisfaction in the event of difficulties. Although S.17 of the *Companies Act, 1948*, provided that 'no company shall be registered by a name which in the opinion of the Board of Trade is undesirable', the *Companies Act, 1985*, makes changes in this area. Whereas previously the Registrar of Companies ensured that all proposed names were checked and the undesirable ones rejected, the new Act places the onus on self-regulation. An index of company names is maintained by the Registrar and the Act prohibits certain names, i.e. those of existing companies or offensive names. If an undesirable name is registered and subsequently discovered within 12 months, the company may be forced to change its name. The Act basically reduces the work of the Registrar and reduces public costs, thereby requiring established companies to do more checking for themselves.

(*b*) *Whether the registered office is situated in England, Wales or Scotland.* If the address of the registered office does not appear in the memorandum, it must be provided separately within 14 days of incorporation.

(*c*) *The objects of the company*. The objects clause states the powers (*vires*) of the company; what it will do when it is established; and forms the legal basis for its activities within the fields specified. Other activities are *ultra vires* (outside its powers). This is a protection to the shareholders. Suppose I invested £500 in a company that was to develop a revolutionary type of aero engine, which I believed had a great future. I suddenly discover that the directors are using my money to buy sugar, which happens to be rising on world markets. I would naturally feel that this was not the purpose for which I had subscribed my capital, and would be able to obtain an injunction restraining the directors from using my money in this *ultra vires* way. For example, in *Ashbury Railway Carriage and Iron Co. v. Riche* (*1875*) a statutory company's objects allowed it to make and sell or lend or hire, railway carriages and wagons. However, the company contracted to finance the construction of a railway in Belgium. The company ratified its action subsequently by passing a resolution in accordance with its articles of association. The company later repudiated its contract and when sued by Messrs Riche for breach of contract, the company set up the defence of *'ultra vires'*. The House of Lords held unanimously that the contract was *ultra vires* the company and hence void; no subsequent agreement of the members could ratify the company's action. According to

Lord Cairns, L.C.: '. . . it is not a question whether the contract ever was ratified or was not ratified. If it was a contract void at its beginning, it was void because the company could not make the contract.'

In *A.G. v. Great Eastern Railway* (1880) it was held that a company's objects shall include not simply the stated objects in its memorandum but also by implication power to do anything which is reasonably incidental to the carrying out of those objects. Further, *Re Jon Beauforte, Ltd (1953)* provides evidence that where goods are supplied to a company under a *prima facie ultra vires* contract and if the company uses those goods for *intra vires* purposes and the person supplying the goods has no knowledge that the goods will be used for *ultra vires* purposes, then the contract may not be held to be *ultra vires.*

In *Introductions Ltd v. National Provincial Bank Ltd (1969)*, a company was formed and its objects enabled it to provide services and accommodation for visitors to the Festival of Britain in 1951. At a later date, as a result of a change in management, the company began pig-farming contrary to its objects, and borrowed money. The pig scheme failed and when sued by the bank the liquidator put forward the defence of *ultra vires* while the bank placed reliance on an independent objects clause under which the company could borrow for any purpose which in the opinion of the directors could be advantageously carried out either in connection with or as ancillary to the business of the company. The Court of Appeal held the borrowing as *ultra vires* since the power of borrowing could not be exercised independently of the objects of the company. It must be noted, however, that the objects clauses of modern companies are elaborately drawn and may allow a company to engage in numerous types of business activities. The wording used in modern memorandums allows a certain amount of interpretation. Legal advice should be sought by a person dealing with a company whose objectives cannot be clearly identified.

The *ultra vires* doctrine has been modified and weakened as a result of the UK becoming a member of European Economic Community. The *European Communities Act* changed the law (since the principle is not known in other European countries) and the 1985 Act S.35 now provides:

(*a*)'In favour of a person dealing with a company in good faith, any transaction decided on by the directors is deemed to be one which it is within the capacity of the company to enter into, and the power of the directors to bind the company is deemed to be free of any limitation under the memorandum or articles.

(*b*) A party to a transaction so decided on is not bound to enquire as to the capacity of the company to enter into it or as to any such limitation on the powers of the directors, and is presumed to have acted in good faith unless the contrary is proved.'

The essence of the above provision seems to be that while an outsider dealing with the company can put forward the plea of *ultra vires* if the company has exceeded its authority, the company itself cannot rely on the *ultra vires* rule as a defence against someone dealing with the company in good faith. Other important aspects of this provision are: (*a*) that it only applies to a transaction decided on by the directors, which presumably includes the managing director where authority has been properly delegated to the latter; and (*b*) action can be *ultra vires* the articles as well as *ultra vires* the objects clause of the memorandum of association.

The effect of S.9(i) seems to be that the cases mentioned above would be decided differently today. However, until such time as this section has been tested and interpreted in the courts, its exact legal implications will remain unknown (see 1982 case on page 88).

It must be noted that protection is also afforded to an outsider under the rule established in *Royal British Bank v. Turquand* (*1856*). It was held in this case that in dealing with a company an outsider can assume that all the internal requirements or formalities have been completed by the company (e.g. the passing of a resolution at a general meeting) and a director or directors acting without authority in such circumstances will bind the company on any contracts entered into.

(*d*) *A statement that the liability of the members is limited.*

(*e*) *The amount of share capital to be issued and the type of shares.*

Note: Besides the above points a memorandum of association must be accompanied by a statement in the prescribed form giving the names and relevant particulars of the first director or directors, and the first secretary or joint secretaries, and their consents to the appointments.

Alterations to the essential clauses mentioned above may be made provided the statutory requirements laid down in the *Companies Act, 1985*, are satisfied. For example, the name may be changed by a special resolution under S.18 of the Act; the objects of the company may be changed by special resolution and by fulfilling the requirements of S.4, 5 and 6; alterations of capital must comply with S.121; the creation of reserve capital must comply with S.120 and S.124; reduction of capital with S.135; if the liability of directors is made unlimited it must comply with S.307 and in the case of a private company if the limited liability clause is altered S.49, 50 and 516 must be complied with.

The Articles of Association

Having drawn up and signed the memorandum of association, the promoters usually then draw up detailed articles of association which control the internal affairs of the company. Such matters as the procedure to be followed at meetings, appointment and duties of the directors and the managing director, the borrowing powers that may be exercised, and so on, are considered and agreed. A set of model articles, called Table A, is printed as a statutory instrument (at present 1984 No.1717). These articles will be effective and binding on all companies issuing shares, unless the company's own articles specifically invalidate them on some point.

S.9 of the 1985 Act provides that the articles may be altered by special resolution. The case of *Allen v. Gold Reefs of West Africa Ltd* (*1900*) suggests that not only the statutory requirements must be fulfilled for any alteration but that the alteration must be '*bona fide* for the benefit of the company as a whole . . .' (per Lord Lindley, M.R.). The case is also authority for the proposition that alterations may have retrospective effect.

All the documents relating to a company are kept in a file at the Companies Registry at Companies House. The file is open for inspection by anyone for a nominal fee.

5.4 The Consequences of Incorporation

As a consequence of registration and the issue of a Certificate of Incorporation a company comes into existence. One of the fundamental results of this is that the company acquires its own independent legal personality. The law regards the company as a separate legal entity, distinct from and independent of the persons who manage it (the directors) or those who own it (the shareholders). This separate legal personality of a company was confirmed by The House of Lords decision in *Salomon v. Salomon and Co. Ltd (1897)*.

Salomon v. Salomon (1897). Salomon owned a profitable boot manufacturing business and converted to a limited company. The company then issued a debenture to Salomon for £10,000, secured on the total assets of the company. Later the company got into difficulties and became insolvent. When the creditors attempted to recover their money Salomon claimed all the assets which were his security for the debenture. **Held:** the debenture took priority. The company was a different person in law from the controlling shareholder and the unsecured creditors could not defeat his claim.

The principle of separate corporate personality of a company established in Salomon's case is also referred to as 'the veil of incorporation'. As a general rule the courts will not go beyond this veil of incorporation except in some of the following instances where the separate personality of a company may either be ignored or modified:

(*a*) In time of war in order to find out who the members of the company are to determine whether or not the company has enemy characteristics (*Daimler Co. Ltd v. Continental Tyre & Rubber Co. (Gt Britain) Ltd (1916)*).

(*b*) In circumstances indicating that the company was formed for a fraudulent purpose (*Re F.G. Films Ltd (1953)*). S.458 and S.630 of the 1985 Act provide that if a company engages in fraudulent trading, any persons who knowingly become partners to the fraud are personally liable for the debts and other liabilities of the company.

(*c*) Where a company makes a loan to a director, as in *Wallersteiner v. Moir (1974)*. A director made a loan to another company which was his puppet. **Held:** The loan should be treated as made to the director personally.

(*d*) If a company carries on business for more than six months with less than the statutory minimum of members (two for both private and public companies – *Companies Act, 1985*), the person carrying on business may be made personally liable to the creditors for the debts of the company (S.24, 1985 Act).

(*e*) In some cases the courts may want to investigate the control structures of companies to determine the question of residence for tax purposes (*Unit Construction Co. Ltd v. Bullock (1960)*).

Liability for Torts

A company is liable for the torts committed by its servants in the course of their employment, e.g. negligence, fraud or libel (*Citizens Life Assurance Co. v. Brown* (*1904*) and *Houldsworth v. City of Glasgow Bank* (*1880*)). A company may also be criminally liable for the acts of its organs. In *R. v. I.C.R. Haulage Ltd* (*1944*), the fraud committed by the managing director was imputed to the company, although the court accepted that there were some crimes which a company was not capable of committing. The company can own land, buy property and employ people. Company property belongs to the company itself and not to any individual member. A company may enter into contracts, it can sue and be sued. The death of any members of the company does not affect the company since it enjoys perpetual succession unless wound up or dissolved. The liability of the company is limited to the amount of its share capital and the liability of its members is limited to any outstanding amount on the shares the members hold.

5.5 Share Capital of a Company, and Debentures

A person will invest in a company either by taking up shares and thus becoming a member of the company or by making a loan to the company usually against a security – he will then be issued with a debenture certificate, thus becoming a debenture holder. A debenture holder is not a member of the company and does not therefore have voting rights. He is a creditor of the company who is entitled to interest at a fixed rate on his loan to the company.

When a person takes up a share he is issued with a share certificate. The basic characteristics of a share were described by Farwell J. in *Borland's Trustee v. Steel Bros. & Co. Ltd* (*1901*) as follows:

> 'A share is the interest of a shareholder in the company measured by a sum of money, for the purpose of liability in the first place, and of interest in the second, but also consisting of a series of mutual covenants entered into by all the shareholders *inter se*.'

Note that the word 'interest' here may be confusing. It does not refer to any rate of interest, but to the extent that the shareholder is financially interested in the company. The reward enjoyed by the shareholder for buying a share takes the form of a dividend, which depends upon the type of share held, the profitability of the enterprise and the recommendations of the directors. The interest of a shareholder is the extent to which his ownership of the company extends.

Various terms are used to describe the share capital of a company: the **authorised or nominal capital** is the amount that a company may raise ultimately by issuing its shares; the **issued capital** is that portion of the authorised capital which has been issued by the company and the **uncalled capital** is that part of the issued capital which has not been called and/or paid by the shareholders; the **reserve capital** is that part of the uncalled capital which has been set aside by special resolution and will only be called up in the event of the company being wound up (S.120, 1985 Act).

When a share is issued **at par**, it is issued at its present nominal value. If issued above the nominal value it is said to be issued at a **premium** and if issued below its nominal value it is said to be issued at a **discount**. (Shares may no longer be issued at a discount, even by leave of the court.)

The share capital of a company may consist of different types of shares and the rights of different classes of shareholders will be set out in the company's articles. A company's share capital may consist of:

(*a*) **Ordinary Shares.** The holders of these shares do not have any special rights apart from voting rights. Companies may issue non-voting ordinary shares. The holders of ordinary shares receive any dividend that the directors may recommend after the preference shareholders have received their dividend. The extent of the dividend paid to these shareholders will vary with the fortunes of the company. Ordinary share capital is also called 'equity' share capital, since all shares participate equally in the profits, or share equally in any losses. Because the risks are greater for equity shares than for preference shares equity capital is also spoken of as 'risk' capital.

(*b*) **Preference Shares.** The issue of these shares is authorised by the memorandum or the articles and the holders of the shares receive priority over other shareholders of the company. The holders are paid a fixed rate of dividend and usually also have preferential rights to repayment of capital in the event of winding up. The rights of holders of these shares may vary considerably from company to company and they may or may not be eligible to vote at a general meeting. Preference shares may be **cumulative**, in which case the fixed rate of dividend payable is carried to future years until the company makes sufficient profits. When they are **non-cumulative** the shortfall or dividend will not be made good in future years. Holders of **'participating'** preference shares will participate in any further distribution of funds to equity shareholders. Thus if shares are designated as 7 per cent participating preference shares the preference shareholders will first be awarded 7 per cent. If the ordinary shareholders are then awarded 20 per cent the preference shareholders would be entitled to participate in this more extensive distribution of profits and would be entitled to a further 13 per cent dividend.

The 1981 Act repealed S.58 of the Companies Act (which authorised the issue of **redeemable** preference shares). Instead S.159 of the 1985 Act permits companies to issue redeemable shares of any type. The shares may only be redeemed out of the distributable profits of the company, or out of the proceeds of a fresh issue of shares made for the purposes of the redemption. Any premium payable on redemption must also be paid out of distributable profits of the company, except where they were originally issued at a premium, when special rules apply. Shares redeemed in this way may be treated as cancelled on redemption, and reduce the amount of the company's issued share capital, but the authorised capital is not reduced – and hence the shares could be reissued at a future date.

Another innovation under S.162 of the 1985 Act is the power granted to companies to purchase their own shares. Certain safeguards are built into the Act, but the general effect is that the company may use the distributable profits to purchase and cancel shares, if authorised to do so by its articles.

(*c*) **Deferred or Founders' Shares.** The holders of these shares receive a dividend after the declaration of dividends on the preference and ordinary shares. These shares are usually held by promoters and directors of the company and are also known as management shares. The extent of the dividends will vary according to the profits made by the company, and may be very lucrative. The willingness of a founder of a business to accept 'founders'' shares in part settlement of the purchase price when selling the business to a company is evidence of his belief in the future viability of the business, since they rank for dividend only after the other shareholders have received some reward.

(*d*) **Stocks and Shares.** A company's share capital may consist of stocks and shares. The difference between the two is that whereas stocks are fully-paid and may be assigned in fragments in fractional amounts, shares may have been partly paid and cannot be divided up. Fully-paid shares may be converted by the company into stock, e.g. 100 £1 shares may be converted into four stock certificates of £25.

(*e*) **Debentures.** Apart from raising capital through the issue of shares, an important and common means of raising capital for the company is by the issue of debentures. A debenture is a document issued to a person who extends a loan to the company. The document acknowledges the debt owed by the company and the debenture holder becomes a creditor of the company, receiving a fixed rate of interest. The debenture holder, unlike a shareholder, is not a member of the company and hence does not have any voting rights.

A debenture is normally secured by a fixed or floating charge over the company's assets. Where specific assets (e.g. plant and machinery) are given as security the debenture holder is said to have a **fixed charge** over the company's assets. In the circumstances, the company cannot deal with the assets or sell them without the consent of the debenture holder. A **floating charge** exists where the circulating assets (e.g. stock in trade) are given as security. Here the company does not require express permission of the debenture holder in order to deal with or sell the assets charged. Whether a debenture is secured by a fixed charge or a floating charge, the debenture holder has the ultimate power to enforce the security in the event of default by the company on the loan. S.395 of the *Companies Act, 1985*, requires charges to be registered with the Registrar of Companies within 21 days of their creation. Failure to register will mean that the charges will be void against a creditor or a liquidator of the company.

5.6 The Management of Companies

Since a company is an artificial legal person it can act only through natural persons – the directors and other officers who are empowered to act on its behalf. The type and extent of these powers will depend on the company's articles. A typical company structure may look something like the one shown in Fig. 5.1.

Whereas in a private company the directors and shareholders are usually the same persons, in a public company this is not the case as the officials may hold only a few shares in the company and hence effectively the management is divorced from the ownership of the company. Although the shareholders appoint and can dismiss the directors, once appointed the management of the company rests with the directors. Their powers, con-

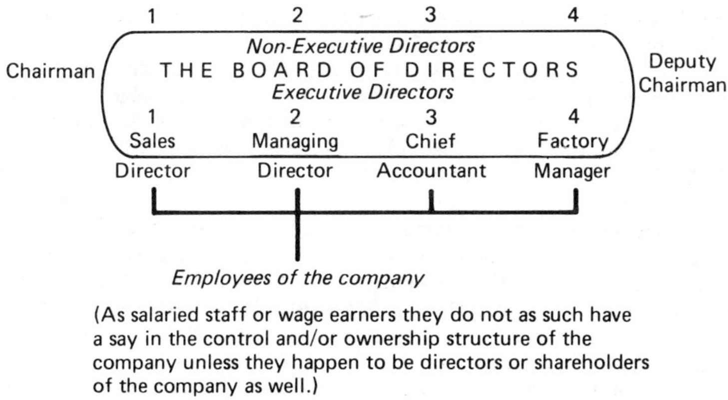

Fig. 5.1. A typical company structure

tained in the articles of association, must be exercised *bona fide* for the benefit of the company as a whole. The shareholders cannot interfere with the exercise of the directors' powers unless these are exceeded and neither can they interfere with the day-to-day management of the company.

The directors together form a board of directors which then constitutes the governing body of the company. The board may in turn appoint a managing director as provided in the memorandum or the articles. His status depends on the powers conferred on him by the company.

5.7 Company Directors

The management of the company is entrusted to a small group of persons called directors. As trustees and agents of the company, onerous liabilities and responsibilities are placed on them. Directors are appointed by the shareholders and hold office in accordance with the terms of the articles. These may require that they hold qualification shares in the company. The minimum number of directors required in a public company is two (S.282, 1985 Act), while for a private company there need only be one director but he cannot also be appointed as a secretary (S.283). Certain persons cannot be appointed as directors and these are:

(*a*) A person aged 70 or over, with certain exceptions – for example, if the company is a private company, or if the articles otherwise provide, or the appointment is by a resolution in which special notice of the age is given (S.293, 1985 Act).

(*b*) An undischarged bankrupt (S. 302).

(*c*) A person convicted of an indictable offence connected with the promotion, formation or management of a company (S.295–299). These offences have now been extended to include offences connected with liquidation, receivership or management of a company.

(*d*) A person found guilty of fraud or any breach of duty in relation to a company while an officer of the company.

(*e*) A person who has been persistently in default of compliance with the Companies Acts (S.297, 1985 Act).

(*f*) A person who is, or has been, a director of an insolvent company and is, or has been, a director of another such company which has gone into liquidation whithin five years of the first mentioned company and whose conduct as a director in any of those companies makes him unfit (S.300, 1985 Act).

A director may resign at any time and provision for this is made in the articles. Provision for retirement is also made in the articles, and under S.303 of the 1985 Act the company can remove a director by ordinary resolution before his period of office has expired, notwithstanding anything in the articles. Provisions may exist in the articles on disqualifications from acting or continuing to act as a director, over and above those contained in the 1985 Act – for example, under S.302 it is an offence for an undischarged bankrupt to act as a director without authority of the court.

S.288 of the 1985 Act requires the company to keep at its registered office a register of all its directors and secretaries. The register must contain their names, addresses, nationalities and business occupations and must give particulars of any other directorships held. S.324 of the 1985 Act and S.325), oblige a director to notify the company of his interests in shares or debentures held in the company or any associated companies. These must be registered. In this respect, the interests of a director's spouse and infant children are considered that of the director. The 1985 Act has tightened up and extended the law on the disclosure of interests in shares – for example, by requiring disclosure by persons acting together to acquire an interest in a 'target company'. S.325 of the 1985 Act obliges the company to keep a register containing information about a directors' interests in the company or any associated companies. The registers containing information on company directors must be kept at the registered office and be available for inspection by members of the company without any charge and by non-members for a minimal charge.

Also available for inspection must be copies of each of the directors' contracts of service as required by S.318 of the 1985 Act. S.323 of the 1985 Act penalises the directors, and any shadow directors, for any option dealing, i.e. buying or selling any quoted shares or debentures of the company or associated companies. This prohibition is intended to further the interests of fairness by denying directors an opportunity to use 'inside' information which the ordinary members do not possess. It can also be justified as a means of preventing 'insiders' from manipulating the stock-markets. The primary aim of this section is to protect members. A new bill on insider dealing is currently (1987) being considered by Parliament.

Directors are managers or controllers of the company and normally receive remuneration in accordance with the terms of the articles. Accordingly, directors cannot claim payment for their services unless provision is made in the articles. The remuneration of the directors is normally determined by the company at general meetings. Directors cannot be compensated for loss of office or when retiring unless the amount is disclosed to the members and approved by the company (S.312, 1985 Act). It is illegal for a company to make tax-free payments to any of its directors as the law considers any such payments made to be subject to tax (S.311, 1985 Act). Particulars of directors' salaries, pensions, etc., must be mentioned in the company accounts and laid before the company at general meetings (S.231, 1985 Act). S.231 and 237 of the 1985 Act further provide that these accounts must contain certain additional information on the directors' emoluments. S.330 of the 1985 Act prohibits the company from making a loan to a director of the company or its holding company or to provide guarantee or security for a loan made to a director by any other person.

Let us now consider the directors' positions and their other duties. As a general rule directors cannot be regarded as servants of the company but there are cases to the effect that a managing director who devotes his full time to the affairs of the company may be regarded as employed by the company (*Trussed Steel Concrete Co. Ltd v. Green* (1946)). It is also recognised that for some purposes a director may be regarded as a servant of the company. For example, in *Lee v. Lee's Air Farming Ltd* (*1961*) the Privy Council held that a person who happened to hold all the shares except one and to be managing director and pilot of a company engaged in crop-spraying could also be regarded as a servant of the company and his widow could therefore recover under the *Workmen's Compensation Act*, effective at that time.

Essentially directors occupy twin roles within a company as trustees and agents. 'The directors are the mere trustees or agents of the company – trustees of the company's money and property, agents in the transactions which they enter into on behalf of the company' (per Lord Selbourne, L.C., in *Great Eastern Railway Co. v. Turner* (*1872*)). As trustees of the company's money and property they must ensure that these are used solely for the benefit of the company. Any misapplication of funds or property is regarded as a breach of trust for which the directors may be called to account (*Wallersteiner v. Moir* (*No. 2*) (*1975*)).

As trustees of the powers conferred on them the directors must ensure that these are used *bona fide* for the benefit of the company as a whole – for example, where powers are given to issue shares, these must be used for raising capital when required by the company and not for the purpose of maintaining control of the company and preventing the election of additional directors (*Piercy v. S. Mills & Co. Ltd* (*1920*)). As trustees of the powers, they cannot fetter their future discretion, i.e. they cannot contract either with one another or third parties on how they shall vote at future board meetings (*Selangor United Rubber Estates Ltd v. Cradock* (*1968*)).

As agents of the company directors bind the company on contracts with outsiders so long as they act within the scope of their authority. They will not incur personal liability for *intra vires* contracts (*Elkington & Co. v. Hürter* (*1892*)). However, if the directors were to exceed the authority conferred on them by the articles and memorandum they might be liable for breach of warranty of authority (*Firbank's Executors v. Humphreys* (*1886*)). **Ultra vires** contracts made by directors can be ratified by a resolution at a general meeting or the articles of the company may be altered retrospectively by a special resolution. Note that the foregoing will only apply to contracts *ultra vires* the directors and not the contracts *ultra vires* the company, which are void and cannot be ratified (*Ashbury Rail Carriage & Iron Co. v. Riche* – see page 62). For principles of agency, see Chapter 13.

The directors of a company owe the following duties to the company:

(*a*) *A duty of care and skill.* Directors are required to exercise ordinary care and skill in discharging their duties. They will be held liable for neglecting their duties only if they are guilty of 'gross or culpable negligence in a business sense' (Romer, J., in *Re City Equitable Fire Insurance Co. Ltd* (*1925*)): on the question of the duties, the judge said that a director is not required to display in performing his duties a greater degree of skill than can reasonably be expected from a person of the director's knowledge and experience, e.g. 'a director of a life insurance company . . . does not guarantee that he has the skill of an actuary or physician'. Further, a director is not bound to give continuous attention to the affairs of the company as his duties are of an intermittent nature. Lastly, a director can properly delegate his duties and be justified in trusting that the duties will be performed honestly. In *Re Duomatic Ltd* (*1969*), where the directors had compensated a former director for loss of office without notifying the shareholders (S.191, 1948 Act – now S.312, 1985 Act), it was held they had acted unreasonably in failing to take legal advice on the point.

(*b*) *Duty of loyalty and good faith.* Since directors occupy a fiduciary position *vis-à-vis* the company they owe their duties to the whole company as a corporate body. They do not therefore owe a fiduciary duty to any individual shareholder (*Percival v. Wright* (*1902*)), and neither should the directors when considering what is in the best interests of the company give prominence to their duty to employees only as opposed to their prime duty to the shareholders (*Parke v. Daily News Ltd* (*1962*)). Directors are barred from any sort of 'insider' dealings.

Because of their position, directors should not allow themselves to be placed in a situation where their personal interests may conflict with their duties to the company.

Transvaal Lands Co. v. New Belgium (*Transvaal*) *Land Co.* (*1914*). The articles of T.L.Co. provided that its directors could not vote in respect of contracts in which they had an interest. H was a shareholder in both the companies and a director of T.L.Co. H voted in favour of the purchase but did not disclose his interest in the N.B.Co. as required also by the articles of T.L.Co. **Held:** the contract was voidable.

S.317 of the 1985 Act provides that 'it shall be the duty of a director of a company who is in any way, whether directly or indirectly, interested in a contract or proposed contract with the company to declare the nature of his interest at a meeting of the directors of the company'. A fine is imposed for failure to comply with this duty and this section in no way prejudices the right of a company to impose a more rigorous penalty in accordance with its articles, nor does it 'prejudice the operation of any rule of law restricting directors of a company from having interests in contracts with the company' (S.317(9)).

A breach of S.317 does not mean that the contract is a nullity; it means that the contract is *prima facie* voidable at the option of the company (*Hely-Hutchinson v. Brayhead Ltd* (*1968*)). Any secret profits made or benefits received by a director on such a contract must be accounted for by the director. In *Boston Deep Sea Fishing & Ice Co. v. Ansell* (*1888*), Bowen, L.J., stated: 'There can be no question that an agent employed by a principal or master to do business with another, who, unknown to that principal or master, takes from that other person a profit arising out of the business which he is employed to transact, is doing a wrongful act inconsistent with his duty towards his master, and the continuance of confidence between them. . . . If it is a profit which arises out of the transaction, it belongs to his master, and the agent or servant has no right to take it, or keep it, or bargain for it, or receive it without bargain, unless his master knows of it.' The facts of the case were that A was a director of B.Co. and on the company's behalf contracted for the building of fishing smacks. Unknown to the company, A was paid a commission on the contract from the other party to the contract. In addition A received a bonus from B.Co. of which he was a shareholder and which supplied ice to the fishing smacks. **Held:** A must account to B.Co. for both the commission and the bonus.

Finally, concerning directors' duties, S.310 of the 1985 Act provides that any exclusion of liability in respect of a director for 'any negligence, default, breach of duty or breach of trust of which he may be guilty in relation to the company shall be void'.

The 1985 Act embodies numerous measures introduced by Parliament to ensure fair dealing by directors. In particular:

(*a*) Directors are required to have regard to employees' interests; employees cannot, however, enforce the duty.

(*b*) Service contracts for more than five years require the approval of a general meeting.

(*c*) Any 'substantial' property transaction between a director and the company also requires the sanction of a general meeting.

(*d*) Increased provisions for disclosure in the accounts of loans and contracts in which directors have an interest are imposed.

(*e*) Regarding insider dealings, the exclusion from dealings on the open market now includes a person who is, or during the last six months has been, knowingly connected with a company. Such a person may not deal in the securities of the company, or a related company, or one which the company has had dealings with, if he has unpublished price-sensitive information. Nor may he counsel or procure another to deal, or communicate the information to another. The maximum penalty is two years imprisonment and/or an unlimited fine.

On the question of enforcing director's duties, the rule established in *Foss v. Harbottle* (*1843*) and as stated by Lord Davey in *Burland v. Earle* (*1902*) is that 'in order to redress a wrong done to the company or to recover moneys or damages alleged to be due to the company, the action should *prima facie* be brought by the company itself'. No outsider, member or director of a company may bring an action for an alleged wrong done to the company except the company itself. In *Foss v. Harbottle*, two members of the company had instigated proceedings against the company directors, alleging fraud and mismanagement of the company's assets. Upholding the corporate principle of a company, the court held that in such a case the proper plaintiff was the company and the matter was considered to be a matter of internal management which could have been ratified by a majority of the members.

The rule in *Foss v. Harbottle* has a number of exceptions when a shareholder may sue depending on the situation, either in his personal capacity or in a representative capacity on behalf of the other shareholders, in order to redress a wrong. These exceptions are as follows:

(*a*) Where the alleged action is illegal or *ultra vires* since the action cannot be ratified by the members (*Moseley v. Koffyfontein Mines Ltd* (*1911*)).

(*b*) Where a resolution is not validly passed, i.e. a matter has been decided by a simple majority whereas it requires the passing of a special or extraordinary resolution (*Edwards v. Halliwell* (*1950*)).

(*c*) Where personal rights of a plaintiff shareholder have been infringed or are about to be infringed, i.e. rights conferred by the articles (*Pender v. Lushington* (*1877*)).

(*d*) In circumstances where those who control the company are perpetrating a fraud on the minority shareholders. According to Lord Davey in *Burland v. Earle* (*1902*), fraud takes place when the 'majority in the company are endeavouring directly or indirectly to appropriate for themselves money, property or advantages belonging to the company or in which other shareholders are entitled to participate'.

(*e*) In cases where the interests of justice require departure from the rule in *Foss v. Harbottle* – for example, in *Heyting v. Dupont (1964)* it was intimated that a member might be allowed to sue to restrain misfeasance without alleging fraud.

(*f*) Under the statutory provisions of the 1986 Act a member of the company can petition the court to wind up the company alleging 'that it is just and equitable that the company should be wound up' (I.A.: S.122). Some of the varied circumstances when this would occur would be where the substratum of the company has failed (the company concerned had been unable to obtain a patent essential to its activities) (*Re German Date Coffee Co.* (*1882*)) or where there is a deadlock in the management of the company (*Re Yenidje Tobacco Co. Ltd* (*1916*)), or where the petitioner is kept from his rightful share in the management of the company (*Re Westbourne Galleries Ltd* (*1973*)), or where no *bona fide* intention exists for carrying on business in a proper manner (*Re London & County Coal Co.* (*1866*)), or where the company was formed for a fraudulent or illegal purpose (*Re Thomas Edward Brinsmead* (*1897*)). Under S.459 of the 1985 Act, a member can petition for an alternative remedy to a winding-up where 'the affairs of the company are being conducted in a manner unfairly prejudicial to some part of the membership (including himself) or that any actual or proposed act or omission of the company is, or would be so prejudicial.

The 1985 Act imposes increased penalties for many of the offences in the Companies Acts. There are over 20 pages in schedule 24 of penalties imposed for offences under the Act.

Further provisions in the 1985 Act under which members can bring an action are: S.5 (where objects are being altered), S.127 (where class rights are being varied) and under SS.431 and 442 (where a certain statutory minimum number of shareholders may apply for the Department of Trade to conduct an investigation into the company's affairs).

5.8 Other Officers of the Company

The Secretary. The law requires that a company must have a secretary who may be an individual or a corporation. The 1985 Act requires the company secretary of a *public* company to be qualified as a solicitor, barrister, accountant or chartered secretary. In a public company one of the two directors may be the secretary while in a private company a sole director cannot also be the secretary (S.293, 1985 Act). Being the main administrative officer in the company, he has varied duties and responsibilities depending on the company. He is regarded as an officer of the company, being included in the section of the Act dealing with the officers. A deputy secretary may be appointed. A secretary can sign administrative contracts on behalf of the company (e.g. employing staff, ordering cars, etc.), whereas other contracts require specific authority and hence he cannot bind the company (*Houghton & Co. v. Nothard, Lowe and Willis Ltd* (*1928*)).

As a clerk, he is present at all meetings of the company and board. He prepares proper minutes of the proceedings and issues all notices to members and others. He is responsible for all matters connected with the shares – for example, he certifies transfers of shares, keeps the register of members, makes returns to the Registrar and maintains the books of the company, etc. As a clerk or servant of the company he is entitled to preferential payment of his salary in the event of a winding-up of the company.

Auditors. They can be appointed by the directors at any time before the first general meeting of the company. If the auditors have not been appointed by the directors, the company can do so at the general meeting (S.384, 1985 Act). Auditors appointed at a general meeting are to hold office from the end of that meeting until the end of the next (S.384, 1985 Act). The Secretary of State must be given notice where no auditor is appointed or reappointed at a general meeting and failure to do so makes the company and every officer in default liable to a fine (S.384(5), 1985 Act). The remuneration of the auditors is fixed by the company at general meeting. The auditors are required to be independent persons and as such an officer or servant of the company, a body corporate or a partner or employee of an officer or servant of the company cannot be appointed as an auditor. To be appointed an auditor, a person must be a member of a recognised body of accountants. The 1976 Act recognises the three Institutes of Chartered Accountants (England and Wales, Scotland, and Northern Ireland) and the Association of Certified Accountants. Alternatively, the person must have been authorised by the Department of Trade. A company can remove an auditor by ordinary resolution before his term of office expires and notwithstanding anything in any agreement with him (S.386, 1985 Act). An auditor is an officer of the company for some purposes and an agent of the company for other purposes.

The duty of an auditor, depending on the articles, is essentially to examine the company accounts in order to ascertain the true financial position of the company and lay a report before the members of the company. S.221 of the 1985 Act requires every company to keep accounting records which must be available for inspection by the company's officers; the form and content of the accounts are prescribed in the Fourth Schedule to the

1985 Act. The auditor's duty is owed primarily to the members of the company and not to the directors as such (*Re London & General Bank* (*No. 2*) (*1895*)). Auditors are required to act honestly and with reasonable care and skill in discharging their duties. An auditor will be liable to the company for any loss resulting from negligence or default in the performance of his duties although a court may grant him relief against liability in certain circumstances – for example, where he has acted honestly and reasonably (S.727, 1985 Act).

5.9 Meetings and Proceedings

S.366 of the 1985 Act requires the company to call an annual general meeting every year and an interval of not more than 15 months should elapse between meetings. Under S.368 an extraordinary general meeting may be requisitioned, irrespective of anything in the articles, by the holders of at least one tenth of the paid-up capital with voting rights at a general meeting or members representing one tenth of the voting rights in the case of a company without share capital.

Notice of the meetings of the company must be given, and should contain the place, date and the time of the meeting. On the question of length of notice for calling meetings, S.369 requires 21 days' written notice in the case of an annual meeting whereas other general meetings require 14 days' written notice unless a special resolution is proposed, when not less than 21 days' notice is required. The period of notice can be shortened in particular cases if specified in the articles, e.g. with agreement of all members at an annual general meeting. Where the 1985 Act requires special notice then at least 28 days' notice of the meeting must be given (S.379).

Notice of the meeting must be served on each member of the company (S.370) and also served on the auditors (S.387, 1985 Act). Where a notice of such a meeting is not given to every entitled person, any resolution passed becomes a nullity (*Young v. Ladies' Imperial Club Ltd* (*1920*)). However, company articles can provide that accidental omission does not invalidate the company proceedings at the meeting.

Members themselves have a right to move a resolution or to circulate statements on any proposed resolution at the meeting (S.376). Proceedings at general meetings will be valid only if an effective quorum is present and this may depend on the articles. However, S.370(4) of the 1985 Act provides that the quorum duly constituted for both public and private companies is two members personally present.

At the meeting any member can be elected as chairman (S.370) and the manner in which the meeting is conducted depends on the meeting itself. Although the chairman cannot adjourn a meeting at his will, he may do so in case of disorder. Voting at the meeting is decided by a show of hands if the articles do not provide otherwise.

Subject to the articles of a company, a poll may be demanded, when every member is normally entitled to one vote per share (S.370). S.372 grants a right to vote by proxy in a poll. At the general meetings some matters are decided by ordinary resolution requiring a simple majority while more important matters are decided by extraordinary resolution requiring a three-quarter majority of those present and entitled to vote. Special resolutions require the same majority as extraordinary resolutions but in addition also require the serving of at least 21 days' notice.

A statutory right exists to demand a poll when passing a special resolution or an extraordinary resolution (S.378(4) and (5)) or where the articles so provide.

Lastly, S.380 of the 1985 Act requires that copies of certain resolutions and agreements are to be forwarded to the Registrar within 15 days, either in printed form or in a form approved by the Registrar.

5.10 Winding up of a Company

Although a company cannot die it will cease to exist if dissolved and removed from the register of companies. The process leading up to dissolution is called winding up or liquidation, and this can take the following forms:

(*a*) **Compulsory Winding up.** Under S.122 of the 1986 Act a company may be wound up by the court. The High Court and in some cases the County Court may make such an order if:

(i) By special resolution the company has so resolved.

(ii) The company has not been issued with a certificate under S.117 of the Companies Act 1985 (public companies).

(iii) The company does not commence business within a year from its incorporation or suspends its business for a year.

(iv) The minimum membership is reduced below two.

(v) The company is unable to pay its debts (S.123 defines what this means).

(vi) The court is of the opinion that it is just and equitable that the company be wound up. The various grounds under this head are mentioned on page 74, at (*f*).

Petitions for winding up may be presented, depending on the circumstances, by either the company, a creditor, a contributory (those liable to contribute to the assets of the company in case of winding up), the Official Receiver or the Department of Trade. The court controls the winding up and appoints the liquidator, whose role is to dispose of all the remaining assets of the company in order to pay the various creditors in the order of their ranking.

(*b*) **Voluntary Winding up.** This can take three forms:

(i) *Members' voluntary winding up.* Here the company is able to pay all its debts in full within 12 months and the company directors file a statutory declaration of solvency in accordance with the terms of S.89 of the 1986 Act. Members of the company appoint a liquidator and the powers of the directors cease forthwith (I.A.: S.91).

(ii) *Creditors voluntary winding up.* Apart from the above all other types of voluntary winding up will take this form. The company is unable to meet the creditors' claims in full and they will be able to appoint a liquidator (I.A.: S.100) to control the winding up.

(iii) *Winding up supervised by the court.* As a result of a court order or a petition by a creditor, this voluntary winding up is supervised by the court. This type of winding up is a rare occurrence.

Note: The 1985 Companies Act is the most comprehensive re-statement of Company Law for forty years, and a similar exercise is unlikely to be repeated for an equally long period, although minor Acts are sure to appear from time to time. Therefore the purchase of a comprehensive edition of the Acts at the moment is likely to be long-lasting and extremely valuable as a reference book. One of the best is published by ICSA Publishing Ltd., for the Institute of Chartered Secretaries and Administrators. It is *Companies Act 1985 and Related Legislation, with Index*. It is available from ICSA Publishing Ltd., Fitzwilliam House, 32 Trumpington St., Cambridge, CB2 IQY, England. Students cannot do better than read the actual Acts for company law studies, and the indexes in this volume are particularly helpful.

5.11 Advantages of the 'Limited Company' as a Form of Business Entity

When compared with a partnership or a sole trader a company has the following advantages:

(*a*) Being a separate legal person, the debts of the company can only be claimed against the company. The liability of the shareholders is limited to any outstanding amount of the shares taken. In a partnership the partners are jointly liable for the debts of the firm (except a limited partner) and a creditor can make claim against the personal assets of a partner. The same would also apply to a sole trader who is personally liable for all his debts.

(*b*) Once formed, a company enjoys perpetual succession and the death, bankruptcy, mental disorder or retirement of a member does not affect the existence of the company. A partnership dissolves on grounds of death, bankruptcy or insanity of a partner.

(*c*) A new partner cannot be introduced in a partnership without the consent of all existing partners whereas in a company shares can be transferred without the consent of other shareholders.

(*d*) A company can enter into contracts with its members and can sue and be sued on the contracts. A partner cannot enter into a contract with the firm.

(*e*) Since the property of a company belongs to the company, any changes in the ownership of shares does not affect the ownership of the company property. In a partnership, changes due to death or retirement of a partner will result in changes to the ownership of the firm's property.

(*f*) Each partner can take part in the management of the firm (except a limited partner) and as an agent of the firm can bind the firm on contracts entered with outsiders. Shareholders of a company are not agents of the company and they do not participate in the management of the company; management is entrusted to a body of persons called directors whose status, function and powers are determined by the articles and the memorandum.

(*g*) A company can raise large amounts of capital because of its huge membership whereas a firm has to be content with the personal contributions of the individual partners which, due to the restricted membership, cannot be large. A company has greater facilities for borrowing – e.g. through the issue of debentures – than a firm or a sole trader.

5.12 Disadvantages of Limited Companies

Some of the disadvantages associated with a company are:

(*a*) Members who own the company are not necessarily those who run the company and hence management is divorced from ownership. This leaves it open for the directors to abuse their position although safeguards are provided by the *Companies Act, 1985*. It is also possible that since directors do not own the company they may not devote all their energies to the success of the company. A sole trader or a partner, being the owner of the business, would probably work harder to promote that business.

(*b*) A company will not be able to preserve the privacy of its business affairs as most of its important documents are filed at the Companies Registry and are available for public inspection. Privacy of business affairs may be considered important to some businessmen and a partnership or sole tradership may appear more attractive in this regard.

Note: A private company can maintain some privacy on its affairs. Under the 1985 Act small companies (those with a turnover less than £2.0 million and assets of less than £975 000) need not file a profit and loss account, and need only submit a modified balance sheet. Medium companies (those with turnover less than £8.0 million and assets of less than £3.9 million) need not reveal their turnover, and may submit a modified profit and loss account as laid down in Sch. 8, Part 1 of the 1985 Act.

5.13 Revision Test

Answers	*Questions*
–	**1.** What is the principle of limited liability?
1. Shareholders cannot be held liable for losses suffered by a company beyond the amount of nominal share capital they agreed to contribute.	**2.** As a result, on whom do such losses fall?
2. On creditors, who cannot secure payment for goods and services supplied to an insolvent company.	**3.** What are the three types of company?
3. Chartered, statutory and registered companies.	**4.** What are the types of registered companies?

Answers	*Questions*
4. Public companies and private companies.	**5.** How is a company formed?
5. By registering with the Registrar of Companies: (*a*) a memorandum of association; (*b*) articles of association; (*c*) a statutory declaration that the requirements of the Companies Act have been complied with; (*d*) a statement of the capital required, and how it will be contributed; (*e*) the names and addresses of the first director or directors and first secretary or joint secretaries with their written consent to take office.	**6.** What is the most important clause in a memorandum of association?
6. The objects clause, because it establishes which activities a company may perform and which acts are *ultra vires*.	**7.** How does S.35 of the 1985 Act affect the *ultra vires* principle in English law?
7. It makes it possible for those who have dealings with a company in good faith to secure redress of any grievance even though the dealing was outside the powers of the company. It reduces the severity of English law.	**8.** What is the rule in *Royal British Bank v. Turquand (1856)*?
8. The rule is that those dealing with a company can expect that the internal requirements and formalities have been complied with. Thus if the company should have passed a resolution to authorise the directors to act for the company one can assume it has been done.	**9.** What was *Saloman v. Saloman (1897)* about?
9. It established that the company was a different legal person from the directors of the company.	**10.** What are the commonest classes of shares?

Answers	*Questions*
10. (*a*) Ordinary shares; (*b*) preference shares; (*c*) deferred or founders' shares.	**11.** What duties do directors owe to the company?
11. (*a*) A duty of care and skill; (*b*) a duty of loyalty and good faith; (*c*) a duty to have regard of the employees' interests.	**12.** What was *Foss v. Harbottle (1843)* about?
12. It held that individual members could not sue the directors for fraud and mismanagement for the proper plaintiff was the company itself. However, there are several exceptions to this rule, where a shareholder may sue.	**13.** Go over the questions again until you are sure of all the answers. Then try the written questions in Appendix 1.

Part 3: The Law of Contract

6
The Nature of Contracts

6.1 Agreement as the Basis of Contracts

The whole basis of the law of contract is agreement. In particular, a contract is an agreement bringing with it obligations which will be enforced by the courts.

Most of the principles of modern contract date from the eighteenth and nineteenth centuries, when great importance was placed upon the commercial freedom of individuals. The concept of a contract at that time was of equals coming together to bargain and reach agreement: an agreement which they would wish to be upheld by the courts. Whilst it is still true that individuals come together to form agreements, it must also be recognised that countless contracts are entered into between parties who are not equals in any way, even if the law may pretend they are. A major criticism of contract law over the years has been that rich, experienced and legally advised corporations have been able to make bargains with many people who are of limited resources, relatively unsophisticated and totally unrepresented legally for fear of incurring costs beyond their means. Because of this the law of contract has gradually moved away from a total commitment to enforce, without qualification, any agreement which has the basic elements of a contract. In particular, Parliament has introduced statutes which are often designed to protect relatively weak consumers from businessmen having greater bargaining power. Despite this, the courts are still reluctant to set aside an agreement having all the elements of a contract and in this respect follow their nineteenth century predecessors.

6.2 A Definition of a Contract

A contract has been defined by Sir William Anson as '*a legally binding agreement made between two or more parties, by which rights are acquired by one or more to acts or forbearances on the part of the other, or others*'.

The essential elements of this definition are as follows:

(*a*) **Legally binding.** Not all agreements are contracts, for not all agreements are legally binding. In particular we may notice *social arrangements*, *domestic arrangements* and *agreements specifically stated to be entered into without any intention of creating legal arrangements* (see Section 6.5 below.)

(*b*) **Two or more parties.** To have an agreement there must be at least two parties. One cannot make bargains with oneself.

(*c*) **Rights are acquired.** An essential feature of a contract is that legal rights are acquired. One person promises to do a certain thing, or supply a certain object. The other person promises to pay the price, or do something else in return.

(*d*) **Forbearances.** To forbear is to refrain from doing something. It may still be a benefit to one party to have the other promise not to do something. Thus the owner of a right of way across land might agree, in consideration of a payment of £200, to use the footpath only on weekdays, leaving the other party to enjoy the privacy of the land at weekends.

6.3 The Elements of a Contract

The elements of a contract may be listed as follows:

(*a*) Capacity to contract.
(*b*) Intention to create legal relations.
(*c*) Agreement to the same idea (*consensus ad idem*).
(*d*) A clear offer, communicated to the offeree.
(*e*) A valid acceptance of the offer.
(*f*) Valuable consideration.
(*g*) Absence of duress or undue influence.
(*h*) Absence of mistake amounting to 'operative mistake'.
(*i*) Absence of misrepresentation.
(*j*) Legality of the objects of the contract.

A diagrammatic representation of these points is given in Fig. 6.1. The chief points about items (*a*), (*b*) and (*c*) above are raised in this chapter. The rest are dealt with in Chapters 7 and 8.

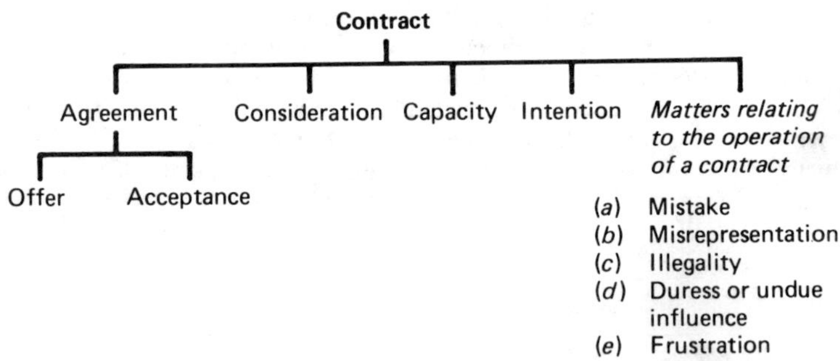

Fig. 6.1. The elements of a contract

6.4 Capacity to Contract

In general every person has full legal powers to enter into whatever contracts they might choose. There are, however, some exceptions to this general rule and they are:

(*a*) Infants and minors.
(*b*) Persons drunk or mentally disordered.
(*c*) Corporations.

(*a*) **Infants.** An infant is anyone under the age of 18 years (S.12, *Family Law Reform Act, 1969*) – previously the age was 21 years. The basic intention of the law is to protect infants from exploitation, whilst at the same time to avoid impairing in total their right to enter into contracts. It is possible to put contracts made by infants into three groups: (i) valid contracts; (ii) voidable contracts; and (iii) contracts void within the meaning of the *Infants Relief Act, 1874*.

(i) *Valid contracts*, i.e. contracts which the courts will enforce against minors. There are two types of contract within this group: contracts for necessaries and beneficial contracts (usually contracts of employment).

Contracts for necessaries. For a long time it has been the law that a minor is bound to pay a *reasonable* price (not necessarily the contractual price) for necessaries supplied to him. Necessaries may be goods and services and are those things reasonably necessary to maintain the minor in the station in life in which he moves. So far as goods are concerned necessaries have been defined in S.3 of the *Sale of Goods Act, 1979*, as meaning: 'goods suitable to the condition in life of the minor or other person concerned and to his actual requirements at the time of the sale and delivery.' This means that there are two factors determining whether a particular article is a necessity: (i) the condition in life of the minor and (ii) his actual requirements at the time of sale and delivery. Should the minor be sufficiently supplied with goods of the kind in question then, even though the fact is not known to the plaintiff, the price is irrecoverable:

Nash v. Inman (1908). The plaintiff was a tailor in Savile Row and the defendant an undergraduate at Trinity College, Cambridge. While under 21 (the age has been reduced to 18 since that time) the defendant ordered certain clothes from the plaintiff, including 11 fancy waistcoats at two guineas each, and the plaintiff instituted proceedings to recover the cost of the clothes supplied. Evidence given by the defendant's father showed that the defendant already had an adequate supply of clothes suitable and necessary for his condition in life. **Held:** in view of this fact the goods ordered from the plaintiff were not necessaries and the plaintiff's action must fail. (Courtesy of *Cracknell's Law Students' Companion*)

The tests are the same for necessary services as for goods. Necessary services include education, medical and legal advice. In *Chapple v. Cooper (1844)* it was held that the provision of a funeral service ordered by a minor for her deceased husband was a necessary.

Beneficial contracts of service. A contract of employment is binding on a minor if *viewed as a whole when made it is for the minor's benefit*. The court looks at the whole contract, weighs the onerous against the beneficial terms and then decides whether the balance is in favour of the infant. Compare the following cases:

Clements v. London and North Western Railway Co. (1894). The plaintiff, who was an infant, entered the service of the defendants as a porter and agreed to become a member of the defendants' insurance scheme, to the funds of which the defendants contributed, and to forfeit his right to sue the defendants under the *Employers' Liability Acts*. The insurance scheme did not restrict the payment of compensation to those cases for which the employers would otherwise be liable, but the amount of benefit payable under the scheme was rather less than that which could be recovered under the Acts. The scheme also provided that claims should be forfeited in certain circumstances and that all disputes should be settled by arbitration. The plaintiff was injured in the course of his employment and sued to recover damages from the defendants. **Held:** the action must fail as the plaintiff's contract of service, which contained a clause prohibiting the proceedings of this kind, was binding upon him because it was, taken as a whole, advantageous to him. (Courtesy of *Cracknell's Law Students' Companion*)

De Francesco v. Barnum (1890). An infant and her mother executed a deed whereby the infant, who was to be apprenticed to the plaintiff for seven years with a view to being taught stage dancing, agreed that she would not marry or accept any professional engagements during the period of her apprenticeship without the consent of the plaintiff. The contract also contained terms whereby the infant was to be paid a certain small sum for such engagements as she should fulfil, but there was no stipulation that the plaintiff should provide engagements for the infant or maintain her while she was unemployed. In breach of this agreement the infant signed a contract to dance for the defendant and the plaintiff sought to enforce the provisions of the deed and claimed damages for breach of contract. **Held:** the claim must fail as the provisions of the deed were unreasonable and could not be enforced against the infant or her mother and no action would lie against the defendant for enticing the infant away from the plaintiff's employment. (Courtesy of *Cracknell's Law Students' Companion*)

Benefit to the minor is the vital factor when considering such contracts. However, there is no *general* principle that any kind of agreement is binding merely because it confers benefit upon the infant. For example, it has long been established that a minor is not bound by a trading contract even if it is financially beneficial for him. He is not liable for the price of goods supplied to him in trade; he cannot be made bankrupt for trade debts; and he is not liable for the non-delivery of goods which he has sold as a trader. For example:

Cowern v. Nield (1912). The defendant, an infant, carried on business as a hay and straw merchant. The plaintiff ordered some clover and hay and sent his cheque in settlement. The goods were never delivered and the plaintiff brought an action to recover the amount which he had paid. **Held:** the plaintiff's claim must fail as the transaction in question was a trading contract and whether or not it was for the benefit of the defendant, in the absence of fraud, he could not be liable under such an agreement. (Courtesy of *Cracknell's Law Students' Companion*)

For a beneficial agreement to be valid it must either be a service or apprenticeship contract or analogous to such a contract. For example:

Doyle v. White City Stadium, Ltd. (1935). The infant plaintiff was a boxer and the terms of the contract with the British Boxing Board of Control by which he was granted a licence to box provided that payment of the money due to a boxer might be withheld if he was disqualified for one of various reasons. The plaintiff took part in a contest for the heavy-weight championship of Great Britain but was disqualified in the second round. The plaintiff sought to recover the amount due to him in respect of the fight and contended that he was not bound by the terms of the contract with the British Boxing Board of Control as he was an infant. **Held:** the plaintiff's action must fail as he was bound by the agreement, which was closely analogous to a contract of employment, because it was, on the whole, for his benefit. (Courtesy of *Cracknell's Law Students' Companion*)

(ii) *Voidable contracts.* Contracts falling within this group are voidable in the sense that they are valid and binding upon the minor unless he repudiates them during his minority or within a reasonable time thereafter. The other party cannot repudiate.

Contracts in this category are those which confer a continuous interest on a minor. There are four main kinds:

1. Contracts concerning land – particularly contracts to buy or rent land.
2. Contracts to subscribe for, or buy in the market, company shares.
3. Partnership contracts.
4. Marriage settlements.

When a minor repudiates such contracts he is relieved of all liabilities (e.g. rent) which accrue after the repudiation but probably not those which accrued before repudiation.

Steinberg v. Scala (Leeds) Ltd (1923). An infant applied for and was allotted certain shares. She paid the amount due on allotment and also the first call. Eighteen months later, while still an infant, she purported to repudiate the contract and sought repayment of the money she had paid. **Held:** her claim must fail as there had not been a total failure of consideration, the only ground on which she could have succeeded. (Courtesy of *Cracknell's Law Students' Companion*)

An infant partner is not liable for debts that the firm has acquired during his infancy (*Lovell and Christmas v. Beauchamp (1894)*). However, when he reaches the age of majority, i.e. the commencement of the eighteenth birthday, he is liable for all the debts incurred during the period of his majority unless he takes steps within a reasonable time to avoid the partnership contract (*Goode v. Harrison (1821)*).

(iii) *Contracts within the Infants' Relief Act, 1874.* At common law there was a third group of contracts which were neither valid nor voidable. They became binding on the minor only if he ratified them on attaining full age. This position was modified by the *Infants Relief Act, 1874*, and two groups of contracts are covered by this Act. They are (*a*) those that can still be ratified and (*b*) those absolutely void. The latter include accounts stated (a balance of account agreed between debtor and creditor), non-necessary goods or services supplied, and loans. Even a guarantee of a void contract is itself void, for example:

Coutts & Co. v. Browne-Lecky (1946). An infant's bank account was overdrawn and the bank sought to recover the amount which he owed from two guarantors. **Held:** their action must fail as the loan itself was void under the *Infants' Relief Act, 1874* (S.1) and so was any guarantee made in respect of such a loan. (Courtesy of *Cracknell's Law Students' Companion*)

(*b*) **Persons Drunk or Mentally Disordered.** Some persons of unsound mind have their property controlled for them by the courts under Part 8 of the *Mental Health Act, 1959*. Such persons can never make a valid contract.

Other persons of unsound mind and those 'unbalanced' by intoxication are treated alike. Their contracts are divided into two types: those for necessary goods (the situation is as with minors) and other contracts (where the presumption is one of validity unless the person of unsound mind or the drunkard can show: (i) he did not know what he was doing, and (ii) the other party was aware of this). In this case the contract is voidable at the option of the person of unsound mind, or the drunkard. In *Hart v. O'Connor (1985)* the Judicial Committee of the Privy Council held that the validity of a contract entered into by a lunatic *who is ostensibly sane* is to be judged by the same standards as a contract by a person of sound mind and is *not* voidable by the lunatic or his representative by reason of unfairness unless such unfairness amounts to equitable fraud, which would have enabled the complaining party to avoid the contract even if he had been sane.

(*c*) **Corporations.** A corporation is a legal entity created by a process of law. It has a separate legal entity from the person or persons who actually represent it in human form. Thus a company which is a corporation has a separate legal entity from the shareholders who own it and the directors of the board that conduct its business. It can own property, employ staff and sue and be sued in the courts under its corporate name. There are two kinds of corporation: **corporations sole** and **corporations aggregate**.

A corporation sole is a high office held by an individual, who therefore has a corporate capacity as well as a personal capacity. Examples are the bishops of the Church of England and the Lord Warden of the Cinque Ports.

A corporation aggregate can be created under:

(*a*) Common law.
(*b*) Royal charter.
(*c*) Special statute. Many early railway companies were set up under private statutes, and in recent times statutes have been passed to set up many public corporations – for example, the Atomic Energy Authority was set up under the *Atomic Energy Act, 1954*.
(*d*) The *Companies Acts 1985*. As already explained in Chapter 5 this Act has consolidated into a single statute the five Acts of 1948, 1967, 1976, 1980 and 1981. One or two specialised items, such as the provisions about Business Names have been put into separate minor statutes.

These changes aside, there are detailed provisions in the new statute which contain rules for the formation, registration, conduct and liquidation of limited and unlimited companies. One such provision is that there shall be a memorandum of association in which those wishing to form the company express their willingness to associate together. It contains the **objects clause** which governs the capacity of the company to contract. A company can only contract on matters falling within its objects clause, and since the records of companies are matters of public record available for inspection at Companies House it used to be the case that a company could not have a contract enforced against it if it lay outside its object clause. The presumption was that those entering into contracts with the company knew or ought to have known the contents of the objects clause. Consequently anyone making an *ultra vires* (outside the powers) contract with a company only had themselves to blame. On entry into the European Community in 1973 this *ultra vires* doctrine had to be revised, since it is not followed in the other countries of the Community. This matter has been fully discussed already in Chapter 5 (see page 63) and need not be restated here, except to reiterate that those who enter into contracts with companies can enforce such contracts even though they are outside the objects clause, providing of course that they have acted in good faith themselves. Despite the amelioration of hardship to unsophisticated contractors, the fact remains that the capacity of a company is limited to activities authorised by its objects clause. It has been clearly laid down in *International Sales and Agencies Ltd v. Marcus (1982)* that the clause which is now Section 35 in the 1985 Act was designed to protect innocent third parties dealing with the company unaware of its objects clause. It was not designed to protect sophisticated businessmen, or to defeat the duties of a trustee or contructive trustee (which were the facts in the case).

A more detailed coverage of companies has been given in Chapter 5.

6.5 Intention to Create Legal Relations

As mentioned in Section 6.1 above, merely because there is an agreement it cannot be assumed that an enforceable contract exists. English law requires that the parties to a contract actually intended to enter into legal relations (by which is meant relations actionable and enforceable in the courts). If it can be demonstrated that no such intention existed then the courts will not intervene, despite the presence of agreement and consideration.

When the courts are called upon to examine agreements from the point of view of intention, they classify them into two broad groups:

(*a*) Social, family, and other domestic agreements, where the general rule is that the courts presume that there is *no* intention to enter into legal relations.

(*b*) Commercial agreements, where the courts presume that the parties *do* intend to enter into legal relations.

Though the above are the general rules it is possible to demonstrate to the court that in the first group of agreements the form of words used, and the circumstances in which they were used, amounted to an intention to enter into legal relations. It is equally possible to rebut the presumption in the second group by showing that in fact the parties clearly expressed their desire to exclude legally enforceable relations.

(*a*) **Social, family and other domestic agreements.** The following cases demonstrate the view of the courts in relation to the basic presumption, i.e. lack of intention:

Balfour v. Balfour (1919). The defendant Balfour, a civil servant, returned to his work in Ceylon leaving his wife in England – doctors advised that her health would not allow her to accompany him. He promised that, whilst away, he would send her £30 per month on which she might live. He did not keep this promise and his wife sued. At first she succeeded but on appeal it was said by Atkin, L.J., that of the forms of agreement which do not constitute a contract one of the most usual consists of arrangements made between husband and wife. They are not contracts because the parties do not intend that legal consequences should follow from them. In this particular case the parties were amicable and living together normally when the arrangements were made and clearly they did not envisage any legal developments.

Buckpitt v. Oates (1968). The parties were two friends who occasionally rode in each other's cars. Neither had passenger insurance and whilst Oates was driving his negligence caused an accident in which Buckpitt was injured. Prior to the trip Buckpitt had paid Oates 10 shillings (50 pence) towards the fuel costs. Also Oates had displayed on his dashboard a notice disclaiming liability for injuries to passengers. Buckpitt sued Oates, however, (*a*) for breach of contract and (*b*) in tort for negligence. He failed in (*a*) because it was regarded that the carrying of Buckpitt was a friendly gentleman's agreement and there was no intention to enter into legal relations. He also failed in (*b*) because of the notice disclaiming liability – a situation which has been changed by the *Road Traffic Act, 1972* (S.148(3)).

The following cases demonstrate how the presumption of non-intention might be rebutted:

Merrit v. Merrit (*1970*). The husband left his wife and began living with another woman. The family home was in the names of both Mr and Mrs Merritt and £180 was still owed on the mortgage. A document was signed whereby Mr Merritt agreed to transfer the property into the sole ownership of his wife providing she met all charges associated with the property until such times as the mortgage was discharged. Mrs Merritt paid off the mortgage but her husband refused to transfer the property. **Held:** at the time the agreement was made the pair were not living happily together as man and wife and therefore the usual presumption relating to non-intention did not apply. There was a binding contract and the property must be transferred.

Parker v. Clarke (*1960*). The Clarkes, an elderly couple, invited the Parkers to sell their cottage and come to live with them (Mrs Parker was Mrs Clarke's niece). The Clarkes promised that the house and contents would belong to the Parkers once the Clarkes died. The move took place. After two years though the Clarkes asked the Parkers to leave. The Parkers sued for breach of contract and succeeded. An intention to create legal relations was found and was thought to be particularly strong since the Parkers had been induced to sell their own home.

(*b*) **Commercial Agreements.** The following cases demonstrate the view of the courts in relation to commercial agreements, i.e. that there *is* an intention to create legal relations:

Edwards v. Skyways Ltd (*1964*). Skyways made Edwards, a pilot, redundant. They eventually agreed to make all redundant pilots an *ex gratia* payment amounting to the sum each had paid into the pension fund. Skyways then refused to make any payments. Edwards sued for breach of contract. **Held:** in business arrangements it is presumed that the parties intend legal relations, and the use of words such as '*ex gratia*' is insufficient to rebut that presumption.

The following case demonstrates how the presumption to enter legal relations might be rebutted:

Jones v. Vernons Pools Ltd (*1938*). Jones claimed to have sent a winning coupon to Vernons who did not receive it. All coupons issued by the company contained the clause 'binding in honour only' and required a signature accepting the clause. Jones agreed that he had signed the coupon (unsigned it would have been invalid). **Held:** there was clearly no intention to enter into legal relations, and there could be no contract.

There are two rather special cases where what appear to be situations involving commercial agreements are in fact regarded as if the parties do not intend to enter into legal relations. They are:

(i) *Collective bargaining agreements*, e.g. *Ford Motor Co. v. Amalgamated Union of Engineering and Foundry Workers* (*1969*), where Lane J. held that agreements relating to pay and working conditions arrived at between the company and the trade union were not intended to create legal relations.

It should be noted that most of the collective agreements contain provisions expressly stating that no legal intention is intended. Those agreements that are silent on the matter are covered by the *Trade Union and Labour Relations Act, 1974* (S.18), which provided that it will be presumed that no legal intention is intended. Some politicians have called for the enactment of a contrary presumption but this has not transpired to date.

(ii) Cases where a public body is acting under a statutory duty, e.g. *Willmore v. S.E. Electricity Board* (*1957*). Here it was held that a public body under a statutory duty to supply a service such as electricity and having agreed to supply electricity to a consumer, intends only to fulfil its statutory duty – *not* to enter into legal relations. Hence if the electricity supply fails and chickens die (as did Willmore's) the Electricity Board is not liable for breach of contract.

6.6 Agreement to the Same Idea (*Consensus ad Idem*)

It is said that the UK Cabinet Secretariat was originally set up after a certain Prime Minister had said: 'Well gentlemen, then we are all agreed!' After a chorus of assents had carried this proposition, one diffident voice was heard to say: 'But Prime Minister, on what have we all agreed?' In contract law, no less than in Cabinet, we need to know what we have agreed. It is possible for two parties to use words which are susceptible to interpretation in different ways, so that they do not have the same idea in mind when they 'agree'. If A says 'I will sell you my car for £800 (thinking of his rather battered 1300 cc family saloon) and B replies 'Done!' (thinking of A's vintage Rolls Royce) they have not agreed to the same idea. The classic case is:

Raffles v. Wichelhaus (*1864*). The defendants agreed to buy '125 bales of Surat cotton . . . to arrive *ex Peerless* from Bombay. . . .' It appeared that the ship mentioned in the agreement was intended by the defendants to be the *Peerless*, which sailed from Bombay in October, whereas the plaintiff ordered 125 bales of Surat cotton from another ship called the *Peerless* which sailed from Bombay in December. **Held:** there was no binding contract between the parties as the defendant meant one ship and the plaintiff another. (Courtesy of *Cracknell's Law Students' Companion*)

Other cases of interest are *Smith v. Hughes* (*1871*) and *Scriven Brothers v. Hindley* (*1913*). The question in each of these three cases was: 'Were the parties in agreement to the same idea' or, in Latin, was there a *consensus ad idem*.

6.7 Revision Test

Answers	*Questions*
–	**1.** What is the basis of a contract?
1. Agreement between the parties.	**2.** Why is *consensus ad idem* important in contract law?

Answers	*Questions*
2. It means 'agreement to the same idea'. If the parties have not agreed to the same idea then there is no true agreement.	**3.** How did Sir William Anson define a contract?
3. As 'a legally binding agreement made between two or more parties, by which rights are acquired by one or more to act or forbearances on the part of the other, or others'.	**4.** What agreements are not contracts?
4. Social arrangements, domestic arrangements and agreements specifically made without intention of creating legal arrangements.	**5.** What is capacity?
5. The ability to make a legally binding contract.	**6.** What is an infant?
6. A person under 18 years of age.	**7.** What contracts are binding against infants?
7. (*a*) Contracts for the supply of necessaries; (*b*) contracts which are beneficial to the infant, i.e. apprenticeships.	**8.** What is the classic case about necessaries supplied to an infant?
8. *Nash v. Inman (1908)* – the 'fancy waistcoats' case, in which it was held that clothing supplied to an infant who already had adequate clothing was not a necessary.	**9.** What was *Doyle v. White City Stadium Ltd* about?
9. It was a 1935 case about an infant boxer who was not paid his fee because he struck a low blow and was disqualified. The contract specifically forbade payment if he struck a low blow. **Held:** it was a beneficial contract and he was bound by it.	**10.** What is the *Infants Relief Act, 1874*?
10. An act to protect infants. In particular all loans of money to infants are absolutely void under the Act.	**11.** What is the basis for the legality of the contracts made by corporations?

Answers	*Questions*
11. The 'objects clause' of the memorandum of association outlines the objects which the company may pursue. Contracts must be *intra vires*, within the objects clause and therefore 'within the law'.	**12.** What Act modifies this rule about the objects clause?
12. Section 35 of the *Companies Act 1985*, which reduces the severity of the rule to innocent parties who have made contracts with a company not knowing what the objects clause said.	**13.** What was *Balfour* v. *Balfour* (*1919*)?
13. A 1919 case between a husband and wife. Its conclusion was that a domestic arrangement is not a contract.	**14.** What was *Raffles* v. *Wichelhaus* (*1864*)?
14. A case in which the parties agreed to ship cotton from Bombay to England in a vessel called SS *Peerless*. There were two ships of that name and the conclusion was that the parties had not agreed to the same idea.	**15.** Go over the questions until you are sure of all the answers. Then try the written questions in Appendix 1.

7
Offer, Acceptance and Valuable Consideration

7.1 A Clear Offer, Communicated to the Offeree

An offer is a promise that the person making the offer (known as the offeror) is prepared to be legally bound upon specified terms. It is susceptible to acceptance by the offeree at any time, unless it is revoked by the offeror.

For example, Jack might offer his car to John providing that John pays £250 for it. Jack is prepared to be legally bound to deliver the car provided that John complies with the specified term of the offer and pays the £250.

It might be thought that the area of offer is one which is simple and clear, but this is not so. A number of situations arise which at first sight appear to be offers capable of being accepted by the offeree, but which the courts have ruled are not 'offers'. These situations are:

(*a*) Invitations to treat.
(*b*) The supply of information.
(*c*) Declarations of intent.

Other matters of interest are:

(*d*) That offers must be clear – not vague and uncertain.
(*e*) That offers may be specific (addressed to a particular individual) or general (addressed to the world at large).

(*a*) **Invitations to treat are not offers.** An invitation to treat is an invitation to do business with another party. It is not an offer but an invitation to others to make offers. Examples are:

(i) *The display of goods in a shop window or a self-service store.* Such a display is an invitation to the public to buy – in other words, to offer to buy. It is not an offer to sell, which would be immediately susceptible to acceptance. The classic case is:

Pharmaceutical Society of Great Britain, Ltd v. Boots Cash Chemists (Southern) Ltd (1953). According to the *Pharmacy and Poisons Act, 1933* (S.18) specific drugs could only be sold under the supervision of a registered pharmacist. At Boots customers took the goods from a self-service counter and paid for them at a check-out till *supervised* by a registered pharmacist. The point at issue centred upon where the goods were *sold*. If the display constituted an offer, then the goods were sold when customers accepted the offer by placing drugs in their self-service baskets. If the display was an invitation to treat then the customers offered to purchase at the check-out and Boots accepted the offer – sale being supervised by the pharmacist. The court held that the display was an invitation to treat – it solicited offers which the cashier could accept or reject.

Similarly, in *Fisher v. Bell* (*1960*), where a shopkeeper had displayed a flick-knife with a price tag in his shop window, it was held that this did not constitute an offer for sale; the display was merely an invitation to treat.

(ii) *An auctioneer's invitation for bids*. Under the *Sale of Goods Act, 1979* (S.57) the bids at an auction constitute offers. The auctioneer's invitation for bids is only an invitation to treat, and the bids are offers to buy. Acceptance is completed by the fall of the auctioneer's hammer. Up to that point any offer made can be withdrawn. The case of *Payne v. Cave* (*1789*) illustrates the point.

(iii) *Circulars and advertisements*. These are not considered as offers. This is illustrated by the following case:

Partridge v. Crittenden (*1968*). P advertised for sale bramblefinch cocks and hens. It is illegal to offer wild birds for sale under the *Wild Birds Act, 1954*. However, on appeal the court held that such an advertisement was *not* an offer for sale but an invitation to treat.

In the above case Lord Parker, L.C.J., did make one important qualification, however, and that was that where advertisements or circulars came direct from the manufacturers they can be construed as offers. No doubt the decision in *Carlill v. Carbolic Smoke Ball Co.* (*1892*) (see below) brought forth this qualification.

(*b*) **A supply of information is not an offer.** Those who may well decide to sell often provide details of what they might sell without any intention of making a legally binding offer. The following case illustrates the point:

Harvey v. Facey (*1893*). The appellants sent a telegram to the respondents: 'Will you sell us Bumper Hall Pen? Telegraph lowest cash price.' The respondants telegraphed back: 'Lowest cash price for Bumper Hall Pen £900.' The appellants then sent a further telegram purporting to accept this 'offer' and when it was ignored, they sued for specific performance. The court held that the respondents' original reply did not constitute an offer – it was merely information about the lowest cash price required if they did decide to sell.

(*c*) **A statement of intention.** Quite often a businessman may make a mistake about matters which, when he makes it, he intends to perform, but which he does not envisage as leading to legal relations. For example, the case of *Harris v. Nickerson* (*1873*) was as follows:

Harris v. Nickerson (*1873*). An auctioneer advertised that particular goods were to be auctioned at a specific time and place. The particular goods were withdrawn from the sale and Harris sued the auctioneer for loss of time and expense incurred in going to the sale. The action failed on the grounds that information about the auction amounted only to a declaration of intent – not an offer which was susceptible of acceptance.

(*d*) **An offer must not be vague.** The terms of an offer must be clear and certain, not vague. Where a contract is left deliberately vague, the courts will hesitate to uphold it, since the vagueness must not be interpreted to the benefit of one particular party. However, there is a rule which says 'that is not vague which may be reduced to certainty'. The cases of *Scammell and Nephew Ltd v. Ouston* (*1941*) and *Hillas and Co. v. Arcos Ltd*

(*1932*) may be contrasted. Both were vague contracts, but in the case of the latter the vagueness could be reduced to certainty by referring to previous transactions, and the customs of business in the trade concerned. Another similar case was *Loftus v. Roberts* (*1902*).

Scammell and Nephew Ltd v. Ouston (*1941*) (House of Lords). The respondents agreed to purchase a motor van from the appellants but their order was given on the understanding 'that the balance of the purchase price can be had on hire-purchase terms over a period of two years'. **Held:** no precise meaning could be attributed to this clause as hire-purchase agreements varied widely and consequently there was no enforceable contract. There were no previous dealings between the parties or an accepted trade practice to which the court could refer to determine the hire-purchase terms and, in any case, their lordships found that the matter had not passed the stage of negotiation. (Courtesy of *Cracknell's Law Students' Companion*)

Hillas and Co. v. Arcos Ltd (*1932*) (House of Lords). There was an agreement in writing for the supply of wood during 1930 and it contained an option to buy more wood during the following year but the option clause did not specify the precise kind or size of timber to be supplied, the ports to which it was to be shipped or the manner of shipment. The suppliers argued that the option clause was not binding as it was intended merely to form the basis of a future agreement. **Held:** the agreement in respect of the supply of timber during 1930 was couched in similar terms and had been duly observed. The option clause showed a sufficient intention to be bound and could create a valid contract, as those points which were not specifically resolved in the option clause could be determined by reference to the previous dealings between the parties and normal business practice in the timber trade. (Courtesy of *Cracknell's Law Students' Companion*)

Loftus v. Roberts (*1902*). Roberts engaged an actress for a play 'at a West End salary to be agreed between us'. **Held:** that the reference to salary was too vague to be enforced.

(*e*) **An offer may be specific or general (to the world at large).** If an offer is made to a specific individual it can only be accepted by that individual. Other offers may be general offers, made to the world at large. The following case is of interest:

Carlill v. Carbolic Smoke Ball Co. Ltd (*1893*). The company advertised a promised payment of £100 to anyone who contracted influenza after using the smoke ball as specified. The advertisement further stated that £1000 had been lodged at the company's bank to show their good faith. Mrs Carlill purchased a smoke ball but still contracted influenza. She sued for her £100. In defence the company argued that the advertisement was only an invitation to treat, being made to no specific person. **Held:** the advertisement was an offer to the whole world, the sincerity of which was demonstrated by the £1000 lodged to pay those who accepted the offer and were dissatisfied. Mrs Carlill had accepted the offer by purchasing the article and paying the price. (Courtesy of *Cracknell's Law Students' Companion*)

It should be noted, however, that not all advertisements are serious offers. In this case it was held to be an offer because the defendant company had deposited £1000 with its bankers. In the absence of this deposit the court might well have come to a different conclusion. Hence each advertisement has to be judged individually having regard to the circumstances of each case. It is probably best to say that most advertisements are examples of invitations to treat, as was held in the case of *Partridge v. Crittenden* (*1968*).

(*f*) **Communication of the offer.** An offer is effective only when it is communicated to the offeree. In *Taylor v. Laird* (*1856*) a sailor who helped work a ship home failed in a claim for wages due, since the owners knew nothing of the offer and had not accepted it. The so-called 'reward cases' are a further illustration. A person supplying information or returning items cannot 'accept' the offer of a reward if he supplied the information or returned the items without knowledge of the offer of reward.

7.2 Termination of the Offer

Once an offer has been made, how long does it remain open? There are several ways in which an offer may cease to be available. Since the primary purpose of an offer is that some other party should accept, the offer ceases as soon as acceptance takes place, and is then said to be 'merged' into the contract. Between the moment of 'offer' and the moment of 'acceptance' the following events might lead to a termination of the offer.

(*a*) **Revocation of the offer.** An offeror can withdraw his offer at any time before it is accepted. The revocation must be communicated to the offeree. The offeror cannot just change his mind and not tell anyone about it. Revocation by post is not complete until the letter is received by the offeree. The following case illustrates this:

Byrne v. Van Tienhoven (*1880*). Van Tienhoven in Cardiff posted a letter offering to sell goods to Byrne, a New York customer, on 1st October. On 8th October Van Tienhoven posted a letter withdrawing the offer. On October 11th Byrne telegraphed acceptance and this was confirmed with a letter on 15th October. By 20th October the letter of revocation reached Byrne. **Held:** the revocation was ineffective since acceptance took place before the revocation was received by Byrne.

There are however, some exceptions to the rule that revocation must be 'brought to the mind' of the offeree. A withdrawal would be effective if the offeree just neglected to read it after it had reached him. Similarly, a withdrawal sent to the last known address of the offeree would be effective if the offeree had failed to inform the offeror of a change of address. In addition, an offer made to the general public can be withdrawn by taking 'reasonable steps' to bring the withdrawal to the notice of those persons who knew of the offer.

A bid at an auction may be retracted up to the moment when the auctioneer announces the completion of the sale by the fall of the hammer (*Sale of Goods Act, 1979*, S.57).

Providing the communication of the revocation takes place it need not be communicated by the actual offeror. In *Dickinson v. Dodds* it was established that a third party will suffice providing that a reasonable person would regard the information as true.

Dickinson v. Dodds (*1876*). Dodds offered in writing to sell a house for £800, the offer to be kept open to 12th June. On 11th June, a third party informed Dickinson that the house had already been sold. Dickinson then purported to accept the offer. **Held:** that the revocation had been received by Dickinson and he could not accept an offer which had been revoked even though the revocation only reached him indirectly.

One further point about revocation is that a revocation can take place at any time before acceptance, regardless of any *gratuitous* promise to keep the offer open. *Routledge v. Grant* illustrates this point.

Routledge v. Grant (*1828*). Grant offered to buy Routledge's house, a definite answer to be given by Routledge within six weeks. He then withdrew the offer before the six weeks ended. **Held:** that Grant could revoke at any time during this six week period – providing that acceptance had not taken place. There had been no consideration for the promise to hold the offer open, and consequently it was not binding on Grant.

(*b*) **Rejection of the offer, or a counter-offer.** Once rejection takes place an offer is terminated. The offeree cannot go back at a later date and attempt to accept the 'offer'. Also acceptance must *exactly fit the offer*. An attempt to accept an offer on new terms not contained in the offer amounts to a rejection of the original offer accompanied by a counter-offer. This is illustrated by the following case:

Hyde v. Wrench (*1840*). Wrench offered to sell land for £1000. Hyde wrote back offering £950, which was refused. Later Hyde wrote saying he was prepared to pay £1000 and he accepted the original offer. **Held:** the second letter could not accept the original offer since this original offer had been terminated by Hyde's counter-offer.

On the other hand, a request for further information will not amount to rejection of an offer, as in *Stevenson v. McLean* (*1880*). Details of this case are given in Section 7.3 below.

(*c*) **Lapse of time.** An offer may lapse (go out of existence) through the passage of time. Obviously an offer which is expressly stated to run for a fixed period of time cannot be accepted after that time. If there is no time stated in the offer then the offer lapses after a reasonable time. What is reasonable depends upon the facts surrounding each case, in particular with regard to the subject matter of the contract and the means of communication used. In *Ramsgate Victoria Hotel Co. v. Montefiore* (*1866*), the defendant had intended to purchase shares in the plaintiff company. He applied in June and paid a deposit. Not until the end of November was he informed that he had been allotted shares and that he should therefore pay the balance outstanding on the shares. The defendant's refusal to accept the shares was upheld on the grounds that his offer to purchase the shares in June should have been accepted by the company within a reasonable time. Since the company did not accept the offer until November, his offer had lapsed.

(*d*) **Failure of a condition subject to which the offer was made.** An offer which is expressly or impliedly made subject to some condition cannot be accepted if the condition fails. For example, an offer to buy goods is subject to an implied condition that they will not deteriorate before the offer is accepted.

(*e*) **Death of the offeror.** In *Dickinson v. Dodds* (*1876*) Mellish, L.J., said: 'If a man who makes an offer dies, the offer cannot be accepted after he is dead.' However, in the case of *Bradbury v. Morgan* (*1862*) the estate of a guarantor was held liable for the guarantee of a deceased man whose promise to honour the debts of another was held to be a standing offer which did not lapse on his death. The plaintiff had no notice of his death and had relied on the guarantee in supplying the goods.

7.3 Acceptance

An acceptance is an assent to all the terms of an offer. As with offer, acceptance can be either oral, in writing or implied by conduct. The acceptance must exactly fit the offers; additions or qualifications constitute a counter-offer which renders the purported 'acceptance' invalid. We have already seen this in *Hyde v. Wrench* (*1840*). However, if the court considers that the offeree is enquiring after details rather than making a counter-offer, then the original offer is not destroyed and is still capable of acceptance, as in *Stevenson v. McLean* (*1880*):

Stevenson, Jaques & Co. v. McLean (*1880*). The defendant offered to sell iron to the plaintiffs at 40*s*. per ton. The plaintiffs telegraphed to the defendant: 'Please wire whether you would accept forty for delivery over two months, or if not, longest limit you could give.' Later in the day a further telegram was sent to the defendant in which the plaintiffs accepted the original offer and when the plaintiffs sought to recover damages for breach of contract the defendant maintained that the first telegram was a counter-offer which had destroyed the offer which he originally made. **Held:** the plaintiffs' first telegram was not a rejection of the defendant's offer but an inquiry as to whether he would be prepared to modify its terms. (Courtesy of *Cracknell's Law Students' Companion*).

There is no binding acceptance in the following cases:

(*a*) *Where there is an express statement by the offeree that his acceptance is 'subject to contract'.* There are two reasons why this does not create a contract. First, it negates the intention to create legal relations. Second, it is an acceptance which does not correspond with the terms of the offer, because it imposes a further condition.

Branca v. Cobarro (*1947*). The parties negotiated for the sale of a mushroom farm and signed a document containing the terms of their agreement which concluded: 'This is a provisional agreement until a fully legalised agreement drawn up by a solicitor and embodying all the conditions herewith stated is signed.' The purchaser sued for the return of his deposit and the vendor contended that their 'provisional agreement' was a binding contract. **Held:** there was *no* immediately binding contract 'until' the document was replaced by one expressed in more precise and formal language. If the parties had used the word 'tentative' instead of 'provisional' it would probably have been held otherwise, but each case depends on the intention of the parties as found by the court. (But see *Chillingworth v. Esche* (*1924*).) (Courtesy of *Cracknell's Law Students' Companion*)

(*b*) *Where the terms of the alleged contract are too vague for the court to ascribe legal meaning to them.* However, the court might attempt to make a vague contract certain by implying unstated terms as the basis of:

(i) Previous dealings between the parties, as in the case of *Hillas and Co. v. Arcos Ltd* (*1932*) already described.

(ii) Accepted business practice, as in the case of *Foley v. Classique Coaches Ltd* (*1934*).

Foley v. Classique Coaches Ltd (*1934*). Foley supplied petrol to Classique 'at the price to be agreed by the parties in writing from time to time', with a provision for arbitration in the case of dispute. **Held:** that the lack of a stated price did not invalidate the contract. A term would be implied that the quantity and price of the petrol would be reasonable, and this, together with the arbitration clause, gave the contract its own machinery by which the price could be set.

7.4 Communication of Acceptance

The offeree might have decided in his own mind that he will accept the offer, but this is not sufficient to amount to acceptance in law. There has to be some 'external act', words spoken or written which communicate acceptance to the offeror. Communication is said to have taken place when the acceptance is actually brought to the notice of the offeror by the offeree or his authorised agent. The case of *Powell v. Lee* (*1908*) illustrates this.

Powell v. Lee (*1908*). The defendants resolved to appoint the plaintiff headmaster of a school of which they were managers. The terms of the resolution were never communicated to the plaintiff. **Held:** there was no contract between the parties as the defendants' acceptance of the plaintiff's offer of his services had not been communicated to him. (Courtesy of *Cracknell's Law Students' Companion*)

In *Entores Ltd v. Miles Far East Corporation* (*1955*), Lord Denning (*obiter*) considered in detail the rule that acceptance must be communicated and said that if he shouted an offer to a man across a courtyard and the reply was drowned by the noise of a passing aircraft then there would be no contract. The rule that acceptance is incomplete until received by the offeror governs conversations over the telephone and all other methods where communication is virtually instantaneous, such as telex. There is one major exception to this rule of communication though, and it relates to the less speedy means of dealing through the post. It is known as the 'postal rule'.

The general rule with regard to postal communications is that acceptance is complete upon posting. For example:

Adams v. Lindsell (*1818*). Lindsell wrote to Adams offering to sell wool and asking for a reply 'in course of post'. Lindsell had wrongly addressed the letter and the acceptance arrived later than they expected. In the intervening period Lindsell had sold the wool elsewhere. **Held:** Lindsell had breached the contract which came into existence when Adam's letter of acceptance was posted.

Note: 'Posted' means put into the control of the Post Office, or one of its employees authorised to receive letters. Posting does not take place at the time when a letter is handed to an employee of the Post Office authorised to deliver letters (*Re London and Northern Bank* (*1900*)).

The postal rule is obviously in existence because of convenience. It is clearly to the benefit of contracting parties that they know as soon as possible whether or not they have a contract. In this respect the postal rule obviously favours the offeree. The reason for this is that the offeror who chooses to commence negotiations by post takes the risk of delay and accidents in the post, but he can protect himself by stipulating that he is not bound until actual receipt of the acceptance.

The following points are important as regards the postal rule:

(i) Where a party uses the post as a means of acceptance it must be reasonable to do so. It would not, for example, normally be regarded as reasonable to reply by post to an offer made by telegram or telex. In addition, it would not be reasonable to reply by post if the acceptor knew that the postal service was disrupted.

(ii) A posted acceptance prevails over a withdrawal of the offer which was posted before acceptance, but which has not yet reached the offeree when the acceptance was posted, i.e. acceptance is complete when posted but withdrawal is complete only when received by an offeree.

(iii) A posted acceptance takes effect even though it never reaches the offeror because it is lost through an accident in the post.

(iv) The postal rule has been extended as far as telegrams (*Cowan v. O'Connor* (*1888*)) but not as far as telex.

7.5 Other Points on Acceptance

(*a*) *You cannot take silence as acceptance.* An offeror cannot, without the offeree's consent, put a condition in his offer that silence shall amount to an acceptance. For example:

Felthouse v. Bindley (*1862*). Felthouse wrote to a person J. offering to buy a horse saying 'If I hear no more about him, I consider him mine'. J. did not reply but told the auctioneer B. not to sell the horse. B. sold by mistake and F. sued B. for conversion. *Held:* there could be no conversion because there was no contract between F. and J. since J. had not communicated acceptance of F.'s offer to F.

(*b*) *The offeror can waive acceptance.* While the offeror may not impose a condition on the offeree that silence will amount to acceptance, he may waive the need to communicate acceptance, i.e. he may himself run the risk of incurring an uncommunicated obligation, though he may not impose one upon others. Such a waiver may be express or may be inferred from the circumstances, e.g. *Carlill v. Carbolic Smoke Ball Co.* (*1893*), referred to earlier.

(*c*) *The acceptance must usually be made in the same manner as the offer.* Where an offer explicitly or implicitly calls for acceptance in a certain way, the offeror will not generally be bound unless acceptance is made in that way.

Eliason v. Henshaw (*1819*). A offered to purchase flour from B and the letter which contained this offer stipulated the price to be paid and mode of transport, and in a postscript A added: 'Please write by return of wagon whether you accept our offer.' B accepted the offer but in a letter sent by the first regular mail and A contended that it was not a valid acceptance as it was not sent 'by return of wagon'. **Held:** there was no contract as an offer creates no obligation unless it is accepted according to the terms on which the offer was made. Any departure from these terms invalidates the offer unless the different mode of acceptance is agreed to by the person who made the offer. (Courtesy of *Cracknell's Law Student's Companion*)

If the requirement is at all tentative, acceptance by some other method may still bind the offeror. The rule is expressed in *Manchester Diocesan Council for Education v. Commercial and General Investments Ltd* (*1969*) by Buckley, J. 'It may be that an offeror who by the terms of his offer insists upon acceptance in a particular manner, is entitled to insist that he is not bound unless acceptance is affected or communicated in that precise way. Where, however, the offeror has prescribed a particular method of acceptance, but not in terms insisting that only acceptance in that mode shall be binding, I am of the opinion that acceptance communicated to the offeror by any other mode, which is no less advantageous to him, will conclude the contract.'

7.6 Valuable Consideration

English law will not enforce a simple contract (a contract that is not signed and sealed, i.e. is not a deed) unless it is supported by a valuable consideration. This rule is based upon the principle that English law enforces bargains, i.e. the exchange of valuable promises, not gratuitous promises.

The question then arises 'What is "consideration"?' The answer is 'anything of value'. The supply of goods; the performance of a service; exercising forebearance from the performance of an act, or promising to act, or forbear – can all amount to consideration.

Some confusion might arise here over the status of a promise as regards consideration. The following examples may illustrate the various situations:

(*a*) Aunt Julia promises nephew Ben that she will give him a motorcycle. Such a promise is gratuitous and will not be upheld by the courts – Ben did nothing with which to 'buy' Julia's promise.

(*b*) Aunt Julia promises to supply Ben with a motorcycle and in return Ben promises to pay Julia £250. Here Julia's promise is 'bought' by Ben's promise of payment. In return of course, Ben's promise of payment is bought by Julia's own promise to deliver the machine.

Although both of the above situations involve promises only (*b*) involves a 'bargain'. Only (*b*) will be upheld by the courts, because only (*b*) has consideration, which has been provided by both parties.

(*c*) Aunt Julia promises Ben that on his eighteenth birthday she will give him £5000. The promise is drawn up in a 'deed of gift' and witnessed formally in her solicitor's office. Although there is no valuable consideration from Ben the promise will be binding upon Aunt Julia because of the formality of the promise. A gratuitous promise made in a formal deed will be upheld by the courts.

7.7 General Requirements of Valuable Consideration

(*a*) *Consideration must be real and of some value but it need not be adequate.* Some acts or promises are not regarded by the courts as being valid consideration (see below). However, in all other situations where the courts are prepared to find consideration, they will not investigate its commercial adequacy, or even fairness. So long as the consideration has *some* value in the eyes of the law then that is enough.

'The adequacy of the consideration is for the parties to consider at the time of making the agreement, not for the court when it is sought to be enforced.' – Lord Blackburn in *Bolton v. Madden (1873)*.

Were the above rule not strictly followed then the freedom of parties to contract would be very much impaired, and the courts see no reason why an individual who, say, wants to sell his kingdom for a horse, should be prevented from doing so.

A sentimental or similar motive for making a promise will not make that promise binding. Thus in *White v. Bluett (1853)* the facts were:

White v. Bluett (1853). A father promised not to sue his son on a promissory note provided that the son did not bore his father with complaints. **Held:** that the son had not provided consideration for his father's promise.

In similar vein it has been held that a moral obligation is not good consideration, as in *Eastwood v. Kenyon (1840).*

Eastwood v. Kenyon (1840). Eastwood was the guardian of an infant who eventually married Kenyon. Upon coming of age the infant had agreed to repay debts entered into by Eastwood to improve her (the infant's) property – a promise also entered into by her eventual husband, Kenyon. In the event Kenyon did not pay. Eastwood sued, but failed in his case because he had not provided consideration to Kenyon for his promise. Though Kenyon might be morally bound to repay the debt he was not legally bound because of this lack of consideration.

Even trivial acts or worthless items may constitute consideration, e.g. *De La Bere v. Pearson (1908)* and *Chapell & Co. Ltd v. Nestlé Co. Ltd (1959).*

De La Bere v. Pearson (1908). A newspaper offered financial advice to its readers. The plaintiff wrote and asked for the name of a good stockbroker. He was supplied instead with the name of an undischarged bankrupt, who made off with the £1400 forwarded to him. The plaintiff sued the newspaper. **Held:** that the plaintiff had provided consideration by paying for his copy of the newspaper.

Chapell and Co. Ltd v. Nestlé Co. Ltd (1959). Chappell & Co. Ltd owned the copyright in a dance tune. Another firm X made recordings which they sold to the defendants for four pence a copy. The defendants then sold them to the public for 18 pence and three wrappers from their chocolate bars. These were of no value, and were thrown away. A royalty, as required by the *Copyright Act, 1956*, was paid at 6¼ per cent of the 'ordinary retail price'. The defendant's claimed that this was 18 pence, the plaintiffs' that it was 18 pence plus the retail price of three chocolate bars. **Held:** the plaintiffs must succeed. It was unrealistic to maintain that the wrappers were not part of the valuable consideration. 'A peppercorn does not cease to be valuable consideration if it is established that the promisee does not like pepper and will throw away the corn.' (*per* Lord Somervell)

(*b*) *Forbearance to sue may constitute consideration.* Suppose G owes H £200 at 12 per cent interest, the money now being due. G says that he will pay H a higher rate of interest providing that H does not sue for the time being. H forbears and this will amount to consideration for G's promise which thereby becomes enforceable.

Alliance Bank v. Broom (1864). B. owed the bank £22,000 and the bank asked for security, which B promised to give. The bank gave no promise not to sue, but in fact did not sue. **Held:** the bank's forbearance amounted to consideration received by B.

(*c*) *Existing obligations cannot be consideration for a further promise.* In a number of cases the courts have decided that certain acts or promises to perform acts do not constitute sufficient consideration because they believe such acts or promises do not contribute anything to the bargain. These are:

(*a*) *Performance of a public duty*. A contracting party cannot claim that he is providing consideration if he is merely performing duties which he is bound to do. For example:

Collins v. Godefroy (1831). Collins was subpoenaed to attend court as a potential witness for Godefroy. Collins was not called but demanded payment for his attendance. **Held:** The subpoena put him under a public duty to attend and even if Godefroy had promised him payment, he, Collins, had provided no consideration.

By contrast, in *Glasbrook Brothers v. Glamorgan County Council* (*1925*) Glasbrook Brothers as owners of a mine asked for police protection during a strike. The police were of the opinion that a small mobile guard would be enough for the task. The mine owners wanted a number of stationary guards posted around the mine. This the police agreed to provide at a total cost of £2200. The company refused to pay, contending that the police had not provided any consideration since they were already obliged by law to provide protection. The House of Lords held that in providing the stationary guards, the police had exceeded their normal duty and this therefore constituted valuable consideration that merited the payment of £2200.

(*b*) *Performance of an existing contractual duty owed to the promisor*. It cannot be regarded as consideration if the person receiving the promise (promisee) agrees to perform for the giver of the promise (the promisor) some act which he is *already* contractually bound to perform.

Stilk v. Myrick (1809). Two members of a ship's crew deserted at a port of call. The captain offered the rest of the crew the deserters' wages – if they worked the ship home shorthanded. When the captain did not pay the crew sued. **Held:** They were already contractually bound to work the ship home in foreseeable emergencies and had therefore not provided consideration.

(*c*) *Part payment of a debt*. Part payment of a debt is generally not regarded as consideration for a promise not to sue for the rest. The creditor normally has the option of subsequently suing for the rest of the sum should he so wish. This basic rule was laid down in *Pinnel's case* (*1602*), when the court stated that 'payment of a lesser sum on the day (due) in satisfaction of a greater cannot be any satisfaction for the whole'.

Such a view was reinforced by the decision in *Foakes v. Beer* (*1884*).

Foakes v. Beer (*1884*). Mrs Beer obtained a judgement against Foakes for a sum owed. Mrs Beer allowed time to pay and agreed not to take proceedings on the judgement. Foakes paid the sum, but then Mrs Beer realised she had not charged interest. Foakes refused to pay this and Mrs Beer sued. **Held:** she must succeed. She was entitled to the interest, and payment of the debt *less* interest could not be consideration for a promise not to take proceedings on the judgement.

There are four situations where the creditor might not be able to obtain full payment:

1. Qualifications outlined in Pinnel's case:

(i) Payment of a smaller sum *before* the due date, at the creditor's request.

(ii) Payment of a smaller sum at a *different* place, at the creditor's request.

(iii) Payment of a smaller sum accompanied by delivery of a chattel (or just delivery of a chattel) 'The gift of a hawk, horse, or robe etc.' at the creditor's request.

The above situations all recognise the fact that the new element must provide some benefit to the creditor and that this benefit will amount to consideration.

2. Composition with creditors. This is an agreement by all creditors of the debtor that they will accept a proportion of what they are owed in full settlement of their claims. A creditor who participates in a composition will fail if he sues separately for the remainder of his debt.

3. Payment of a smaller sum by a third party. For example:

Hirachand Punamchand v. Temple (1911). Temple owed money to Hirachand. Hirachand accepted a smaller sum from Temple's father in full settlement. **Held:** Hirachand could not subsequently sue Temple for the remainder of the sum.

4. The equitable doctrine of promissory estoppel. This is sometimes known as quasi-estoppel, or the 'rule in the High Trees House case'. This rule is a major qualification to *Pinnel's case* and *Foakes v. Beer.* It states that once a person has made a promise to another party, *and that party has acted upon it,* the party making the promise will be prevented in equity – estopped – from going back upon it.

Central London Property Trust Ltd v. High Trees House Ltd (1947). In 1937 the plaintiffs let a block of flats to the defendants for a term of 99 years at a ground rent of £2500 p.a. In 1940, as few of the flats were occupied because of the war the plaintiffs agreed to reduce the rent to £1250 as from the beginning of the term. The defendants continued to pay the reduced rent until 1945, when all the flats were let and the plaintiffs claimed that the full rent was again payable. **Held:** the plaintiffs were entitled to recover the full rent from the time when the flats were again occupied; had they sued for the full rent between 1940 and 1945 they would have been estopped from asserting their strict legal right to demand payment in full, as when parties enter into an arrangement which is intended to create legal relations and in pursuance of such arrangement one party makes a promise to the other which he knows will be acted on and which is in fact acted on by the promisee, the promise is binding on the promisor to the extent that it will not allow him to act inconsistently with it, although the promise may not be supported by consideration in the strict sense. 'I . . . apply the principle that the promise, intended to be binding, intended to be acted on and in fact acted on, is binding so far as its terms properly apply. It is binding as covering the period down to 1945, and from that time full rent is payable.' (*per* Denning, L.J.)

This principle operates as 'a shield and not a sword' and hence can only be used in defence. It follows that a plaintiff would not be able to plead it when instituting legal proceedings. As Denning, L.J., explained in *Combe v. Combe (1951).* 'The principle stated in the High Trees case . . . does not create new causes of action where none existed before. It only prevents a party from insisting upon his strict legal rights, when it would be unjust to allow him to enforce them, having regard to the dealings which have taken place between the parties . . .'. (Courtesy of *Cracknell's Law Students' Companion*)

(*iv*) *Consideration must not be past.* Consideration cannot consist of something wholly performed before the promise which it is seeking to support was made. Consideration must be given in response to the promise. The rule is that past consideration is no consideration. The promise and the consideration must form part of the same transaction.

Roscorla v. Thomas (*1842*). Roscorla bought a horse from Thomas for £30. After the sale had taken place Thomas made a promise to Roscorla that the horse was an animal which was sound and free from vice. In fact the horse was not. Roscorla failed in an action for breach of contract since the consideration for the promise (the sale) was past.

There are some exceptions to this rule that past consideration is no consideration. They are:

(*a*) If the act was done at the promisor's request *and* it was assumed by both parties that payment would ultimately be made, then past consideration will be good consideration.

Lamplaigh v. Braithwait (*1615*). The defendant had feloniously slain another and, at his request, the plaintiff did all that he could to obtain the King's pardon for the defendant. This involved 'many days labour' and much 'riding and journeying at his own charges' and in consideration of this the defendant afterwards promised to pay the plaintiff £100. **Held:** there was a binding contract to make this payment as the promise to pay £100 'couples itself' with the request to obtain the King's pardon and the plaintiff's efforts on the defendant's behalf were executed in consideration for the defendant's promise. (Courtesy of *Cracknell's Law Students' Companion*)

(*b*) S.27 of the *Bills of Exchange Act, 1882*, states that a bill of exchange may be supported by an earlier debt or liability.

(*v*) *Consideration must move from the promisee.* Consideration must move from the promisee to the promisor or some other party nominated by the promisor. There are two aspects to this rule:

(*a*) The promisor cannot escape from the contract by showing that he received no benefit from the promisee (a third party could be beneficiary).

(*b*) Only those providing consideration get any rights under a contract. A third party may well be a beneficiary but cannot sue on the contract since he has provided no consideration. This rule is also known as the **doctrine of privity of contract**. It means that a stranger to a contract cannot enforce it although the contract is for his benefit. He can only enforce the contract if he was a party to the contract and has given valuable consideration for the promise. The classic case is:

Dunlop Pneumatic Tyre Co. Ltd v. Selfridge & Co. Ltd (*1915*). The defendants, who were large storekeepers and sold tyres retail to the public, ordered tyres made by the plaintiffs from Messrs A. J. Dew & Co., who were motor accessory factors. In accordance with the requirements of a contract between the plaintiffs and Messrs A. J. Dew & Co., an agreement purporting to be made between the defendants and Messrs A. J. Dew & Co. provided that in consideration of Messrs A. J. Dew & Co. allowing them certain discounts off the plaintiff's list prices, the defendants would not sell or offer any tyres made by the plaintiffs at less than list prices. The plaintiffs sued the defendants for breach of this agreement. **Held:** their action could not succeed as 'only a person who is a party to a contract can sue on it' (per Viscount Haldane, L.C.). (Courtesy of *Cracknell's Law Students' Companion*)

(*vi*) *The consideration must be lawful.* The courts will not uphold a bargain made for an illegal purpose, or where the consideration is unlawful. Thus an action for non-payment of a bribe would obviously never come to court.

7.8 Revision Test

Answers	*Questions*
	1. What is an offer?
1. A promise that the offeror is prepared to be legally bound, upon specified terms.	**2.** What is an invitation to treat?
2. An invitation to do business with other parties. They are invited to make offers which will be considered.	**3.** What was *Pharmaceutical Society of Great Britain v. Boots* about?
3. It was a 1953 test case about the display of goods in self-service shops. It was held that the display is only an invitation to treat.	**4.** What was *Fisher v. Bell* about?
4. It was a 1960 case about the display of a flickknife in a shop. It was held to be an invitation to treat, not an offer.	**5.** Who makes the offers at an auction?
5. The bidder. The fall of the hammer is the auctioneer's acceptance of the highest offer made.	**6.** What are the requirements for an offer?
6. (*a*) It must be clear – a vague offer will not be upheld; (*b*) it must be communicated to the offeree.	**7.** When does an offer terminate?
7. (*a*) On acceptance – it is merged into the contract; (*b*) on revocation, but the revocation must be communicated to the offeree; (*c*) on rejection, or on a counter-offer; (*d*) after lapse of the	

Answers	*Questions*
stated time, or a reasonable time; (*e*) on the death of an offeror; (*f*) on failure of a condition subject to which the offer was made.	**8.** What is an acceptance?
8. Assent to all the terms of an offer.	**9.** How may it be made?
9. Orally, in writing or by conduct – such as stepping on a bus at a bus stop.	**10.** When is an acceptance not binding?
10. (*a*) When it is expressed 'subject to contract'; (*b*) where the terms are too vague for the courts to tell what was agreed upon.	**11.** Contrast *Hillas v. Arcos* and *Scammell & Nephew v. Ousten.*
11. Both were cases about vague contracts. *Hillas v. Arcos* was a 1933 case about the supply of timber. **Held:** 'that is not vague which can be reduced to certainty'. *Scammell & Nephew v. Ousten* was a case about the hire purchase of a car in 1941. **Held:** the matter had not got past the negotiation stage.	**12.** What are the rules about communication of acceptance?
12. The acceptance must be communicated to the offeror. You cannot take silence as acceptance.	**13.** What are the postal rules about acceptance?
13. In general acceptance occurs when the letter is put into the pillar box. This rule is defeated if the offeror specified that acceptance must reach him before he would be bound. A withdrawal of an offer must reach the offeree before it takes effect, so an acceptance of the offer posted before the withdrawal is received is binding.	**14.** What is consideration?

Answers	*Questions*
14. Anything valuable that supports a contract by proving that the parties have struck a bargain.	**15.** When is valuable consideration not required?
15. When the contract is formal – signed sealed and delivered – rather than a simple contract.	**16.** What are the rules about consideration?
16. (*a*) Consideration must be real, but it need not be adequate – it is for the parties to decide what is adequate; (*b*) existing obligations cannot be consideration for a further promise; (*c*) consideration must not be past; (*d*) consideration must move from the promisee.	**17.** List some important cases about valuable consideration. Make sure you know the facts of each.
17. (*a*) *Pinnel's case* (*1602*); (*b*) *White* v. *Bluett* (*1853*); (*c*) *Glasbrook Brothers* v. *Glamorgan County Council* (*1925*); (*d*) *Stilk* v. *Myrick* (*1809*); (*e*) *Foakes* v. *Beer* (*1884*); (*f*) *Central London Property Trust* v. *High Trees House Ltd* (*1947*); (*g*) *Roscorla* v. *Thomas* (*1842*).	**18.** Go over the questions again until you are sure of all the points. Then try some of the questions in Appendix 1.

8
Circumstances Affecting the Validity of Contracts

8.1 Introduction

Agreements where a valid offer is validly accepted and valuable consideration is present are almost always legally binding, but in certain circumstances the contract may be rendered invalid, and either void or voidable by one of the parties. The most common circumstances may be listed as follows:

(*a*) Where either duress, or undue influence is present.
(*b*) Where certain types of mistake have been made.
(*c*) Where the contract is illegal.

8.2 Duress and Undue Influence

Duress is actual or threatened violence to, or restraint of the person of, a contracting party. If a contract is made under duress it is at once suspect, because consent has not been freely given to the bargain supposedly made. The contract is voidable at the option of the party concerned.

Duress is a common law doctrine which relates entirely to the person and has no relation to that person's goods. As such it is a very limited doctrine and is one where cases are rare. However, one came to the Judicial Committee of the Privy Council in 1975, and this illustrates the principles of duress:

Barton v. Armstrong (1975). Armstrong was the Chairman and Barton was the Managing Director of a group of property companies in New South Wales. Hostility developed between them in 1966, and Barton and the other directors removed Armstrong from his chairmanship of some of the companies. Armstrong then threatened to withdraw his money from them, and he also told Barton: 'The city is not as safe as you may think between office and home.' He telephoned him on various mornings between 4 and 5 a.m. saying, 'You will be killed' or simply breathing heavily. He told Barton: 'You can get killed.' These threats were issued to make Barton sign an agreement giving Armstrong excessive compensation in return for resigning from the boards of the companies. Barton signed. **Held:** that there had been duress and the agreements entered into by Barton were void. The onus is upon the person uttering threats to prove that the contract was not made as a result of them.

Undue Influence. Because of the very narrow application of duress under the common law, equity found it necessary to develop related principles where free will or judgement had been excessively influenced – without threats to the person. The equitable doctrine of undue influence is extremely difficult to define since a narrow line divides what might be undue influence from what might be mere persuasion.

The common law doctrine of duress and the equitable doctrine of undue influence are in the process of merging to cover all cases where a contract is entered into under compulsion, from physical or moral pressures, which the law considers unfair. The cases where a contract will be regarded as voidable by the party under duress are extended to cover the following cases of undue influence:

(*a*) Threatened criminal proceedings.
(*b*) Wrongful detention of property.
(*c*) A fiduciary relationship (one of trust) between the parties.

In general the requirements relating to undue influence are:

(*a*) The plaintiff must prove undue influence if there is no special relationship between the parties. A case illustrating this is:

Williams v. Bayley (1866). A son forged his father's signature on certain promissory notes. When the forgery, which the son did not deny, was discovered the bankers arranged a meeting with his father and issued veiled threats to the effect that if some settlement was not made the son would be prosecuted. The father thereupon executed an agreement to make an equitable mortgage of his property and the forged promissory notes were returned to him. **Held:** the agreement was invalid as in these circumstances the father could not be said to have entered into it freely and voluntarily.

(*b*) Where there is a special relationship between the parties then it is up to the defendant to *disprove* undue influence. There is a presumption in contracts between solicitor and client, religious adviser and disciple, doctor and patient, parent and child, etc., that there is undue influence. It can be rebutted by proof of independent advice. For example:

Lancashire Loans Ltd v. Black (1934). A daughter married at 18 and after the marriage went to live with her husband. Some time after the daughter came of age her mother, who was very extravagant and a frequent borrower from moneylenders, requested her daughter to raise certain money to pay off her debts, sign promissory notes and give a second charge on a vested interest in remainder without which the moneylenders refused to make any further loans. The only advice which the daughter received was from a solicitor who acted for the mother and the moneylenders. The moneylenders sued to enforce a promissory note given by the daughter. **Held:** so far as the daughter was concerned, the transaction must be set aside. She had given the note under her mother's influence and as the moneylenders had notice of the fact that the mother had exercised undue influence they were in no stronger position than she was. (Courtesy of *Cracknell's Law Students' Companion*)

(*c*) The effect of undue influence is to render the contract voidable at the option of the injured party, i.e. they can set it aside if they choose. However, the usual equitable bars to relief apply – for example, there should be no prolonged delay in seeking relief.

Allcard v. Skinner (1887). When Miss Allcard was about 35 years of age she felt a desire to devote her life to good works. She became associated with the Sisters of the Poor and after a few years became a professed member of that sisterhood and bound herself to observe the rules of poverty, chastity and obedience. The rule as to poverty required a member to surrender all her property either to her relatives, the poor or to the sisterhood itself. The rules also provided that no sister should seek advice from anyone outside the order without the consent of the lady superior. Within a few days of becoming a member Miss Allcard made a will bequeathing all her property to Miss Skinner, the lady superior, and in succeeding years made gifts to the value of about £7000 to the same person. When Miss Allcard left the sisterhood about eight years later she immediately revoked her will but waited a further six years before commencing an action to recover what was left of the money given to Miss Skinner. **Held:** if she had sued to recover the amount of her gifts which had not been expended on the fulfilment of the purposes of the sisterhood at an earlier date she would have succeeded on the ground of undue influence, but as it was her acquiescence rendered her claim barred by laches. ('Laches' is laxity in performing a legal duty.) (Courtesy of *Cracknell's Law Students' Companion*)

8.3 Mistake

Sometimes parties enter into a contract on the basis of a mistake. At common law mistake is 'operative' (i.e. its presence has an effect on the contract) only in a limited class of cases: a person may enter into a contract under a serious mistake and yet (unless the case is covered by the law relating to **misrepresentation**) have no remedy. The main reason for this is that where mistake is operative at common law it makes the contract void *ab initio* (from the very beginning). This may have a serious effect, not only for the parties to the contract, but also for third parties (see, for example, *Cundy v. Lindsay* below).

Where a mistake is present, but is not such as to make the contract void at common law, *equity* may give relief to a party who would otherwise suffer as a result of the mistake. Both at common law and in equity, only a **mistake of fact** (as opposed to a mistake of *law*) has an effect on the contract. There is a general presumption that everyone knows the law. The rule *'ignorantia juris haud excusat'* (ignorance of the law excuses no one) rules out all mistakes of law except two: one is not expected to know the law of other countries, so *foreign laws* are not regarded as law and have to be proved in court as facts which the court can then take note of; and one is not expected to know *private rights* even when they are legal and these again must be proved in court as facts. Any mistake of private rights or of foreign law is therefore regarded as a mistake of fact and not a mistake of law, and therefore might be an operative mistake.

Ignorantia juris haud excusat also accounts for the rule that a misrepresentation of the law is not actionable. If we are all deemed to know the law, it is not possible for anyone to misrepresent it to us.

The different types of mistake are usually classified as follows:

(*a*) **Common Mistake.** Here both parties make the same mistake – e.g. A sells B a picture which they both mistakenly believe to be a Warhol.

(*b*) **Mutual Mistake.** Here the parties are at cross-purposes – e.g. A has two cars, a Ford and a Leyland: he contracts to sell a car to B; A means the Ford whereas B thinks he means the Leyland.

(*c*) **Unilateral Mistake.** Here one party is mistaken, and the other knows of his mistake – e.g. A sells B a picture which B mistakenly believes to be a Warhol: A knows the picture is not a Warhol, and knows of B's mistake.

Note: In common mistake the parties have reached an agreement, but on the basis of a mistake; in mutual and unilateral mistake, there is no agreement at all.

It will be seen from the above that there is an overlap between the law relating to mistake and the law relating to misrepresentation. In cases of common mistake there has been an innocent or negligent misrepresentation (e.g. in *Leaf v. International Galleries*, where the galleries sold what they believed to be a genuine Constable painting to the plaintiff, who discovered five years later that it was not genuine – see below).

In unilateral mistake there has often been a fraudulent misrepresentation (as in (*c*) above). In cases where both mistake and misrepresentation are present, the effect of mistake should be considered first, because if it is operative at common law it makes the contract *void*: thus there will normally be no remedy for misrepresentation, since any misrepresentation made has not induced a contract. However, if the misrepresentation was fraudulent, there may be damages for the tort of deceit. If the misrepresentation was *negligent*, there may be damages for the tort of negligence under the rule in Hedley Byrne (see page 329). Even if the misrepresentation was innocent the *Misrepresentation Act, 1967*, gives certain reliefs, including rescission of the contract in certain cases.

(*a*) **Common Mistake: the Effects at Common Law.** To ascertain the effect of common mistake at common law, the following points are helpful:

(i) *Cases of res extincta*, i.e. cases where, unknown to both parties, the subject matter of the contract has never existed, or has ceased to exist at the time when the contract is made.

Couturier v. Hastie (1852). The plaintiffs, who were merchants, shipped 1180 quarters of Indian corn and the defendants, their *del credere* agents, successfully negotiated a sale. (A *del credere* agent is one who agrees, in return for extra commission, to run the risk of any bad debts.) In fact the corn had to be disposed of before reaching its destination, because it had fermented. The buyer refused to pay, no corn having arrived, and Couturier claimed that Hastie must honour this bad debt. On a technicality, the *del credere* arrangement not being in writing as required by the *Statute of Frauds, 1677*, Hastie denied liability. This argument was rejected by the court, but on appeal the House of Lords rejected the claims of Couturier anyway. It was a case of *res extincta.* The contract contemplated that there was an existing something to be sold and bought and capable of transfer but as the corn had already been sold at the time of the sale by the defendants this was not the case and the defendants were not liable. There was no contract, and consequently no bad debt. (Adapted from *Cracknell's Law Students' Companion*)

(ii) *Cases of res sua*, i.e. cases where A agrees to sell or lease to B property which already belongs to B.

Cooper v. Phibbs (1867). The appellant sought to be relieved from an agreement whereby he contracted to take from the respondent a three-year lease of a salmon fishery. At the time of making the agreement the appellant believed that the fishery belonged to the respondent but it afterwards appeared that the fishery was the property of the appellant himself. **Held:** the appellant was entitled to have the agree ment for the lease set aside subject to the respondent having a lien on the property in respect of money spent on purchasing certain fishing rights and improving the fishery. (Courtesy of *Cracknell's Law Students' Companion*)

In cases of *res extincta* and *res sua* the contracts have been held to be void. *The reason for this is the absence of any contractual subject matter.*

It is rare for operative mistake to be extended to situations where there is mistake as to the quality of the subject matter of the contract. For example:

Leaf v. International Galleries (1950). (Court of Appeal.) The plaintiff bought an oil painting of Salisbury Cathedral and accepted it as a genuine Constable on the representations of the sellers, the defendants. Five years after the sale the plaintiff discovered that the painting was not by Constable and he claimed rescission on the grounds of innocent misrepresentation. **Held:** his claim must fail as the action had not been commenced within a reasonable time and, further, the mistake in question was not one which would entitle the plaintiff to avoid the contract. (Courtesy of *Cracknell's Law Students' Companion*)

Note that the rescission of a contract entered into after an innocent misrepresentation is now permitted under the *Misrepresentation Act, 1967*, but it is an equitable remedy which will be refused if there has been an undue lapse of time. This would not prevent damages for innocent misrepresentation being given under S.2(2) of the Act. Whatever the effect of misrepresentation the court ruled that the mistake made was not one which would entitle the plaintiff to avoid the contract.

However, the House of Lords in *Bell v. Lever Bros. Ltd (1932)* did state that it would be possible for a contract to be void at common law for a common mistake as to the quality of the subject matter if the mistake was 'fundamental' to the contract.

The effect in equity. Where the contract is void at common law (e.g. cases of *res extincta* and *res sua*) it is also void in equity. In addition, the court may impose terms on either party (*Cooper v. Phibbs*, where the respondent was allowed a lien on a property for work done).

Even where the contract is not void at common law, equity may give relief in one of two ways:

(i) It may set the contract aside, with or without imposing terms. For example:

Grist v. Bailey (1966). B. agreed to sell a freehold house to G. at a price of £850, in the belief that the house was subject to an existing statutory tenancy. In fact the house was not subject to a statutory tenancy, and on a vacant possession basis was worth £2250. G. sought specific performance of the agreement, and B. pleaded the existence of a common mistake of fact, and counterclaimed for rescission of the sale agreement. **Held:** the sale agreement would be set aside for a fundamental common mistake of fact, on terms which gave G. the option to buy the house at the vacant possession price. (Courtesy of *Cracknell's Law Students' Companion*)

(ii) It may grant the equitable remedy of **rectification**. Where the parties have made an agreement or reached a common intention, and have attempted to incorporate this in a document, and, because of a mistake, the document does not accurately reflect their prior agreement or intention, then the court may order rectification of the document, and specific performance of it as rectified.

Joscelyne v. Nissen (1970). J. agreed with his daughter (N.) that she should take over his car-hire business. Throughout the negotiations it was agreed that she should pay all the household expenses. However, when the written contract was concluded no reference was made to household expenses. **Held:** The court would rectify the document to include the daughter's agreement to pay the expenses.

(*b*) **Mutual Mistake.** Where the parties are at cross-purposes the court applies an objective test, and tries to determine the 'sense of the promise': i.e. would a sensible third party, looking at the externals of the contract, come to the conclusion that the contract meant what A intended or what B intended? If such a third party could not conclude that the contract meant what A intended or what B intended, then the contract is void. The classic case is *Raffles v. Wichelhaus (1864)* – see page 93.

The effect in equity of mutual mistake. Equity follows the common law in holding that, where the sense of the promise can be ascertained, a contract to that effect exists and **specific performance** may be ordered, even though the effect may be harsh. For example,

Tamplin v. James (1880). 'The Ship Inn' and a saddler's shop adjoining were put up for sale by auction and the extent of the property to be sold was clearly marked on plans which were on view in the auction room. At the back of the property were two pieces of garden which originally belonged to the vendors, the plaintiffs, but which were now let to them by the present owners. The tenants of the inn and shop used and enjoyed these gardens and the defendant, who purchased the inn and shop at the auction, refused to complete his purchase on the ground that he believed that he was buying the freehold of all that was in the occupation of the plaintiffs' tenants. The defendant said that he had not seen the plans which correctly delineated the property to be sold. **Held:** the plaintiffs were entitled to specific performance as the fact that the purchaser had made this mistake without any excuse ought not to enable him to escape from his bargain. (Courtesy of *Cracknell's Law Students' Companion*)

(*c*) **Unilateral Mistake.** Where we are considering whether one party knows of the other's mistake, he is taken to know what would be obvious to a reasonable person. For example, in *Hartog v. Colin and Shields*:

Hartog v. Colin and Shields (1939)). The defendants offered to sell the plaintiff 30,000 Argentine hare skins at certain prices per pound but after the plaintiff had accepted this offer the defendants failed to deliver the skins as they had intended, as was the usual practice, that they should be sold at the specific prices per *piece*. **Held:** the plaintiff's action for damages would not succeed as he must have realised that the offer made by the defendants contained a mistake. (Courtesy of *Cracknell's Law Students' Companion*)

There are several special cases of unilateral mistake: (*a*) mistaken identity; (*b*) mistakes about documents; (*c*) mistakes in equity.

(*a*) **Mistaken Identity.** Cases of mistaken identity usually arise from fraudulent misrepresentation: e.g. R, a rogue, by pretending to be X, a reputable person, obtains goods on credit from O, the owner. R then disposes of the goods for value to T, a third party acting in good faith. O's contract with R is voidable for fraudulent misrepresentation, but this will not enable him to recover the goods from T. This is shown by the case of *Phillips v. Brooks*:

Phillips v. Brooks Ltd (*1919*). A man entered the plaintiff's shop and asked to inspect some jewellery. He selected some pearls and rings to the value of £3000 and when he was signing a cheque for that amount he stated: 'You see who I am, I am Sir George Bullough', and he gave an address in St James's Square. The plaintiff knew that there was such a man as Sir George Bullough and reference to a directory confirmed that Sir George lived at the address mentioned. The plaintiff asked the man in the shop if he would like to take the jewels with him but was told: 'You had better have the cheque cleared first, but I should like to take the ring as it is my wife's birthday tomorrow.' The plaintiff let the man have the ring but his cheque was dishonoured. The rogue pledged the ring to the defendants from whom the plaintiff sought to recover either the ring or its value. **Held:** the plaintiff intended to contract with the man who came into the shop although he believed (mistakenly) that he was Sir George Bullough. The property in the ring had therefore passed to the actual purchaser who was able to give a good title to the defendants. For this reason the plaintiff's action failed. (Courtesy of *Cracknell's Law Students' Companion*)

In order to recover property, O must prove that his contract with R is void *ab initio* for operative mistake, with the result that no title can pass to or from R. There is a presumption that a contract exists and the court will not hold it void unless the mistaken party can prove the following four points:

(i) *That his mistake as to identity was known to the person with whom he dealt.*

(ii) *That he intended to deal with some third person, i.e. some person other than the person with whom he apparently made the contract.* Thus if there is no third person in existence to point to, the contract will not normally be void.

King's Norton Metal Co. Ltd v. Edridge, Merrett & Co. Ltd (*1897*). Both parties were metal manufacturers and the plaintiffs had received a letter ordering certain goods which purported to come from Hallam & Co., Soho Hackle Pin and Wire Works, Sheffield. At the head of the paper on which the letter was written there was a representation of a large factory with a number of chimneys and a statement that the firm had depots and agencies in Belfast, Lille and Ghent. The plaintiffs supplied the goods but it afterwards appeared that they had been ordered by a man called Wallis who in turn had sold them to the defendants. The firm Hallam & Co. did not exist but the plaintiffs had received payment in respect of previous orders made in the name of that firm. On the occasion in question Wallis did not pay for the goods and the plaintiffs brought an action for damages for conversion. **Held:** their action must fail as they were found to have contracted with the writer of the letter. The property in the goods had therefore passed to Wallis who was able to give the defendants a good title to the goods when they purchased them. (Courtesy of *Cracknell's Law Students' Companion*)

(iii) *That at the time of negotiating the agreement, he regarded the identity of the other contracting party as a matter of crucial importance.*

Cundy v. Lindsay (*1878*). Messrs Lindsay & Co. were linen manufacturers in Belfast and Alfred Blenkarn, who occupied a room in a house looking into Wood Street, Cheapside, wrote to them and proposed buying a quantity of their goods. Blenkarn used the address '37, Wood Street, Cheapside' and signed the letters, without using an initial or Christian name, in such a way that his signature appeared to be 'Blenkiron & Co.'. There was a highly respectable firm of W. Blenkiron & Son carrying on business at 123 Wood Street and Messrs Lindsay & Co., who knew of this firm's reputation but not the number of the premises where they carried on business, supplied the goods ordered by Blenkarn and addressed them to Messrs Blenkiron & Co., 37 Wood Street, Cheapside. Blenkarn did not pay for the goods but disposed of them to the defendants who were sued by Messrs Lindsay & Co. for unlawful conversion. **Held:** no contract had been concluded with Blenkarn who therefore had no property in the goods to transfer to the defendants; consequently the defendants were liable to the extent of their value. (Courtesy of *Cracknell's Law Students' Companion*)

(iv) *That he took reasonable steps to verify the identity of the person with whom he was invited to deal.*

Ingram v. Little (1960). The plaintiffs, who were two sisters and a third person, advertised for sale the car of which they were joint owners. A man called on them, and agreed to buy the car for £717. In order to persuade the plaintiffs to accept a cheque in payment the man said that he was H, and gave an address in Surrey. Having checked the name and address in the telephone directory, the plaintiffs accepted the cheque and parted with the car. The man, who was not H, sold the car to the defendant and then disappeared, his cheque being dishonoured. The plaintiffs sought to recover the car or its value from the defendant who had bought it in good faith. **Held:** the plaintiff's offer to sell on payment by cheque was made only to H, and could not be accepted by the man representing himself to be H; no contract had been formed, therefore, and the plaintiffs were entitled to recover the car or damages from the defendant. (Courtesy of *Cracknell's Law Students' Companion*)

Some doubt has been cast on the correctness of this decision, because in rather similar circumstances the Court of Appeal refused to follow *Ingram v. Little*, and referred in the judgement to 'a presumption that where a transaction takes place between people face-to-face the offer by one person is made to the other, and not to someone he says he is.' The case was:

Lewis v. Averay (1971). The plaintiff advertised a car for sale. A man telephoned for an appointment to view the car, but did not give his name. He came along and tested the car and the plaintiff took him to a flat to discuss the details. At the flat the potential buyer stated that he was 'Richard Green', the well-known actor, and he agreed to buy the car at £450. He tendered a cheque in payment, signed 'R. A. Green', and on producing evidence of his identity he was allowed to take the car away. The cheque proved worthless. The buyer was a rogue, not Richard Green, and later sold the car to the defendant, who bought it in good faith. The plaintiff sued the defendant in conversion. **Held:** where a transaction takes place between people face to face there is a presumption that the offer by one person is made to the other and not to any person that other says he is, and there was nothing on the facts of the case to rebut this presumption. Thus, the plaintiff's offer was made to the rogue and not to 'Richard Green'. The rogue accordingly got a voidable title to the car, under which he sold the car to the defendant before the contract between the plaintiff and the rogue had been avoided. The plaintiff's claim therefore failed.

(*b*) **Documents Mistakenly Signed.** Often documents are signed by mistake. It may be that one party, A, induces another party, B, to sign a document different in class or contents from that which B contemplated. The question then arises as to B's liability to any third party who might subsequently hold such documents. The matter revolves around the point as to whether the law will allow B to say in his own defence that the document is 'not his act' ('*non est factum*').

The basic position as regards *non est factum* follows from the cases listed below, which rest upon two points.

(i) Was the document which was signed totally different in nature from the document which the party believed he was signing? If it was, the court may feel that he should be released from his obligations. If it was substantially the same he must honour the contract. This was the case in *Saunders v. Anglia Building Society* (*1970*).

Saunders v. Anglia Building Society (*1970*). An elderly widow signed without reading a document which X told her was a deed of gift of her house in favour of her nephew. In fact, it was a purported assignment of the leasehold to X, and the old lady would not have signed had she known the facts. X mortgaged the house to the building society, and on his defaulting on the repayments due under the mortgage, they sought possession. **Held:** The plaintiff could not rely on a plea of *non est factum* as against the building society, because on the facts the transaction she intended and what she actually carried out were the same character, and she was bound by what she had signed. (Courtesy of *Cracknell's Law Students' Companion*)

(ii) Was the signee negligent in signing? In *Foster v. Mackinnon* the document was totally different and the feeble-sighted old man was held not to be negligent in signing:

Foster v. Mackinnon (*1869*). The defendant, an old man of feeble sight, was induced to sign his name on the back of a bill of exchange by a fraudulent misrepresentation that he was signing a guarantee. **Held:** if the defendant signed without knowing that it was a bill of exchange under the belief that it was a guarantee, and if he had not been guilty of negligence in so signing, he was entitled to be released from liability under the bill. (Courtesy of *Cracknell's Law Students' Companion*)

(*c*) **Mistake in Equity.** Where a mistake occurs as a slip of the pen (or these days as a slip of the typewriter) equity will not allow the error to go uncorrected. In *Webster v. Cecil* (*1861*) a purported acceptance of an offer to sell land at £1250 when previous offers at £2000 had been rejected was not upheld. The defendant Cecil had intended to offer to sell at £2250. Performance of a sale at £1250 was refused, for Webster must have known it was a slip of the pen.

8.4 Illegal Contracts

Any contract where the promise, the consideration or the object of the contract is unlawful will be void and cannot be enforced in the courts. Where a contract is prohibited by statute or contrary to public policy because it encourages immorality, or crime, or is against the public interest in some other way, it is illegal and the courts will not lend their support to anyone on the matter. It is said to be **void by illegality**. Sometimes a contract is merely denied its full validity, because of a technicality, and it is said to be unenforceable. The words illegal, void and unenforceable are often used loosely and precise understanding of what is meant by each is not easy to attain. The general rule is that all illegal contracts are void. The maxim is *ex turpi causa non oritur actio* (no action arises from a base or wrongful cause).

Some writers suggest that there is virtually no difference between illegal and void contracts, others still maintain that the distinction is worth making, especially since a contract void by illegality will render unenforceable any contracts depending upon it, whilst a contract void for other reasons will not.

Illegal contracts may be illegal by virtue of an infringement of a statute or they may be illegal at common law. However, this does not necessarily mean that the courts will view all infringements with equal severity; some contracts may be strictly illegal and the court will not offer redress to either party, while others may be only nominally illegal and the court may sever the illegal part from the legal part.

8.5 Contracts Illegal at Common Law

These include agreements to commit crimes or torts; agreements to defraud the revenue or other public authority; agreements to commit immoral acts or make immoral acts possible and other contracts which are against public policy.

(i) *Contracts where the object is the commission of a crime or a civil wrong*. Any contract which purports to commit a crime or a tort is illegal and void. Even where the crime is to be committed outside UK jurisdiction it is illegal to make a contract which envisages crime in a foreign and friendly country. In *Foster v. Driscoll* (*1929*) a contract was made to smuggle whisky into the United States during prohibition. It was held to be illegal and void.

(ii) *Contracts to defraud the revenue or other public authority*. Any attempt to defraud the public purse is illegal and cannot be relied upon in a court of law. In *Alexander v. Rayson* (*1936*), 1 KB 169, Alexander and Rayson entered into an agreement whereby the agreed rent was split into two parts, one part declared to be rent and the other declared to be for services to the flat concerned. The object was to reduce the assessment for rates. When A. sued R. for failure to pay for the 'services' the arrangement was held to be void.

(iii) *Contracts depending for their performance upon sexually immoral acts*. In *Pearce v. Brooks* (*1866*) a prostitute failed to pay a carriage-maker for a coach which had been specially built for the attraction of male customers. It was held to be an illegal contract, and the carriage-maker could not recover the price.

(iv) *Other contracts against public policy*. The term 'against public policy' means that crime would be encouraged, or the public interest would suffer. Thus it is against public policy for a person to be allowed to insure property in which they have no interest, for they might just be tempted to make the event occur which they are insuring against, since they will not suffer if the risk occurs. Thus I may insure my own life, my wife's life or our mutual property, for I have an interest in them and would suffer a loss if they were adversely affected by the risk covered. I am not entitled to insure the property (for example) of others, for I have no insurable interest in it.

It is in general against public policy if private activity is curtailed unnecessarily. Everyone has the right to use his personal talents or skills in any lawful way he chooses. Therefore **contracts in restraint of trade** are *prima facie* illegal. This is such an important topic that it is worth separate consideration

(v) *Contracts in restraint of trade.* It is frequently the case that an employee may find out things in the course of his employment that would be helpful to him should he decide to set up in business on his own. This might harm his former employer. Similarly, a vendor of a business is usually paid a sum for goodwill, the money being compensation for the hard work done in establishing a clientèle locally. To set up in business next door to the previous business would clearly be unfair. The question then arises how shall the employer, or the purchaser of a business protect himself from such unfairness? The answer is to insert clauses 'in restraint of trade' in the contract of employment or the agreement to purchase which prohibit the employee or the vendor from setting up in business again. However, it is against public policy to impose such a restriction on the use of one's talents and labours.

The solution is to permit clauses in restraint of trade which are fair and reasonable but to declare unreasonable restrictions against public policy and void. To restrict an employee from setting up next door to his employer might be held reasonable. To restrict him from setting up anywhere in the UK would be unreasonable. The following cases illustrate the problem.

British Reinforced Concrete Co. Ltd v. Schelff (1921). A company took over the local business of S. and included a clause in the agreement restricting him from setting up in business again within 10 miles of any branch of their organisation *which was nationwide.* **Held:** it was too wide a restriction and void.

Nordenfeldt v. Maxim Nordenfeldt Gun Co. (1894). The inventor of a famous machine gun promised that for 25 years he would not make or sell guns or ammunition anywhere in the world. In return he was generously compensated. When he found this restriction irksome and tried to break it the court found it reasonable and binding.

8.6 Illegality Declared by Statute

In modern society a wide range of statutes is passed by the legislative body. They are designed to fulfil a range of purposes and it is often a question put to the judiciary as to what the exact meaning of a statute might be. Some statutes are such that those who neglect their contents render contracts made in that area illegal. Others do not have such a serious impact upon contracts. It is up to the court to interpret and decide in the light of the facts of each case.

Examples of specific declarations about illegality are as follows:

(*a*) **Gaming and Wagering.** By S.18 of the *Gaming Act, 1845*: (i) contracts by way of gaming or wagering are null and void; and (ii) no action can be brought to recover money won upon any wagers. The *Gaming Act, 1968*, drew a distinction between 'hard gaming' and 'bingo' and permitted relaxations in the rules about gaming premises when used for this more innocent activity.

(*b*) **Loans to Infants.** Contracts for the loan of money to infants are absolutely void under the *Infants Relief Act, 1874*.

(*c*) **Restrictive Practices.** The *Restrictive Trade Practices Acts, 1976 and 1977*, and the *Resale Prices Act, 1976*, make it illegal to impose restrictive practices unless these are registered for consideration by the Restrictive Practices Court.

As examples of less specific cases of illegality we may maintain the following:

(*a*) **The 'Ultra Vires' Doctrine.** This had already been fully discussed (see pages 63 and 90). Here it is sufficient to state again that when a company is registered under the *Companies Act, 1985* it includes in its memorandum of association an 'objects clause'. Since this is a matter of public record everybody may be deemed to know what the objects of every company are. If I engage in a contract with a company which is *ultra vires* the company (outside the powers of the company) the contract is strictly speaking illegal. Although S.35 of the Act (see page 63) now protects innocent third parties who make contracts with companies it still remains a fact that as far as the directors of the company are concerned the contract is illegal, and the *ultra vires* principle is therefore still a good example of a situation where a contract may be held to be void by illegality.

(*b*) **Statutes Requiring a Licence.** Many statutes require a person engaging in certain activities to take out a licence. If contracts are made by unlicensed persons the contract is void *ab initio* (from the very beginning). Neither party can acquire rights, whether there is any intention to break the law or not. However, even where a contract is lawfully formed it is possible that the performance of the contract may be illegal. In *Anderson Ltd v. Daniel* (*1924*) a statute required that a seller of artificial fertilisers must give the buyer an invoice stating the composition of the fertiliser. The sellers had failed to do this when supplying 10 tons of fertiliser and when suing for the price were held to have no rights or remedies under the contract, which had been illegally performed.

It must be emphasised, however, that a contract is not automatically rendered illegal as performed merely because some statutory requirement has been violated in the course of its completion. It is all a question of the construction of a statute to determine whether it was the express or implied intention of the legislation that such a violation as that which the guilty party has committed should deprive him of all remedies.

The effects of illegality. The effect is to render the contract void, and unenforceable. This means that the courts will do nothing to implement the contract, even if unfairness results. Where there is equal wrongdoing the court will do nothing to help either party. Thus the coachmaker in *Pearce v. Brooks* could not obtain either payment or the return of the coach. The rule is 'where there is equal wrongdoing' the position of the defendant is the stronger. Where there is unequal wrongdoing the court may order in favour of one of the parties if there is genuine repentance.

Sometimes a contract may be like the curate's egg – good in parts. In that case the court may try to sever the contract into its good and bad parts, and uphold the good part while rejecting the illegal part. This is called **severance** of the contract.

8.7 Revision Test

Answers	*Questions*
–	**1.** What is duress?
1. Actual or threatened violence to the person (or imprisonment of the person).	**2.** What is undue influence?
2. Excessive influence over the free will or judgement of a party to a contract.	**3.** What is the presumption where there is a special relationship?
3. That there is undue influence.	**4.** How can this presumption be rebutted?
4. By proof that independent legal advice was available to the plaintiff.	**5.** What is an operative mistake?
5. A mistake that goes to the root of the operations following from a contract.	**6.** What is the effect of operative mistake at common law?
6. It renders the contract void *ab initio*.	**7.** What are the classes of operative mistake?
7. (*a*) Common mistake; (*b*) mutual mistake; (*c*) unilateral mistake.	**8.** List common cases of operative mistake.
8. (*a*) Mistake as to the existence of the subject matter; (*b*) mistake as to the quality of the subject matter; (*c*) mistake as to the terms of the agreement; (*d*) mistake as to the identity of the person dealt with; (*e*) mistake in equity – a slip of the pen or the typewriter.	**9.** What is the meaning of *non est factum*?
9. 'Not my act.'	**10.** When is a contract illegal?
10. When it contravenes a statute or the common law.	**11.** What is the effect of illegality?
11. The contract is void and unenforceable, except in certain cases where severance is possible to sever the illegal part from the part that is legal.	**12.** Go over the questions again until you are sure of the answers. Then try some of the written questions in Appendix 1.

9
The Terms of the Contract

9.1 Introduction

The contents of a contract are known as the **terms**. Usually the parties to a contract state the terms *expressly*, and may choose to do so orally, or in writing, or in a combination of these methods. However, as we have already seen, terms can sometimes be *implied* by law into the contract (as for example, in *Hillas v. Arcos* (*1932*) (see page 98) and *Foley v. Classique Coaches* (*1934*) (see page 101). These are instances of judicial implication, but terms are also frequently implied into contracts by Acts of Parliament.

The terms themselves, whether express or implied, have varying degrees of importance and a party will be allowed wider remedies for breach by the other party of an important term than for breach of an unimportant term.

Finally, terms in a contract may not only confer rights on one or both of the parties but may also restrict or exclude a party's rights.

Before considering the terms of a contract in detail there are a few preliminary matters to be considered. These are:

(*a*) The distinction between representations and terms.
(*b*) The form of the contract.

(*a*) **The Distinction between Representations and Terms.** A term is part of the contract. A representation is not: it is a statement which *induces* the making of the contract. The distinction between a term and a representation is important, because the remedies are different (see Misrepresentation in Chapter 10). Three tests have been used by judges in determining whether a statement made by a party is a term or a mere representation. None of these tests is, by itself, conclusive.

(i) *The time test*. If the statement was made *at the time the contract was formed*, or shortly before, then it is more likely to be a term than a representation. For example:

Routledge v. McKay (*1954*). A Douglas motorcycle combination was first registered in 1930 but when a new registration book was issued the date of original registration was given as '9.9.41'. In October 1949, the seller, who was not responsible for the incorrect entry in the registration book, in answer to a question by the buyer as to the date of the machine, said that it was a late 1941 or a 1942 model and seven days later the buyer and seller entered into a contract of sale. The memorandum of agreement made no mention of the date of the machine. The buyer claimed damages for breach of warranty. **Held:** the incorrect statement in the registration book was a false representation and not a warranty and, in the absence of fraud, the buyer could not succeed. (Courtesy of *Cracknell's Law Students' Companion*)

(ii) *The writing test.* If the terms are in writing, then any oral statement is more likely to be a mere representation. The court infers that the parties considered it insufficiently important to be reduced to writing, and, therefore, regard it as a representation only. For example:

Heilbut, Symons & Co. v. Buckleton (1913). The appellants' manager had been intructed to obtain applications for shares in the Filisola Rubber and Produce Estates Limited. The respondent telephoned the appellants' manager and said: 'I understand you are bringing out a rubber company', and the manager replied: 'We are.' The respondent asked 'if it was all right' and was told 'We are bringing it out', to which the respondent rejoined: 'That is good enough for me.' As a result of this conversation 6000 shares were allotted to the respondent but they quickly fell in value. The respondent contended that as the company could not be properly described as a rubber company there was a breach of warranty that it was a rubber company whose main object was to produce rubber. **Held:** the words of the appellants' manager constituted a mere representation and not a warranty. (Courtesy of *Cracknell's Law Students' Companion*)

(iii) *The skill and knowledge test.* If the maker of the statement possessed special skill and knowledge compared with the other party, then it is probably a term. This is probably the test to which the courts attach the greatest weight. For example:

Dick Bentley Productions Ltd v. Harold Smith (Motors) Ltd (1965). The plaintiff told the defendant dealer that he was on the look-out for a well-vetted Bentley car and the defendant truthfully assured the plaintiff that he (the defendant) was in a position to find out the history of cars. Later, the defendant informed the plaintiff that he had just purchased 'one of the nicest cars we have had in for quite a long time', that it had been fitted with a replacement engine and gearbox and (falsely but not fraudulently) that it had done 20,000 miles only since it had been so fitted (the speedometer read 20,000 miles). The plaintiff purchased the car for £1850 but it was a considerable disappointment to him and he brought an action for breach of warranty. **Held:** he was entitled to succeed as the inference that the representation was intended as a warranty had not been rebutted. 'If a representation is made in the course of dealings for a contract for the very purpose of inducing the other party to act on it, and it actually induces him to act on it by entering into the contract, that is *prima facie* ground for inferring that the representation was intended as a warranty. . . . But the maker of the representation can rebut this inference if he can show that it really was an innocent misrepresentation, in that he was in fact innocent of fault in making it, and that it would not be reasonable in the circumstances for him to be bound by it' (*per* Lord Denning, M.R.). (Courtesy of *Cracknell's Law Students' Companion*)

(*b*) **The Form of the Contract.** As outlined earlier, a contract may as a general rule be in any form; but where the parties chose to put the contract into writing the courts used not to allow evidence of any unwritten terms to be given. However, this rule is of little importance now as the courts have created very wide exceptions to it. There is, for example, a 'doctrine of the implied term (a custom or trade usage)'. This is explained below. There is sometimes an oral condition precedent, under offer or acceptance, while sometimes the parties intended the contract to be partly written and partly oral. This last exception has been used in so many cases that the general rule would appear to have lost its original value. For example:

S.S. Ardennes (Cargo Owners) v. Ardennes (Owners) (1950). The defendants orally promised that their ship would proceed direct to London and in reliance upon this promise the plaintiffs agreed to the shipment of 3000 cases of their mandarines for sale in the London market. The bill of lading provided that the defendants were able to carry the goods to London proceeding by any route, and whether 'directly or indirectly to such port' and were permitted 'to carry the goods beyond their port of destination'. The ship did not sail straight to London but went first to Antwerp and as a result the cargo was delivered later than could have reasonably been expected. The plaintiffs obtained a lower price for their fruit, had to pay a higher import duty and claimed damages for breach of contract in respect of this loss. **Held:** they were entitled to succeed as the bill of lading was not, in itself, the contract between the parties but merely evidence of its terms. The promise to proceed direct to London was part of the contract and the plaintiffs were awarded damages for breach of this provision. (Courtesy of *Cracknell's Law Students' Companion*)

9.2 Express Terms: Conditions and Warranties

An express term is a clear stipulation in the contract which the parties intend should be binding upon them. Traditionally, the common law has divided terms into two categories. First there are **conditions**, which are terms going to the root of the contract, and for breach of which the remedies of repudiation or rescission of the contract *and* damages are allowed. Second, there are **warranties**, which are minor terms of the contract, for breach of which the *only* remedy is damages. The following cases illustrate the distinction.

Bettini v. Gye (1876). The plaintiff entered into a contract to sing for the defendant for a certain period and at a fixed salary and agreed to be in London six days before the commencement of his engagement for the purpose of rehearsal. In fact, due to illness, he arrived four days later than he had promised and the defendant refused to proceed with the engagement. **Held:** the provision as to rehearsal was not a condition precedent as it did not go to the root of the matter and for this reason the defendant was not entitled to avoid the contract. (Courtesy of *Cracknell's Law Students' Companion*)

Poussard v. Spiers and Pond (1876). The plaintiff agreed with the defendants to sing the chief female part for a period of three months in a new opera which was about to be produced at the defendants' theatre. Owing to illness the plaintiff was not able to attend the final rehearsals or the first four performances and when she offered to take her part in the fifth performance the defendants refused to accept her services and the plaintiff brought an action for wrongful dismissal. **Held:** the plaintiff could not recover as her inability to perform on the opening day and early performances was a breach of a condition precedent which went to the root of the matter and hence entitled the defendants to treat the contract as discharged. (Courtesy of *Cracknell's Law Students' Companion*)

In *Heyworth v. Hutchinson (1867)* Lord Blackburn defined a condition as a term 'going to the essence of the contract' or which 'goes to the root of the matter', and a warranty as a clause 'only collateral to the contract'.

Parliament followed this classification of terms in codifying the law relating to the sale of goods. By S.11.3 of the *Sale of Goods Act, 1979*, a condition is stated to be a term 'the breach of which may give rise to a right to treat the contract as repudiated', while S.61 defines a warranty as a term 'collateral to the main purpose of the contract'.

While the basic distinction between a condition and a warranty in a contract still holds good today, there may be circumstances in which the court will find it difficult to assign a term to either category.

Faced with a term which involves several obligations which are actually or potentially of varying importance, the modern tendency of the courts is not to attempt to label the term as a 'condition' or a 'warranty'. Instead, they look *to the effect of the breach*: if it is serious, then the injured party can repudiate and obtain damages. An example was given by Upjohn, L.J., in the first case in which this approach was adopted (*Hong Kong Fir Shipping Co. Ltd v. Kawasaki Kisen Kaisha Ltd* (*1962*)). He said:

'If a nail is missing from one of the timbers of a wooden vessel . . . the owners are in breach of the seaworthiness stipulation. It is contrary to common sense to suppose that . . . the charterer should at once be entitled to treat the contract as at an end for such a trifling breach.'

This approach has tended to be followed in the majority of subsequent cases dealing with this point, e.g.

Reardon Smith Line Ltd v. Hansen-Tangen (*1976*). The appellants chartered a ship which was described in the charterparty as to be built by a named Japanese shipbuilding company and having a particular hull number. When delivered, the ship had been built by subcontractors under the supervision of the named company, many of whose personnel had been seconded to work on the vessel. The hull number was also different. The appellants appealed against a decision that the ship in fact complied with the description having regard to Japanese custom. They contended that the words specifying the builders and the number were contractual terms forming part of the description and that because of the departure from the description they were entitled to reject the vessel. **Held:** Dismissing the appeal, in reaching its decision the court had to place itself in the same factual position as that in which the parties had been when contracting. The relevant words were only intended as a means of identification. The strict rule of compliance with description which applied in sale of goods cases did not apply to a contract like the present which came under the general law of contract. Even if it did apply, the description had been complied with in the strict sense. The words fulfilled their function of providing a means of identifying the vessel. They could not be read as essential terms of the contract which must be complied with literally. (Courtesy of *Cracknell's Law Students' Companion*)

Apart from this, however, there are three matters which can affect the remedies of the innocent party, in relation to breach of contract:

(i) *Acceptance of goods*. The right to repudiate a contract for the sale of goods will be lost if the buyer has *accepted* the goods (S.11(4)) of the *Sale of Goods Act, 1979*. 'Acceptance', according to S.35 of the Act, occurs if he *indicates acceptance*, or if he *retains the goods* beyond a reasonable time, or if he does anything *inconsistent* with the seller's ownership (such as resale). Effectively then, the condition must be treated as a warranty, with a right only to claim damages, e.g. *Leaf v. International Galleries* (see page 113).

(ii) *If a representation becomes a warranty* in the contract – which could happen if a statement was made before the contract, and then repeated at the time of the contract – then the innocent party could not only obtain damages if it were untrue, but also obtain rescission of the contract under S.1 of the *Misrepresentation Act, 1967*. This right will be considered again in Chapter 10 on Misrepresentation.

(iii) *Waiver*. A breach of condition can be waived. This extinguishes the right to repudiate, e.g.

Aquis Estates Ltd v. Minton (1975). The plaintiff appellants contracted to buy the residue of a lease from the defendants 'subject to no adverse land charge entry'. Unknown to both parties, there was an adverse entry (the property was a 'listed building' for planning purposes) but after discovering it the plaintiffs negotiated (unsuccessfully) with the freeholders for the purchase of the freehold. The court held that the plaintiffs had thereby *waived* the breach of condition of no adverse entries, and so were liable to forfeit their deposit and pay damages for wrongful repudiation. (Courtesy of *Cracknell's Law Students' Companion*)

9.3 Implied Terms

Implied terms are those terms which, although not expressly stated by the parties by words or conduct, are by law deemed to be part of the contract.

Terms may be implied into contracts by (*a*) custom, (*b*) statute, or (*c*) the courts.

(*a*) **Terms Implied By Custom.** By custom, a lawyer means an established practice or usage in a trade, locality, type of transaction, or between parties.

If two or more people enter into a contract against a common background of business, it is considered that they expressly intend the trade usage of that business unless they expressly exclude this.

Trade custom is illustrated by the following case:

British Crane Hire Corporation v. Ipswich Plant Hire Ltd (1974). A crane was hired under an oral agreement between two large companies who were both engaged in the plant hire business. The owner's usual printed conditions of hire, which were standard in the trade, were sent on later. **Held:** the conditions of hire were part of the contract not withstanding that there had been no 'course of dealing'. The standard conditions were fair and reasonable and the hirers knew that the conditions were always applied. (Courtesy of *Cracknell's Law Students' Companion*)

A course of dealing between two parties can also give rise to an implied term in a subsequent contract between two parties, as in *Hillas v. Arcos* (see page 98).

If an express term conflicts with a custom, then the former prevails. For example:

Affréteurs Réunis Société Anonyme, Les, v. Leopold Watford (London) Ltd (1919). A charterparty provided that commission was due to the charterers' brokers on the signing of the charter whereas by custom commission was only payable if hire was earned. **Held:** commission was payable on the signing of the charter as custom was entirely inconsistent with the plain words of the agreement and therefore, in the circumstances of the case, of no effect. The charterers, as trustees for the brokers, could enforce this provision against the shipowners. (Courtesy of *Cracknell's Law Students' Companion*)

(*b*) **Terms Implied by Statute.** There are many areas of the civil law where Parliament has interfered with the right of parties to regulate their own affairs; this interference mainly occurs where one party has used his dominant bargaining position to abuse this freedom.

Thus, in sale of goods, the general principle *'caveat emptor'* ('buyer beware') has been greatly modified, particularly in favour of the consumer, by the provisions in SS.12 to 15 of the *Sale of Goods Act, 1979*. These points are dealt with fully in Chapter 14 on the Sale of Goods.

In addition important changes in relation to exemption clauses have been brought about by the *Unfair Contracts Terms Act, 1977*. Such changes are discussed later.

(*c*) **Terms Implied by the Courts.** The court will imply a term into a contract, under **the doctrine of the implied term**, if it was the *presumed* intention of the parties that there should have been a particular term, but they have omitted to state it expressly.

Although the implied term is one which the parties probably never contemplated when making the contract, the courts justify this by saying that the implication is necessary in order to give 'business efficacy' to the contract.

'Moorcock', The (*1889*). The appellants made an agreement with the respondent for the use of their wharf and jetty for the purpose of loading and storing cargo from the *Moorcock*. The bed of the river adjoining the jetty was vested in a third party: it was beyond the control of the appellants and they had taken no steps to ascertain whether it was a safe place for the *Moorcock* to lie as was inevitable at low water on every tide. The vessel grounded and suffered damages because of the uneven condition of the riverbed. **Held:** the appellants were liable as the jetty could not have been used without the *Moorcock* grounding and in these circumstances they would be deemed to have impliedly represented that they had taken reasonable care to ascertain that the riverbed adjoining the jetty was in such a condition as not to cause injury to the vessel. (Courtesy of *Cracknell's Law Students' Companion*)

Reed v. Dean (*1949*). Reed hired a motor launch which subsequently caught fire. They had to abandon the launch since fire-fighting equipment was out of order. Reed suffered personal injury and loss of belongings. **Held:** that Reed was entitled to recompense since there was an implied undertaking by Dean that the launch was fit for the purpose for which it was supplied; both the (unexplained) fire and the lack of correct fire-fighting equipment amounted to a breach of this implied undertaking.

9.4 Excluding and Limiting Terms

Background. Contractual clauses designed to exonerate a party wholly or partly from liability for breaches of express or implied terms, or for tort, first appeared in the early nineteenth century. The common law did not interfere, but took the view that the parties were free to make a bargain, within the limits of legality, upon such terms as they thought fit.

This is still the general rule today, but the growth and amalgamation of large trading concerns controlling large areas of the market have led to the increase of excluding and restricting clauses – both in number and stringency – to the severe detriment of other parties.

These clauses may be imposed by means of notices, receipts, tickets or other documents which do not contain all the terms of the contract. On the other hand, they may appear in documents which purport to include the whole contract, and which are printed or reproduced in a stereotyped form. The latter are often called **standard form contracts** and Lord Diplock has pointed out that they can be subdivided into those which operate between commercial concerns of roughly equal bargaining power, and those which are imposed by big concerns on consumers on a 'take it or leave it' basis. Unfortunately, the common law does not differentiate between these two kinds of standard form contract.

Many standard form contracts are used in the field of transport, where the common law treated the carrier very harshly, as a person liable for every loss that occurs. Nineteenth- and twentieth-century legislation in this field is very complex (see Chapter 16) and there are at least five international conventions to sort out the problems arising from exemption clauses in carriage contracts. In other areas, until 1977, legislative intervention had been piecemeal and there were still large areas of contract where any party was free to impose total or partial exclusion of his liability on the other, if his bargaining strength permitted. The *Unfair Contracts Terms Act, 1977*, remedied many of these defects and is considered below. First though, it is necessary to consider the ways in which objectionable clauses have been circumvented by the courts using the general rules of contract. These are:

(*a*) *The writing must be a contractual document*. It is assumed that no reasonable man would expect to find contractual terms in a mere receipt for money:

Chapelton v. Barry Urban District Council (*1940*). Deckchairs were stacked up on the beach and beside them was a notice which said 'Barry Urban District Council. Cold Knap. Hire of chairs, 2p per session of 3 hours. . . .' The appellant paid for the hire of two chairs and was given two tickets on the back of which was a condition which purported to exclude the respondents' liability for any injury which the hirer should sustain. The appellant did not read this condition. The canvas on one of the chairs was defective and the appellant claimed damages in respect of the injuries which resulted. **Held:** damages would be awarded as the appellant was entitled to assume that the conditions of hire were to be found in the notice near the stack of chairs. The ticket was a mere voucher or receipt to prove payment or the time of commencement of hire. (Courtesy of *Cracknell's Law Students' Companion*)

But a receipt for *goods* would be regarded as a contractual document, as it is frequently evidence of a contract of bailment (i.e. one whereby the possession of goods is transferred by bailor to bailee), and must be produced by the bailor in order to recover the goods. Common examples are receipts for left luggage, car parking tickets, laundry tickets, and tickets for carriage of goods by land or sea.

(*b*) *Reasonable steps must be taken to bring the existence of the excepting terms to the notice of the other party*. This does *not* mean that he must actually know of the terms. In the case of *Thompson v. LMS Railway* (*1930*) Mrs Thompson was unaware of the terms, but as the railway company had taken reasonable steps to notify the ordinary passenger (by referring to the conditions on the front of the ticket) Mrs Thompson too was bound. A copy of the full conditions was available on request, but, if it had not been, no passenger would be bound by them.

Where the exclusion sought is of a serious nature, such as liability for death or injury, then the reasonable steps taken to notify on tickets requires that such notices be especially prominent:

Thornton v. Shoe Lane Parking Ltd (1971). The plaintiff parked his car at the defendants' automatic car-park. On entering the car-park he passed through an automatic barrier, taking a ticket from the machine at the barrier. On the ticket, in small print, it was stated that the ticket was issued subject to conditions displayed on the premises. To find where the conditions were displayed the plaintiff would have to drive the car into the garage and walk around. The conditions were lengthy but included one exempting the defendants not only from liability for damage to cars but also from liability for any injury to a customer, howsoever caused, whilst his car was in the car-park. The plaintiff later returned to collect his car and there was an accident in which he was severely injured. **Held:** the defendants were not protected by the exemption clause. In order to show that the plaintiff was bound by it, it was necessary to show either that he knew of it or that the defendants had done what was reasonably necessary to draw it to his attention. For this purpose, where the clause was exceptionally wide and was one which was not usual in that class of contract, it was not enough to show that the plaintiff had been given notice that the ticket was issued subject to conditions. It must be shown that adequate steps had been taken to draw his attention in the most explicit way to the particular exempting conditions relied on. Here the defendants had failed to show that the plaintiff knew of the condition or that they had taken sufficient steps to draw his attention to it. (Courtesy of *Cracknell's Law Students' Companion*)

Similarly, a notice displayed on premises must be sufficiently prominent for a reasonable man to see it *before* he makes the contract.

There have been many cases where the Courts had laid down that the term *must be notified before or at the time of contracting*. *Chapelton v. Barry UDC* was one, and the most famous case is:

Olley v. Marlborough Court Ltd (1949). The plaintiff was a guest at the defendant's hotel and during her stay some of her property was stolen. There was a notice in her room which stated that 'The proprietors will not hold themselves responsible for articles lost or stolen . . .' **Held:** This notice could not be read into the contract between the parties as the contract was concluded before the plaintiff was shown to her room and therefore before she saw the notice which purported to exclude liability. (Courtesy of *Cracknell's Law Students' Companion*)

The question of what are 'reasonable steps' is an objective one, and the answer to the question is ultimately one of fact, based on the circumstances of each case.

Yet, even if a defendant is found to have failed to take reasonable steps, the plaintiff may still be bound by the conditions because he knew them from *previous dealings* with the defendant. However, this method of imposing terms is not often likely to succeed.

(*c*) *If the exclusion clause is a document signed by a party, then it is presumed that he has agreed to it, whether or not he has read it*. In such a case, it is not easy to escape the effects of the clause.

L'Estrange v. F. Graucob Ltd (1934). The plaintiff ordered an automatic slot machine by signing a printed form supplied by the defendants for this purpose and on this form in very small print were certain special terms. One of these terms provided that 'any express or implied condition, statement or warranty . . . is hereby excluded'. The machine did not work satisfactorily and the plaintiff, who contended that she was not bound by the condition as she had not read it and knew nothing of its contents, claimed damages. **Held:** her action must fail as, having signed the contract, in the absence of misrepresentation, she was bound by its terms and the provision in the contract had successfully excluded the defendants' liability under the implied warranty that the machine was fit for the purpose for which it was sold. (Courtesy of *Cracknell's Law Students' Companion*)

But if the effect of the clause was *misrepresented* to him by the other party, it may only take effect as he understood it at the time of the contract:

Curtis v. Chemical Cleaning and Dyeing Co. Ltd (1951). The plaintiff took a white satin wedding dress to the defendants for cleaning. She was asked to sign a document which contained a clause that the dress 'is accepted on condition that the company is not liable for any damage howsoever arising' but, before she signed, she was told that the effect of the document which she was about to sign was to exclude liability for damage to beads or sequins. Without reading all the terms of the document the plaintiff then signed as she was asked. The dress was stained due to the negligence of the defendants. **Held:** the defendants were liable as the innocent misrepresentation as to the extent of the exception clause had the effect of excluding the clause from the contract between the parties. (Courtesy of *Cracknell's Law Students' Companion*)

However, while signature of the document containing the clause makes it difficult to show that it was not in a contractual document, yet most of the other methods of avoiding the impact of the clause would still be available (e.g. fundamental breach – see (*f*) below).

(*d*) *Any ambiguity in the clause will be interpreted against the party who put it forward.* It is a general rule of construction of any document that it will be construed *'contra proferentem'* – that is, against the person who prepared the document. As an exclusion clause is invariably drafted by the imposer of it, this is an extremely useful weapon against exclusion clauses.

The effect of the rule is to give the party who proposed the ambiguous clause only the lesser of the protections possible. Thus where an insurance company inserted a clause excluding liability to members of the assured's family (which might mean his wife and children) but they claimed it meant any relative at all (when his sister was injured in a crash) they were held liable. If they wanted the wider meaning of the word 'family' they could easily have chosen words which gave them the wider meaning. They did not, and so much the worse for them. The one who draws up the contract has the choice of words, and must choose them to show clearly the intention he had in mind.

(*e*) *The exclusion clause cannot protect a third party:* this is an application of the rule of privity of contract, that a third party cannot enforce, or take a benefit from a contract.

Scruttons Ltd v. Midland Silicones Ltd (1962). The respondents were the consignees and owners of a drum of chemicals shipped in New York for carriage to London on the terms of the shipowners' standard bill of lading, one clause of which had the effect of limiting the carrier's (i.e. the shipowners') liability for damage to the drum to 500 dollars. For some years the shipowners had engaged the appellant stevedores to discharge their vessels at the Port of London and the agreement between them provided that the appellants have 'such protection as is afforded by the terms . . . of . . . bills of lading'. While lowering the drum into a lorry the appellants negligently dropped it, causing damage to it amounting to £593. The act of lowering the drum into the lorry was one which, by the terms of their agreement with the shipowners, the appellants had contracted with the shipowners to do and which, by the terms of the bill of lading, the shipowners had contracted with the respondents to do. The appellants admitted negligence but contended that they were entitled to rely on the provisions in the bill of lading limiting liability to 500 dollars (then £179). **Held:** They were not so entitled as they were strangers to the bill of lading and it is a general principle (to which this case was not an exception) that a stranger cannot rely for his protection on provisions in a contract (i.e. the bill of lading) to which he is not a party. (Courtesy of *Cracknell's Law Students' Companion*)

(*f*) *The doctrine of fundamental breach.* This doctrine (which is no longer effective) was developed to prevent anyone relying on an exemption clause if he had failed to carry out the basic purpose of the contract. As Lord Abinger said in *Chanter v. Hopkins* (*1838*):

'If a man offers to buy peas of another, and he sends him beans, he does not perform his contract. . . . That is not a warranty.'

Such a breach is more serious, or 'fundamental', than a breach of a condition or warranty, and so an excluding clause which protects a party against a breach of condition or warranty, could not shield him from the consequences of a fundamental breach of the contract.

Originally, the doctrine was applied only to the so-called 'deviation cases', where shipowners diverted ships from their agreed course for their own purposes, thereby causing loss to the charterers or cargo-owners whose cargo was delayed.

In *Hain SS Co. v. Tate & Lyle Ltd* (*1936*), where the appellants unjustifiably diverted their ship from its course, causing loss to the respondents in respect of their cargo of sugar on board, Lord Atkin said: 'The departure from the voyage contracted to be made is a breach by the shipowner of . . . such a serious character that however slight the deviation the other party is entitled to treat it as going to the root of the contract, and to declare himself as no longer bound by *any of its terms.*' Since then, however, the courts have extended the doctrine to other types of contract. For example:

Karsales (*Harrow*) *Ltd v. Wallis* (*1956*). Wallis inspected and agreed to purchase a car in excellent condition. He took finance. On attempted delivery the car was seen to have changed dramatically to be a virtual wreck incapable of moving. Wallis refused delivery, but it was towed to his place of business and left there. The finance company involved assigned its rights to Karsales and they sought to recover the payments relying on the following clause in the agreement assigned to them: 'No condition or warranty that the vehicle is roadworthy . . . or of fitness for any purpose is given by the owner or implied herein.' **Held:** exemption clauses only avail the party which included them when they are carrying out their part of the contract in its essential respects. Here breach was such as to amount to non-performance – 'a car which will not go is no car at all' (Birkett, L.J.).

Thus the doctrine of fundamental breach was developed by the courts into an extremely effective way of combating exclusion clauses. This was subject nevertheless to two qualifications:

(i) *Waiver of the breach.* It has always been clear that, in the words of Lord Atkin in *Hain SS Co. Ltd v. Tate & Lyle Ltd* (*1936*), 'the innocent party can elect to treat the contract as subsisting: and if he does this with knowledge of his rights he must in accordance with the general law of contract be held bound'. In that case, Tate & Lyle lost their claim because they had earlier waived their rights, and so the charterparty remained in force.

(ii) *Excluding liability for a fundamental breach.* It is possible to frame an exclusion clause in such wide terms that it covers even a fundamental breach. In the *Suisse Atlantique Case* (1966) Viscount Dilhorne stated: 'It is not right to say that the law prohibits and nullifies a clause exempting or limiting liability for a fundamental breach.' The House of Lords laid down that there is no rule of law that an exemption clause is nullified by a 'fundamental breach of contract' or breach of a 'fundamental term'; in each case the question is one of construction of the contract.

Theoretically, therefore, such an exclusion clause is possible, but the courts would be slow to construe a clause so widely that it would protect a party from the lawful consequences of total non-performance of the contract. In the words of Lord Reid in the same case, 'It is generally reasonable to draw the line at fundamental breaches. A case of this type soon followed:

Photo Production Ltd. v. Securicor Ltd (1980). Securicor agreed to carry out a nightly patrol service against burglary and fire at the plaintiff's premises, under standard terms and conditions which stated that Securicor should not be responsible for losses by fire except if caused by the negligence of their servants in the course of carrying out their duties. One of their employees deliberately set fire to the premises which were destroyed. **Held:** on the true construction of the exclusion clause Securicor were not liable – they had chosen words which successfully excluded their liability for the deliberate act of their employee.

The whole situation has been clarified and to some extent simplified by the *Unfair Contract Terms Act, 1977* to which we must now turn our attention.

9.5 The *Unfair Contract Terms Act, 1977*

The efforts of the courts to mitigate the worst effects of objectionable exclusion clauses have been reinforced by the passage of the above Act, which restricts the extent to which liability can be avoided for breach of contract and negligence. The main points of the Act are:

(*a*) The Act relates to 'business liability' – that which arises in the course of business or through the occupation of business premises. Transactions between private persons are therefore not covered.

(*b*) Liability for death or personal injury resulting from negligence cannot be excluded at all. Attempts to exclude or restrict liability for *other* loss or damage are viewed from the point of view of 'reasonableness'. The party seeking to justify the clause must show that it is fair and reasonable in the circumstances of the contract.

(*c*) Where breach occurs and is not a result of negligence (dealt with in (*b*) above), attempts to exclude liability will be interpreted in favour of the party who 'deals as consumer' and against those dealing as businessmen or using 'written standard terms of business'. Once again the 'reasonableness test' is used.

(*d*) The 'reasonableness test' is further extended to situations where parties attempt to exclude liability for fundamental breach, i.e. where performance is substantially different from that reasonably expected or there is no performance at all of the whole or any part of the contractual obligations.

Contracts between business parties not on standard terms or between private parties are not covered here and the doctrine of fundamental breach continues to operate.

(*e*) In addition to the above, the following are subject to the Act's provisions:

(i) Making liability or its enforcement subject to restrictive or onerous conditions.

(ii) Excluding or restricting any right or remedy.

(iii) Excluding or restricting rules of evidence or procedure.

(*f*) Any contractual term requiring a party dealing as consumer to indemnify any other person for any liability by reason of the other's negligence or breach of contract is again subject to the test of reasonableness.

(*g*) Goods in consumer use and subject to a guarantee cannot have liability for defects excluded by a term of guarantee.

(*h*) Evasion of the provisions of the Act by use of a secondary contract is prohibited.

The case law on exclusion clauses is gathering momentum under the influence of the Act. Two typical cases are given below:

Phillips Products Ltd v. Hyland and Another (*1984*). Hyland was the driver of a JCB hired by Another to Phillips Products Ltd. Hyland drove the vehicle negligently into Phillips' building and did £3000 damage to it. A clause in the hire contract said that for the period when the driver was operating the JCB he was to be under the hirer (Phillips') direction and was to be regarded as their emplyee in the event of any claim arising from the operation.

The Court found this to be unreasonable. On appeal this opinion was confirmed, and Slade L.J. expressed the view that the meaning of the 'test of reasonableness' is not a general matter that can be interpreted away from the facts of the case. The test is 'Was the clause reasonable in the *particular* contract under consideration?'

Stag Line Ltd v. Tyne Shiprepair Group Ltd and Others (*The Zinnia*) (*1984*). This case was one where repairs to a vessel were defective in quality. When the ship got into difficulty claims were made for various losses including consequential losses, but the case established that the defective repairs played no part in the actual losses which were caused by something else entirely. The point of interest to us is that certain exclusion clauses were considered and in the course of dealing with them Staughton J. expressed the opinion that they were in such small print and used such convoluted and prolix language that they might be considered unreasonable from that point of view alone. As one commentator said 'For one judge, apparently, legal gobbledegook is unreasonable'.

9.6 Revision Test

Answers	*Questions*
–	**1.** What are stipulations in a contract called?
1. The terms of the contract.	**2.** What is an express term in a contract?
2. One that is actually stipulated by one of the parties, requiring the other party to do certain things.	**3.** What is an implied term?
3. A term which will be read into the contract either by custom, or a course of dealing between the parties, or by statute, or under the doctrine of the implied term (where a term has to be implied to give business efficacy to the contract).	**4.** What is a representation?
4. A statement made in the course of negotiations leading to a contract which induces the other party to enter into the contract.	**5.** What tests help a judge decide whether a statement is a representation or a term of the contract?
5. (*a*) The time test; (*b*) the writing test; (*c*) the skill and knowledge test.	**6.** What types of express terms are there?
6. (a) Conditions; (*b*) warranties.	**7.** Distinguish between them.
7. A condition goes to the root of the contract and breach of the condition is breach of contract. A warranty is only collateral to the contract, a less serious term. Breach of a warranty is not breach of contract, but it does entitle the disappointed party to damages.	**8.** What is an exclusionary clause?

Answers	*Questions*
8. One which excludes one party to a contract from some legal or statutory duty and forces the other party to trade on unsatisfactory terms.	**9.** How has the law traditionally reduced the severity of exclusionary clauses?
9. (*a*) By insisting that if they are to be valid they must be in a document which is clearly contractual – not a mere receipt. (*b*) By insisting that the other party must have notice of the effect of the term and have its importance drawn to his attention. (*c*) If it is misrepresented to him the clause will only be effective to the extent represented. (*d*) The *contra proferentem* rule applies. (*e*) The doctrine of fundamental breach applies.	**10.** What are the chief points made in the *Unfair Contract Terms Act, 1977*?
10. (*a*) The Act only relates to business contracts. (*b*) Liability for death or personal injury resulting from negligence cannot be excluded. (*c*) Other exclusions must be viewed from the point of view of reasonableness. (*d*) It is for the party inserting the exclusion clause to show that it is fair and reasonable in the particular circumstances of the contract.	**11.** Go over the questions until you are sure of all the answers. Then try some of the questions in Appendix 1.

10
Misrepresentation

10.1 What is Misrepresentation?

Representations are statements made in order to induce a party to enter into a contract. They differ from conditions or warranties in that they do not form part of the contract themselves. However, they are extremely important, for without such representations the contract might not be entered into at all. They may be distinguished from mere puffs, which are statements made in the course of the negotiations which are not intended to be taken seriously but are recognised by both parties as being mere hyperbole (exaggeration for the sake of effect). Thus to say that a horse is 'the finest creature on four legs today' is a mere puff, and not intended to lead to legal action should the other party find a finer animal. A representation does lead to legal relations. *A misrepresentation is a false statement made in the course of negotiations leading to a contract which was intended to induce, and did induce, the other party to enter into that contract.*

The nature of misrepresentation. It is necessary to consider in detail the various elements of the above definition:

(*a*) As a general rule, there must be a positive statement; this is often expressed by saying that *'silence is not a misrepresentation'*. This was shown in the case of *Keates v. Lord Cadogan* (*1851*). Here a landlord was held not liable when he failed to inform a tenant that a house being let was in a dilapidated condition – even though he knew that it was required for immediate occupation. In some circumstances this rule operates unjustly, and the courts have long recognised exceptions to it.

(*i*) *When silence distorts or falsifies a positive representation.* Thus, if a vendor of land states that the farms are let, he must not omit to state the further fact that the tenants have given notice to quit. This is illustrated by *Dimmock v. Hallet* (*1866*).

Dimmock v. Hallet (*1866*). A vendor of farms induced their sale by saying that they were let. Whilst this was true the statement was held to be a misrepresentation because the tenants had given notice to quit.

The principle also applies even if the original statement was full and correct, but subsequent events make it incorrect:

With v. O'Flanagan (*1936*). In January 1934 a medical practice was represented to the plaintiffs by the doctor selling it as worth £2000 p.a. In May 1934 the plaintiffs contracted to buy, but by then the practice was producing less than £5 p.w. (due to the illness of the defendant). The Court of Appeal held that the duty to disclose had been broken – rescission of the contract was allowed, and so the defendant had to repay.

(ii) *Contracts uberrimae fidei* (see below).
(iii) *Fiduciary relationships* (see below).

(*b*) The statement need not be expressed in words, but can be made by conduct. Thus it could be 'a nod, or a wink, or a shake of the head or a smile' Lord Campbell in *Walters v Morgan (1861)*.

(*c*) The statement must be one of fact, and not of law, opinion or intention. However, if a person expresses an opinion *fraudulently*, this is regarded as a statement of *fact*, and therefore actionable. Here we can contrast the cases of *Bisset v. Wilkinson (1927)* and *Smith v. Land and House Property Corporation (1884)*.

Bisset v. Wilkinson (1927). The appellant sought to recover the purchase money under an agreement for the sale of certain land but the respondents claimed to be entitled to rescind the contract on the ground of misrepresentation. It was shown that the appellant had stated that it was his belief that the land in question would carry 2000 sheep if properly worked but in fact it had never been able to support that number. **Held:** the contract would not be rescinded on the ground of misrepresentation as the statement as to the carrying capacity of the land was merely an opinion which the appellant honestly entertained. (Courtesy of *Cracknell's Law Students' Companion*)

Smith v. Land and House Property Corporation (1884). In the particulars of sale the plaintiffs said that their hotel was 'now held by a very desirable tenant . . . for an unexpired term of twenty-eight years, at a rent of £400 p.a.' The defendants resisted the plaintiffs' claim for specific performance on the ground of misdescription in that it afterwards appeared that the rent was in arrear at the time of the sale and the tenant shortly afterwards filed his petition for liquidation. **Held:** the contract should be rescinded as the description of the tenant as 'very desirable' was not an expression of opinion but a misrepresentation on the faith of which the defendants contracted to purchase the hotel. (Courtesy of *Cracknell's Law Students' Companion*)

In similar fashion a fraudulent statement of intention can lead to misrepresentation. For example:

Edgington v. Fitzmaurice (1885). The directors of a company issued a prospectus inviting subscriptions for debentures and stating that their purpose in issuing debentures was to complete alterations to the company's premises, purchase horses and vans and develop trade. The plaintiff advanced money on certain of these debentures in reliance upon the statements in the prospectus and in the erroneous belief that the debenture holders would have a charge upon the property, but it turned out that the real object of the loan was to enable the directors to pay off pressing liabilities. **Held:** the mis-statement of the objects for which the debentures were issued was a material mis-statement of fact which rendered the directors liable in deceit although the plaintiff was influenced by his own mistake as to the effect of the transaction. (Courtesy of *Cracknell's Law Students' Companion*)

(*d*) The misrepresentation must at least partly induce the contract.

Smith v. Chadwick (1884). A prospectus contained a statement that 'the present value of the turnover or output of the entire works is over £1 000 000 sterling per annum'. This statement was ambiguous in that it could mean that in one year the works produced goods worth £1 000 000, in which case it was untrue, or that the works were capable of this output, in which case it was correct. **Held:** in order to succeed in an action of deceit for fraudulent misrepresentation, the plaintiff had to prove that he had interpreted the statement in the sense in which it was false and that he had in fact been influenced by it in making his decision to take shares. The plaintiff failed to satisfy the court on these points. (Courtesy of *Cracknell's Law Students' Companion*)

It would follow that a misrepresentation that does not affect a plaintiff's mind or his judgement (*Attwood v. Small* (*1838*)) or where the plaintiff is aware of the untruth of a misrepresentation (*Jennings v. Broughton* (*1854*)) is legally harmless.

10.2 Types of Misrepresentation

There are three types of misrepresentation; innocent, fraudulent and negligent.

(*a*) An **innocent misrepresentation** is one made honestly, and with reasonable grounds for believing in its truth.

(*b*) A **negligent misrepresentation** is a statement made honestly, but without reasonable grounds for belief in its truth. It is really a special case of innocent misrepresentation, for although the statement is made in the belief that it is true, insufficient care has been taken to check it. Thus where the plaintiff can show that the statement made was made without reasonable care, and that this negligence resulted to the plaintiff's detriment, he will be able to secure redress of the grievance by an action in tort. The classic case is *Hedley Byrne & Co. Ltd. v. Heller and Partners Ltd* (*1963*) – see page 339 for details.

(*c*) A **fraudulent misrepresentation** is one made dishonestly, knowing it to be untrue. It was defined in *Derry v. Peek* (*1889*) by Lord Herschell as a false statement *'made knowingly or without belief in its truth or recklessly, careless whether it be true or false'*. The court must be satisfied, if a statement was made carelessly, that it was so grossly careless that its maker could not honestly have believed it to be true.

Derry v. Peek (*1889*). The Plymouth, Devonport and District Tramways Co. was authorised to make certain tramways by special Act of Parliament which provided that the carriages might be moved by animal power and, with the consent of the Board of Trade, by steam or any mechanical power for fixed periods and subject to the regulations of the Board. The company issued a prospectus stating that 'one great feature of this undertaking, to which considerable importance should be attached, is that by special Act of Parliament obtained, the company has the right to use steam or mechanical motive power, instead of horses'. The plaintiff bought shares on the faith of this statement but the Board of Trade afterwards refused their consent to the use of steam power and the company was wound up. At the time of issuing the prospectus the company honestly believed that consent would be granted as a matter of course. **Held:** the plaintiff's action in deceit must fail, as the statement contained in the prospectus was not a fraudulent misrepresentation as the company entertained an honest belief that it was true. (Courtesy of *Cracknell's Law Students' Companion*)

(*Note:* The *Directors' Liability Act, 1890*, altered the law to make directors liable for untrue statements made in prospectuses without reasonable grounds for believing them to be true. This is now contained in S.43 of the *Companies Act, 1985*.)

(*d*) **Non-disclosure.** Although as a general rule silence *is not* a misrepresentation, there is a duty in the following kinds of contract to disclose relevant information:

(i) *Contracts uberrimae fidei.* These comprise contracts which involve one party alone possessing full knowledge of all the material facts, and the other being unable to obtain them from any other source. The law therefore requires *'uberrima fides'* (utmost good faith) from the first party. Examples are contracts of insurance, contracts to take shares from companies and family arrangements. A duty to disclose also arises in fiduciary relationships.

The contract of insurance. The insured must disclose all material facts, i.e. all circumstances 'which would influence the judgement of a prudent insurer in fixing the premium or determining whether he will take the risk'. This definition in S.18 (2) of the *Marine Insurance Act, 1906*, was held applicable to other types of insurance in:

Locker and Woolf Ltd v. Western Australian Insurance Co. Ltd (*1936*). When proposing for fire insurance in respect of their premises the claimants failed to disclose that an insurance on their motorcars had been declined by another company on the grounds of misrepresentation and non-disclosure. **Held:** the non-disclosure of this previous refusal was a material fact in the proposal for fire insurance which entitled the respondents to avoid the policy. In all classes of insurance what constitutes a 'material fact' is decided by reference to S.18 of the *Marine Insurance Act, 1906*. (Courtesy of *Cracknell's Law Students' Companion*)

But you are not liable to disclose what you do not know (Fletcher Moulton, L.J., in *Joel v. Law Union and Commercial Assurance Co.* (*1908*).

(ii) *Contracts to take shares from companies.* An omission of a fact from a company's prospectus may be a misrepresentation because it contravenes the *Companies Act, 1985*.

(iii) *Family arrangements.* The classic case here is *Gordon v. Gordon* (*1821*):

Gordon v. Gordon (*1821*). There was an agreement between two brothers, the elder of whom was believed to be illegitimate, for the division of the family estates. It turned out that the younger brother, who had obtained an advantage because of this belief, had known all along that his brother was legitimate. **Held:** even after a lapse of nineteen years, the agreement should be rescinded, because family arrangements of this sort are uberrimae fidei. (Courtesy of *Cracknell's Law Students' Companion*)

(iv) *Fiduciary relationships.* This is a relationship of trust – for example, those of doctor and patient, principal and agent, solicitor and client, religious superior and inferior, trustee and beneficiary, parent and child, and guardian and ward. This list is not exhaustive, and if any party to a contract uses his influence, obtained through the confidence necessarily reposed in him by the other, to obtain an advantage at the expense of the confiding party, rescission will be allowed for non-disclosure, or misrepresentation.

This is because the first party has been guilty of *fraud* in the equitable sense – unconscionable conduct. For example:

Tate v. Williamson (1866). Tate was a spendthrift Oxford undergraduate. He relied upon Williamson (his cousin) for financial advice as Tate was estranged from his father because of his extravagance. Williamson, who had been recommended by Tate's great-uncle, advised Tate to sell his estate for £7500 to Williamson (its true value was £20 000), and he duly sold it as advised. **Held:** Williamson's non-disclosure was a misrepresentation and so the sale was set aside.

(Tate's heir was the plaintiff, Tate having died an alcoholic at 24.)

10.3 Remedies for Misrepresentation

Under the common law the remedies for misrepresentation were unsatisfactory, in particular with regard to innocent misrepresentation. To correct the position the *Misrepresentation Act, 1967*, removed certain bars to the rescission of a contract for innocent misrepresentation, and also clarified the position about damages.

In general, the plaintiff is interested in three possibilities: (*a*) may he repudiate the contract if it has not yet been executed, and do nothing more about it; (*b*) may he obtain rescission of the contract, if it has been performed and return to the situation before the contract was made; (*c*) are damages available? Whether these remedies are available depends upon the type of misrepresentation made, and whether the misrepresentation was embodied as a term in the contract, either as a condition of the contract, or a warranty of the contract. It is in the nature of a representation that it occurs before the contract is finally made, and under the common law if the misrepresentation was embodied in the contract it was only possible to rescind the contract if the plaintiff alleged fraud. This bar to rescission was removed by S.1 of the *Misrepresentation Act, 1967*. Consequently, whether fraud is alleged or not it is possible to obtain rescission of the contract.

If the misrepresentation has become a term of the contract, then the party who has been deceived has the following remedies:

(*a*) *If the term is a condition* he has the right to repudiate the contract if it has not been performed, and the right to have it rescinded if it has been performed. The nature of rescission, which is a discretionary remedy which the courts may, or may not, apply is explained below. Damages will be payable for non-performance.

(*b*) *If the misrepresentation is a warranty*, the plaintiff is entitled to damages and, since the *Misrepresentation Act, 1967*, rescission (S.1 of the Act).

If the misrepresentation has not become a term of the contract, then the remedies available to the innocent party depend on whether the misrepresentation was made to him fraudulently, or negligently, or innocently.

For *fraudulent misrepresentation* the party misled is entitled to damages for the tort of deceit, the measure of damages being the loss incurred as a result, and to repudiate or rescind the contract.

For *innocent misrepresentation* the Act gives the party misled the right to repudiate the contract, or to have it rescinded. Damages may also be payable, depending on the nature of the misrepresentation. The Act says that damages will be payable 'unless the defendant proves that he had reasonable ground to believe, and did believe up to the time the contract was made, that the facts represented were true' (S.2.1). Note that the usual rule that 'he who alleges must prove' is reversed here; there is a presumption that the misrepresentation was negligent, and the defendant must prove that it was not. Thus, for example, a misrepresentation affecting the state of buildings might be justified if a recent surveyor's report led the defendant to believe that they were in fact in good condition. The Act divides innocent misrepresentation into two categories; namely, negligent misrepresentation and representation which is not negligent. In many cases, negligent misrepresentation is equated with fraudulent misrepresentation.

The working of the Act is illustrated by:

Watts v. Spence (1975). The plaintiff, Watts, contracted to buy a house from the first defendant, John Spence who, prior to the contract, told the plaintiff that Mrs Spence (the second defendant) who was a joint owner of the house with her husband, would join in the subsequent conveyance. In fact, she refused to do so.

Graham, J., in the Chancery Division held that the first defendant was liable to pay damages for *loss of bargain* under S.2(1) of the 1967 Act.

Where the innocence of the misrepresentation is established the misled party is in the same situation as before the 1967 Act; he is entitled only to rescission of the contract, with the possible addition of an indemnity for expenses he has *necessarily* incurred under the contract.

Whittington v. Seale-Hayne (1900). The plaintiffs, who were lessees of certain premises which they used for breeding prize poultry, alleged that they had been induced to take up the lease by the representations of the defendant's agents, made during oral negotiations for the lease, that the premises were in a sanitary condition and in a good state of repair. The plaintiffs further alleged that in consequence of the insanitary condition of the premises their manager and his family became very ill and the poultry either died or became valueless for the purpose of breeding. The local authority declared that because of defective drainage the premises were unfit for human habitation. The plaintiffs contended that they were entitled to an indemnity against the consequences of entering into the contract, which included losses in respect of stock and medical expenses. **Held:** their claim would fail as it was really a claim for damages which could not be awarded at that time in a case of innocent misrepresentation, but they were entitled to an indemnity in respect of those things which were required to be performed by the terms of the lease and this included rent, rates and repairs. (Courtesy of *Cracknell's Law Students' Companion*)

Exclusion of liability for misrepresentation. Under S.3 of the *misrepresentation Act, 1967*, any exclusion clause in a contract which excludes or restricts any liability to which a representor may become liable as a result of misrepresentation, shall be of no effect except in so far as the court or an arbitrator allows reliance on it as being fair and reasonable in the circumstances. This is now the standard of reasonableness in S.11.1 of the *Unfair Contract Terms Act, 1977.*

Even the right of rescission is subject to the approval of the court, which may hold the contract to be subsisting, and award damages in lieu of rescission. This is explained below.

Limitations on the remedy of rescission. Rescission is a remedy available for all three types of misrepresentation; it has been developed in equity decisions and is limited by general principles common to all the equitable doctrines and remedies (rescission, rectification, injunction and decree of specific performance) with some limitations peculiar to itself. These limitations mean that in some situations a plaintiff will have no remedy. The limitations are:

(*a*) *It is a discretionary remedy*. This means that the court will refuse to grant it to a plaintiff who has himself been guilty of inequitable conduct.

(*b*) *Delay*. If the plaintiff has been guilty of unreasonable delay (termed laches) in seeking rescission, he will be barred. In *Leaf v. International Galleries* (*1950*) (see page 116) the Court of Appeal decided against Leaf (*inter alia*) because he delayed five years in bringing his action; but in *Gordon v. Gordon* (*1821*) (see page 142) the elder son obtained rescission despite the 19 years which had elapsed, because he had acted as soon as he eventually discovered the truth, and therefore the delay was reasonable.

(*c*) *Affirmation*. The representee cannot rescind after expressly or impliedly affirming the contract with full knowledge of the true facts. For example:

Long v. Lloyd (*1958*). The defendant advertised for sale a motor lorry which he described as being in 'exceptional condition' and told the plaintiff, who purchased it, that it was capable of 40 m.p.h. and did 11 miles to the gallon. Two days later certain defects appeared and the plaintiff accepted the defendant's offer to pay half the cost of a reconditioned dynamo. On the following day the plaintiff's brother set out to drive the lorry to Middlesbrough but it broke down on the way and an expert found that it was not in a roadworthy condition. The defendant's representations concerning the vehicle were untrue, although honestly made, and the plaintiff sought to rescind the contract on the ground of the defendant's innocent misrepresentation. **Held:** the plaintiff had finally accepted the lorry and any right of rescission which he might otherwise have had was lost. (Courtesy of *Cracknell's Law Students' Companion*)

(*d*) *'Restitutio in integrum' impossible*. Because rescission involves 'a giving back and a taking back on both sides' it clearly cannot apply where the subject-matter of the contract has substantially ceased to exist, or has changed its identity. For example:

Vigers v. Pike (*1842*). B had agreed in his lifetime to let mines in return for £165 000. The mines were operated and a part of the payment made. Pike, B's executor, sued the managing director of the company operating the mine for the rest of the money. In defence it was claimed that a number of misrepresentations had been made to induce the lease. **Held:** the lease could not be set aside since the mines had substantially been worked and the parties could not be restored to their original positions.

However, a minor change in subject-matter will not preclude rescission; instead, the court will grant rescission, with an indemnity to compensate for the loss, under the *Whittington v. Seale-Hayne* principle referred to above.

(*e*) *Damages in lieu of rescission*. Under S.2(2) of the 1967 Act, the court *may* declare the contract subsisting, if it would be equitable to do so, having regard to the nature of the misrepresentation, and the loss that would be caused by it if the contract were upheld, as well as to the loss that rescission would cause to the other party. Instead the court will award damages to the victims of the innocent or negligent misrepresentation.

(*f*) Intervention of third-party rights. It has always been a fundamental principle of equity that it will protect a person who has in good faith and for value acquired rights in property. The effect of a misrepresentation of any kind is to make the contract voidable at the misled party's option, and if he has transferred property under it to the misrepresentor, the title to it will pass to the latter under the voidable contract, and from him to any third party who acquires it in good faith and for value. This was the case in *Phillips v. Brooks* (*1919*) and *Lewis v. Averay* (*1971*) referred to earlier (see Section 8.3).

10.4 Revision Test

Answers	*Questions*
–	**1.** What is a misrepresentation?
1. It is a false statement made in the course of negotiations leading up to a contract which was intended to induce, and did induce, the other party to enter into the contract.	**2.** What are the three types of misrepresentation?
2. (*a*) Innocent misrepresentation; (*b*) negligent misrepresentation; (*c*) fraudulent misrepresentation.	**3.** When is a misrepresentation innocent?
3. When the representor honestly believes it to be true.	**4.** What was the case of *Hedley Byrne & Co. v. Heller and Partners Ltd* (*1963*) about?
4. Heller and Partners were bankers who gave a credit reference on a customer to Hedley Byrne. It proved to be false and the judge ruled there was a duty of care, i.e. a negligent misrepresentation.	**5.** Why were damages not awarded against Heller and Partners?
5. Because they had disclaimed any responsibility when giving the reference.	**6.** Is silence misrepresentation?
6. Not generally – there is no general duty to disclose.	**7.** What special cases are there where silence is misrepresentation?

Answers	*Questions*
7. (*a*) Contracts of the utmost good faith; (*b*) contracts where a statute calls for disclosure; (*c*) family arrangements; (*d*) fiduciary relationships (based on trust).	**8.** What are the remedies for fraudulent misrepresentation?
8. (*a*) The right to repudiate the contract and claim damages for loss of bargain; (*b*) the right to have the contract rescinded and claim damages.	**9.** (*a*) What are the remedies for innocent misrepresentation?
9. (*a*) The right to repudiate the contract; (*b*) the right to have the contract rescinded (unless damages in lieu of rescission are ordered by the court); (*c*) the right to damages unless the party at fault can prove that they had reasonable grounds for believing the statement to be true.	**10.** What is the nature of the remedy 'rescission of the contract'?
10. (*a*) It is an equitable remedy; (*b*) the court will not exercise it if there has been delay; (*c*) or if the aggrieved party has reaffirmed the contract after being made aware of the misrepresentation; or (*d*) if third parties have acquired rights which will be disturbed unfairly.	**11.** Go over the page again. Then try some of the questions in Appendix 1.

11
The Discharge of Contracts

11.1 The Meaning of Discharge

When a contract is entered into it confers upon the parties to it certain rights and obligations. These rights and obligations, though, persist for only as long as the contract is in existence. Once the contract comes to an end (for whatever reason) the rights and obligations are said to have been 'discharged'.

There are four ways in which a contract may be discharged.

(*a*) By performance.
(*b*) By express agreement.
(*c*) Under the doctrine of frustration.
(*d*) By breach.

11.2 Discharge of the Contract by Performance

The normal way in which a contract is discharged is that both parties perform their obligations under it. If only one party performs his obligations, then he alone is discharged, and he acquires the right of action against the other (see later under discharge by breach). *The general rule is that performance must be precise and exact.* This rule is very strict, as is shown by:

Cutter v. Powell (*1795*). The defendant agreed to pay Cutter 30 guineas 'provided he proceeds, continues and does his duty as second mate' on a voyage from Kingston, Jamaica, to Liverpool. Cutter began the journey but died when the ship was about one week's sail from Liverpool. His administratrix sought to recover a proportion of the agreed wage in respect of the part of the journey for which Cutter had acted as second mate. **Held:** she was unable to succeed as Cutter had not performed his part of the contract. (Courtesy of *Cracknell's Law Students' Companion*)

For practical reasons the common law has been driven in some circumstances to adopt a lower standard than that of precise and exact performance, and to create exceptions to the general rule in *Cutter v. Powell.* These cover a wide field and represent a considerable inroad upon the doctrine. They all enable a party at fault to recover to the extent of his performance.

(*a*) *Divisible contracts.* Most contracts are 'entire' (i.e. indivisible): the obligations of the parties are interdependent: *neither* party can demand performance from the other unless he himself performs or is ready to perform, his obligations.

However, with a contract to work materials into the property of another, or an instalment contract, the presumption is that payment is to keep pace with performance, so that a party can claim a certain sum even though he has not completed his obligations under the contract. Such contracts are said to be divisible.

Roberts v. Havelock (1832). The defendant's ship was sailing from Cardiff to Alexandria with a cargo of iron when it was damaged and forced to dock at Milford Haven to allow necessary repairs to be carried out. The plaintiff, a shipwright, was employed and undertook to put the ship into thorough repair. Before the work was completed the plaintiff asked for payment in respect of that part which he had carried out, but when payment was refused he sued to recover the amount to which he maintained he was entitled at that stage. **Held:** the plaintiff would succeed as there was no agreement to the effect that the plaintiff would make no demand for payment until all the repairs were completed. (Courtesy of *Cracknell's Law Students' Companion*)

(*b*) Where a party is prevented from completing his obligations by the action of the other party, he can claim for what he has done:

Planché v. Colburn (1831). P. agreed to write a book on items of historical interest, and was to be paid £100 on completion of the book. Before he could finish the work the publishers abandoned the idea. P. sued and on a '*quantum meruit*' (as much as he has deserved) claim succeeded in getting payment for what he had done.

(*c*) Where one party has accepted partial performance by the other, that other can claim for the partial performance on the basis of an implied promise of payment, but there must be a true option to accept. This was not the case in *Sumpter v. Hedges, 1898*:

Sumpter v. Hedges (1898). The plaintiff, a builder, contracted to build two houses and stables upon the defendant's land for the sum of £565. The plaintiff did part of the work, amounting in value to about £333, and then abandoned the contract. The defendant completed the buildings and the plaintiff claimed payment in respect of that part of the work which he had carried out. **Held:** the defendent was not liable to pay on a *quantum meruit* as there was no inference of a fresh contract to do so. (Courtesy of *Cracknell's Law Students' Companion*)

(*d*) At an early point in time the courts developed the **doctrine of substantial performance**, i.e. that a party can claim if his performance has been substantial, even though not exact and literal (although, of course, he cannot claim the full price in such case).

Hoenig v. Isaacs (1952). The defendant agreed to pay the plaintiff £750 to redecorate and refurnish his flat. When the job was done he paid only £400, saying there was faulty design and bad workmanship. **Held:** by the Court of Appeal – there were only defects in the furniture and this would cost £55 to remedy. Therefore the defendant was liable to pay £750 less £55.

11.3 Discharge by Express Agreement

The basic legal rule is 'that which has been created by agreement can be extinguished by agreement'. An agreement to extinguish a contract though is itself a contract, and unless under seal, must be supported by consideration. It is in this area surrounding consideration that difficulties arise. The position as regards consideration depends upon whether discharge is bilateral or unilateral.

Bilateral Discharge. This occurs when both parties to the contract have some rights to surrender. For example, where there has been no performance or only part performance from one or both parties. Agreement in such circumstances can be reduced to one of three possible situations which the parties might intend:

(*a*) To rescind the existing agreement. This is called **termination**.
(*b*) Rescission plus agreement on the terms of a new contract.
(*c*) Variation of the existing contract.

Providing that the original contract is a simple one (where evidence in writing is *not* required), then words of agreement will achieve any of the three situations described above.

With bilateral discharge both parties have rights to surrender and in this way the new agreement generates its own consideration. The consideration given by each party is the surrender of his rights under the contract.

Unilateral Discharge. This occurs where only one party has rights to surrender. For example, where one party has performed his part of the contract he is no longer under an obligation himself but has acquired rights to compel the other party to perform. If for some reason (perhaps out of sympathy) the party with rights agrees not to insist upon them such an agreement will not be enforceable (unless under seal) without the provision of consideration by the party receiving benefit. The process is known as one of 'accord and satisfaction', the accord being the discharge of the obligation, the satisfaction the consideration with which the discharge is 'bought'. An example is:

British Russian Gazette and Trade Outlook Ltd v. Associated Newspapers Ltd (1933). Talbot, a director of the Gazette Company, sued the defendants for an alleged libel. A representative of the defendants met Talbot and terms of settlement were arranged whereby Talbot agreed to accept one thousand guineas in full discharge and settlement of his claims and that of his company and undertook to discontinue the action against the defendants. Before the agreed amount was paid Talbot proceeded with the action in breach of the agreement. **Held:** he was not entitled to do so as he was bound by the terms of the settlement, consideration for which was to be found in the executory promises made by the defendants. (Courtesy of *Cracknell's Law Students' Companion*)

There are two further situations where discharge can be by agreement. They are:

(*a*) *Novation.* Novation occurs when two existing contracts are replaced by a new one. Suppose one party, X, is involved in two contracts. In one he owes Y £1000, in the other he is owed £1000 by Z. If the parties agree X can be released from his obligation to Y if Z enters into an agreement to pay £1000 directly to Y, by-passing X.

(*b*) *Condition Subsequent.* Here the parties to a contract agree, at the time of its formation, that in the event of specific things happening the contract will come to an end.

11.4 Discharge of a Contract by Frustration

At common law, a contract will be discharged if something occurs which is not the fault of the parties, and was not contemplated by them, and prevents the contract from being performed as intended. Generally, where there is a positive contract to do a thing which is not unlawful the promiser must perform the contract or pay damages. This was laid down in:

Paradine v. Jane (1647). The defendant was lessee of land and when sued for arrears of rent he contended that he was not liable to pay as the land in question had been occupied by a German Prince who had 'invaded the realm with an hostile army of men', thus preventing the defendant from receiving the profits from the land. **Held:** the plaintiff was entitled to recover as the defendant had covenanted to pay the rent and if he had wished to be excused payment in circumstances such as this he should have inserted a term to that effect in the contract. (Courtesy of *Cracknell's Law Students' Companion*)

Eventually this rule was seen to be harsh and inappropriate to the developing commercial world of the nineteenth century. From *Taylor v. Caldwell (1863)* (see below) the doctrine of frustration was developed. Three requirements must be satisfied for frustration to occur:

(*a*) An event has taken place which could not have been foreseen by the parties when they entered into the contract.
(*b*) None of the parties to the contract is in any way responsible for the event.
(*c*) If the contract was to be performed now despite the event, the contract would be different from the one originally entered into.

There are many areas in which the doctrine of frustration has been held to apply:

(*a*) *The destruction or non-availability of the subject-matter of the contract* (i.e. of a thing essential to the performance of the contract):

Taylor v. Caldwell (1863). The plaintiffs entered into an agreement with the defendants for the hire of a certain music hall for the purpose of giving a series of concerts. Before the series was due to begin the hall was destroyed by accidental fire. **Held:** the plaintiffs could not recover damages as the destruction of the hall excused both parties from the performance of their promises. (Courtesy of *Cracknell's Law Students' Companion*)

(*b*) *The non-availability of a person*. This will frustrate a contract involving personal service – for example, where death, insanity or illness is serious enough to put an end to the contract in a business sense. An example is:

Robinson v. Davison (1871). The defendant contracted to play in a concert on a particular day but fell ill. **Held:** the performer's illness on that particular day was sufficient to frustrate the contract.

In longer-term contracts the courts are reluctant to find that illness frustrates the contract. For example:

Storey v. Fulham Steel Works (1907). S was employed by the steel works for five years as a manager. After working for two years he became ill and needed time away from work. Six months later he had recovered, but during his illness his employment had been terminated. S. sued for breach and the defendants claimed that

S.'s illness discharged the contract. **Held:** S.'s absence for six months did not go to the root of the five-year contract and termination could not be allowed.

(*c*) The non-happening of an event. The most famous cases here arose from the cancellation of the coronation of King Edward VII.

Krell v. Henry (1903). The processions in connection with the coronation of Edward VII were due to be held on 26th and 27th June, 1902, and shortly before this the defendant agreed to hire the plaintiff a flat in Pall Mall along which the processions were to pass. The contract made no mention of the purpose of letting but when the processions were not held on the days originally appointed the defendant refused to pay the balance of the rent. **Held:** the plaintiff's claim to recover such amount would fail as, by a necessary inference drawn from the surrounding circumstances, the holding of the procession on the days planned was regarded by both parties as the foundation of the contract. (Courtesy of *Cracknell's Law Students' Companion*)

Such grounds for frustration, however, are not extended to slight changes in circumstances.

Herne Bay Steam Boat Co. v. Hutton (1903). The parties entered into an agreement whereby the plaintiffs' ship was to be 'at the disposal' of the defendant on a certain date 'for the purpose of viewing the naval review and for a day's cruise round the fleet'. The Royal review was afterwards cancelled but the fleet was still at Spithead on the day in question. In view of the cancellation of the review the defendant did not use the ship and declined to pay the balance of the hire. The plaintiffs claimed damages for breach of contract. **Held:** the plaintiffs should succeed. The naval review was not the sole foundation of the contract as the object of the voyage was also to cruise round the fleet. (Courtesy of *Cracknell's Law Students' Companion*)

(*d*) *Supervening illegality*. This occurs where a contract is entered into the object of which subsequently becomes illegal.

Denny, Mott and Dickson Ltd v. Fraser and Co. Ltd (1944). In 1929 the two parties made an agreement relating to the sale of timber and the option to purchase or lease a timber yard. Both parties agreed that the sale of timber was frustrated in 1939 by timber control orders. However, in 1941 D., M. & D. attempted to exercise their option to purchase the timber yard. **Held:** that looked at as a whole the main purpose of the contract was the sale of timber and when this had been frustrated the option to purchase no longer existed.

(*e*) *Administrative (Governmental) interference*. This is the most important and frequent example of frustration:

Metropolitan Water Board v. Dick, Kerr and Co. Ltd (1918). In July 1914 the appellants contracted to construct extensive reservoirs near Staines within six years. The agreement contained a proviso to the effect that if the work should be 'unduly delayed or impeded' an extension of the time for the completion of the work would be granted. War broke out and in February 1916 the Minister of Munitions ordered the work to stop and the plant to be sold. This prohibition was still in force in November 1917. The appellants claimed that the order had put an end to the contract. **Held:** this plea would be upheld as the interruption caused by the prohibition was of such a character and duration as to make the contract when resumed essentially different from that the performance of which was compulsorily brought to an end. (Courtesy of *Cracknell's Law Students' Companion*)

The mere fact that the change in circumstances makes the contract more difficult to execute or less profitable does *not* frustrate the contract:

Davis Contractors Ltd v. Fareham Urban District Council (1956). The plaintiffs contracted to build the defendants 78 council houses within eight months for a fixed price. Through no fault of the plaintiffs there was a scarcity of skilled labour and the work took 22 months to complete. The plaintiffs maintained that by reason of the scarcity of labour the contract had been brought to an end and that they were entitled to recover a sum in excess of the contract price on the basis of a quantum meruit. **Held:** their claim should fail, as the scarcity of labour had not frustrated the contract and the plaintiffs had not been released from its terms as regards price.

The Effects of Frustration. The effect is that the contract is ended at once, but for the future only; it is not void *ab initio*, as with mistake. The financial adjustment that is necessary is now governed by the *Law Reform (Frustrated Contracts) Act, 1943*. The effects of the Act are that the payer can recover money prepaid and ceases to be liable to pay, even though there was no total failure of consideration. However, if the payee has incurred expenses the Act says:

(*a*) If money has already been paid to him, the court has a discretion to allow him to keep some or all of it;
(*b*) If money has not yet been paid to him, the court has a discretion to allow him to claim some or all, but only to the extent that the money was payable before the date of frustration.

The Act further says that if a party has done something in the performance of the contract prior to the frustrating event he may be allowed compensation for any benefit conferred on the other party. This is an exception to the rule, discussed in Section 11.2, that unless performance is *precise and exact*, the plaintiff can recover nothing; formerly this rule applied even though there was frustration.

The Act can be excluded by an express provision in the contract, and it does not apply to the following classes of contract:

(i) Contracts for the carriage of goods by sea, and charterparties.
(ii) Contracts of insurance.
(iii) Contracts to which S.7 of the *Sale of Goods Act, 1979*, applies. These are contracts where the specific goods which are the subject matter of an agreement to sell, perish through no fault of either party. The contract is avoided, not frustrated.

11.5 Discharge of a Contract by Breach

In many respects it is incorrect to say that breach of a contract will bring about that contract's discharge. Breach means the failure of one party to the contract to comply with the terms of that contract. The rights and actions of the innocent party following on from that breach are what will determine if the contract is discharged. We have seen that the terms of a contract fall into two main sections:

(*a*) Warranties – those terms which are minor in nature.
(*b*) Conditions – those terms which are of greater importance and go to the root of the contract.

Breach of a warranty will not discharge the contract. It merely provides the injured party with the opportunity to sue for damages; in all other respects the contract continues as before.

Breach of a condition gives the injured party the *option* of treating the contract as ended (with the right to sue for damages). However, this is an option and it might be that the injured party sees benefit in continuing with the contract and *then* suing for non-performance. An illustration is:

White and Carter (Councils) Ltd v. McGregor (1961). The respondent's sales manager, acting within his authority, entered into a contract with the appellants for the fixing to litter-bins of plates advertising the respondent's business. On the same day, upon hearing of the contract the respondent wrote to the appellants to cancel the agreement, but the appellants refused to accept his cancellation. The contract was for a period of 156 weeks and, under the terms of the contract, if any instalment was unpaid for four weeks, the whole of the amount due for the 156 weeks, or the remainder of that period, became due and payable. The respondent did not pay the first instalment within the time allowed and the appellants sought to recover the whole price. **Held:** they were entitled to succeed. 'If one party to a contract repudiates it . . . the other party, the innocent party, has an option. He may accept that repudiation and sue for damages for breach of contract whether or not the time for performance has come; or he may if he chooses disregard or refuse to accept it and then the contract remains in full effect. . . . It is . . . impossible to say that the appellants should be deprived of their right to claim the contract price merely because the benefit to them as against claiming damages and reletting their advertising space might be small in comparison with the loss to the respondent' (per Lord Reid). (Courtesy of *Cracknell's Law Students' Companion*)

Those who choose to continue with the contract, though, do face some risk that subsequent events might undermine their position, as in:

Avery v. Bowden (1855). B. chartered a ship from A. and agreed to put a cargo on board at Odessa within 45 days. The ship went to Odessa and stood there for almost 45 days without cargo being loaded. B. then told the Captain there was no cargo and he ought to go elsewhere. The Captain remained, hoping that the cargo would turn up. Before the end of the 45-day period the Crimean War broke out and performance of the contract would have been illegal. **Held:** A. had an option to treat the defendants' refusal to load cargo as anticipatory breach, but this option had been waived by staying on at Odessa. Now the contract was discharged by the outbreak of war.

Whether a particular act of non-performance breaches a warranty or a condition is usually decided by the courts taking into account all the facts surrounding a particular contract. Some outline on this question was given by the Court of Appeal in the case of:

Mapleflock Co. Ltd v. Universal Furniture Products (Wembley) Ltd (1934). A contract was concluded for the sale and delivery of 100 tons of rag flock to be dispatched in instalments of $1\frac{1}{2}$ tons three times per week. The sixteenth instalment had excessive amounts of chlorine in it and the buyers wished to repudiate stating that the contract had been breached. **Held:** no entitlement to repudiate since the breach bore only a small quantitative ratio to the contract as a whole.

Generally, breaches of contract can be divided into two types: (*a*) anticipatory breach and (*b*) actual breach.

(*a*) Anticipatory Breach. This means a breach which occurs before the date specified in the contract for performance. It can occur in two ways: (i) expressly – where the defaulting party notifies his intention not to perform the contract, and (ii) implicitly – where the defaulting party through some action shows that he will not be performing the contract.

Anticipatory breach gives the injured party the *option* of treating the contract as ended.

(*b*) **Actual breach** can occur in three ways:

(i) *Non-performance*, i.e. the due date for performance arrives and the other party does not perform his part of the bargain.

(ii) *Defective Performance*. Here performance is not precise and exact. For example, turning up late where time is important.

(iii) *Untruth as regards a term of the contract*. Where the promise made has deliberately concealed the true intentions, as where a cattle truck was sent to do a removal where it was specified that a removal van would be used.

It is cases of actual, as opposed to anticipatory, breach which usually create problems for the courts. As suggested above, the difficulty is in deciding whether a major or minor term of the contract has been breached. With anticipatory breach it is usually the whole of the contract which has been breached.

11.6 Assignment of Contracts

It sometimes happens that one party to a contract wishes to dispose of his obligations under it, but the extent to which this is permitted is limited. The other party may have valid reasons why he prefers the obligations to be performed by the original contractor. If I have contracted with Rembrandt to paint my picture it is unlikely that Rembrandt's pupil, or any other acquaintance of Rembrandt, will produce the picture I require. The rule is that liabilities can only be assigned by **novation**. Novation is the formation of a new contract between the party who wishes performance and a new contractor, whom he accepts is as adequately qualified to perform as the original contractor. Liabilities can only be assigned by consent.

By contrast, rights under a contract can usually be assigned without consent of the other party, except where the subject matter involves personal service. Thus if you owe me £50, it should not make any difference to you if I say: 'Don't pay me – pay Smith.' This is the basis of many debt collection activities. The debtor who is a slow payer finds that his debt has been sold (at a discount) to a debt collector who specialises in collecting debts and will make clear arrangements about settlement and insist that they are carried out. It is a different matter if personal service is involved. If A engages to teach B the piano, and has been paid for a course of lessons, B cannot say 'Don't teach me – teach C'. C may not have any musical potential. The rights to personal services cannot be transferred without the consent of the person giving the service.

Even if the contract does not involve personal service, but specifically restricts the right to assign the contract or any interest in it to third parties, the assignment of rights will not be permitted. In *Helstan Securities Ltd v. Hertfordshire County Council (1978)* the County Council specifically restricted the right of their contractors to assign the contract in any way. A contractor who got into financial difficulties assigned his rights to the plaintiffs, but payment was refused. **Held:** the assignment was invalid.

Contracts may be assigned in four ways. These are: (*a*) novation; (*b*) legal assignment; (*c*) equitable assignment; (*d*) operation of the law.

(*a*) *Novation.* This has been referred to above. The old contract is discharged and a new contract is made between one of the original parties (the creditor) to whom the liability (whether goods, services or money) is owed, and the new debtor who has agreed to undertake the obligations. In many cases the matter is quite routine, as where an existing partnership is dissolved and a new partnership is formed. The existing obligations of the old firm are usually honoured by the new firm with the consent of the customers, and no difficulty arises.

(*b*) **Legal Assignment.** A legal assignment is one made under the *Law of Property Act, 1925*, S.136. All debts and other things in action (formerly called *choses in action*) may be assigned in the following manner:

(i) The assignment must be in writing, signed by the assignor;
(ii) It must be absolute, and not by way of a pledge or charge;
(iii) Express notice must be given to the debtor, trustee or other person from whom the assignor is entitled to demand payment or other right. This is to ensure that the debtor knows that the assignor has surrendered his rights completely in favour of the assignee.

Choses in action are rights of property which can only be enforced in the courts, and not by taking possession. A right under a contract is the commonest example of a *chose in action.*

It is not possible to assign part of a debt, for this puts the debtor to the inconvenience of seeking out two creditors.

The effect of a legal assignment. The effects are that the assignor transfers the legal rights to the debt, or other *choses in action*, together with the legal and other remedies available to the assignee, who may demand payment or satisfaction in the agreed manner laid down in the original contract, and sue if dissatisfied in his own name. He is also free to make such arrangements as he wishes to achieve satisfaction and may give a good discharge to the other party without reference to the assignor.

One defect in assignments from the assignee's point of view is that he always takes **'subject to the equities'**. This means that if, on seeking to enforce the assignment, the debtor is able to show that it is inequitable for the full rights to be enforced, the assignee will not be able to enforce them. Thus if a debtor has paid the debt before receiving notice of the assignment, or is able to raise a set-off against the original obligation, the assignee will be able to enforce only the balance and will be thrown back for redress upon the assignor.

(*c*) **Equitable Assignments.** An equitable assignment is one that will be recognised by equity, even if the common law will not recognise it (because, for example, it lacks the form required by S.136 of the *Law of Property*

Act, 1925). If there has been a clear intention to assign, equity will recognise the assignment and enforce it, even if it is not in writing or only for part of a debt. Thus where K agreed with B, who was his financial backer, that all moneys due to K from customers should be paid direct to B, there was a clear intention to assign. K sold goods to D, who were given notice of assignment by B and asked to pay B. D ignored the request and paid K. When sued by B it was held that D must pay B again, even if they had already paid K. It would be inequitable for B to suffer a loss when they had given clear notice of the assignment (*Brandt v. Dunlop Rubber Co.* (*1905*)).

This is an example of an equitable assignment of a legal *chose in action.* It must be distinguished from the assignment of an equitable *chose in action* – for example, the assignment of a claim by a legatee on an executor.

(*d*) **Other Assignments.** Certain contractual documents are not assigned in the manner laid down in the *Law of Property Act, 1925*, but are governed by special statutes. They include bills of exchange and promissory notes (see Chapter 17), bills of lading, shares in companies, marine insurance policies and life assurance policies.

Assignments by operation of the law occur at death or bankruptcy.

At **death** all liabilities and rights on a contract pass to the personal representatives, and are dealt with as part of the estate. Contracts for personal skill and service are not assignable, and terminate at death.

At **bankruptcy** the rights and liabilities under a contract pass to the trustee in bankruptcy, and are dealt with as part of the process of settling the bankrupt's affairs.

11.7 Revision Test

Answers	*Questions*
–	**1.** How is a contract usually discharged?
1. By performance.	**2.** In what other ways may it be discharged?
2. (*a*) By agreement; (*b*) by frustration; (*c*) by breach.	**3.** What are the criteria for discharge by performance?
3. Traditionally performance must be *precise and exact*. More recently the doctrines of *substantial performance*, *divisible contracts* and *quantum meruit* have reduced the severity of the traditional rule.	**4.** What was the case of *Hoenig v. Isaacs* (*1952*) about?

Answers	*Questions*
4. Substantial performance. Isaacs refused to pay fully for redecoration and refurnishing, but the contract was held to have been substantially performed.	**5.** What are the rules in discharge by agreement?
5. (*a*) That which has been created by agreement can be extinguished by agreement; (*b*) the new agreement is a contract in its own right and requires consideration unless under seal.	**6.** What is meant by the doctrine of frustration?
6. The doctrine that holds that in certain circumstances a contract may be discharged by events which render it impossible to perform.	**7.** What are the common instances of frustration?
7. (*a*) Destruction of the subject matter; (*b*) non-availability of a person in a contract for personal service; (*c*) non-occurrence of an event; (*d*) supervening illegality.	**8.** What Act of Parliament controls frustrated contracts?
8. The *Law Reform (Frustrated Contracts) Act, 1943.*	**9.** What are its rules?
9. (*a*) Money prepaid can be reclaimed; (*b*) money not paid need not be paid; (*c*) if a party has incurred expenses he may retain these out of any repayment, or claim them, if they have conferred a benefit on the other party.	**10.** What is the result of a breach of a warranty in a contract?
10. The injured party may claim damages, but the contract subsists.	**11.** What is the result of a breach of condition?
11. (*a*) The aggrieved party has an option to treat the contract as ended and sue for breach. (*b*) Alternatively, he may complete the contract and sue for non-performance. In this case he runs the risk that subsequent events may worsen his legal position.	**12.** What is a legal assignment?

Answers	*Questions*
12. The passing of legal rights or obligations on a contract to another party.	**13.** How are obligations on a contract assigned?
13. By novation with consent of the creditor to whom money, goods or services are due. The old contract ceases and a new contract is made between the new parties.	**14.** How are rights assigned?
14. By the rules of the *Law of Property Act, 1925*, S.136.	**15.** What are these rules?
15. (*a*) The assignment must be in writing, signed by the assignor; (*b*) it must be absolute, not by way of charge or pledge; (*c*) notice must be given to the debtor.	**16.** What is an equitable assignment?
16. An assignment which equity will recognise even though it lacks the formality required by the *Law of Property Act, 1925*.	**17.** Go over the questions until you are sure of the answers. Then try some of the written questions in Appendix 1.

12 How the Law Enforces Contractual Obligations

12.1 The Nature of Contractual Enforcement

The law of contract is concerned with 'enforceable' agreements. The question then arises as to what 'enforceable' means in this context. It means that should one of the parties to the contract fail to perform his contractual obligations, the courts, at the request of the aggrieved party, will impose conditions upon the defaulting party. These conditions are intended to provide a remedy for the aggrieved rather than a punishment for the defaulter. In this respect the law of contract is quite unlike criminal law; remedies are designed to compensate, not to penalise.

As with many branches of the law, remedies available for those injured by breach of contract fall into two groups:

(*a*) Those available at common law.
(*b*) Those available in equity.

12.2 Common Law Remedies

The remedies available at common law are: (*a*) repudiation of the contract, (*b*) damages and (*c*) a *quantum meruit*.

(*a*) **Repudiation of the Contract.** Where there has been anticipatory breach or breach of a vital condition of the contract, the injured party has the option of repudiating the contract, i.e. treating it as ended. Of course he may decide not to exercise this option (see *White v. McGregor*, page 154). Should he choose to repudiate he will do nothing further on the contract. He will escape from all further contractual obligations and in addition will normally sue for damages.

(*b*) **Damages.** These are available not only to those who have suffered through anticipatory breach or breach of condition, but also those disadvantaged through breach of warranty.

Damages are a money payment designed to put the injured party in the position he would have been in had the contract been performed. Therefore the injured party can never get more in damages than the extent of his loss. If he suffers no loss he may still win his action for breach but will receive only nominal damages (a token payment). He may not recover his costs. The following are the main areas of concern as regards contractual damages:

(i) *Remoteness of damage.* A situation might arise where a breach of contract leads not only to the loss immediate upon the breach itself, but to further consequences which give rise to additional loss. The question then arises as to whether the injured party can recover for all of these consequences. In other words, how are the damages to be assessed, and how extensive are the consequences to be considered?

The line of demarcation between the losses recoverable through an action for damages, and those not recoverable because the damage is too remote, was laid down in the case of *Hadley v. Baxendale* (*1854*). This is the most important case:

Hadley v. Baxendale (*1854*). The plaintiffs were millers and mealmen in Gloucester. The crankshaft of the steam engine which worked their mill was fractured and they ordered another from a firm in Greenwich who asked that the old shaft should be sent to them for use as a pattern. The plaintiffs gave the shaft to the defendants, who were common carriers, and the defendants promised to deliver the shaft on the following day. In fact they took a week to deliver it and because their mill was out of action for longer than would otherwise have been the case the plaintiffs claimed damages for loss of profit. **Held:** the plaintiffs would not succeed as the loss of profit could not reasonably be considered a consequence of the breach of contract which could have been fairly and reasonably contemplated by both parties when they entered into the contract of carriage. 'Where two parties have made a contract which one of them has broken, the damages which the other party ought to receive in respect of such breach of contract should be such as *may fairly and reasonably be considered either arising naturally, i.e. according to the usual course of things, from such breach of contract itself, or such as may reasonably be supposed to have been in the contemplation of both parties, at the time they made the contract, as the probable result of the breach of it.* Now, if the special circumstances under which the contract was actually made were communicated by the plaintiffs to the defendants, and thus known to both parties, the damages resulting from the breach of such a contract, which they would reasonably contemplate, would be the amount of injury which would ordinarily follow from a breach of the contract under the special circumstances so known and communicated. But, on the other hand, if these special circumstances were wholly unknown to the party breaking the contract, he, at the most, could only be supposed to have had in his contemplation the amount of injury which would arise generally, and in the great multitude of cases not affected by any special circumstances, from such a breach of contract. For, had the special circumstances been known, the parties might have specially provided for the breach of contract by special terms as to damages in that case; and of this advantage it would be very unjust to deprive them' (per Alderson, B.). (Courtesy of *Cracknell's Law Students' Companion*)

The rule in this case has been applied in many subsequent cases and is well established. The following cases further illustrate this rule:

Diamond v. Campbell-Jones (*1960*). The defendants wrongly repudiated an agreement for the sale by the defendants to the plaintiff of a leasehold property in Mayfair and the question arose as to the amount of damages that the plaintiff was entitled to recover. The agreement was subject to and with the benefit of a contract for the grant of a new lease and this contract required the premises to be converted by the lessee into ground-floor office accommodation and residential maisonettes. The plaintiff was a dealer in real property but it was not shown that the defendants were aware of this or that he intended to carry out a conversion of the premises. **Held:**

the amount of damages should be limited to the difference between the purchase price and the market value at the date of the breach of contract as there were no special circumstances sufficient to impute to the defendants knowledge that the plaintiff intended to convert the property for profit. (Courtesy of *Cracknell's Law Students' Companion*)

Cottrill v. Steyning and Littlehampton Building Society (1966). Here it was held that the vendors, knowing that the purchaser intended to develop the land himself, were liable for loss of profits which the purchaser would have made by carrying out the development.

Koufos v. C. Czarnikow Ltd 'The Heron II' (1967). A vessel was chartered for a voyage from Constanza to Basrah for the carriage of sugar. She deviated to Berbera to load livestock for the shipowners. If she had not deviated, she would have arrived at Basrah 10 days earlier than she did in fact. The charterers claimed damages for the difference between the market value of the sugar at the due date of delivery and at the actual date of delivery. **Held:** their claim should succeed. Although the shipowners did not know what the charterers intended to do with the sugar, they knew that there was a market for sugar in Basrah. They must have realised that at least it was not unlikely that the sugar would be sold there on arrival, and that in any ordinary market prices were apt to fluctuate daily. It was an even chance that the fluctuation would be downwards. The loss was of a kind which the shipowners, when they made the contract, ought to have realised was liable to result from a breach causing delay in delivery. (*N.B.* The Law Lords emphasised that the measure of damages in contract and the measure of damages in tort are not the same. In contract there is opportunity for the injured party to protect himself against risk by directing the other party's attention to it before the contract is made; in tort there is no such opportunity, and the tortfeasor cannot reasonably complain if he has to pay for unusual but foreseeable damage resulting from his wrongdoing.) (Courtesy of *Cracknell's Law Students' Companion*)

(ii) *Quantification of damages*. Once the courts have established the cause for which the injured party may receive damages its attention is turned to the size of those damages, i.e. how to express the loss suffered in terms of money.

Where the contract is for the sale of goods or the carriage of goods the normal way of quantifying damages will be with reference to the market. This is known as the **'market rule'**. Should a seller fail to deliver goods then the buyer must buy similar goods in the market and his loss will be the difference between the market price and the contract price.

In other cases there are no such specific rules, and often the assessment of damages is reduced virtually to guesswork. The damages which the plaintiff claims may be **liquidated** or **unliquidated**.

Liquidated damages. These are a genuine pre-estimate of the loss likely to be suffered by the plaintiff if there is a breach of contract. They are written into the contract itself. For example, if the parties provide in the contract that failure to complete a construction job on time will lead to a claim for damages of £100 a day, this would be a genuine attempt to liquidate (express in money terms) the loss to be suffered. If the sum mentioned is not a genuine pre-estimate of the loss, but is excessive and inserted *in terrorem* (to frighten the other party), it is called a penalty and the law will not enforce it. Thus a claim for £1 000 000 a day would be a penalty, *in terrorem*, and void. If the amount is liquidated damages, the court will enforce it, even though in the event the pre-estimate turns out to have been wrong. If, however, the court comes to the conclusion that the amount is a penalty, then the plaintiff cannot enforce it, but can simply claim unliquidated damages.

Often it is difficult to tell whether an agreed sum is liquidated damages or a penalty; it is a matter of construction. The fact that a sum is described as one thing or another is not conclusive, although there is a rebuttable presumption that the clause is what it says it is.

Willson v. Love (1896). A tenant farmer agreed to pay the additional rent of £3 per ton by way of penalty for every ton of hay or straw which shall be sold off the premises during the last 12 months of the tenancy. The clause was regarded as penal because at the time hay was worth five shillings a ton more than straw.

Dunlop Pneumatic Tyre Co. Ltd v. New Garage and Motor Co. Ltd (1915). The appellants, manufacturers of motor tyres, supplied goods to the respondents under a contract which provided that the respondents would not sell tyres at less than the appellants' list price. It was further provided that if the respondents sold a tyre in breach of this agreement they would pay the appellants £5. **Held:** this sum would be regarded as liquidated damages and not as a penalty.

In this case certain rules for guidance were laid down by Lord Dunedin:

(i) The sum is a penalty if it is greater than the greatest loss which could be suffered from the breach – in other words, if it is 'extravagant and unconscionable'.

(ii) If it is agreed that a larger sum shall be payable in default of paying a smaller sum, this is a penalty.

(iii) If a single sum is payable on different events of varying importance this is *prima facie* a penalty. (But this presumption may be rebutted if it is impossible to prove the exact monetary loss.)

Ford Motor Co. (England) Ltd v. Armstrong (1915). A dealer, the defendant, agreed to sell the plaintiff's motorcars and, in the event of his selling any car or parts below list price, to pay £250 for every breach of such undertaking 'such sum being the agreed damages which the manufacturer will sustain'. **Held:** the sum of £250 was a penalty and not liquidated damages.

Unliquidated damages. The term means that no attempt has been made by the parties to express the loss in money terms, and the amount payable will be assessed by the court.

(iii) *Taxation*. There are circumstances where the incidence of taxation has to be taken into account when quantifying damages. The guiding case here is:

British Transport Commission v. Gourley (1956). Gourley was injured an accident as a result of the negligence of BTC. His claim for £37,000 loss of earnings for the rest of his working life was reduced to £6000 by the House of Lords since this was the amount he would have received after tax.

The principle behind this decision is that individuals ought not to make a profit out of damages. It is therefore necessary, if the case is to be applied, for there to be a combination of non-taxable damages and a liability for taxation in the earnings which the damages represent. Where the damages will eventually be taxed in the hands of the recipient – for example, where he is a trader, or where they represent a non-taxable item – the court will make no deduction for taxation.

The *Income and Corporation Taxes Act, 1970* (SS.187 and 188), has slightly modified the position. Damages for wrongful dismissal in excess of £5000 are now taxed in the hands of the recipient: only the initial £5000 is now subject in such cases to the rule in *BTC v. Gourley* (*1956*).

(iv) *Mitigation of damage.* It is the duty of the plaintiff to take all reasonable steps to mitigate his loss. In *Brace v. Calder and Others* (*1895*) four men in partnership agreed to employ Brace for two years in the capacity of manager. Five months later two of the partners retired. The partnership was automatically dissolved but the remaining two partners offered Brace employment on the same terms. Brace chose to sue for breach and claimed as damages the salary for the remainder of the two year contract period. **Held:** he was entitled to nominal damages only because it was his duty to mitigate his loss which he could easily have done by accepting re-employment.

This rule is subject to two qualifications:

(*a*) The burden is on the defendant of proving that the plaintiff has failed to mitigate his damage.

Pilkington v. Wood (*1953*). When the plaintiff bought a house in Hampshire he employed the defendant, a solicitor, to act for him. Over a year later the plaintiff decided to sell the house and it was then that a defect in the plaintiff's title came to light. The defendant admitted that he had been guilty of negligence and the question arose as to the amount of damages which he should pay. In addition to the difference between the market value of the house with a good title and its value when the title was defective, the plaintiff claimed certain hotel, travelling and telephone expenses which he would not have incurred if he had been able to sell the house and move to Lancashire, his new place of employment. He also claimed interest on a bank overdraft which would have been paid off when the house was sold. The defendant maintained that it was the duty of the plaintiff to mitigate the damage which he had suffered by suing the vendor in respect of a breach of his implied covenant for title. **Held:** the plaintiff's duty to mitigate the damage did not go so far as to require him to undertake a difficult piece of litigation, but his claim for additional damages would fail as it arose out of facts which could not reasonably be supposed to have been in contemplation of the parties at the time at which the plaintiff bought the house.

(*b*) The principle is completely at variance with the rule that, in the case of anticipatory breach, the plaintiff has the option to hold the defendant to his contract and await the date of performance. If he chooses this course, he may well inflate his damages rather than mitigate them (*White and Carter* (*Councils*) *Ltd v. McGregor* (*1962*)). However, it seems he is entitled to do this, since the contract remains alive and the question of damages or of mitigation has not yet arisen.

(*c*) ***Quantum Meruit.*** At common law a party injured by breach of contract might be able to make a claim other than for damages. He may be able to claim for what he has done under the contract. This right to sue on a *quantum meruit* does not depend upon the original contract but flows from an implied promise by the other party, who has had executed consideration, that a reasonable sum will be paid for it. Such cases are often described as 'quasi-contractual' (almost contractual). See *Planché v. Colburn* (page 149), and a more recent case *British Steel Corporation v. Cleveland Bridge and Engineering Co. Ltd.* (*1984*).

12.3 Equitable Remedies

Throughout its development equity has attempted to mitigate the harshness of common law rules to provide for omissions in the common law. In respect to breach of contract the common law remedies of damages and repudiation may not be adequate to compensate the injured party effectively for his loss. Equity therefore developed the equitable remedies of specific performance and injunction.

(*a*) **Specific Performance.** Specific performance is a decree issued by the court which orders a defendant to perform the promises he has made. Such a decree is likely to be made only where the injured party has no solution to his problem by ordinary dealings in the market. Thus where a contract for the supply of a motor vehicle is broken the court would expect the customer to buy elsewhere and only money damages would be payable. It might be different if the motor vehicle was a unique vintage model which could not therefore be obtained elsewhere.

One of the main difficulties with specific performance is that it involves the courts in the business of supervision and therefore there are many limitations to its application by the courts. The following are the main ones:

(i) *Where damages is an adequate remedy* specific performance will not be awarded. This means that where the contract is for the sale of goods specific performance is rarely given. For example:

Cohen v. Roche (*1927*). Cohen sued for specific performance against Roche, an auctioneer, claiming that he was entitled to a set of eight Hepplewhite chairs after an auction. **Held:** he could have damages, but not specific performance, because the chairs were not special items of interest but ordinary articles of commerce.

Specific performance will be awarded though for an obligation to pay money, where damages would not be an adequate recompense. This is illustrated by:

Beswick v. Beswick (*1967*). By a written agreement P.B. assigned his business as a coal merchant to his nephew, J.B. In consideration, J.B. agreed to employ P.B. as a consultant at £6 10s. 0d a week for the rest of his life, and further to pay P.B.'s wife an annuity of £5 a week for her life, after P.B.'s death. P.B.'s wife was not a party to the contract. After P.B.'s death, J.B. paid one sum of £5 to the widow, but refused to pay any more. The widow sought an order for specific performance of the agreement in her capacity as administratrix of her husband's estate and in her personal capacity. **Held:** the widow as administratrix was entitled to enforce the agreement by an order for specific performance in her own personal favour. However, the House of Lords rejected the argument that S.56, *Law of Property Act, 1925*, applied to such an agreement, and hence the widow would be unable to enforce the agreement in her personal capacity as she was not a party to the original contract. Fortunately she could rely on her position as administratrix of her husband's will.

(ii) *Where the court hesitates to exercise discretion.* As with all equitable remedies, specific performance is not available as of right, but at the court's discretion. In this respect it is unlike damages. The case of *Wood v. Scarth* (*1858*) illustrates the court's attitude:

Wood v. Scarth (*1858*). Wood sued Scarth alleging that Scarth had contracted to grant Wood the lease of a public house but then had refused to convey the property. Scarth acted through an agent and the agent had failed to make clear to Wood the terms which Scarth required. Wood agreed to one set of terms, Scarth to another – in other words, non-identical bilateral mistake. In 1855 Wood sued for specific performance but the court withheld this on the grounds that in view of the mistake performance would be hard on Scarth. In this (1858) action Wood sued at common law for damages and was granted them on the grounds that it was reasonable for Wood to feel that he had entered a contract on the basis of the terms he had agreed.

The principles followed by the court when deciding whether or not to award specific performance depend upon the justness and equity of its application. For example:

Flight v. Bolland (*1828*). In this case Sir John Leach, MR, stated that: 'No case of a bill filed by an infant for the specific performance of a contract made by him has been found in the books. It is not disputed that it is a general principle of courts of equity to interpose only where the remedy is mutual.' Since the infant, had he been the defaulting party, would have been insusceptible to legal action, equity felt it would be unfair to grant an equitable remedy in his favour.

(iii) *Where the contract will be difficult to enforce.* There are two main areas:

(iii*a*) Contracts requiring constant supervision by the courts. For example:

Ryan v. Mutual Tontine Westminster Chambers Association (*1893*). By the term of a lease of a residential flat the landlords covenanted to provide a porter, who was to be constantly in attendance, or during his temporary absence, a trustworthy assistant. The landlords appointed one Benton to be porter but, while he spent much of his time acting as chef at a neighbouring club, boys and charwomen performed his duties as porter. **Held:** the landlords were in breach of their covenant but the court would not grant an injunction to restrain the continuance of the breach or order the covenant to be specifically enforced. (Courtesy of *Cracknell's Law Students' Companion*)

(iii*b*) Contracts for personal services, since this would interfere with personal liberty.

(*b*) **Injunction.** An injunction is a decree which compels a party to do an act (**a mandatory injunction**) or to refrain from doing an act (**a prohibitory injunction**). In relation to the law of contract it can be used in order to prevent a party from committing a breach of contract, i.e. a negative stipulation. For example, if I enter into a contract promising to take all my electricity supply from you, then I can be prevented from obtaining electricity supply from anyone else (*Metropolitan Electric Supply Co. v. Ginder* (*1901*)). Negative stipulation applies also to contracts of personal services where an actor or a singer has undertaken to act or sing at the plaintiff's theatre. This actor or singer can be prevented by an injunction from acting or singing for someone else (*Lumley v. Wagner* (*1852*); *Warner Bros. v. Nelson* (*1937*)).

Warner Brothers Pictures Inc. v. Nelson (1936). Bette Davis entered into a contract with the plaintiffs, initially for a term of one year, but giving the plaintiffs the option of extending it, whereby she agreed that she would not undertake other film work without obtaining their written consent. The plaintiffs sought an injunction to restrain her from doing film work for another in breach of this agreement. **Held:** the injunction would be granted for the period of the continuance of the contract, or for three years, whichever was the shorter. (Courtesy of *Cracknell's Law Students' Companion*)

However, an injunction will not be granted where the effect is to compel a party to do that which specific performance would not order.

Page One Records, Ltd v. Britton (1967). By a written agreement made in 1966, the defendants, a group of pop musicians, appointed the plaintiffs as their managers for five years. The agreement was world-wide. The plaintiffs agreed to use their best endeavours to advance the defendants' careers, and the defendants said they would not engage any other person to act as their manager or agent. The plaintiffs were to receive 20 per cent of all moneys earned by the defendants during the currency of the agreement. As a result of the plaintiffs' services, the defendants achieved success, but in 1967 purported to repudiate the management agreement. The court then held that there had been no breaches of duty by the plaintiffs to justify repudiation. The plaintiffs claimed damages for breach of contact and, pending trial, sought an **interlocutory injunction** restraining the defendants from engaging anyone else as their manager. **Held:** dismissing the application, the injunction would be refused because, if granted, it would enforce a contract for personal services of a fiduciary nature to be performed by the plaintiffs and not specifically enforceable by the defendants against them. (Courtesy of *Cracknell's Law Students' Companion*)

12.4 Limitation of Actions

Generally speaking, litigation is a costly and time-consuming process which becomes more difficult as the time between the disputed events and the litigation increases. For this reason Parliament has enacted Limitation Acts which set a time limit on the commencement of litigation. The current Act is the *Limitation Act, 1980*.

The right to bring an action can be discharged in three ways:

(*a*) The parties to the contract might agree to discharge their rights. This agreement will either be under seal, or through accord and satisfaction.

(*b*) Through the judgement of a court.

(*c*) Through lapse of time. If an action is not commenced within a certain time the right to sue is extinguished. Specific provision for lapse of time is now governed by the *Limitation Act, 1980*. Actions in simple contract and tort become 'statute barred' after six years. In the case of specialties (deeds) the time allowed is 12 years. The Act does permit certain extensions to these time limits. For example, where a person is under a disability (he may be unconscious as the result of an accident) the time limit does not begin to run until the disability is removed, or the person dies.

A number of international conventions, particularly with regard to the law of carriage, lay down shorter limitation periods for action than those specified in the *Limitation Act, 1980*. For example, in carriage by sea the limitation period is normally one year, but this may be extended by mutual agreement. In carriage by air under the Warsaw Rules the period is two years. Such conventions are enacted into British law in relevant acts of Parliament, in the above cases the *Carriage of Goods by Sea Act, 1971*, and the *Carriage by Air Act, 1961*.

12.5 Revision Test

Answers	*Questions*
–	**1.** What is meant by 'enforcement of contracts'?
1. It is the imposition of sanctions upon the defaulting party in a contract to compensate the aggrieved other party.	**2.** What common law sanctions are available?
2. (*a*) Repudiation of the contract; (*b*) damages; (*c*) a *quantum meruit*.	**3.** What happens with repudiation of the contract?
3. The aggrieved party does nothing further on the contract, and may also sue for damages for non-performance.	**4.** What case laid down the principles on money damages payable?
4. *Hadley* v. *Baxendale* (*1854*).	**5.** What was this case about?
5. A mill owner sent a crankshaft for repair, the carrier promising delivery next day. There was a considerable delay and his factory was idle. He claimed for this loss.	**6.** What was the principle laid down in the case?
6. Damages would be limited to those naturally following from the breach of contract, or those in the contemplation of both parties when they made the contract.	**7.** What other rules apply?
7. (*a*) The rule that the plaintiff must mitigate his losses so far as possible. (*b*) The rule that taxation may need to be taken into account unless it is taxable on the recipient.	**8.** What are liquidated damages?

Answers	*Questions*
8. Damages laid down as a term in the contract and believed to be a fair pre-estimate of the loss likely to be suffered if a breach of contract occurs.	**9.** What does *quantum meruit* mean?
9. 'How much is it worth?' The aggrieved party sues for the value of the work done.	**10.** What is an equitable remedy?
10. A remedy given at the discretion of the court to see fair play in a situation where money damages are not a satisfactory remedy.	**11.** What are the equitable remedies?
11. (*a*) Specific performance; (*b*) injunction. The court may also order rescission of the contract.	**12.** When is specific performance used?
12. (*a*) Where the object of the contract is unique – such as the ownership of a particular parcel of land, or a work of art. (*b*) Where the supervision required is not great, since the courts hesitate to undertake continuous supervision of any situation.	**13.** What is an injunction?
13. An order of the court requiring a party to do a certain thing, or to refrain from doing a certain thing.	**14.** What limitations are placed on ordinary actions by the *Limitation Act, 1980*.
14. (*a*) Simple contracts – 6 years; (*b*) torts (civil wrongs) – 6 years; (*c*) specialties (deeds) – 12 years.	**15.** Go over the questions until you are sure of all the answers. Then try some of the questions in Appendix 1 which require a written answer.

13
Agency

13.1 The Nature of Agency

Any legal person, whether it be an individual, a firm or an incorporation like a company or nationalised corporation can appoint someone to act on his behalf in a particular matter, or in all matters. Thus a householder may appoint an 'estate agent' to sell his property, or an explorer may appoint a friend to act on his behalf in any matters that arise during his absence from home. The essence of agency is that the agent is empowered to make binding contracts between his principal and third parties. The Latin rule ***Qui facit per alium, facit per se*** ('He who does something by another does it himself') applies, and the principal is bound by the acts of his agent, to the extent that he has authorised them, either expressly or impliedly.

The more sophisticated an economy is the more agency arrangements are made. It is part of specialisation into trades and professions that expertise should be developed in special fields, and that the specialists thus developed should act for others who are not knowledgeable in that particular area. Solicitors, estate agents, freight forwarders, bankers, factors, brokers and many others specialise in their fields and offer their services to the business world around them.

The essential aspects of agency may be listed as follows:

(*a*) *Appointment.* The agent's appointment determines the extent of his authority and is clearly of crucial importance. There is also an **agency of necessity**.

(*b*) *The nature of contracts made under agency.* The relationship is a triangular one, as explained below (see Fig. 13.1).

(*c*) *Ratification of an unauthorised act.* Sometimes an agent will exceed his authority, but it is always open to the principal to ratify the unauthorised act and thus make it legally binding upon him.

(*d*) *Breach of warranty of authority.* In acting with third parties the agent holds himself out as authorised to act for his principal. If this proves to be untrue, and he acts outside his authority, the disappointed third party may sue the agent for breach of warranty of authority.

(*e*) *The duties of the agent to the principal.*

(*f*) *The duties of the principal to the agent.*

(*g*) *The agent as servant, or as independent contractor.* Sometimes servants act as agents of their employers. Other agents are not servants, but independent contractors acting for a principal, but not under the principal's direct control.

(*h*) *The doctrine of the undisclosed principal.* Sometimes a principal requires the agent to keep the principal's identity a secret. This presents special problems, and rules have evolved to deal with them.

(*i*) *The termination of the agency.* Agencies come to an end in a variety of ways. One is express revocation of the agency by the principal. Agency of necessity comes to an end when the emergency – whatever it was – is over.

All these matters need careful study, and are dealt with below.

13.2 The Appointment of Agents

Agency relationships can start in a variety of ways. For convenience they are grouped here under the general heading of 'appointments' but not all agency relationships involve a formal or informal appointment of the agent by the principal. If I have your strawberries on my lorry and am unable to reach the market because of floods, I may become your agent of necessity, authorised to do whatever is necessary to ensure that they fetch a reasonable price and do not rot for lack of attention.

The most common types of relationship are as follows:

(*a*) **Express authority** given by the principal to the agent. The relationship between a principal and an agent is a contractual relationship. It follows that the parties to it must have the capacity to contract if the relationships between them are to be enforceable. Taking the more usual circumstances, where a principal with full capacity to contract appoints an agent, who also has full capacity to contract, to act for him in some matter, how is the appointment made? No formal appointment is necessary in most cases. An oral appointment will do, even if the agent is to make contracts which by law must be expressed in writing (for example, guarantees). The chief exceptions to this rule about lack of formality are:

(i) Where the agent is to be authorised to make contracts which are required to be made under seal, the agent's appointment must also be under seal. This is known as a **power of attorney**. The rules about powers of attorney are laid down in the *Powers of Attorney Act, 1971*.

(ii) A statute may require that an agent is appointed in writing. Thus S.10 of the *Companies Act, 1985*, with regard to the appointment of directors and first secretaries says that if the document required to be registered with the Registrar is provided by an agent for the subscribers to the memorandum it must contain a statement specifying that fact, and giving the agent's name and address. Thus an oral appointment without a written acknowledgement in the registration document would not do.

(*b*) **Implied authority.** The term 'implied' in law is the opposite of 'express'. The authority follows not from an express statement in front of witnesses, or a written statement or a formal declaration (in a deed) but from the look of the thing. If I repeatedly send my servant to collect goods from A and in due course settle A's account from time to time, the servant has an implied authority to collect goods from A on my behalf. If I decide to discontinue the man's employment I must not just assume that he will cease to collect goods. I must notify A that the servant is no longer entitled to collect goods on my behalf. Until the implied authority I have conferred on the man is countermanded by an express revocation of authority I shall be liable if he dishonestly obtains further supplies ostensibly on my behalf. The implication is that the servant is my agent and I shall be estopped from denying the fact of this agency (*Ryan v. Pilkington* (*1959*)).

Similarly, a manager frequently is taken to have implied authority to make contracts on behalf of his employers. It is also unwise to allow letterheads to be in full circulation in an office, where copies could be used by unauthorised persons who would appear, by the use of the letterhead, to have authority.

An example of implied authority is the following case:

Australia and New Zealand Bank v. Ateliers de Constructions Electriques de Charleroi (*1966*). The Australian agent of the Belgian company had been in the habit of paying large sums of the company's money into his personal bank account at the Australia and New Zealand Bank. The Belgian company had no bank account in Australia, and had made no previous enquiries about the agent's method of receiving money and making remittances to them. When they did discover how things were being arranged they made no complaint, until the agent went into liquidation and a large sum due to the Belgian company could not be paid. They then sued the bank for conversion of cheques made out to the Belgian company and endorsed and paid into the agent's personal account. The agent had authority to bank cash received in his own account, but had no express authority to bank cheques. **Held:** the Privy Council held that authority could be implied in the agent, and the Belgian company failed in its action.

A particular case of implied authority is agency by **estoppel**. The word 'estoppel' means that a person is prevented from taking a particular course of action because of a previous faulty action of his own. Suppose that a person has allowed another to believe that a certain state of affairs exists, with the result that there is reliance upon such belief. He cannot afterwards be allowed to say that the true state of affairs was far different, if to do so would involve the other person suffering some kind of detriment. Applied to agency this means that a person who by words or conduct has allowed another to appear to the outside world to be his agent, with the result that third parties deal with him as an agent, cannot afterwards repudiate this apparent agency if to do so would cause harm to the third parties. He is treated as being in the same position as if he had in fact authorised the agent to act in the way he had done. Slade, J., in *Rama Corporation v. Proved Tin and General Investment Ltd* (*1952*), summed up the requirements for agency by estoppel as follows:

(i) *A representation.* There must be some statement or conduct on the part of the principal which can amount to a representation that the agent has authority to act on his behalf in the way he is acting.

(ii) *A reliance on the representation.* The representation must be made to the person who relies upon it. This means that it must be made either to the particular individual who transacts business with the agent, or to the public at large in circumstances in which it is to be expected that the general public would be likely to transact business with the agent.

(iii) *Suffering or 'detriment'*. There must be a suffering or 'detriment' as a result of a change in position because of faith in the representation.

If these requirements are present the principal will be estopped from denying that the agent had authority to act on his behalf. Suppose a partnership has over a period transacted business with a supplier. The partners then quarrel and cease to trade in partnership, but the active partner keeps the name of both partners over the premises and continues to use the partnership letterhead. Suppose now that the non-active partner orders goods from the supplier ostensibly for use in the business. The active partner will be estopped from denying that the purchase has been made on behalf of the business, for he has 'held his former partner out' as being an agent of the firm. An example of estoppel is the following case:

Henderson & Co. v. Williams (1895). The plaintiffs were sugar merchants and the defendant a warehouseman. The owner of goods lying in the warehouse was induced by the fraud of one Fletcher to instruct the defendant to transfer the goods to the order of Fletcher and the goods were accordingly placed at his disposal. Fletcher sold the goods to innocent purchasers, the plaintiffs, but when Fletcher's fraud was discovered the defendant refused to deliver the goods to the plaintiffs. **Held:** the plaintiffs' action for damages would succeed. The original owners had enabled Fletcher to hold himself out as owner of the goods in such a way as to induce the plaintiffs to enter into a contract and the defendant was estopped from afterwards denying Fletcher's title to the goods. (Courtesy of *Cracknell's Law Students' Companion*)

(*c*) **Agency of Necessity.** As the name implies, agency of necessity arises out of exceptional circumstances – for example, accidents, fires, flooding, etc. In the commercial field it may be that perishable cargoes are threatened by such developments as strikes, power failures, natural disasters, etc. The emergency must be a genuine one, and actually threaten the goods. It must also be impossible to contact the principal in time to secure proper authority. Thus, in these days of instantaneous communication, it is usually possible to contact the owner of goods by telephone or telex and seek authority for the course of action proposed.

In *Great Northern Railway v. Swaffield (1874)* a horse arrived at a station and there was no one to receive it. The railway company incurred livery stable expenses in accommodating the animal overnight, and were held entitled to recover these charges as agents of necessity.

In *Springer v. Great Western Railway (1921)* the plaintiffs were the owners of tomatoes delayed in Weymouth by a rail strike. The railway's traffic agent decided to sell the whole consignment locally since he believed they could not have reached Covent Garden market in saleable condition. The plaintiffs argued that had the traffic agent contacted them they would have moved the goods by road, and earned the high prices prevailing due to the rail strike. **Held:** There was no agency of necessity, since the traffic agent could easily have communicated with the owners and taken instructions. Damages awarded to the plaintiff.

(*d*) **Agency of the Wife.** Although usually referred to as agency of the wife, this class of agencies springs from the relationship of a man with those living in the same house, and could equally apply to a mistress, a housekeeper or a servant. Where a husband actually authorises a wife to buy goods needed by the family (real authority) or habitually pays for such goods and therefore gives the tradesmen the impression that she has authority (apparent authority) or manifestly cohabits with her (implied authority) the wife will be the agent of her husband.

These authorities may be removed by the husband either by giving notice to traders with whom the wife has had dealings, or by a general notice in the press which is effective against all traders. There is no implied authority where the husband has specifically forbidden his wife to pledge his credit, or where she is adequately provided for or has an adequate allowance. A separated wife has no authority to pledge her husband's credit if she has adequate private means, or is adequately provided for. Third parties must therefore be cautious when assuming that a husband will always stand as principal for the wife's transactions. The assumption may not be well founded.

13.3 The Nature of Contracts Made Under Agency

When contracts are made by agents on behalf of their principals a triangular relationship results which has legal implications for the three parties. This is most simply illustrated in diagrammatic form, as in Fig. 13.1. A note of explanation appears below the diagram.

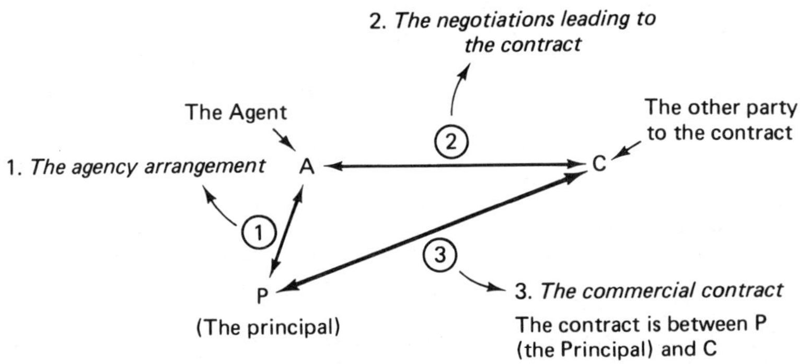

Fig. 13.1. A simple agency arrangement

Notes

(i) The arrangement is a triangular one in which A, the agent, arranges a contract between P, his principal, and C. (C may be a customer, or a supplier, or the owner of property or a person who performs a service.)

(ii) The link between A and P is that of agent and principal. P has appointed A to act for him and their respective rights and duties follow from the appointment. The link is partly contractual and partly fiduciary – a matter of trust between them. The relationship between them is of a confidential nature, and there are other rights and duties between them besides those that follow from the contractual arrangement they have made with one another.

(iii) The link between A and C is a nebulous one, since A is acting for P and any contract that results will be between P and C. In acting as agent, A warrants that he has authority, and if this proves to be untrue because A has acted outside his authority C will be disappointed and unable to enforce the contract against P. In this situation C will sue A for breach of warranty of authority. This is explained more fully later in this chapter.

(iv) The link between P and C is a binding contract. A has arranged the contract, but the parties to it are P and C. In any dispute about it P will sue C, or C will sue P, but A is not involved in any way. The intermediary drops out of the dispute, leaving the parties to the contract confronting one another.

13.4 Subsequent Ratification of an Unauthorised Act

An agent will usually act within his authority, but if the relationship with his principal is well established he may occasionally act outside it, if he feels that the principal will subsequently ratify it. Imagine A, who is authorised to act for P in the purchase of pre-Columbian artefacts, to a limit of £2500. A particularly beautiful example of Inca gold work is auctioned and although the price climbs above £2500 he continues to bid and secures it for £2900. The principal would be perfectly entitled to reject the artefact, but in fact he ratifies the purchase and adds it to his collection. The unauthorised act has been ratified subsequently, making the contract sound.

The effects of subsequent ratification are as follows:

(*a*) The principal and the third party are now in contractual relations with one another and may sue and be sued on the contract.

(*b*) The agent cannot be sued by the third party for breach of warranty of authority, for his act has been accorded full authority.

(*c*) The principal cannot claim that the agent has exceeded his authority, for the principal has extended the authority far enough to cover the action on *this* occasion.

(*d*) The ratification only applies to the act already done, and does not extend the authority to cover a repetition of the act – which would be outside the agent's authority again.

(*e*) The agent will be entitled to his remuneration and to indemnity for the expenses incurred.

Some rules about ratification are as follows:

(i) The agent must contract expressly as an agent for a principal who is either named or described sufficiently for the other party to know that it is not the agent with whom he is making the contract. In such circumstances a contract made which is outside the agent's authority may be ratified subsequently. The principal is able to embrace the contract which his former limitation on the agent's authority had prevented, and he enjoys the benefits of it and assumes the duties under it. Such a ratification is not possible if the principal is not disclosed, for if a man keeps his intention to act 'locked up in his own breast', who is to know whether he did in fact act for the undisclosed principal? 'Civil obligations are not to be created by, or founded upon, undisclosed intentions.' (*Keighley Maxstead and Co. v. Durrant* (*1901*).)

(ii) The principal must exist when the contract is made. It is not possible for an act to be ratified subsequently if the principal did not exist at the time of the act. This frequently presents difficulties when a company is formed to take over an existing business. The benefits of the old business can only be secured for the new business if a management appointed in the interim period carries on the business until the legal formalities can be complete. At the moment of incorporation the company cannot ratify the acts done before incorporation to make them valid, nor can it accept as profits the profits earned in the interim period. The management which has been continuing the business is deemed to have acted as principal, and must make a contract with the new company to hand over its affairs. The profits made in the interim period must be treated as part of the capital transaction on taking over the business and they become part of the capital reserves, which are not available for distribution as profits to the shareholders. They are known as 'profits prior to incorporation'.

In *Kelner v. Baxter (1866)* the proposed directors of a company which had not yet been registered took delivery of wine purported to be sold to the company. They were held liable as principals, since the agents' acts could not be ratified subsequently. Having received the wine, they must pay for it. However, this case was subsequently distinguished by Lord Goddard from a case where the goods had not been delivered. In *Newborne v. Sensolid (Great Britain) Ltd (1954)* Lord Goddard held that a contract made with a non-registered projected company was a nullity, and not susceptible of subsequent ratification. Therefore the person who had signed quite clearly as the representative of the company and who had made it clear that he was not personally a party, could not be forced to accept the goods by the disappointed 'seller'.

The situation has now been clarified (but perhaps not improved) by S.36(4) of the *Companies Act, 1985*, which consolidates the rules of the *European Communities Act, 1972* into company law. It renders the agent liable for contracts made on behalf of an unformed company. This obviously protects innocent third parties, but leans over backwards in their favour. The agent therefore carries a serious personal responsibility in these situations and must be sure that his principal (presumably an intending director) is a worthy individual able to afford to honour the obligations entered into.

(iii) The principal must have capacity to contract at the time the act was done by an agent. In *Boston Deep Sea Fishing & Ice Co. Ltd v. Farnham (1957)* the case concerned the tax liability of an English company which was acting as an agent for a French company during the war. It was held that the English company was liable to pay tax locally on the profits accruing to the business, unless the French company as principals could ratify the English company's actions after the war. This the French company could not do as it was considered an alien enemy during the period of the war and lacked capacity to contract.

(iv) Subsequent ratification will be implied if a principal who has been informed of an act outside the agent's authority takes no action to reject the bargain made. If he uses goods obtained this will imply ratification of the act which procured them.

(v) Ratification must be of the whole contract, and not just the beneficial parts. The principal ratifies what the agent has done in its entirety. If this were not so, the other party would be left with something less than the bargain he thought he had concluded with the agent.

13.5 Breach of Warranty of Authority

An agent who purports to act on behalf of another impliedly warrants that he has the authority to make binding contracts on behalf of his principal. Remember that a warranty is an undertaking which, if broken, can lead to a claim for damages at the suit of the aggrieved party. It follows that if an agent acts without authority, so that there is no contract between his principal and the third party concerned, this third party will be entitled to bring an action for 'breach of implied warranty of authority' against the agent, provided the third party did not know of the lack of authority and has suffered loss as a result. This action is said to be quasi-contractual (quasi = almost). It cannot be brought in contract law, because there is no contract between A and C.

The agent's liability is said to be 'strict' – a term which means that he is liable even if he fully believed he had authority, or if the authority had been terminated without his knowledge by some circumstance such as the death or insanity of his principal. (*Yonge v. Toynbee,* (*1910*).)

13.6 The Duties of the Agent

The relationship between principals and agents is a fiduciary relationship (a relationship based on trust). McCardie, J, pointed out in *Armstrong v. Jackson* (*1917*) that the position of agent is confidential and readily lends itself to abuse. To meet this special situation the behaviour of the agent must be above reproach, and conform to strict rules. The duties of an agent may be listed as follows:

(*a*) To perform his duties in person, using ordinary skill and diligence, or if he purports to have special skills using those special skills as well. The rule which requires the agent to act personally is '*delegatus non potest delegare*' (a delegate cannot delegate). For example, it was held in *John McCann & Co. v. Pow* (*1974*) that a person who had been appointed a sole agent had no implied authority to appoint a sub-agent. However, this rule is relaxed to permit the agent to delegate for normal business reasons – for example, to a clerk or secretary: he does not have to do everything himself.

(*b*) To obey the lawful instructions of his principal, and in so far as he is not instructed on any particular point to act in the principal's best interests. If he fails to act in the best interests of his principal he will be liable to the principal for any loss that is suffered.

(*c*) To disclose to the principal all details of the agency, avoiding any conflict of interest with his principal. Thus, unless the principal was fully aware and agreeable to the situation, an agent may not buy the property of the principal.

(*d*) To maintain confidentiality about any matters communicated to him as agent, and not to disclose them to prospective third parties or anyone else. The relationship between principal and agent is a fiduciary relationship, depending upon mutual trust.

(*e*) To keep proper accounts of all transactions and render them to the principal on request. This includes a duty to keep the principal's property separate. Any failure to do so will raise a presumption that the property is the principal's, and it will be necessary for the agent to prove his ownership of any particular item, or of any money in a mixed account.

(*f*) To avoid any secret profits from the transaction. If the agency results in extra profits they must be disclosed to the principal.

13.7 The Duties of the Principal

The principal's duties may be listed as follows:

(*a*) A duty to pay the agreed commission or remuneration following from the contract. Where the remuneration is expressly stated it will be payable according to the contract. Where it is not expressly stated the court may imply that payment was intended in order to make the agency effective. This means that if the court holds that the parties could not possibly have intended the agent to act gratuitously, then payment must have been intended and this intention will be implied. The remuneration will then be what is reasonable in the circumstances.

The courts will not over-ride the terms agreed between the parties, even if the terms are extremely unfavourable to one party. Thus where it was agreed that the directors should determine the sum payable, and they failed to determine that any sum was payable, it was held that no remuneration could be claimed (*Re Richmond Gate Property Co. Ltd* (*1964*)).

(*b*) The duty to reimburse the agent for any expenses, losses or liabilities incurred as a result of the agency. This duty may arise from an express term in the contract or from a term which the court will imply in order to make the agency effective. This duty will require the principal to indemnify the agent for all expenses incurred by the agent acting within the scope of his authority, both actual authority and implied authority. Thus expenses or liabilities incurred as a result of some 'custom of the trade', known to the principal, must be reimbursed to the agent appointed to act for him. The test is whether the principal, had he acted for himself, would have incurred those same costs or liabilities.

The duty does not extend to circumstances where the agent acts outside his authority, or acts negligently or wrongly having failed to exercise the skills he purported to have. Nor will the agent be able to claim reimbursement of expenses incurred when acting in an illegal way.

(*c*) The question whether a principal has a duty not to prevent the agent from earning his commission is one that has exercised the courts to a considerable extent. Usually such cases arise in connection with the work of estate agents, where a principal may sell privately and thus prevent the agent earning his commission. The rule is that if such a term is expressed in the contract, or may be implied, the agent may sue his principal for the commission, but the courts will be unwilling to imply such a term (that the principal agrees not to do anything which prevents the agent from earning his commission) unless it is essential to give the contract business efficacy. Most contracts to sell property already have business efficacy without such a clause. The agent agrees to act to try to sell the property for the principal, and if he succeeds a commission will be earned. If the agent wishes to put in a more onerous clause, let him do so; he cannot normally expect the court to imply one for him. This illustrates two very important aspects of English law:

(i) Words do not always convey a correct impression – in this case the terms 'principal' and 'agent' give an impression that the principal is the stronger of the two. While this is true as far as contractual responsibility occurs, the principal (especially in the sale of landed property) is often less sophisticated than the agent, who handles such transactions every day. It is the agent who lays down the terms of the bargain between them. If he states those terms less clearly than he intended, so much the worse for him.

(ii) In interpreting contracts the courts will always interpret them strictly against the one who drew the contract up. This means they will interpret any clause in favour of this person in the narrower sense, rather than the wider sense. If the agent wishes to be paid commission whether the sale results from his own work or is the result of the principal's private efforts, let him say so in the contract. If he does not say so expressly, he cannot look to the courts to imply it. This is called the 'contra proferentem' rule.

13.8 The Agent as Servant or Independent Contractor

An employee frequently acts as an agent for his employer in the course of his employment, and as a result is in a dual capacity; he is both a servant of, and an agent for, the employer. This is important in certain circumstances because an employer is **vicariously liable** for the torts of his employees. The term 'vicariously liable' derives from the Latin (*vicarius* = substitute). The employer is required to substitute himself for the wrongdoer, his servant, as he is generally a more worthy target for a legal action than the servant. The classic case is *Lloyd v. Grace Smith*; the facts were as follows:

Lloyd v. Grace, Smith & Co. (1912). The appellant, a widow, sought advice from the respondents, a firm of solicitors of high repute, and in fact saw one Sandles, a managing clerk who conducted their conveyancing work without supervision. Sandles advised the appellant to sell two cottages and induced her to sign two documents which he said would enable the properties to be sold. The documents were in fact conveyances to Sandles and he dishonestly proceeded to dispose of the cottages to his advantage. **Held:** although the fraud was not committed for the benefit of the respondents, they were liable as Sandles had acted in the course of his employment. (Courtesy of *Cracknell's Law Students' Companion*)

The test is whether the servant performed the tort in the course of the employment, and to this extent the matter is really one for the law of master and servant and not the law of agency. The fact that the employee acts as an agent is incidental.

Where the person is an independent contractor, and definitely not the servant of the principal, the principal will not be liable for the torts, and the independent contractor will be the target for legal action brought by any aggrieved person. The test as to whether a person is an independent contractor or not is the question: 'Is this person instructed not only what to do, but how to do it?' If the individual is under the detailed control of the principal as to the manner in which he performs the work concerned he is probably a servant of the principal. If he is instructed what to do, but himself determines completely the manner in which the work should be done and the order of priority to be used between various tasks, he is probably an independent contractor. In *Mersey Docks and Harbour Board v. Coggins* the facts were as follows:

Mersey Docks and Harbour Board v. Coggins & Griffith (Liverpool) Ltd (1946). The question arose as to who was liable for the negligent act of a crane driver. The harbour authority, who let the crane to a firm of stevedores, employed, paid and had the power to dismiss him, but the conditions of hire stated that the crane driver should be regarded as a servant of the hirers (the stevedores). The stevedores were entitled to control the moving of the cargo but had no power to tell the driver how to work his crane. **Held:** the harbour authority were liable for the crane driver's negligence as they were entitled to give the orders as to how the work should be done. (Courtesy of *Cracknell's Law Students' Companion*)

13.9 The Doctrine of the Undisclosed Principal

Where an agent acts on behalf of a principal three possible situations may exist as to the arrangements between the agent and third parties:

(*a*) The agent may say 'In this matter I am acting for B, who is interested in . . .' etc. In this situation the third party knows who the other principal is, and is not under any illusions that he is contracting with the agent, for the agent has declared his agency.

(*b*) The agent may say 'In this matter I am acting on behalf of a principal, who wishes to remain anonymous.' Here again the third party knows that the agent is acting for someone else, and is not personally a party to any contract that may be concluded. The unsatisfactory part of this situation is that the third party does not know who the other principal is. It may be a little old lady of 90, with nothing but an old-age pension as resources. It may be the most powerful multinational in the country.

(*c*) The agent may not say anything at all about his agency, and lead the third party to conclude that he is contracting with a principal. In this situation, should anything go wrong, the third party may find that when he sues on the contract the person he believed to be principal says 'I was only acting as an agent; you must sue X.' The third party may then discover that X is a person of no resources, or (perhaps worse) is the most powerful multinational in the land.

The question arises whether it is fair for this undisclosed principal to become a party to a contract with a person who was ignorant of his existence at the time the contract was made. The courts have justified the view that it is fair, on the grounds of commercial expedience. In many contracts the parties do not mind who assumes the rights and duties upon the contract so long as the bargain made is honoured in every detail. To this extent it would contradict the principle that 'the courts will always uphold the reasonable expectations of businessmen' if the undisclosed principal was not allowed to step in and assume the benefits of, and the duties upon, the contract.

The doctrine of the undisclosed principal holds that where a person has contracted in his own name **in general terms** he may subsequently introduce oral evidence to prove that in fact he did not act on his own behalf but on behalf of some undisclosed principal. The phrase 'in general terms' means that he did not expressly state that he was the real and only principal. If the contract was made in terms which exclude the possibility of any other party being the principal, the undisclosed principal will not be allowed to enforce the contract. For example:

(*a*) Where the agent contracts as 'owner', a word without ambiguity, oral evidence cannot be admitted to vary the written evidence. In *Humble v. Hunter (1848)* an agent signed a charterparty in his own name, describing himself as **owner of the ship**. It was held that his undisclosed principal could not sue. If the agent contracts in some more general way – such as 'as a party interested in the ownership of . . ., etc.' – the oral evidence would have been permissible to explain the ambiguous term used.

(*b*) Where the personality of the parties is important – as where a particular skill is required and the third party contracted with the agent for the use of the agent's personal skills – the agent cannot then claim that he acted on behalf of another.

(*c*) Where the third party expressly inquired whether the agent acted for a particular third party, and was misled by a statement to the contrary, the undisclosed principal will not be allowed to enforce specific performance of the contract.

In *Said v. Butt (1920)* the defendant had specifically asked the agent whether he acted on behalf of Said, and had been told that he did not. A long-standing dispute between Said and Butt had led Butt (a theatre owner) to regard Said's presence at a 'first night' performance as undesirable. It was held that Said's action must fail; the 'personal element' was strong and Butt had no intention of entering into a contract with the undisclosed principal, who consequently could not intervene.

In all cases where the agent has acted in a manner which is not totally inconsistent with behaviour as an agent, the true principal may emerge from the shadows and exert his rights upon, and assume the duties under, the contract.

Further aspects of these matters are the legal effects that follow from an undisclosed agency. Until the principal is revealed the third party believes the agent to be the principal and may sue the agent. When the true principal is revealed the third party has a right to elect whom he will sue. He will naturally sue the most worthy, and this may not be the principal. If sued by the true principal the third party may set off against the claim all sums owed by the agent, and may use any defences available to him against the agent as defences against the principal.

13.10 The Termination of Agency

An agency may be terminated in the following ways:

(*a*) **By complete performance of the agent's function.** Thus when an estate agent appointed to sell a property completes the sale the agency comes to an end and the commission or other remuneration is paid.

(*b*) **By effluxion of time, when the agency is for a fixed term.** Normally a fixed-term appointment is a matter of express agreement between the parties. It is convenient where the parties are uncertain of one another's abilities, or where inflation may erode the arrangements made for remuneration. The expiry of the term gives an opportunity for reappraisal and re-statement of the terms of the appointment.

(*c*) **By voluntary discharge of the agency arrangement.** This occurs when the parties agree to discontinue the relationship.

(*d*) **By revocation or renunciation.** Generally speaking, if the principal gives notice to the agent of his intention to revoke the agency, or if the agent gives notice that he renounces the agency, the agency comes to an end. However, there are special cases where an agency is irrevocable on the part of the principal. For example, where the authority is coupled with an interest having been given to the agent in order that the agent may recover some loss previously suffered or some debt owed to him, the principal cannot revoke the agency. The fact that the authority was granted to benefit the donee in some particular way – and not just by earning a fee or commission for services rendered – means that it would be inequitable to allow the principal to revoke the agency.

(*e*) **By the death or bankruptcy of either party.** Agency is a personal contract between agent and principal and except in those cases where the agency is irrevocable the death of either party ends the contract between them. The death of the principal terminates the agent's authority, and even if he is not aware of the death any subsequent acts on behalf of the principal will lack authority. The agent may still claim from the estate for services rendered before the death occurred, but will not be entitled to commission on services rendered after death, unless the executors subsequently ratify the agent's acts.

Similarly, the bankruptcy of either party normally brings an agency relationship to an end. Bankruptcy is a form of incapacity which precludes the bankrupt from making further contracts, and consequently brings the agency to an end whichever party is affected.

(*f*) **By the mental disorder of either party.** The mental disorder of either party automatically ends the agency relationship. A mentally disordered agent can no longer act for his principal while a principal in the same situation is held to be unable to act for himself, and therefore unable to act through an agent. These rules do not present any difficulties, but difficulties can arise where an agent who acts for his principal who has become mentally disordered contracts on the principal's behalf with third parties who are unaware of the principal's disability. In such circumstances the law is somewhat unclear, and is under review at present. The agent has been held, in *Yonge v. Toynbee* (*1910*), to be liable for breach of warranty of authority, for in acting for the principal who had become insane they had impliedly warranted that they had authority. An earlier case, *Drew v. Nunn* (*1879*), concerned a principal whose wife had purchased goods as his agent during his temporary insanity. It was held that the principal could not claim that his wife's agency ceased entirely on the commencement of his insanity. Though her actual authority had ceased, she still had apparent authority to bind the principal.

(*g*) **By frustration.** As with all other contracts, an agency contract is liable to be frustrated by supervening events. Thus where the contract is rendered illegal, or impossible of performance, the agency comes to an end (see Chapter 11 for the doctrine of frustration).

The Effects of Termination. In general, the effects of termination are that the agent's actual authority ceases at once and he may no longer act for the principal. He may claim commission on work already performed before termination.

As explained in Fig. 13.1, the agency arrangement is a three-cornered one, in which third parties are brought into legal relationship with the principal as a result of the agent's action. The termination of the agency must be brought to the notice of third parties either known to be involved in negotiations with the agent or potentially likely to be involved. If the principal fails to give notice to third parties, or holds his agent out as having authority in any way on letterheads or similar documents, he will be liable to third parties who are misled.

13.11 Revision Test

Answers	*Questions*
–	**1.** What Latin rule is at the root of the law of agency?
1. *Qui facit per alium facit per se.*	**2.** What does it mean?
2. He who does something by another, does it himself.	**3.** What does this mean as far as the law of contract is concerned?
3. A principal can be brought into contractual relationships with another party as a result of the actions of his agent, and will be bound by them just as much as if he had made the contract himself.	**4.** What are the essential elements of agency?
4. (*a*) Appointment of the agent by the principal. (*b*) Negotiations by the agent with a third party. (*c*) The conclusion of a contract between the third party and the principal. (*d*) The agent is rewarded for his efforts. (*e*) Termination of the agency.	**5.** In what ways may one person become the agent of another?
5. (*a*) By express appointment. (*b*) By implication, as a result of repeated behaviour, or holding out of the person by the principal, to give the impression that he has appointed him. (*c*) By necessity – in a genuine emergency.	**6.** What was *Great Northern Railway* v. *Swaffield* (*1874*) about?

Answers	*Questions*
6. A horse arrived at a station and there was no one to meet it. The railway company lodged it at a livery stable overnight. **Held:** they were agents of necessity and were entitled to recover their charges from the consignee.	**7.** What is 'subsequent ratification' in the law of agency'?
7. It is the ratification of an act outside the agent's authority, to bring the act within the agency arrangement. The principal who ratifies in this way is bound by the contract made as if he had authorised it originally.	**8.** What is 'breach of warranty of authority'?
8. An action brought against an agent by a third party who has been disappointed to discover that the agent acted outside his authority and consequently the contract he believed he had made with the agent's principal is not valid.	**9.** List the duties of an agent to his principal.
9. (*a*) To perform the duties personally, using that degree of skill he purports to have. (*b*) To obey the principal's instructions and to act in the best interests of the principal at all times. (*c*) To disclose to the principal the full facts of the agency, and avoid any conflict of interest. (*d*) To maintain confidence about any matters disclosed to him. (*e*) To keep proper accounts and not to make any secret profit. (*f*) To keep the principal's property separate from his own.	**10.** What are the duties of the principal to his agent?
10. (*a*) A duty to pay the agreed remuneration. (*b*) A duty to reimburse the agent for any expenses incurred.	**11.** What is the doctrine of the undisclosed principal?

Answers	*Questions*
11. A doctrine which holds that if an agent has contracted with third parties in general terms he may subsequently introduce oral evidence to prove that he acted for an undisclosed principal, but if he contracts expressly as principal, in terms which do not admit of any ambiguity, he will be precluded from introducing the principal at a later date.	**12.** How may an agency be terminated?
12. (*a*) By performance; (*b*) by effluxion of time; (*c*) by voluntary discharge; (*d*) by revocation of the authority; (*e*) by renunciation by the agent; (*f*) by death, bankruptcy or mental disorder of either party; (*g*) by frustration.	**13.** Go over the questions until you are sure of all the answers. Then try some of the written questions in Appendix 1.

Part 4: Some Specialised Sections of Law

14
Contracts for the Sale of Goods

14.1 Development of the Law of the Sale of Goods

The sale of goods is a very ancient activity. In a modern advanced society the volume of goods that changes hands daily is enormous. Raw materials flow into our factories and finished goods pour off production lines. The distribution of these goods is a science in itself (physical distribution management) and their exchange, from manufacturer to wholesaler, to retailer, to consumer is the art of commerce.

Naturally disputes arise. The law of 'sale of goods' has a long history, beginning in the merchant courts outside the national systems of laws and later becoming part of English common law under the principle that the courts will always uphold the reasonable expectations of businessmen. Later the many rules of law developed in countless cases over the years were 'codified' by Parliament into the *Sale of Goods Act, 1893*.

The *Sale of Goods Act, 1893*. The test of a good Act of Parliament is that it should last a great many years without major amendment. The 1893 Act was a product of its age, a carefully drawn and fully debated bill became an enduring Act embodying all the rules of law about the sale of goods. Drawn in an age of triumphant capitalism it reflected the principles of that age, that '*laisser faire*' was the wisest policy. If businessmen are largely left to themselves they will do the best both for themselves, and for the nation. Thus the rules embodied in the *Sale of Goods Act, 1893*, could be avoided by contractual stipulations called 'exemption clauses' by which the merchant stated that he exempted himself from any duties implied under the Act. Such clauses were 'fair' because the other party who did not wish to accept them was free to go elsewhere, and obtain goods from the supplier's competitors. The Victorians believed strongly that all were equal before the law, and either party to a contract was free to strike a bargain in the most favourable terms for himself. This philosophy ignores the very real inequalities in bargaining strengths between the parties – for example, between monopolists and their customers who have no chance to go elsewhere. Powerful industrialists may easily escape liability for poor-quality goods supplied to consumers – who are frequently unsophisticated, unrepresented and too poor to employ lawyers to fight cases where the actual sum of money involved is small but the loss in proportion to the individual's total income is great.

Gradually pressure developed for a change of emphasis in the law towards the protection of the consumer, and following the Moloney Commission of 1962, which made 214 recommendations for improvements in the law, a succession of Acts was passed to improve the outdated 1893 Act. Finally the *Sale of Goods Act, 1979*, consolidated the new legislation by re-enacting the 1893 Act *as amended.* That the two Acts are very similar is a tribute to the enduring work of the Victorian legislators, but the modifications reflect the social legislation of the twentieth century and the improved status of the consumer in society.

The *Sale of Goods Act, 1979.* This Act forms the basis of the chapter which follows. As explained above, it is a consolidating Act, which re-enacts most of the rules of the 1893 Act and the new rules of later statutes to give in a single Act all the current statutory provisions. The reader is strongly urged to obtain a copy of the Act itself, although it is extensively quoted in the chapter. It is a particularly good Act to study as an example of the legislative process. Law students must become familiar with the format of Acts of Parliament, and discover for themselves the precision achieved by the legislature even in the most complex matters. Such detailed study highlights the problems faced by the courts in construing legislation and discovering the meaning of Parliament.

14.2 The Meaning of 'Goods'

The *Sale of Goods Act, 1979*, does not define 'goods', but in S.61, the 'interpretation' section, it states:

'Goods' includes all personal chattels other than things in action and money.

Chattels are items of property, and in law they are divided into 'chattels real' and 'chattels personal'. **Chattels real** refers to 'real estate' – landed property – which means leases of the use of land. **Chattels personal** are all other personal property. Since goods are stated to include all personal chattels other than things in action and money the list of items covered by the word 'goods' is very long – from a million tons of iron ore to a box of chocolates.

The rather awkward phrase 'things in action' means property which can only be recognised as property when it comes up for discussion in court. Thus a debt is a form of property which has no physical existence, though it may be represented by a piece of paper like an IOU or a promissory note. I may sell my debts to a debt collector – but it will not be a sale of 'goods'. 'Things in action' have traditionally been called '*choses in action*' but the 1979 Act set a precedent for doing away with obscure French and Latin terms, as we shall see later.

Money is the means for settling payments, and it would be contrary to common sense to call money 'goods' and talk of 'selling it' to others.

These items aside, all personal chattels are included in the term 'goods'. This is not the end of the definition, for the Act goes on to say that emblements (crops growing on the land which will come to fruition within a year), industrial growing crops (which take longer than a year) and '*things attached to or forming part of the land, which are agreed to be severed before sale or under the contract of sale*' are goods. If I sell you my beech trees, and you fell them and take them away, I have sold you a 'good' under the Act.

14.3 The Contract of Sale

S.2(1) of the Act says:

A contract for the sale of goods is a contract by which the seller transfers or agrees to transfer the property in goods to the buyer, for a money consideration called the price.

Implicit in this definition is the idea that the seller must be the owner of the goods, for no one can transfer the property in goods except the owner, or an agent acting on his behalf. The section goes on to say that there can be a contract of sale between one part-owner and another. A contract of sale may be absolute (**a sale**) or conditional upon the performance of some act, or the passage of time, in which case we have an **agreement to sell**. An agreement to sell becomes a sale after the elapse of the time or the fulfilment of the condition prescribed in the contract.

Capacity to buy and sell is regulated by the general law concerning capacity to contract (see S.3.1) but the Act makes a special point about necessaries. Even those with no capacity to contract must be able to obtain necessaries. The Act provides that minors, drunkards and those suffering from mental incapacity must pay a reasonable price for necessaries *sold* and *delivered* to them. Consequently such people could not be forced to pay an agreed contractual price if it was an unreasonable price. Necessaries are defined as '*goods suitable to the condition in life of the minor or other person concerned, and to his actual requirements at the time of the sale and delivery*' (S.3.3). This is of course the rule in the 'fancy waistcoats' case, *Nash v. Inman (1908)* – see page 87. Note that the minor is still not bound by the contract, so that even if goods were delivered to him he could refuse them and send them back. All that the section means is that if he takes delivery and uses the necessaries, he must then pay a reasonable price for them. A minor who is the *seller* cannot be held liable on a contract, for the general rule applies that all contracts made with minors are unenforceable under the *Infants Relief Act, 1874*.

The Form of the Contract. There is no special form for contracts of sale, unless required by some Act of Parliament – as, for example, the hire purchase regulations. Ordinary sales contracts may be made by word of mouth, in writing (with or without seal), partly in writing and partly by word of mouth and may be implied from the conduct of the parties.

The following contracts are not contracts of sale:

(*a*) *A contract of barter or exchange.* Since the definition of a sale refers to the payment of a 'price', a simple exchange of goods is not a sale of goods. However, since part-exchange is a common practice in some trades like the motor-vehicle trade, the courts have held that part-exchange is a sale if a significant proportion of the consideration is in money form.

(*b*) *A contract of hire*. Here the hirer obtains *possession* of the goods, but the property does not pass, and is not intended to pass.

(*c*) *A contract of hire purchase*. This is a contract of hire until the clause in the contract which stipulates how the hirer becomes the purchaser is fulfilled. Often this take place on the payment of the last instalment, or on the payment of a nominal sum of money added to the final instalment. Until that moment the hirer is not the buyer, and the property does not pass, so it is not a sale of goods.

(*d*) *A contract for the use of skill and materials*. When a customer approaches a tradesman to carry out work for him, some sort of goods are usually involved. The landscape gardener who lays my patio supplies paving stones and other materials. Am I really paying for these as goods, or as a part of the work at which he is skilled and I am not? Such questions can be difficult to decide, but in general they are not sales of goods, though in some respects – for example, an obligation to supply materials of merchantable quality – they are very similar. In *Robinson v. Graves* (*1935*) a contract under which Robinson, an artist, was commissioned to paint a portrait was held to be a contract for the use of skill and materials, and not a sale of goods, even though Robinson supplied the canvas etc.

(*e*) *Mortgages, pledges and charges*. Any transaction where goods are used as security for a loan are not 'sales of goods'. The 'seller' never intends to transfer the property in the goods to the person holding them as security, and the money paid is not the 'price', but the return of a loan, with interest.

The Subject Matter of the Contract. In any contract for the sale of goods, the goods which are the subject matter of the contract are prone to the same hazards as all goods. The Act therefore makes several stipulations about them, in SS.5, 6 and 7.

First, if the goods are actually in existence at the time the sale is made they are called 'existing goods'. If the contract is for the sale of goods which have yet to be manufactured or obtained, these are called 'future goods', and the contract operates as an agreement to sell.

If at the time the bargain is struck the goods in question have already perished without the knowledge of the seller (for example, they may have been lost at sea the night before), the contract is void (S.6). For example, in *Barrow, Lane and Ballard Ltd v. Phillip, Phillip and Co*. (*1929*) a contract for the sale of 700 bags of groundnuts was held to be void, since, unknown to the parties, 109 bags had been stolen.

Where the goods are specific goods and the seller has agreed to sell them, but before the time for delivery arrives they perish through no fault of the seller, the contract is again rendered void (S.7). Specific goods are goods identified at the time the contract of sale is made. Thus if I agree to sell you my Rolls Royce car next week, but it is wrecked before the time arrives, the contract is void. If I agreed to sell you 20 tonnes of wheat which I do not own, and some I am interested in is destroyed, this will not render the contract void for I can still obtain wheat elsewhere. Unless the wheat was actually identified at the time of the contract it will not be 'specific goods'.

The Price. The definition of a sale in S.2 specifically refers to 'a money consideration called the price'. Normally the price will be clearly fixed in the contract, or a manner for fixing it will be agreed. Thus a car might be sold according to the recommended price in a certain popular guide to the values of second-hand cars. A price may be determined by a course of dealing between the parties – though in present inflationary times this is less common than in years gone by. If no method for fixing the price is laid down, the buyer must pay a reasonable price, and this, the Act says (S.8.3), is always a question of fact dependent on the circumstances of every case.

S.9 says that where price is to be decided by valuation by a third party, and he cannot or does not make a valuation, the contract is void. If the goods have already been delivered to the buyer he must then pay a reasonable price.

Finally, if the third party cannot make a valuation because of the fault of either the buyer, or the seller, the disappointed party may bring an action for damages against the party at fault.

14.4 Conditions and Warranties in the Contract

It is this subject area of the Act which has been most subject to modification in recent years. A condition is of course a term in the contract which goes to the root of the contract. If a condition is broken it entitles the disappointed party to repudiate the contract and sue for damages. A warranty is a term in a contract which is not of the essence of the contract, but a less important term. Breach of warranty can lead to an action for damages, but the contract itself is left intact.

The sections of the Act about conditions and warranties are SS.10–15. They are very detailed, and must be studied from the Act itself. Because certain contracts made before the 1979 Act was passed may still become the subject of disputes in the courts, certain residual features of earlier law are preserved in Schedule 1 of the Act. These features have been ignored in the following description of the Act, the rules of which may be summarised as follows:

(*a*) *The time for performance* (*S.10*). Apart from the fact that the word 'month' is defined as meaning *prima facie* a calendar month, it is the terms of the contract which decide whether time for performance of the contract is of the essence or not. However, as regards payment, unless the contract stipulates that the time of payment is of the essence of the contract, it is taken not to be a condition but only a warranty.

(*b*) *Conditions treated as warranties*. Those who draw up contracts do not always use the correct terminology and in any dispute it is for the courts to construe the contract. Thus a stipulation that 'It is a condition of the contract, etc.' may in fact prove to be only a warranty, while a stipulation stated to be a warranty may be found by the court to go to the root of the contract, and in fact be a condition. For example:

Cehave NV v. Bremer Handelsgesellschaft m.b.h.; The Hansa Nord (*1976*). A written contract stated specifically that a shipment was to be made in good condition. Some of the goods were not in good condition and the buyers rejected the goods for breach of what they held to be a condition of the contract. **Held:** the buyers could not reject the goods as only a breach of warranty had been committed; the buyers were entitled to damages only.

If a contract is conditional upon some act being performed by the seller, and he does not perform it, the buyer may waive the condition, or treat it only as a warranty, and consequently may insist that the seller fulfils the contract.

If a contract of sale is not severable into parts and the buyer has accepted the goods or part of them, the breach of a condition by the seller cannot be used by the buyer as a reason for repudiating the contract, but may only be treated as a breach of warranty, unless the contract is absolutely clear that the buyer is entitled to treat the contract as repudiated.

(*c*) *Implied terms in the contract*. By S.12 of the Act and other sections a number of important terms are implied in the contract. There is an implied condition that the seller has the right to sell, or in an agreement to sell that he *will* have the right to sell, the goods at the time when the property is to pass. Except where the seller only purports to sell such rights as he, or a third person for whom he is acting, has, there is an implied warranty that the goods are free from any charge or encumbrance not disclosed to the buyer, and will remain so. There is also an implied warranty that the buyer will enjoy **quiet possession of the goods**, other than disturbances caused by any encumbrances revealed at the time of the contract. There is an implied warranty that all the encumbrances known to the seller will be revealed to the buyer, and that neither the seller, nor any third party named, nor anyone claiming under them, will disturb the buyer's quiet possession.

This implied condition is commonly broken by someone selling goods which are not his. Very often the seller will have stolen the goods in which case he will normally not be worth suing. However, the condition is broken when a hirer under a hire purchase agreement sells goods which are subject to the agreement. Another type of case was:

Niblett v. Confectioners' Materials Co. (*1921*). An American firm sold to an English buyer a quantity of tins of 'Nissley Brand' condensed milk. These were detained by the Excise authorities in England as constituting an infringement of the Nestlé trade mark. The buyer was forced to remove the offending labels, and re-sold at a loss. **Held:** this constituted a breach of the condition as to title implied by what is now S.12(1) of the *Sale of Goods Act, 1979*, and the buyer was entitled to damages. (Courtesy of *Cracknell's Law Students' Companion*)

Another interesting case, *Microbeads A.G. v. Vinhurst Road Markings* (*1975*), concerned a Swiss firm who had sold road-marking machines to an English firm. It turned out that the machines infringed a British copyright registered at a later date, and the copyright owners threatened to require the delivery-up or destruction of the machines – thus defeating the buyer's quiet enjoyment of the goods for the future. Although the sellers of the foreign machine were quite innocent in the matter, and it was therefore a question of which innocent party must suffer, the court held that the Act threw the load on the vendor.

(*d*) *Sales by description*. Where goods are described there is an implied condition that the goods will correspond with the description. If the sale is by sample as well as by description it is not enough if the bulk of the goods correspond with the sample if they do not correspond with the description, and even if the goods are exposed for sale and are selected by the buyer, this does not prevent the sale being a sale by description (S.13). For example:

Beale v. Taylor (1967). T advertised a car as a Herald 1961 Convertible, but in fact, unknown to T, it was two halves of wrecks welded together, one a 1961 model and the other of earlier date. **Held:** It did not comply with the description.

(e) *Quality and fitness for purpose*. The general rule is that there is no implied condition or warranty about the quality or fitness for purpose of goods supplied under the contract of sale. However, under S.14 there is an implied condition that goods sold *in the course of business* are of merchantable quality, unless defects are drawn to the attention of the buyer at the time, or the buyer examines the goods and ought to have noticed such defects. Where the buyer expressly, or by implication, makes it clear either to the seller, or in the case of hire purchase to the credit broker, that he requires the goods for a particular purpose and relies upon the seller's or credit broker's skill and judgement in choosing the goods, there is an implied condition that the goods supplied are reasonably fit for that purpose. This claim may be rebutted by proof that the buyer did not in fact rely on the seller's skill and judgement, or that it was unreasonable for him to have done so.

Thornett and Fehr v. Beers and Son (1919). T's representative went to B's factory to inspect glue, and was afforded every facility. He did not actually open any of the drums purchased. When it proved unsatisfactory T and F refused to pay. **Held:** There was no condition that the goods were to be of merchantable quality since an opportunity to examine the goods had been afforded.

In particular trades it is possible for implied conditions about quality or fitness for purpose to be attached to contracts by usage of the trade.

The term 'merchantable quality' means that goods are as fit for the purposes for which such goods are commonly bought as is reasonable in the circumstances, taking any description applied – and the price – into account.

(f) *Sale by sample*. Where goods are sold by sample there is an implied condition that the bulk of the goods will correspond to the sample, that the buyer will have a reasonable opportunity to compare the bulk with the sample, and that the goods will be free from any defect rendering them unmerchantable, which would not be apparent on reasonable examination of the sample (S.15). A case about sale by sample was:

Godley v. Perry (1960). Perry, who had supplied a defective catapult which injured G, brought in his wholesalers, X, as third parties, who brought in their wholesalers in Hong Kong, Y, as fourth parties. The sale to P had been made by sample. **Held:** X and Y were both in breach of S.15, the bulk of the goods were not up to the sample.

We see therefore that all these implied conditions and warranties offer some protection to the buyer of goods against unfair trading.

14.5 Effects of a Contract for the Sale of Goods

The whole purpose of a sale of goods is to transfer the ownership of goods from one person to another. There are two reasons why it is important to know when the property passes. First, all goods are at risk to some extent, and S.20 of the Act says that unless otherwise agreed, the risk passes when the property passes. Goods are at the seller's risk until the property passes to the buyer, and then they are at the buyer's risk, whether the actual delivery of the goods has taken place or not. Second, in normal circumstances the price may only be recovered by the seller once the property in the goods has passed to the buyer. For these reasons the Act tries to pinpoint the moment when the property passes from seller to buyer.

Closely associated with the property (ownership) is the title (right of ownership) which may be exerted in the courts by legal action. Generally speaking, no one can transfer ownership except the true owner or some agent acting on behalf of the true owner. The Latin rule '*nemo dat quod non habet*' (no one can give what he does not have) applies. However, in certain circumstances the transfer of goods to a third party by someone else other than the true owner may transfer a valid right of ownership. These cases are listed in the Act, as shown below.

The transfer of the property. Generally speaking, the property in goods passes from one party to another when the parties intend it to be transferred. The Act lays down a number of rules for determining the intention of the parties, but it first of all says that the property in goods which have not been ascertained cannot pass unless or until the goods are ascertained. Thus a sale of bulk oil stored in a tank at a tank farm with other supplies cannot pass to the buyer until it is separated off and identified as the subject matter of the contract, perhaps by being pumped into a delivery vehicle.

The rules for identifying the intentions of the parties as to the time at which the property is to pass are given in S.18. They are:

Rule 1. Where there is an unconditional contract for the sale of **specific goods** in a deliverable state, the property passes to the buyer when the contract is made, and it is immaterial whether the time of payment or the time of delivery, or both, is postponed. The important point here, which is not explained until we reach S.20, is that the risk *prima facie* passes with the property. Thus if goods sold by A to B at noon are destroyed by fire at 1 p.m. the loss is B's, even if the goods were still in A's possession, awaiting delivery. S.20 goes on to explain that if delivery was delayed due to the fault of a particular party, the risk lies with the party that is at fault. Also the duties of any party as bailee or custodier are not affected by the Act.

Rule 2. If the sale is conditional upon the seller doing something to the goods, the property does not pass until the seller has done it, and the buyer has notice of it.

Rule 3. If the seller has to weigh, measure or do some other act to determine the price the property does not pass until the thing is done and the buyer has notice of it.

Rule 4. When goods are on sale or return or on approval the property does not pass until the potential buyer signifies his approval or does some act adopting the transaction. For example, if A sends goods to B on approval and B sells them to C, this is an act which can be carried out only by the owner, and consequently B must have adopted the transaction. If the buyer does not signify his approval or acceptance of the transaction, but retains the goods without notice of rejection, the property will pass at the end of the time fixed for return of the goods, or – if no time was fixed – at the end of a reasonable time.

Rule 5. Where there is a sale of unascertained or future goods by description, and goods of that description are unconditionally appropriated to the contract by the seller with the assent of the buyer, or by the buyer with the assent of the seller, the property in the goods then passes to the buyer. If the seller delivers the goods to the buyer, or to a carrier, bailee or other custodier for the purpose of delivery to the buyer, and does not reserve the right of disposal, the goods are deemed to have been unconditionally appropriated to the contract, and the property has passed to the buyer.

A particular example of the difficulties in deciding whether the property has passed occurs in the carriage of goods by sea. It is quite common for goods to be shipped under a bill of lading which is made out in favour of the seller or his agent. This is *prima facie* taken to mean that the seller reserves his right to dispose of the goods. Where he then sends the bill of lading, with a bill of exchange drawn on the buyer, to the buyer the understanding is that if the bill of exchange is paid (or accepted for future payment) the property passes to the buyer and he may claim the goods from the ship. If he does not pay the bill of exchange or accept it for future payment, the buyer must return the bill of lading, and the property in the goods represented by the bill of lading does not pass to him.

The Transfer of the Title. S.21(1) of the Act embodies two important principles. First, it upholds the rights of the true owner. Anyone else purporting to transfer ownership cannot give a better title to the goods than he has himself (*nemo dat quod non habet*). Second, it seeks to protect commercial transactions by laying down that if the true owner's conduct leads a *bona fide* purchaser to conclude that he is engaging in a *bona fide* transaction he will get a valid title to the goods.

The title to goods is the right of ownership. Only the owner of goods can transfer the title to goods, except in special circumstances, which are listed in the Act. Apart from these circumstances the 'sale' of goods by a person who is not their owner does not transfer to the buyer any better title to the goods than the seller of them had, unless the true owner, by his conduct, is precluded from denying the seller's authority to sell the goods. This situation is called in law 'estoppel'. It is a situation where one party creates an impression which misleads the other party into taking an action which he would not have taken had he known the true facts. If the owner's deliberate conduct makes someone else appear to be the true owner, a person dealing with that 'apparent true owner' will obtain a valid title to the goods.

Eastern Distributors Ltd v. Goldring (1957). A person M, who had provided a car dealer C with documents enabling C to appear to be the true owner of a vehicle, was unable to deny the title of Eastern Distributors Ltd, who bought the car from C. M had regained possession of the car by hire purchase from ED Ltd, and sold it to Goldring. ED Ltd sought to recover it from Goldring. **Held:** M had no title to the car, and could not give one to Goldring, who was forced to surrender the car to ED Ltd. (*Note:* Since 1964 the *private buyer* of a motorcar in these circumstances has been protected, and Goldring would not today have to surrender the vehicle.) The case still illustrates the point of title, that he who deliberately creates an impression that another person has a valid title to goods, cannot later deny the title of someone who took the goods from that person in good faith, for value.

It is debatable whether negligent conduct or omission to do what ought to be done is enough to give rise to an estoppel, but it is possible.

The special circumstances listed in the Act in which an innocent third party does receive a valid title to goods transferred by a person who is not the true owner, are as follows (note that these are exceptions to the *nemo dat quod non habet* rule):

(*a*) *Sales by a factor or other mercantile agent.* A factor is defined in the *Factors Act, 1889*, as 'A mercantile agent having in the customary course of business as such agent authority either to sell goods, or to consign goods for the purpose of sale, or to buy goods, or to raise money on the security of goods.' The Act goes on to say that where such a person transfers goods, which are in his possession with the consent of the owner, to another person who acts in good faith, the transfer gives a valid title as if the factor had been expressly authorised to sell the goods.

Folkes v. King (*1923*). F. delivered a car to H., a mercantile agent, to sell at a specified price. H. sold to K. at a lower price, and absconded with the proceeds. F. tried to recover the car from K. **Held:** he could not do so. H. was in possession as a mercantile agent for the purpose of sale, and when he sold to K. he gave K. a valid title.

(*b*) *Sales under any other Act.* Sale under any Act of Parliament which permits the apparent owner of goods to dispose of them as if he were the true owner, gives a good title to the buyer.

(*c*) *Sales of goods distrained under a court order.* Auctioneers or bailiffs are clearly not the true owner but their sale of the goods with due authority gives a valid title to the buyer.

(*d*) *Sales in market overt* (open market), according to the usage of the market, by a buyer purchasing them in good faith without any notice of defect in title on the part of the seller give a valid title. This ancient part of our law is based on the idea that if we buy openly, where everyone can see, we are presumed to buy honestly. A market overt must be recognised by Royal Charter, or by statute, or by prescription (from long use) and operates from sunrise to sunset.

Bishopsgate Motor Finance Corporation v. Transport Brakes Ltd (*1949*). The hire purchaser of a motor vehicle took it to auctioneers to sell at Maidstone market. They could not sell the vehicle, but later the hire purchaser sold it privately in the market. **Held:** as the rules of the market permitted private sales if the auctioneer had failed to sell, it was a sale in market overt and the purchaser received a valid title.

(*e*) *Sales under a voidable title.* A voidable title is one which is the result of a misrepresentation, mistake as to the identity of the buyer or similar reason. The buyer has a title which can be disturbed by the seller should he discover the misrepresentation or deception. It must be distinguished from a void title, where the so-called seller has no right at all to the goods – as, for example, where he has stolen them. Such a title can never give a third party a valid title, but a voidable title may do so under S.23 of the Act.

The cases of *Cundy v. Linday & Co.* (*1878*) and *Lewis v. Averay* (*1972*) have already been referred to (see pages 118–19). Sales under a voidable title were at one time thought to be straightforward, since it was thought that the title could only be avoided if the original seller found the original buyer and gave notice that it was avoided. In *Car and Universal Finance Ltd v. Caldwell* (*1964*), however, it was held that if the original seller gave notice to the police of the improper conduct of the buyer, and made every attempt to publicise his intention to rescind the contract, the contract would be avoided and the second buyer could not be deemed to have taken the goods in good faith. This leaves the innocent third party in an exposed position. However, the re-enactment of the 1893 Act as the 1979 Act did nothing to remedy the situation and consequently the protection given to the innocent third party by S.23 is less helpful than formerly supposed.

(*f*) *Resale by a seller in possession.* A seller is frequently left in possession of goods, perhaps to repair them, or deliver them. A seller may also be left in possession of the document of title to goods. If the seller then disposes of the goods or the document of title again to an innocent third party taking them in good faith, the third party gets a valid title to the goods, and the original buyer must look to the original seller for satisfaction.

(*g*) *Resale by a buyer in possession after a sale.* This section (S.25) says that if a buyer is in possession of the goods or the documents of title and transfers them to a third party having no notice of a seller's lien or other right, the situation is the same as if the person making the delivery was a mercantile agent in possession of the goods. This is not of much practical interest because it does not really change the legal position. First, a buyer can always sell what he has bought. Second a lien is usually a possessory right to hold onto goods until payment, and is lost when possession is lost to the buyer. The unpaid seller is therefore left in an unsatisfactory position. This also applies to the situation where it is the document of title that is transferred, because S.47.2 specifically refers to the fact that when a document of title is passed to an innocent third party without notice of any unpaid seller's lien or right to stop the goods in transit, these rights are defeated.

S.25(2) goes on to say that a buyer under a conditional sale agreement is not to be regarded as a buyer. A conditional sale agreement is one made under the *Consumer Credit Act, 1974*, whereby a sale is made on condition that the property does not pass to the buyer until the last instalment is paid.

We can conclude that if the property in the goods has already passed to the buyer S.25 does not really have much effect. If the property has not passed the third party taking in good faith may not get a good title. Since the rule is that the situation is the same as that of a mercantile agent in possession of the goods with the consent of the owner, the third party will only get a good title if he buys in accordance with the rules – i.e. in the ordinary course of business from a person who appeared to be a mercantile agent.

(*h*) *Sale of a vehicle under hire purchase to a private buyer*. The *Hire Purchase Act, 1964* (Part III), which is still in force although the rest of the Act has been repealed, gives special protection to innocent third parties who buy a second-hand car unaware that it is not the property of the seller but is in his possession on hire purchase or conditional sales terms. It does not protect motor traders, who are able to check these things out through their professional associations. Where a *private buyer* buys a vehicle in good faith (S.27 of the Act) the effect is as if the ownership of the vehicle had become vested in the hirer or buyer immediately before the sale to the innocent third party, who thus gets a valid title to the vehicle and quiet enjoyment of it. The finance company or other true owner must now look to the customer who has sold the vehicle for satisfaction.

Once the good title of an innocent third party has been established, any subsequent action by the third party also gives a valid title:

Barker v. Bell (1971). A third party sold a car to a dealer, Bell, who sold it to another dealer, Barker, who was found in possession of the car by the original hire purchase company. Barker returned the car to them, and claimed the purchase price from Bell. **Held:** Barker need not have returned the car. The title acquired by Bell was good, and therefore Barker's title was good. The action therefore failed.

14.6 The Duties of the Seller in the Performance of the Contract

S.27 of the Act says 'it is the duty of the seller to deliver the goods . . . in accordance with the terms of the contract of sale'. The following points follow from this simple declaration, or from the wider body of law surrounding the sale of goods:

(*a*) The seller must fulfil his contractual obligations, both express and implied.

(*b*) The word 'delivery' has several implications. S.61 defines 'delivery' as 'the voluntary transfer of possession from one person to another'. The method of delivery and the place and time of delivery may be important.

(*c*) There are other legal aspects of the sale of goods, such as the possibility of tortious liability to third parties not directly involved in the contract, and the need to avoid misrepresentations, or the commission of crimes.

Express Contractual Duties

A seller may make express promises about quality, delivery and price, and certain other implied terms will be read into the contract under SS.10–15 of the *Sales of Goods Act, 1979*, as we have seen in Section 14.4 above. Both these sets of promises must be kept.

The seller must do what he promised to do. Express promises must be carried out exactly, unless the contract can be held to have been frustrated (see S.11.4), but in the absence of frustration any failure to perform the contract to any extent will give a right of action to the disappointed buyer. Whether the breach is of a condition of the contract or only of a warranty is for the court to decide (see S.14.4 above).

Liability to keep these promises is 'strict'. This means that the seller cannot exempt himself from responsibility by saying it is not his fault that some promise was broken. Even if every precaution is taken the seller will be liable to the buyer for any damage or loss that results, though he may have a right of action subsequently against the person at fault. In *Frost v. Aylesbury Dairy Co. Ltd* the facts were as follows:

Frost v. Aylesbury Dairy Co. Ltd (1905). The defendant dairy company supplied milk to the plaintiff, using every possible precaution to ensure it was pure. The plaintiff's wife died of typhoid fever as a result of drinking the milk. **Held:** the plaintiff clearly relied on the seller's skill and judgement in supplying milk for domestic consumption. They were in breach of S.14.1. Although they had taken every precaution they were still liable for all the losses suffered, which included the plaintiff's loss of consortium.

Implied contractual duties. These have already been outlined in S.14.4 above. Their effect is to ensure that the buyer gets what he wants: goods of merchantable quality fit for the purpose for which they were intended free of any charge or encumbrance.

Statutory Requirements about Performance of the Contract

Delivery. S.28 of the Act says that unless otherwise agreed delivery of the goods and payment of the price are concurrent conditions of the contract. Each party must be ready and willing to fulfil his part of the bargain at the same time.

Some rules for delivery are laid down in S.29:

(i) It is a question of fact in every contract whether it is the buyer who shall collect the goods or the seller who shall send them.
(ii) If no agreement was reached then the place of delivery is the seller's place of business, or his home address, or any other place where the specific goods are known to be.
(iii) If the seller is to send the goods to the buyer but no time limit has been given, then the time allowed is a reasonable time.
(iv) Where the goods are in the hands of a third party there is no delivery to the buyer until the third party acknowledges that he holds the goods on the buyer's behalf.
(v) Delivery must be made at a reasonable hour.
(vi) Unless otherwise agreed, expenses of delivery must be borne by the seller.

Delivery of the wrong quantity. Where the wrong quantity is delivered the rules are as follows (see S.30), but if there is a special usage of the trade on such matters it may be held to apply:

(i) If less than the correct quantity is sent the buyer may reject the goods, but if he accepts them he must pay for them *pro rata*.
(ii) If the seller sends more than the correct quantity the buyer may accept the whole consignment, or accept the correct quantity and reject the rest, or he may reject the whole consignment. If he accepts the whole consignment he must pay *pro rata* for the extra supplies.
(iii) If the seller sends a mixture of goods the buyer may accept only those included in the contract, and reject the rest or he may reject the whole consignment.

Delivery by instalments. On instalment deliveries the Act says (S.31) that unless otherwise agreed the buyer is not bound to accept delivery by instalments. Where delivery by instalments is agreed, and a dispute arises about non-delivery (or non-acceptance) of one instalment, it is necessary to look at the whole contract to see whether the breach is a breach of the whole contract or a severable breach giving rise only to a claim for compensation.

Delivery to a carrier. If a seller has to deliver the goods to a carrier this is deemed to be (*prima facie*) delivery to the buyer. The contract of carriage is between the carrier and the owner of the goods, and the seller is the agent of the buyer in effecting this contract. He must therefore make the contract in such a way as is reasonable 'having regard to the nature of the goods and the other circumstances of the case'. Failure to do so may lead to the buyer rejecting the idea that the goods were properly transferred to him. If insurance is required for carriage by sea the seller must notify the buyer in time for him to insure, and if not they are at seller's risk during the sea transit.

Goods delivered to a distant place. If the seller agrees to deliver to a distant place at his own risk this does not apply to deterioration of the goods incidental to the transit (unless this is agreed specifically).

The right to examine the goods. A buyer is entitled to a reasonable time to examine the goods, to determine whether they are in accordance with the contract.

Other Requirements

Absence of misrepresentation. Misrepresentation has been dealt with elsewhere in this book, but the seller of goods frequently misrepresents them. The difference between a mere 'puff' and a statement liable to mislead the buyer and induce the purchase of goods is a fine one, and an action for misrepresentation is frequently possible.

Tortious liability. Any seller of goods is in a contractual relation with the buyer, but has a general liability in tort to any third party injured or suffering loss as a result of defective goods. Liability in tort is not strict, and therefore the plaintiff must prove the point. The action must also be brought against the negligent person, and this may not always be the actual seller, but someone further back in the chain of production, distribution and exchange. The classic case is *Donaghue v. Stevenson* (*1932*), where the person injured was not the buyer, but the buyer's friend, and the negligent person was not the seller, a retailer, but the manufacturer who had supplied the seller. The case is fully discussed later (see page 336).

Criminal liability. Criminal liability for the sale of defective goods exists under a great many Acts of Parliament. It is an offence to sell unsafe motor vehicles under the Road Traffic Acts, or unsafe machinery under the Factories Acts. Under the *Consumer Safety Act, 1978*, the Government is empowered to make regulations about the sale, hire, etc., of any goods which the Secretary of State for the appropriate Department deems to be unsafe. Such regulations are used to prohibit further sales of goods found by experience to be dangerous – such as children's cots which have caused cot deaths. The Act also permits those injured by a breach of safety regulations to recover damages for breach of the statutory duty.

The most important of these Acts is the *Trade Descriptions Act, 1968*, which is discussed separately in S.14.11 below.

14.7 Exclusionary Clauses in Contracts

In the *Sale of Goods Act, 1893*, it was possible to exclude any or all of the rights, duties and obligations under the Act by express agreement in the contract or by a custom of the trade. This was in line with the view at that time that both parties to a contract were equally strong in the eyes of the law when making bargains. Today the law has been changed to help consumers in particular, who tend to be the weaker parties in any bargain. Anyone attempting to exclude liability must surmount a number of obstacles placed in his way by the *Sale of Goods Act, 1979*, and the *Unfair Contract Terms Act, 1977*. S.55 of the *Sale of Goods Act, 1979*, repeats the wording of the 1893 Act but mentions the following points:

(*a*) An express condition or warranty does not negative a condition or warranty implied by the 1979 Act unless it is inconsistent with it. An exclusion clause must therefore be worded clearly if it is to negative the intention of the Act.

(*b*) S.55 is stated to be subject to the *Unfair Contract Terms Act, 1977*.

The Unfair Contract Terms Act, 1977

This Act gives a considerable protection to consumers who are parties to a contract for the sale of goods, but much less protection to businessmen actually engaged in trade with one another, since here they may be held to be equally sophisticated and legally advised.

S.6 says that breaches of obligations under S.12 of the *Sale of Goods Act, 1979* (about title and quiet enjoyment of the goods), and S.8 of the *Supply of Goods* (*Implied Terms*) *Act, 1973* (the same thing in relation to hire purchase), cannot be excluded by an exclusion clause in the contract. Obligations under SS.13, 14 and 15 of the 1979 Act cannot be excluded as against any consumer, and this also applies to SS.9, 10 and 11 of the 1973 Act (the same regulations as applied to hire purchase).

As regards other businessmen, S.12 cannot be excluded but the other sections can be excluded if the seller can show that this is reasonable. Note, however, that these rules only apply to implied conditions and warranties under the Act; express statements can be excluded by a clause, even in a consumer sale – though one wonders why they should be made at all in that case. Even so, they will be caught by S.2 of the Act, which says that no exclusion clause can operate to exclude liability for negligence causing death or injury, and as far as other loss or damage is concerned only succeeds in excluding liability if it is reasonable in the circumstances.

S.3 of the Act deals with the situation where one party is a consumer, or deals with the other party under a set of Standard Terms and Conditions. In these circumstances an exclusion clause cannot be inserted to exclude liability for breach of contract, or less than full performance unless it is reasonable. The presumption is that it is invalid unless the seller proves it is reasonable. Although such contracts are not always 'sales of goods' contracts, S.3 does cover many situations where goods are supplied and attempts are made to exclude liability for breach of express promises made earlier.

Where goods pass as a result of a contract not subject to the law of sale of goods or hire purchase (such as a contract for services and materials) S.7 says that terms purporting to exclude liability for the quality, fitness for purpose, description or correspondence with sample are void if the contract is with a consumer, and if the contract is with another trader the term is only valid in so far as it is reasonable. Terms about the seller's right to transfer ownership or give possession or give quiet possession are only valid in so far as they are reasonable.

14.8 The Duties of the Buyer in the Performance of the Contract

The buyer's duties are to accept the goods and pay for them (S.27, *Sale of Goods Act, 1979*). He has a right to a reasonable time to examine the goods to determine whether they are in accordance with the contract (S.34).

Acceptance of the goods is deemed to take place when the buyer intimates to the seller that he accepts them, or (*a*) when they are delivered to him and he does some act which is inconsistent with the seller's ownership of them (like selling them to someone else) or (*b*) he retains the goods for a reasonable time but does not intimate to the seller his acceptance of them.

The buyer is not bound to return goods he does not accept; he only needs to intimate to the seller his refusal to accept (S.36).

The buyer is liable for any costs or losses incurred if he fails to take delivery within a reasonable time from a seller ready and willing to deliver the goods (S.37).

14.9 The Remedies of the Buyer

Breach of Contract. Failure to deliver the goods is a breach of contract by the seller. The disappointed buyer is entitled to damages for non-delivery, and the measure of damages is the loss directly and naturally resulting from the seller's breach of contract. If there is an available market for the goods the damages is the difference between the price the buyer must pay in that market and the contract price. The time (which may be important when prices are under discussion) is the time when they ought to have been delivered, or if no time was stated the time of refusal to deliver (S.51, 1979 Act). The market must be available, not half a world away.

Specific Performance. Where the goods are specific, or ascertained, goods the court may order specific performance of the contract. This is an equitable remedy which requires the seller to deliver up the goods, and removes his option to retain them and merely pay damages (S.52).

Breach of Warranty. Where there is a breach of warranty, or a breach of condition which the buyer elects to treat as a breach of warranty, the buyer is not entitled to reject the goods, but may commence an action for damages for breach of warranty or for reduction of the price payable. The measure of damages for the former is the estimated loss following from the breach; the damages for the latter is the difference in value between goods in perfect condition and those in the condition as supplied (S.53).

Breach of Condition. Where there is a breach of condition the buyer may treat it as only a breach of warranty, and insist that the contract is still performed. Alternatively, he may reject the goods and treat the contract as terminated. Whether the term was in fact a condition of the contract, or only a warranty, is for the court to decide, but certain implied terms in SS.12–15 are stated to be conditions, and an express term of the contract which was of a serious nature would be upheld as a breach of condition.

14.10 The Remedies of the Unpaid Seller

The unpaid seller of goods has several rights. The Act defines an 'unpaid seller' to include not only the actual seller, but anyone in the same position, such as an agent of the seller or a consignor or other agent who has become liable for the price.

The position arises when the whole of the price has not been paid or tendered, or when a bill of exchange is dishonoured. In these circumstances the unpaid seller may:

(*a*) Exercise a lien on the goods to retain them in his possession until payment is received.

(*b*) Stop the goods in transit if the buyer is insolvent. This was formally called 'stoppage *in transitu*' but the 1979 Act has anglicised this to stoppage in transit.

(*c*) A limited right of resale.

These points need a little explanation, and a further development (which is not part of the 1979 Act) is the use of:

(*d*) Romalpa clauses.

(*a*) **The Lien on the Goods** (pronounced to rhyme with the boy's name Ian). A lien is a right to retain possession of the goods until payment or tender of the price. This right may be exercised where no period of credit has been stipulated, or where the period of credit has expired, or where the buyer is known to be insolvent. The right is lost (*a*) when the goods are delivered to a carrier or other custodier without the rights of disposal being reserved, (*b*) where the buyer or his agent lawfully obtains possession of the goods, or (*c*) by waiver.

(*b*) **Stoppage in Transit.** An unpaid seller who knows that his buyer has become insolvent may stop the goods in transit – that is, resume control over them and retain them until payment or tender of the price. The Act lays down when goods are deemed to be in transit: this is from the time when the goods are handed to the carrier, or other bailee or custodier, until the buyer or his agent takes delivery of them. If the buyer or his agent obtains delivery before their arrival at the stated destination the transit is at an end. If the goods arrive at destination and the carrier acknowledges that he holds them on the buyer's behalf, the transit is at an end even though they are still in the carrier's possession. If the buyer rejects the goods the transit is not at an end. If the carrier wrongfully refuses to deliver the goods to the buyer or his agent the transit is at an end, and the goods cannot be stopped in transit. If goods are delivered to a ship it depends upon the facts of every case as to whether the master holds them as carrier, or as agent for the buyer, as to whether the goods can be stopped. If part of the goods has been delivered the balance can still be stopped in transit, unless delivery of the first part was made in such a way as to show an agreement to give up possession of the whole consignment.

Stoppage is effected by repossessing the goods or by giving notice of the claim to stop the goods to the carrier or other bailee in possession. Notice may be given to the actual custodier or his principal but notice to the principal is ineffective unless, given reasonable diligence, he is able to communicate it to his servant or agent in time to prevent delivery. The carrier of goods stopped in transit must deliver them to, or according to the directions of, the seller, who will bear all the expenses involved.

A sub-sale by the buyer to a third party does not defeat the unpaid seller's right of stoppage in transit, unless the seller has agreed to it. However, where a document of title has been lawfully transferred to an innocent third party acting in good faith and for value, the right to stop the goods is defeated. This means that with such a sale the third party has a valid right to the goods, but where the documents were only pledged the right of lien can still be exercised after the pledgee's rights have been satisfied.

(*c*) **The Right of Resale.** Stoppage in transit or the exercise of a lien does not rescind the contract. If the unpaid seller gives notice to the buyer of his intention to resell, and the buyer does not pay the price within a reasonable time, the seller may resell and claim any difference in proceeds from the buyer. If goods are perishable he may resell at once. If in the original sale the seller reserved the right to resell if the buyer defaulted, the seller may resell at once and still sue the buyer for breach of contract.

Any third party who buys goods from the seller who has exercised a lien or right of stoppage in transit gets a good title to the goods, even though the seller had no right to sell. The seller will be liable to the original buyer for non-delivery if he offers to pay for the goods.

(*d*) **Romalpa Clauses.** Romalpa clauses take their name from a 1976 case entitled *Aluminium Industrie Vasssen B.V. v. Romalpa Aluminium Ltd.* The contract between these two companies had inserted into it a complex clause which entitled the sellers (if unpaid) to claim ownership of the material they had supplied to Romalpa Aluminium Ltd even after the property had passed to the buyer, and even after it had been manufactured into other goods. The rights went even further, stating that even if the goods so manufactured were sold to third parties the debts owed by these customers to Romalpa should be transferred to Aluminium Industrie Vaassen, the original suppliers of the materials from which the goods were made. When Romalpa Aluminium Ltd became insolvent all these claims were upheld. It follows that such clauses have now been adopted by many suppliers to give additional rights to the unpaid seller.

This wide adoption of Romalpa clauses has led to several legal actions, often between the seller which inserted the clauses and the receivers of bankrupt firms or the liquidators of companies. Without going too deeply into the case law on this complex issue the following rules seem to have been established:

(i) If the clauses are worded in such a way as to require the buyer to store the raw materials or finished goods separately, this implies that ownership has not passed until the goods are paid for, and may therefore be recovered by the seller and are not to be included in the realisation of the assets by the receiver.

(ii) If the clauses specifically create a fiduciary relationship (one of trust) between the buyer and the seller so that the buyer is under a duty to keep a separate record of goods sold to third parties (either the actual goods supplied by the seller or manufactured products embodying the materials supplied) then this imposes a duty on the buyer to account (for the proceeds of the sub-sales) to the original supplier, and gives a prior claim over other creditors,

(iii) The wording of all such clauses is crucial and varies with every case. A case very releveant to the Sale of Goods Act S.25 was *Four Point Garage Ltd v. Carter (1985)*. Carter purchased a car from a motor dealer Freeway (Cougar) Ltd, which they had obtained from Four Point Garage Ltd. When Freeway went into liquidation Four Point Garage Ltd tried to reclaim the car from Carter, who had paid for it, on the grounds that Freeway had not paid them, and therefore Carter could not get a good title from Freeway. It was held that the wording of the clauses was inadequate to interfere with the right of title gained by the innocent third party buyer of the car, who had bought in the ordinary course of Freeway's business as a motor dealer. In another case – *Clough Mill v. Martin (1984)* – the Appeal Court decided that the receiver's argument that the Romalpa Clause merely established a charge over the materials was incorrect. The clause clearly reserved the property in the materials supplied, and entitled the seller to enter the buyer's premises to repossess the materials if unpaid for. This the receiver refused to allow. The Court ordered that they must be allowed to re-possess the material.

Other Rights of the Seller. The seller of goods who has not been paid may bring an action against the buyer for the price. If the price was due to be paid on a certain date the seller may bring an action for the price even though the property has not passed and the goods have not been appropriated to the contract.

If a buyer refuses to take delivery the seller may bring an action for non-acceptance of the goods. The measure of damages is the estimated loss directly and naturally arising from the buyer's breach of contract. If there is an available market it will be the difference between the market price and the agreed contract price.

14.11 The *Trade Descriptions Act, 1968*

Traditionally the sale of goods has been a private contractual matter and the question of liability for selling defective goods was resolved by a civil action brought by the aggrieved party. In recent years a number of Acts of Parliament have made it a criminal offencc to supply defective goods, in the interests of public safety. For example, the *Food and Drugs Act, 1955*, makes it an offence to supply food unfit for human consumption, and the *Road Traffic Act, 1972*, makes it illegal to sell a motor vehicle or trailer which is unroadworthy. These are criminal matters for which the offender is prosecuted.

While such Acts deal with particular classes of goods, the *Trade Descriptions Act, 1968* (as amended), is a general Act applying to all who trade in goods, (and offer services). Since it is the description of goods which most consumers take into account when making purchases, the misdescription of goods misleads the public, who may be put to considerable expense in bringing a civil action to redress their grievances. To discourage the practice it became a crime, under the 1968 Act, to apply a false trade description to any goods or to supply or offer for sale goods to which such a false description had been applied.

Originally the Act was purely of use to reduce crime; the Trading Standards Officers would initiate prosecutions against offenders, and the result was a fine or imprisonment. This left the victim to sue for the compensation to which he felt entitled. Later, under the *Powers of Criminal Courts Act, 1973*, courts were empowered to make compensation orders up to £1000 to compensate victims and reduce the need for separate civil actions.

Defences to Prosecution. It is a defence to any proceedings to show: (i) that the description complained of was due to (*a*) a mistake, (*b*) an accident, (*c*) reliance upon information supplied by another person, (*d*) the act or default of another person, or (*e*) some other cause beyond the accused's control; and (ii) that the person accused took all reasonable precautions and exercised due diligence to avoid the commision of such an offence by himself or any person under his control.

14.12 The *Supply of Goods and Services Act, 1982*

This Act might be said to set the seal on recent legislation to control all aspects of the relationships between consumers and those who supply them with goods and services. What it does is carry the ideas developed in recent years about the sale of goods into related fields where similar activities take place, such as the hire of goods and the provision of services. It is concerned with three main areas:

(*a*) *The transfer of property in goods* (other than sales of goods, hire purchase of goods, redemption of trading stamps by goods, transfers of goods by deed as a gift and transfers concerned with mortgages, pledges and charges) (SS.1–5 of the Act).

(*b*) *Contracts for the hire of goods.*

(*c*) *The supply of services* (but this does not apply to personal service or apprenticeships).

In all these cases the Act provides that the implied terms about title, quality, fitness for purpose, description and sample which we are familiar with in the sale of goods shall also apply to the supplies of goods and services. The effect is that however goods are supplied or transferred in England, Wales and Northern Ireland the implied terms are set out in statutory form and consumers cannot be deprived of their rights in these matters by an exclusionary clause. A contract for the transfer of property in goods is affected even if part of the contract is about services. Furthermore the 1982 Act inserts a new clause 3A into the *1977 Unfair Contract Terms Act* to prevent exclusionary clauses being used to exempt those transferring property from liability for breach of the obligations in the 1982 Act. In the case of services the Act sets out in statutory form certain implied terms which apply to most contracts for the supply of services. These are:

(*a*) that the supplier will carry out the service with reasonable care and skill.

(*b*) that the supplier will carry out the service within a reasonable time (and what is reasonable is a question of fact in every case).

(*c*) that the customer will pay a reasonable charge (and what is reasonable is always a question of fact in every case).

However, in the case of services, it is permissible for the parties to agree that these implied terms shall be excluded or varied by express agreement, or a course of dealing between the parties, or such usage as binds both parties to the contract. However such an exclusionary clause would be subject to the test of reasonableness laid down in the *Unfair Contract Terms Act, 1977*. It is for the trader to prove that the clause is reasonable – not for the consumer to prove that it is unreasonable.

This Act seems to bring to an end the long series of legislation about consumer affairs which began with the Maloney Commission in 1962.

14.13 A Note on the Recodification of Statutes

The enactment of the *Sale of Goods Act, 1979* after many years when the *Sale of Goods Act, 1893* was the definitive statute raises the question of whether all the case law of the earlier period is now obsolete and redundant. While a statute is passed to recodify the law, eliminating any errors or unsatisfactory aspects of earlier statutes, it cannot incorporate every detail of earlier *ratio decidendi*, and certainly not *obiter dicta*. Such 'sayings by the way' may therefore still be of interest, and the cases in which they were made are therefore not entirely redundant. It is precisely this aspect of case law which distinguishes English law from other systems, and gives it its rich and intricate texture.

14.14 Revision Test

Answers	*Questions*
–	**1.** Which Act controls the sale of goods?
1. The *Sale of Goods Act, 1979*.	**2.** What are 'goods'?

Answers	*Questions*
2. 'Goods' includes all personal chattels other than 'things in action' and money.	**3.** What is a contract for the sale of goods?
3. One where the seller transfers or agrees to transfer the property in goods to the buyer, for a money consideration called the price.	**4.** Who has capacity to buy and sell?
4. Capacity is the same as for other contracts, but minors, drunkards and those of unsound mind can make valid contracts for necessaries – but they need only pay a reasonable price.	**5.** What was *Nash* v. *Inman* about?
5. The 'fancy waistcoats' case, in which it was established that if an infant has adequate clothing, etc., already, such clothing, etc., is not a necessity.	**6.** Which contracts similar to sales are *not* sales?
6. (*a*) Barter; (*b*) hire; (*c*) hire purchase; (*d*) contracts for skill and materials; (*e*) mortgages, pledges and charges.	**7.** What is S.12 of the Act about?
7. The seller's right to sell and the buyer's quiet enjoyment of the goods.	**8.** What is S.13 about?
8. Sales by description.	**9.** What is S.14 about?
9. Quality, fitness for purposes and reliance upon the seller's skill and judgement.	**10.** What is S.15 about?
10. Sales by sample.	**11.** What is meant by 'an implied condition' or 'an implied warranty'?
11. Although the condition or warranty was not actually expressed in the contract the court will infer that it was, because no sensible person would have engaged in the contract unless it had been.	**12.** When does the property in goods pass?

Answers	*Questions*
12. When the parties intended it to pass. It cannot pass until the goods are ascertained goods.	**13.** What are the five rules for determining the intention of the parties?
13. *Rule 1:* Specific goods in a deliverable state pass when the contract is made, even when payment or delivery are postponed. *Rule 2:* If the seller has to do something the property passes when he has done it and the buyer has notice of it. *Rule 3:* If the seller has to weigh, measure, etc., it does not pass until he has done it and the buyer has notice. *Rule 4:* If goods are on approval the property passes when approval is given, or when the buyer does some act only consistent with ownership which adopts the transaction. If the buyer does nothing the property passes at the end of the fixed time, or in a reasonable time. *Rule 5:* If the goods are unascertained or future goods, and they are produced and appropriated to the contract with the knowledge of both parties, the property passes.	**14.** What is the title to the goods?
14. The right of ownership.	**15.** Who can transfer the title?
15. Only the owner, except in special cases.	**16.** What are the special cases?
16. (*a*) Sales by a factor or mercantile agent; (*b*) sales under distraint; (*c*) sales under an Act of Parliament; (*d*) sales in market overt; (*e*) sales under a voidable title; (*f*) resale by a seller in possession.	**17.** What is stoppage in transit?

Answers	*Questions*
17. It is the right of an unpaid seller to stop goods in transit and divert them to some other destination than the buyer's premises.	**18.** What are Romalpa clauses?
18. Clauses inserted into a contract which give an unpaid seller rights not only over the goods still unpaid for, but also over any goods into which they have been manufactured, or over the moneys to be earned from the sale of such goods.	**19.** Go over the questions again until you are sure of all the answers. Then try some of the written questions in Appendix 1.

15
Insurance

15.1 The Nature of Insurance

Insurance has an ancient history, but at present the insurance industry is under considerable pressure to haul itself into the twentieth century, or perhaps the twenty-first century. For example, the 1978 *Report on Marine Insurance*, produced by the committee on shipping of UNCTAD, pin-pointed many weaknesses in the 'ancient document' used in marine insurance for over 350 years, and called for an international regime of law and practice in this field. The report, as we shall see, has produced striking improvements in the documents used, though not as yet an international regime of law and practice.

The essence of insurance is that we live in a dangerous world, where 'fate' may at any time knock on our doors. In such circumstances it is wise to reduce risks as much as possible. The best way is to find someone who will bear our risks for us. This is what **insurers** do. **Lloyds of London**, a particularly experienced institution in the risk-bearing field, calls its risk-bearing members **underwriters**, so that the terms 'insurers' and 'underwriters' have the same meaning. Insurance is the bearing of risks by specialists in risk-bearing, so that ordinary businessmen operate more confidently, 'and losses fall rather easily upon many, than heavily upon a few'.

The main branches of insurance are as follows:

(*a*) Life assurance
(*b*) Fire insurance
(*c*) Marine insurance
(*d*) Accident insurance
(*e*) Liability insurance

Some of these will only be dealt with briefly in this book, which is more directly concerned with business aspects of insurance.

The words 'insurance' and 'assurance' are really interchangeable, and at least one London company is seeking to put an end to any confusion by using the word 'insurance' only, and calling the one insured the 'insured' and not the 'assured' – the traditional term. The only difference traditionally is that one event (death) occurs for us all and therefore is assured for everyone. Life assurance is therefore traditionally used as a description for life cover. Other types of loss are not so definite: we may never have a fire, or a burglary, or an accident, but we shall surely die.

The consideration for undertaking to provide cover for any risk is called the **premium**. This may be a lump sum payment or a succession of payments. The premiums form a pool of reserves, which is invested to earn further income that is added to the pool. Valid claims are settled by compensation payments from the pool. The adequacy of reserves is always an important consideration for insurers, but provided reserves are adequate profits may be extracted by the insurers as a reward for their activities. It is the reduction of the heavy losses which fall upon individuals in the real world into a wider loss spread over the whole population in the form of premiums paid, that makes insurance such a sound system for risk-bearing.

Reinsurance. Every insurer has a right to insure himself against the chance that the peril he has agreed to insure will occur. This insurance of insurance liabilities is called reinsurance, and is governed by the same rules as an ordinary insurance policy. Where this is arranged as a regular thing, one insurer agreeing to reinsure either a particular class of policies for another insurer, or an agreed percentage of that insurer's total business, it is called a 'reinsurance treaty'.

15.2 The Principles of Insurance

To assume someone's risks is a burden not to be lightly undertaken and there have to be strict rules. These are the **principles of insurance**. They may be listed as follows:

(*a*) Insurable interest
(*b*) Utmost good faith
(*c*) Indemnity
  (*c*1) Contribution
  (*c*2) Subrogation

There is also a doctrine, called the **doctrine of proximate cause**. What do these various terms mean?

(*a*) **Insurable Interest.** This principle holds that no one may insure against any risk unless he/she will suffer loss should the risk insured against occur. Thus I may insure my own life, and my person and my property against accident, fire, flood, tempest, etc., because if I die, or am injured, or my property is damaged or destroyed I shall suffer a loss. I may not insure my neighbour's life, person or property except in very special circumstances, because usually I have no interest in their wellbeing and shall not suffer a loss if they are adversely affected.

A person is considered to have an insurable interest in his/her own life and the life of his/her spouse. Parents do not necessarily have an insurable interest in the lives of their children or vice versa; a pecuniary interest must be shown. This means that the proposer must show that he will suffer financial loss if the person whose life he has insured dies (*Halford v. Kymer* (*1830*)). Hence a creditor has an insurable interest in the life of his debtor; a guarantor has an insurable interest in the life of the debtor he is guaranteeing and an employer has an insurable interest in the life of his employees and vice versa. Everyone may insure property wholly owned, or jointy owned with another, or where there is an equitable or limited interest in property. A shareholder in a company may insure the shares held, but not the property of the company, for a shareholder has no insurable interest in property owned by the company. The person insured is called the **assured** – a name traditionally used, which has the same meaning as *insured*.

(*b*) **Utmost Good Faith.** This principle holds that all contracts of insurance are contracts *uberrimae fidei* (of the utmost good faith). The proposer of an insurance policy is under a duty to disclose to the insurer all the material facts. Any non-disclosure of a material fact makes the insurance contract voidable at the option of the insurer. This doctrine of disclosure of material facts, which applies to all types of insurance, is well described in S.18 of the *Marine Insurance Act, 1906*:

'Subject to the provisions of this section, the assured must disclose to the insurer, before the contract is concluded, every material circumstance which is known to the assured and the assured is deemed to know every circumstance, which, in the ordinary course of business, ought to be known by him. If the assured fails to make such disclosure, the insurer may avoid the contract.

Every circumstance is material which would influence the judgement of a prudent insurer in fixing the premium, or determining whether he will take the risk.'

In *Carter v. Boehm* (*1766*) Lord Mansfield said:

'Good faith forbids either party, by concealing what he privately knows, to draw the other party into the bargain from his ignorance of that fact and his believing the contrary.'

In *Arterial Caravans Ltd v. Yorkshire Insurance Co.* (*1973*) where a company seeking fire insurance failed to reveal that another company managed by them had suffered a loss by fire, it was held that this constituted non-disclosure of a material fact. Similarly, a failure to reveal that a motor insurer had refused cover in circumstances reflecting upon the moral integrity of the insured's character was held to be a breach of utmost good faith by an applicant for a fire policy (*Locker & Woolfe Ltd. v. West Australian Insurance Co. Ltd* (*1936*)).

(*c*) **Indemnity.** This principle holds that the duty of the insurer is to indemnify the assured against the loss he has suffered, and thus restore him (so far as money can) to the same position he was in before the loss occurred. Where indemnity is not the purpose of the contract, as with life assurance and accident insurance, the purpose of the contract is to pay the insured a known sum of money (the benefit) on the happening of the event. Indemnity is restoration to the previous situation, not to a better situation. It is against public policy (which means 'crime would be encouraged') for those who might suffer a loss to be in a position where they could profit from it if the loss occurred. Thus the owner of a wrecked vehicle does not receive a new car, but only the value of the car in the condition it was in immediately prior to the accident. Due allowance will be made for depreciation in deciding the value of the vehicle.

(*d*) **Contribution.** This subprinciple of indemnity holds that an insured person cannot be allowed to recover more than once for any loss – so that if two policies exist to cover the same risk the insurers will contribute to the loss pro rata, according to the terms expressed in the contracts. Any attempt deliberately to insure to a value greater than the interest existing in the life or property may be void under the *Life Assurance Act, 1774*. In other circumstances – for example, where a 'Contents' policy and an 'All Risks' policy cover the same goods – contribution would apply. Where one insured pays in full he may recover from the other insurers. The rule does not apply to cases of life assurance, where a person may take out several policies to yield benefits large enough to support his dependants in the event of his death.

(*c2*) **Subrogation.** To subrogate is to step into the shoes of another individual, and become entitled to every right of that individual, both contractual and in tort, or indeed in any other branch of law. The fact that I have obtained cover against any loss – for example, loss of goods in transit – does not mean that the person who caused the loss escapes liability for his actions, such as dangerous driving, negligent driving, etc. The insurance company is entitled to subrogate into the legal situation of the assured, and to exert the assured's legal rights in its own name. The assured may have been fully compensated, and may no longer be interested, but the insurance company is anxious to restore to the pool of insurance funds what it can recover by way of salvage or from the person at fault. This right is based upon equitable considerations. Since the contract of insurance is a contract to indemnify the assured, once this has been done it would be inequitable if any further sums from the sale of damaged goods, or compensation from those liable for the loss, should also go to the assured. The insurer is entitled to be recouped by having the amount returned to him. However, this recoupment only extends to the limit of the indemnity. In *Yorkshire Insurance Co. Ltd v. Nisbet Shipping Co. Ltd (1962)*, where a refund – due to the delay involved – resulted in an exchange profit which exceeded the indemnity, the insurers were allowed to recover only what they had paid.

The Doctrine of Proximate Cause. A policy of insurance provides cover against named risks, a claim being payable only if the named risk occurs as the proximate cause of the loss (closest in effect, or 'efficiency', not in time). Suppose a property is covered against fire, but in view of its proximity to an airfield damage due to an aviation accident is excluded. If an aircraft crashes and causes a fire is the loss covered by the policy? It would appear not, for the proximate cause of the loss is the aircraft accident, and the fire was a consequence of that event. In making a claim it is for the claimant to prove that the loss comes within the terms of the policy. If a *prima facie* case is established the onus shifts to the insurer to raise the question of proximate cause.

The following complex situations may arise:

(*a*) The loss was caused by a succession of perils, of which the last one was *the insured peril*. If the others were non-insured perils the loss is covered by the insured peril and the insurers are liable. If the others were excluded perils, see below.

(*b*) The insured peril was not the last in the chain of perils, but an earlier link in the chain. The question then arises, did the series of events follow in an unbroken chain? If so, the insured peril is the cause of the loss. If the chain of events was interrupted after the insured peril, and the final event is an uninsured peril, the insurers are not liable, for the cover they provided was not cover for the event that actually caused the loss. This new event is called a *novus actus interveniens* – a new act which intervenes to break the chain of events.

(*c*) An insured peril and an uninsured peril occur at the same time. The loss is deemed to be caused equally by the two perils, and hence the insured peril caused the loss and the insurers are liable.

(*d*) An insured peril and an *excluded* peril operate separately. Since their separate actions can be distinguished we can determine which caused the loss.

(*e*) An insured peril and an *excluded* peril operate in circumstances where it is difficult to distinguish their individual effects. If the insured peril was preceded by the excluded peril and followed from it the excluded peril is the proximate cause and the insurers are not liable. If the insured peril came first, and the excluded peril followed from it, the insured peril is the proximate cause and the insurers are liable. If the insured peril came first, and then the excluded peril as a separate and distinct event, the excluded peril caused the loss, and the insurers are not liable. Finally – if the events are concurrent and equally effective in causing the loss, we have what seems to be a strange result: the insurers are not liable. This is because it can truthfully be said that the excluded peril caused the loss, and in such circumstances the insurance company cannot be held liable. They were careful to exclude this peril and it would be wrong to hold them liable.

15.3 Life Assurance

Life assurance is a contract by which an insurer undertakes to pay a beneficiary a certain sum of money (or succession of payments of money) on the death of the person whose life is insured.

The *Life Assurance Act, 1774*, rules that any life assurance contract taken out by someone who has no interest in the life assured is null and void. The name of the interested person, or the name of the beneficiary, shall be inserted in the policy. Where the insured has an interest (as where a creditor insures the life of his debtor to the value of his debt) he shall not recover more than the amount of the interest. If a life assurance policy is assigned to a third party (perhaps as security for a debt) it is not necessary for the assignee to have an insurable interest in the life concerned.

In business, life assurance is possible for partners, employers and employees. For example, at the death of a partner the estate of the deceased will perhaps wish to withdraw the deceased's share for distribution to the heirs. It is wise to insure the life of your partner, so that at death a sum of money becomes available to pay out the partner's share. An employer may insure the life of a key employee, and an employee may insure the life of the employer upon whom he depends for employment. In *Hebdon v. West* the facts were:

Hebdon v. West (1863). An employee was contracted to serve for seven years at £600 per year to a man named Pedder. He insured Pedder's life for £2500. After two years Pedder died. **Held:** he had an insurable interest in Pedder's life for the amount of unpaid salary (£3000) and the claim would therefore succeed.

Suicide. The general principles of insurance law preclude a claim resulting from a loss deliberately caused by the policy holder. For example, unless the policy expressly provides otherwise the personal representatives of a policy holder who commits suicide while sane will not be able to succeed in a claim. They will succeed if the policy holder committed suicide while mentally disordered since this is not considered a deliberate act, unless the policy provides otherwise.

Cooling-off Period. To prevent difficulties caused when a persuasive insurance salesman deals with an unsophisticated client, insurance companies are now required to send a statutory notice when long-term contracts are entered into. These give clients a 10-day cooling-off period during which they may consider the matter again and withdraw from the contract if they so wish (*S.1 1978 No. 1304 Insurance Companies (Notice of Long-term Policy) Regulations, 1978*).

Assignment of a Life Policy. If a policy is assigned to a third party the assignment must be in writing, either endorsed upon the policy or in a separate document. The assignee's rights will be subject to defences which would have been valid against the assignor (for example, if the policy excluded payment if the life assured ended by suicide). The assignee should give notice to the insurance company at the place specified in the policy for such notice to be given. Assignments may be made under the general terms for assignment of *choses in action* (S.136 of the *Law of Property Act, 1925*) but also under the special terms of the *Policies of Assurance Act, 1867*.

Right of Subrogation and Life Assurance. The right of subrogation does not apply to life assurance, and the company must pay the benefit agreed without any hope of recovery from the offending party if the death was unnatural. The rights of action against anyone concerned lie with the legal representatives of the deceased and any award made will not be subject to any claim for a refund of the benefit paid.

Termination of the Contract. Where a life policy is terminated otherwise than by the death of the insured life, two alternatives are usually available. The insured may surrender the policy and instead accept a sum of money called the **surrender value**. This surrender value will be affected by a claw-back of tax under the *Finance Act, 1975*. Alternatively, he may agree to accept a **'fully paid' policy**. This means that no further payments are called for, but the policy continues until the death of the insured when a reduced benefit – recognising the premiums already paid and the deceased's expectation of life at the time the 'fully paid' policy is issued – becomes payable.

15.4 Fire Insurance

A fire insurance contract is an indemnity contract where the insurer, in consideration of a premium payable either as a lump sum or at regular intervals, agrees to indemnify the insured against the consequences of a fire happening within an agreed period. In general, such a policy covers fires however caused, even if the insured was negligent (*Harris v. Poland* (*1941*)), or some third party deliberately caused the fire. Cover does not extend to the **wilful misconduct** of the insured (though wilful misconduct is very difficult to prove), nor to the insured's deliberate **arson**.

Fire is a different risk from explosion, even if the latter is followed by a fire, and it depends upon the wording of clauses about explosions as to what liability the insurers will accept. Usually they will cover damage due to the fire, but not blast damage attributable to the explosion. A fire requires ignition, so that damage due to overheating is not covered by a fire policy if there is no fire.

Insurable Interest. The insured must have an insurable interest in the premises or goods insured. Owners of property have an interest; occupiers have an interest and a mortgagee may insure property over which he has a mortgage. A bailee (a person in possession of goods for the purpose of performing some service on them) may insure his customer's goods for the full value, and if a loss occurs the sum payable will be for his benefit to the extent of the work done, and the balance will be held as trustee for the owner.

The interest of a person in buildings must exist at the time of taking out the policy and also at the moment when the loss occurred. If the insured dies, or becomes bankrupt, the insurable interest is assigned by process of law to his legal representatives who may enforce the policy if a fire occurs. If the property is conveyed in other circumstances the policy will continue to be effective only if it is assigned, with the consent of the insurers, to the new owner. If a contract is signed for the conveyance of a property, but the actual conveyance has not yet taken place, the purchaser has an equitable interest in the property to be acquired and may insure it. This is advisable in case there is any defect in the previous owner's policy and the premises are destroyed before the legal conveyance takes place.

Being a policy of indemnity, the amount of the loss only can be recovered, but if the policy is a 'valued policy' which recognises that the value is a given figure, this sum will be payable even if the true value at the time the loss occurred was different. This is frequently used with marine insurance. Commodities vary in value from day to day and place to place, and the use of valued policies avoids legal disputes over valuations at a particular time or place. One more unusual case – which confirms the rule – was *Elcock v. Thomson*:

Elcock v. Thomson (*1949*). A house at Wokingham in Berkshire was insured in 1940 at an agreed valuation in excess of £100,000. It was damaged by fire in 1947, when it was found that the true value was less than £20,000 before the fire and damage amounted to 30 per cent of this value. **Held:** The percentage of depreciation due to the fire should be applied to the agreed value, not the true value, and compensation of more than £30,000 was due.

Reinstatement. An early Act (the *Fires Prevention* (*Metropolis*) *Act, 1774*) creates a statutory obligation on insurance companies to reinstate premises damaged by fire at the request of anyone interested in the continued existence of the property. The person interested must serve clear notice upon the insurance company who must then ensure that the insurance moneys are used for this purpose, whoever receives them. In the absence of such notice the insurers are required to pay only money compensation, and it is for the assured to decide whether reinstatement shall be made. Despite its name, this Act applies to the whole country, not just the metropolis.

Inflation and the Value of Property. Most fire policies have a 'subject to average' clause which limits the liability of the insurers if the property is under-insured. For a fully insured property partially damaged by fire the rule is that the assured is entitled to have the damage made good, and to be restored to the indemnity position. If the property is under-insured, the damage will only be restored to the same extent as the insured value bears to the full value, leaving the assured to find any balance of funds for the repairs.

Contribution and Fire Insurance. If property is double insured – i.e. insured for more than its true value (S.32, *Marine Insurance Act, 1906*) – the question of how a claim will be exerted depends upon whether the policy has a contribution clause. This is a clause which prevents the assured from claiming the full amount from any insurer (leaving the insurers to claim contribution) but requires the assured to claim from each insurer the proportion due from him. Thus a property valued at £25,000 and insured for £20,000 with one company and £30,000 with another company would be exerted by claiming £10,000 from one and £15,000 from the other.

15.5 Marine Insurance

The law relating to marine insurance was codified in the *Marine Insurance Act, 1906*, but since the individual arrangements are contractual and by long usage have been reduced to a very large number of standard clauses for the vast majority of contracts, the law depends to a considerable extent on judicial interpretation of these clauses.

In this respect recent criticisms of the traditional legal regime have led to a drastic rethink of the terms and clauses used, which have been greatly changed (and very lucidly set out) in the **1982 Policy Forms and Clauses**. The criticism came in the form of a Report on Marine Insurance published on November 20, 1978, by the United Nations Committee on Trade and Development (UNCTAD). This report – which consisted of a major appraisal of the 'English system' of insurance – took objection to this *de facto* world system of insurance, on the following grounds:

(*a*) It had become a *de facto* world system, but lacked the authority of an international legal regime.

(*b*) It was a unilateral, insurer-developed system, couched in archaic language so that many assureds did not understand the meaning of many of the clauses and terms.

(*c*) In particular the new nations, the developing nations and the Soviet bloc had had no chance to influence the system, or reduce the uncertainties in it for them.

(*d*) The regime took little account of new developments, particularly multi-modal movements. Being British-based it was preoccupied with transits involving sea movements, but for many countries sea transits did not arise, and long-haul road and rail movements were more important.

Accordingly the report called for an *ad hoc* Working Group to study the situation and report on the idea of an International Convention on Marine Insurance to replace the English system. No doubt such a working party is at work, but in the meantime many of the criticisms have been met by a joint working party of the Institute of London Underwriters and the Corporation of Lloyds. This has produced and implemented the 1982 Policy Forms and Clauses, which are gradually being extended into all the trades with specialist **trade clauses**. These new clauses are illustrated in this chapter. Whether they quite meet the call from UNCTAD for an international legal regime remains to be seen, but they are likely to be the *de facto* regime for many years to come – since international agreement on these matters is not easy to achieve.

Nature of Marine Insurance Policies. A marine insurance contract is one where the insurer (or underwriter) undertakes to indemnify the assured (or insured) to the extent agreed against marine losses incurred in any marine adventure. The marine insurance market is a highly organised market, on which only experts may deal. The expert acting on behalf of the assured is called a **broker**. Some brokers are accredited by Lloyds of London, and are called **Lloyds brokers**. Others are members of **BIBA**, the British Insurance Brokers Association. They are not mere agents of the assured, since they are responsible to the underwriters for the payment of the premium. As a result they hold a lien (right of retention) over the policy until such time as the premium they have paid is reimbursed to them by the assured.

The subject matter of marine policies may include the ship itself; the ship's necessaries to be used on the voyage; the cargo and the freight (freight is the reward to a ship-owner for carrying goods); and money lent on a **bottomry bond** (a mortgage on a ship executed by a master in difficulties in a foreign port).

Valued and Unvalued Policies. Most marine policies are **valued policies** – that is, policies where goods and other items to be covered are expressed at a given value which will be the sum to be repaid in the event of a total loss. If the loss is partial the sum payable will be proportional to the agreed value and the percentage of loss suffered. If a policy is **unvalued** the amount payable to the assured will be the value of the goods at the time and place concerned.

Types of Policies

Voyage policies cover the subject matter of the insurance policy for a particular voyage 'at and from' port A to port B.

Time policies cover the subject matter of the insurance policy for a stated period of time.

Floating policies were developed in the nineteenth century to save endless renegotiation of insurance cover for repetitive journeys with similar groups of cargo. Under a floating policy an underwriter agrees to cover all sendings, at an agreed rate, the premium being paid in advance. The exact details of the ship's name, value of cargo moving, etc., are notified subsequent to departure in a separate **declaration**. The premium is then adjusted

The trouble with this system is that the insurance policy covers many sendings by many ships, and cannot therefore be assigned to a foreign cargo owner as required in many export transactions. The solution found was to issue a **certificate of insurance** for each consignment which certifies that insurance cover has been arranged for the consignment in question.

Open covers. Floating policies, as described above, had some major disadvantages. To help underwriters the policy was for a fixed amount of cover (say £1 million) and an average premium was agreed and paid in advance. This was a heavy cost to the assured. The fixed amount also meant that as declarations were made against the policy the sum outstanding declined until the full sum had been used up. Note that any adjustment between the average premium and the true premium for each consignment was adjusted on declaration, a difference either way being paid (or repaid). The difficulty was that if an assured received a spate of urgent orders, the premium falling due at once, he might run out of cover at busy periods. The solution was the introduction of **open covers**. Here the sendings are declared as and when they occur, and the premium is invoiced for on a monthly, quarterly or other agreed basis. All sendings are held covered at a standard premium – which assists costing and quoting to customers – and the insurer has the benefit of a steady stream of business with a residual right of cancellation if required, usually at 30 days notice.

Slip policies. Where insurance is effected facultatively (each cover being decided between the broker and the underwriters rather than by the use of an open cover) the basis for discussion is a slip of paper on which the risk is outlined. The underwriters sign the slip to say what portion of the risk they will accept, and eventually a policy is prepared. The *Marine Insurance Act, 1906*, says that only a policy is evidence for the courts, and other documents like slips, certificates, etc., are not evidence. However, in practice many shipments arrive safely, while many claims are met without dispute, or disputes are settled by arbitration. Therefore the drawing up of many policies is a complete waste of time. In 1972 it was decided that the slip itself should be the policy, and bear a similar wording to the policy itself – but where a formal policy is required one would be issued in substitution for the slip policy, upon request. This resulted in a considerable simplification of arrangements.

The 1.1.82 Policy Forms and Clauses. The 1.1.82 Policy Forms and Clauses replaced the 350-year-old S & G Form (Ship and Goods Form) with its archaic format. Traditionally three main sets of clauses – all risks, WA (with average) and FPA (free of particular average) – had been available. Today there are still three sets of clauses, designated Institute Cargo Clauses (A), Institute Cargo Clauses (B) and Institute Cargo Clauses (C). There is little point in attempting to compare these three sets of clauses with the traditional clauses; suffice to say that the C clauses offer the least cover, the B clauses offer rather more cover, and the A clauses offer something very similar to the all risks cover under the traditional all risks policy. None of the Cargo Clauses offers cover against war, or strikes, and if these risks are to be covered a further set of clauses, the **Institute War Clauses** (there is a choice of three sets) and the **Institute Strikes Clauses** must be adopted (at an extra premium of course).

The new form presents the terms of the contract in a clear format, under eight subheadings. These are:

(*a*) Risks covered
(*b*) Exclusions
(*c*) Duration
(*d*) Claims
(*e*) Benefit of insurance
(*f*) Minimising losses
(*g*) Avoidance of delay
(*h*) Law and practice

The layout of the Institute Cargo Clauses (A) is reproduced on pages 226–233 by kind permission of Witherby & Co. Ltd. Some notes on the various clauses are printed on facing pages, to assist study of the clauses. When reading the clauses please remember that the new format was designed to improve insured's understanding of what the clauses actually meant in terms of cover provided.

The *Marine Insurance Act, 1906*. The *Marine Insurance Act, 1906*, codified the law on marine insurance as it existed at that time, when the old S & G policy had already been in use for over 250 years and a considerable body of case law had grown up. It laid down statutory definitions for many of the phrases used in that policy. Now that the S & G policy is, if not quite dead, at least painlessly laid to rest the wordings have in some cases disappeared, or at least have been expressed in plain modern English. However, the meaning of such words as 'thieves', 'pirates', etc., will still be the same as those laid down in the Act, and the reader is strongly recommended to buy a copy and study it in detail. It is the subject matter for a specialist book on insurance law, rather than a general book like this one.

Claims in Marine Insurance. Claims may be made by the person with an insurable interest for any loss that is proximately caused by one of the perils insured against. The *doctrine of proximate cause* has already been described, the proximate cause being the one that is *proximate in efficiency*, not necessarily in time. Losses may be total, or partial, as explained below.

As there are frequently many parties involved the settlement between the assured and the insurer is called the **adjustment** and is usually settled on behalf of the assured by the broker, who opens a file on the claim, collects together the various documents and reports and negotiates a settlement. Arrangements are sometimes very complex and – with the losses being suffered around the world – some time is taken in collecting the necessary details. Once the type of loss has been established, settlements are made on the basis of established practice. A broad outline of losses and the settlements that result is as follows:

Total losses. These are divided into **actual total losses** and **constructive total losses**.

An actual total loss is one where:

(*a*) The subject matter is actually destroyed, or irretrievably lost, or so badly damaged as to be irreparable.

(*b*) The assured is irretrievably deprived of it, because it no longer exists in recognisable form as the object or equipment insured, or

(*c*) When a court of competent jurisdiction rules that as a result of the peril insured against it is the property of another, and no longer the insured's property (e.g. sale as a prize by a foreign power).

A constructive total loss is one where the costs of repair (or recovery of a sunken vessel) would exceed its value on repair or recovery. In such cases notice of abandonment must be given, so that the rights of the assured are transferred to the insurers who may then take such action as they think fit to recover or repair the vessel or the damaged goods.

SS.67–78 of the *Marine Insurance Act, 1906*, are about the **measure of indemnity** payable to the assured by the insurer. The rules are complicated, being based upon case law over more than 250 years, and a detailed study of these sections is essential for those with a particular interest in marine insurance.

Compensation on a ship, subject to any special clauses in the policy, is either at the agreed value for a total loss if it is a valued policy, or if it is an unvalued policy it is the insurable value of the ship at the commencement of the risk, including her outfit, provisions and stores, the money advanced in wages and other disbursements to make the ship ready for the voyage, and the insurance charges (Sch.1, 1906 Act, rule 15). If a vessel arrives safely after settlement of the claim she is treated as if she had been abandoned and becomes the property of the insurers.

The measure of indemnity for a total loss of goods is payment of the agreed value if it is a valued policy. If unvalued, the figure is once again the insurable value, which is the prime cost of the goods, plus the shipping and insurance charges.

Partial losses. A partial loss may be a **total loss of part** of the goods, or it may be damage to all the goods sent, but not a total loss. In total loss of part of a valued policy the compensation payable is that proportion of the agreed value which the part lost represents of the whole consignment, valued as for an unvalued policy (S.71, *Marine Insurance Act, 1906*). Thus if the value of the policy is £10,000, and the insurable value according to S.16 of the Act is £8000, of which half is lost, the compensation payable is half the agreed value, i.e. £5000. If the policy is unvalued, the sum recoverable is the insurable value of the part lost – in the example above it would be £4000.

General average losses. A very ancient body of law relates to the sacrifices made or expenses incurred by some assureds to save the entire project when a ship is in real danger. Thus cargo may be jettisoned to lighten a vessel; or may be used as fuel; or part of the ship may be cut away, etc. The principle of general average (*average* here is from the Arabic word *awariya* meaning 'damaged goods') is that those whose property was sacrificed must be compensated by those whose goods arrived safely as a result of the sacrifice, so that all suffer equally. The sacrifice or expenditure is called a general average loss, and the contributions are called general average contributions. The carrier is legally responsible for collecting the contributions from those whose goods have arrived safely, and to this end has a lien (a right to retain possession until paid) over their goods on arrival. As this can be very inconvenient he will usually release the goods on receipt of a **general average guarantee** from a reputable security such as a bank, or insurance company. The 1.1.82 clauses reproduced on pages 226–233 carry a General Average Clause giving cover against general average charges. The **York-Antwerp rules 1974** cover the internationally agreed rules on general average, and are available in booklet form from the Institute of Freight Forwarders Ltd, Suffield House, 9 Paradise Road, Richmond, Surrey TW9 ISA.

15.6 Accident Insurance

The general heading of accident insurance covers a number of classes of insurance, such as personal accident insurance, motor vehicle insurance and aviation insurance. They may overlap into liability insurance, since accidents often result in liability to other parties. The general principles of insurance apply to all such policies, but they may not all be indemnity policies.

Personal Accident Insurance. Where an insured arranges cover against the possibility of accidental injury resulting in disablement or death, and the loss of income that results, the policy will not be an indemnity policy, for restoration to the original position is not possible. It will be a benefit policy, securing either a lump sum or a continuation of smaller payments to the policy holder or the dependants.

Motor Vehicle Insurance. Motor vehicle insurance to cover third parties and passengers is compulsory under the *Road Traffic Act, 1972.* There is a statutory duty to obtain cover and both the owner and the driver are liable to prosecution for failure to obtain cover. Proof of cover being obtained is provided by a **certificate of insurance**, which a police officer may require to be produced for inspection. To give immediate cover a **cover note** will be provided while the insurers are preparing a policy and issuing a certificate of insurance. Many people prefer **comprehensive cover**, which means 'including much', but it still does not cover every possibility. The chief difference is that the driver and his vehicle are covered against injury or damage respectively.

The Act provides that the insurer must pay a third party or passenger who has obtained a judgement against the insured. However, if the terms of policy have been breached the insurers are not compelled to honour the policy. In *Seddon v. Binions (1978)* a policy covered the use of the vehicle for 'social, domestic and pleasure purposes' only. The vehicle was being used for business purposes when the accident occurred, and the insurance company was not required to pay.

15.7 Liability Insurance

Liability insurance covers the insured person against liability to others by virtue of some tortious act, such as negligence or trespass. It is often part of accident insurance (most notably in the case of motor vehicle insurance) or building insurance. Cover is usually extensive enough to protect the insured even when the law has been broken, as in careless or dangerous driving, but it would not cover deliberate tortious acts such as defamation

1/1/82 Institute Cargo Clauses (A)
(For use only with the new marine policy form)

RISKS COVERED

1 This insurance covers all risks of loss of or damage to the subject-matter insured except as provided in Clauses 4, 5, 6 and 7 below. Risks Clause

2 This insurance covers general average and salvage charges, adjusted or determined according to the contract of affreightment and/or the governing law and practice, incurred to avoid or in connection with the avoidance of loss from any cause except those excluded in Clauses 4, 5, 6 and 7 or elsewhere in this insurance. General Average Clause

3 This insurance is extended to indemnify the Assured against such proportion of liability under the contract of affreightment 'Both to Blame Collision' Clause as is in respect of a loss recoverable hereunder. In the event of any claim by shipowners under the said Clause the Assured agree to notify the Underwriters who shall have the right, at their own cost and expense, to defend the Assured against such claim. 'Both to Blame Collision' Clause

EXCLUSIONS

4 In no case shall this insurance cover General Exclusions Clause

4.1 loss damage or expense attributable to wilful misconduct of the Assured

4.2 ordinary leakage, ordinary loss in weight or volume, or ordinary wear and tear of the subject-matter insured

4.3 loss damage or expense caused by insufficiency or unsuitability of packing or preparation of the subject-matter insured (for the purpose of this Clause 4.3 'packing' shall be deemed to include stowage in a container or liftvan but only when such stowage is carried out prior to attachment of this insurance or by the Assured or their servants)

4.4 loss damage or expense caused by inherent vice or nature of the subject-matter insured

4.5 loss damage or expense proximately caused by delay, even though the delay be caused by a risk insured against (except expenses payable under Clause 2 above)

4.6 loss damage or expense arising from insolvency or financial default of the owners managers charterers or operators of the vessel

4.7 loss damage or expense arising from the use of any weapon of war employing atomic or nuclear fission and/or fusion or other like reaction or radioactive force or matter.

5 5.1 In no case shall this insurance cover loss damage or expense arising from Unseaworthiness and Unfitness Exclusion Clause

unseaworthiness of vessel or craft,

unfitness of vessel craft conveyance container or liftvan for the safe carriage of the subject-matter insured,

where the Assured or their servants are privy to such unseaworthiness or unfitness, at the time the subject-matter insured is loaded therein.

5.2 The Underwriters waive any breach of the implied warranties of seaworthiness of the ship and fitness of the ship to carry the subject-matter insured to destination, unless the Assured or their servants are privy to such unseaworthiness or unfitness.

6 In no case shall this insurance cover loss damage or expense caused by War Exclusion Clause

6.1 war civil war revolution rebellion insurrection, or civil strife arising therefrom, or any hostile act by or against a belligerent power

Authors' Notes on the Institute Cargo Clauses (A)

Risks covered. The risks clause is clear and unambiguous but it does refer to certain ◀ risks which are *not* covered. These are given in detail in Clauses 4, 5, 6 and 7. They include wilful misconduct of the assured, losses due to fair wear and tear, faulty packing, inherent vice, delay, insolvency of the owners or charterers of the vessel, nuclear accident, unseaworthiness, war and strikes.

◀ The **general average clause** (about losses suffered by cargo owners and the owners of vessels where goods are deliberately sacrificed to save the entire venture) says that general average and salvage charges *are* covered. This is explained more fully on pages 224–5.

◀ The **'both to blame collision' clause.** This is a clause which sometimes arises out of a similar clause in the contract of affreightment. When ships collide and both are to blame the damage suffered by both ships is added together and each carrier is responsible for half. Some contracts of affreightment permit the ship-owner to call on cargo owners to help with such losses. The clause covers the risk that this will occur but also authorises the insurer to act as agent for the cargo owner in rebutting the claim (at the insurer's expense).

◀ **Exclusions.** These are the clauses referred to above, which list the risks not covered by the policy.

6.2 capture seizure arrest restraint or detainment (piracy excepted), and the consequences thereof or any attempt thereat

6.3 derelict mines torpedoes bombs or other derelict weapons of war.

7 In no case shall this insurance cover loss damage or expense — Strikes Exclusion Clause

7.1 caused by strikers, locked-out workmen, or persons taking part in labour disturbances, riots or civil commotions

7.2 resulting from strikes, lock-outs, labour disturbances, riots or civil commotions

7.3 caused by any terrorist or any person acting from a political motive.

DURATION

8 8.1 This insurance attaches from the time the goods leave the warehouse or place of storage at the place named herein for the commencement of the transit, continues during the ordinary course of transit and terminates either — Transit Clause

8.1.1 on delivery to the Consignees' or other final warehouse or place of storage at the destination named herein,

8.1.2 on delivery to any other warehouse or place of storage, whether prior to or at the destination named herein, which the Assured elect to use either

8.1.2.1 for storage other than in the ordinary course of transit

or

8.1.2.2 for allocation or distribution,

or

8.1.3 on the expiry of 60 days after completion of discharge overside of the goods hereby insured from the oversea vessel at the final port of discharge,

whichever shall first occur.

8.2 If, after discharge overside from the oversea vessel at the final port of discharge, but prior to termination of this insurance, the goods are to be forwarded to a destination other than that to which they are insured hereunder, this insurance, whilst remaining subject to termination as provided for above, shall not extend beyond the commencement of transit to such other destination.

8.3 This insurance shall remain in force (subject to termination as provided for above and to the provisions of Clause 9 below) during delay beyond control of the Assured, any deviation, forced discharge, reshipment or trans-shipment and during any variation of the adventure arising from the exercise of a liberty granted to shipowners or charterers under the contract of affreightment.

9 If owing to circumstances beyond the control of the Assured either the contract of carriage is terminated at a port or place other than the destination named therein or the transit is otherwise terminated before delivery of the goods as provided for in Clause 8 above, then this insurance shall also terminate *unless prompt notice is given to the Underwriters and continuation of cover is requested when the insurance shall remain in force, subject to an additional premium if required by the Underwriters*, either — Termination of Contract of Carriage Clause

9.1 until the goods are sold and delivered at such port or place, or, unless otherwise specially agreed, until the expiry of 60 days after arrival of the goods hereby insured at such port or place, whichever shall first occur,

Duration. Naturally the insurer has to know for how long the policy is to be in existence if a fair premium is to be arranged. S.8.1 shows that it is a warehouse-to-warehouse arrangement, but Clause 8.1.3 says that if the assured does not take delivery within 60 days of the goods being discharged from the ship at destination the cover ceases. SS.9 and 10 require prompt notice to be given in the special circumstances outlined if the goods are to be held covered, pending movement elsewhere.

or

9.2 if the goods are forwarded within the said period of 60 days (or any agreed extension thereof) to the destination named herein or to any other destination, until terminated in accordance with the provisions of Clause 8 above.

10 Where, after attachment of this insurance, the destination is changed by the Assured, *held covered at a premium and on conditions to be arranged subject to prompt notice being given to the Underwriters.* Change of Voyage Clause

CLAIMS

11 11.1 In order to recover under this insurance the Assured must have an insurable interest in the subject-matter insured at the time of the loss. Insurable Interest Clause

11.2 Subject to 11.1 above, the Assured shall be entitled to recover for insured loss occurring during the period covered by this insurance, notwithstanding that the loss occurred before the contract of insurance was concluded, unless the Assured were aware of the loss and the Underwriters were not.

12 Where as a result of the operation of a risk covered by this insurance, the insured transit is terminated at a port or place other than that to which the subject-matter is covered under this insurance, the Underwriters will reimburse the Assured for any extra charges properly and reasonably incurred in unloading storing and forwarding the subject-matter to the destination to which it is insured hereunder. Forwarding Charges Clause

This Clause 12, which does not apply to general average or salvage charges, shall be subject to the exclusions contained in Clauses 4, 5, 6 and 7 above, and shall not include charges arising from the fault negligence insolvency or financial default of the Assured or their servants.

13 No claim for Constructive Total Loss shall be recoverable hereunder unless the subject-matter insured is reasonably abandoned either on account of its actual total loss appearing to be unavoidable or because the cost of recovering, reconditioning and forwarding the subject-matter to the destination to which it is insured would exceed its value on arrival. Constructive Total Loss Clause

14 14.1 If any Increased Value insurance is effected by the Assured on the cargo insured herein the agreed value of the cargo shall be deemed to be increased to the total amount insured under this insurance and all Increased Value insurances covering the loss, and liability under this insurance shall be in such proportion as the sum insured herein bears to such total amount insured. Increased Value Clause

In the event of claim the Assured shall provide the Underwriters with evidence of the amounts insured under all other insurances.

14.2 Where this insurance is on Increased Value the following clause shall apply: The agreed value of the cargo shall be deemed to be equal to the total amount insured under the primary insurance and all Increased Value insurances covering the loss and effected on the cargo by the Assured, and liability under this insurance shall be in such proportion as the sum insured herein bears to such total amount insured.

In the event of claim the Assured shall provide the Underwriters with evidence of the amounts insured under all other insurances.

Claims. It is made quite clear that the assured must have an insurable interest at the time of the loss. Three other clauses cover forwarding charges incurred if the goods are discharged elsewhere than at the named destination; what happens when there is a constructive total loss (one where the goods are not lost but so badly damaged that the costs of repair, etc., would be greater than their value when repaired); and what happens when the assured takes out an 'increased value' policy for the cargo in question.

BENEFIT OF INSURANCE

15 This insurance shall not inure to the benefit of the carrier or other bailee. Not to Inure Clause

MINIMISING LOSSES

16 It is the duty of the Assured and their servants and agents in respect of loss recoverable hereunder Duty of Assured Clause

16.1 to take such measures as may be reasonable for the purpose of averting or minimising such loss, and

16.2 to ensure that all rights against carriers, bailees or other third parties are properly preserved and exercised

and the Underwriters will, in addition to any loss recoverable hereunder, reimburse the Assured for any charges properly and reasonably incurred in pursuance of these duties,

17 Measures taken by the Assured or the Underwriters with the object of saving, protecting or recovering the subject-matter insured shall not be considered as a waiver or acceptance of abandonment or otherwise prejudice the rights of either party. Waiver Clause

AVOIDANCE OF DELAY

18 It is a condition of this insurance that the Assured shall act with reasonable despatch in all circumstances within their control. Reasonable Despatch Clause

LAW AND PRACTICE

19 The insurance is subject to English law and practice. English Law and Practice Clause

NOTE: It is necessary for the Assured when they become aware of an event which is 'held covered' under this insurance to give prompt notice to the Underwriters and the right to such cover is dependent upon compliance with this obligation.

(Reproduced by courtesy of Witherby & Co. Ltd)

◀ **Benefit of Insurance.** The 'not to inure' clause makes it clear that under no circumstances can the carrier or any other bailee (like a freight forwarder) claim under the insurance since the insurance company, when it settles a claim, subrogates into the assured's legal position and may sue the one at fault (usually the carrier or multimodal operator). It destroys their subrogation rights if these people can claim under the insurance. If found liable to compensate the insurance company the insurance company would then have to compensate them back again, which would be absurd.

◀ **Minimising losses.** It is a basic rule in insurance that the assured has a duty to do everthing possible to minimise losses. This includes taking what steps are necessary to preserve goods, safeguard them, etc., and any charges incurred are covered by the policy. It also requires the assured to exert all legal rights by giving notice of damage promptly (within the time limits supplied in the contract of carriage) and suing promptly (according to the terms of the international convention or other law applicable in the case). Anything done in these respects does not waive any rights of either party, but is simply done to save the goods or recover from the party at fault.

◀ **Avoidance of delay.** This is part of minimising losses, as explained above.

◀ **Law and practice.** This clause is self-explanatory and simply ensures that English law and practice shall apply, and English courts shall have jurisdiction (though not, of course, exclusive jurisdiction).

Readers wishing to see the full text of other sets of clauses should obtain the *Annual Reference Book of Marine Insurance Clauses*, obtainable from Witherby & Co. Ltd. They also offer an updating service for new clauses or amended clauses as and when they occur. Their offices are at 5 Plantain Place, Crosby Row, London, SE1 1YN.

or deliberate criminal acts. It is even against public policy to allow a claim where the act is foolhardy. In *Gray v. Barr (1971)* Gray was the personal representative of a relative who had been shot and killed in a struggle with Barr. Despite Barr's acquittal of murder and manslaughter the action (under the *Fatal Accidents Act, 1959*) sought compensation from Barr. Barr sought an indemnity under his accident liability policy, but he was not allowed to claim under the policy. Those who engage in struggles with loaded guns cannot be allowed to claim that any calamity that results is an accident.

If a third party has a claim against a person who is insured and that person becomes bankrupt, or makes a composition with his creditors, or if the 'person' is a limited company and it goes into liquidation, or its debenture trustees appoint a receiver or manager, the rights of the insured person against the insurers are transferred to the third party and vest in him, and he may claim the compensation directly from the insurance company.

Under the *Employers' Liability (Compulsory Insurance) Act, 1969*, employers must obtain cover against liability for bodily injury or disease sustained by employees in the course of, and arising from, the employment. A copy of the Certificate issued by the insurers must be displayed at all premises where workers are employed.

15.8 The *Policyholders' Protection Act, 1975*

In recent years some spectacular collapses of insurance companies have left both policyholders and those they injure unprotected. The *Policyholders' Protection Act, 1975*, established a fund for UK policies, financed by levies on the insurance companies, to pay claims in full on compulsory insurance policies (for third parties and passengers in motor accident cases and employers' liability cases). Ninety per cent of the value of other claims will also be met.

15.9 Revision Test

Answers	*Questions*
—	**1.** What is the main purpose of insurance?
1. The bearing of risks by experienced risk-bearers called insurers or underwriters, so that ordinary businessmen are relieved of uncertainty.	**2.** What are the chief types of insurance?
2. (*a*) Life assurance; (*b*) fire insurance; (*c*) marine insurance; (*d*) accident insurance; (*e*) liability insurance.	**3.** What are the contributions to the insurance pool called?

Answers	*Questions*
3. Premiums.	**4.** What are the principles of insurance?
4. (*a*) Insurable interest; (*b*) utmost good faith; (*c*) indemnity – with contribution and subrogation; (*d*) the doctrine of proximate cause.	**5.** What is insurable interest and why is it important?
5. Insurable interest requires that only those who will suffer a loss if a risk occurs may insure against that risk. It is against public policy (crime would be encouraged) if people who did not suffer any loss could profit from the misfortune of others.	**6.** Why is utmost good faith essential in insurance?
6. Only the insured knows the facts of his own situation. Failure to reveal the true facts would mean that insurers would fix premiums too low, and the pool would be drained of resources fraudulently.	**7.** What is indemnity?
7. The restoration of an unfortunate victim of fate to the position he/she was in before fate knocked on the door.	**8.** What is contribution?
8. If double insurance has occurred the insured can only expect to be restored to the indemnity position – the insurers will each contribute to settle the claim.	**9.** What is subrogation?
9. Taking the place of another. On paying a valid claim the insurer succeeds to all the rights of the insured and may recover what can be recovered by legal action, or by sale of the damaged goods, etc.	**10.** What is the proximate cause of a loss?

Answers	*Questions*
10. The loss *closest in efficiency* to the result that occurred.	**11.** A ship is struck by a mine in wartime and is unable to answer the helm. A storm blows up and she sinks. What was the proximate cause of the loss?
11. The war risk, not the peril of the seas. From the moment the mine blew up she was in the grip of the war peril, and the storm was only an incidental cause of the loss.	**12.** What is a *novus actus interveniens*?
12. A new event which intervenes and causes a loss. If the new event was an uninsured peril compensation will not be payable.	**13.** What are the chief policies offered in marine insurance?
13. (*a*) Voyage policies; (*b*) time policies; (*c*) floating policies; (*d*) open covers.	**14.** What are the 1.1.82 Policy Forms and Clauses?
14. New policy forms and clauses introduced to meet criticisms of the archaic S & G Form by UNCTAD.	**15.** What are the chief sets of clauses?
15. Clauses A, B and C, the three sets of Institute War Clauses and the Institutes Strikes Clauses.	**16.** What are the chief features of the new clauses?
16. (*a*) A clear layout with marginal headings to highlight the main points; (*b*) a clear statement of the risks covered in plain English; (*c*) a clear statement of the exclusions; (*d*) English law and practice is contractually adopted.	**17.** Go over the questions until you are sure of all the answers. Then try some of the questions in Appendix 1.

16
Law of Carriage by Land, Sea and Air

16.1 Carriage and the Concept of the Common Carrier

Carriage is an ancient activity. Since time immemorial carriers have gone over the hills and far away with other people's property, and it was soon established that in these circumstances a carrier was liable for *every* loss that occurred. The common law concept of a **common carrier** is of someone who holds himself out as ready to carry goods for anyone who engages him. Under this concept the carrier is held to be liable as an insurer for every loss that occurs. The severity of this rule was later reduced by the development of five **common law exceptions**. These were:

(*a*) Act of God
(*b*) Act of the Queen's (King's) enemies
(*c*) Fault of the consignor
(*d*) Fraud of the consignor
(*e*) Inherent vice

An **Act of God** is one so unusual and rare that anything the carrier might do would not have prevented it. To be struck by lightning is an Act of God; a cyclone or hurricane is an Act of God; etc.

An **Act of the Queen's enemies** applies to enemies in time of war, or perhaps to a major insurrection. In *Curtis and Sons v. Matthews* (*1919*) the acts of rebels in the Dublin insurrection in 1916 were held to be acts of the King's enemies.

Fault of the consignor refers to improper packing and similar faults, while **fraud of the consignor** refers to dishonest behaviour by the consignor – usually failure to declare the true nature and value of the goods. In such circumstances the carrier will not be liable for any loss, however caused.

Inherent vice refers to the nature of goods: strawberries rot, cattle can become frightened, prize bulls develop diseases, etc. Where a consignor sends perishable goods he must himself take the risk that their inherent vices may lead to losses.

Apart from these common law exceptions the common carrier is liable for every loss that occurs. He is also under a **legal duty to carry**, except where the law provides that he may lawfully refuse to carry. These special cases are as follows:

(*a*) He need not carry through a riot (and probably not through a war, or a flood or similar natural disaster).

(*b*) He need not carry dangerous goods.

(*c*) He need not carry goods which are improperly packed.

(*d*) He need not carry if his vehicle is full.

(*e*) He need not carry if the consignor does not pay the freight in advance.

(*f*) He need not carry if the consignor refuses to declare the nature of the goods to be carried.

If a carrier does decide to carry in any of these circumstances he will be under his full liability as a common carrier, unless he makes a special contract with the consignor. Obviously he would usually do so, excluding his liability as a common carrier.

A common carrier holds himself out as being willing to carry for the public at large, though it may be in a restricted field, both as to geographical area and to the class of goods being carried. A carrier of meat cannot be compelled to carry coal, and a carrier offering to carry between Manchester and London cannot be compelled to carry to Glasgow.

A word about this chapter. Underlying the whole relationship between consignors and carriers today is the old concept of the common carrier. The harshness of the ancient rules has made carriers evade them by holding themselves out not as common carriers but as **private carriers**, each using a set of **conditions of carriage** which form the basis of a private contract between the carrier and his customers. It follows that practically every carrier is a private carrier – though since an individual firm may start with as little as one lorry it does happen that some small carriers are unaware of the hazards of being a common carrier and set up with arrangements that leave them vulnerable in this respect. In this chapter the various aspects which affect carriers are dealt with in S.16.3; the position of the common carrier is outlined first and the improvement in his position (if any) by becoming a private carrier is then explained. The rest of the chapter deals with the various modes of carriage – road, rail, sea and air – and the arrangements under which carriers in the real world actually carry. In the course of these explanations constant references inevitably occur to the common carrier and private carrier situations.

Inevitably in a book of this nature an exhaustive treatment of the law of carriage is not possible. The reader with a particular interest is referred to Ridley, J., *The Law of Carriage of Goods by Land, Sea and Air*, published by Shaw & Sons Ltd.

16.2 Carrying as a Private Carrier

Where a carrier does not wish to accept the onerous burdens of the common carrier he can hold himself out as a private carrier, carrying under the terms of private contracts made with his customers, usually based upon a set of conditions of carriage. Under the traditional law of contract all parties were deemed to be equally knowledgeable and equally legally advised, so that any terms in a contract which had been agreed between the parties were perfectly permissible. Early sets of conditions of carriage were therefore frequently very harsh, with the carrier refusing to admit liability of any sort and the less sophisticated customer having to accept the conditions because he could not do anything about them. More recently such Acts as the *Unfair Contract Terms Act, 1977*, have reduced the unfairness in inland carriage. The problem has also been tackled over the years in international trade, and as a result a number of international conventions have been introduced. These are explained in detail later.

The private carrier's position is as follows:

(*a*) He is not under a legal duty to carry, but free to pick and choose his customers with whom he makes a private contract.

(*b*) He is a bailee of the goods carried, and is liable as such for negligence only, and not as an insurer of the goods, liable for every loss that occurs.

(*c*) He may limit or exclude this liability for negligence by a special term in the contract.

As a result of these more favourable terms to the private carrier nearly all carriers today are private carriers, and make it perfectly clear that they are *not* common carriers. A typical clause reads:

1. *The carrier is not a common carrier, and will accept goods for carriage only on these conditions* (*i.e. the set of standard conditions of carriage of which this is clause 1*).

As the private carrier is liable only for negligence (unless he has excluded this possibility) the proof that he has been negligent lies upon the one alleging this. However, the rule *res ipsa loquitur* (the facts speak for themselves) applies where goods arrive damaged and the onus of proof shifts to the carrier to show that he was not negligent (*Joseph Travers and Sons Ltd v. Cooper* (*1915*), 1KB 73). Thus he might prove that the damage was the result of an Act of God, or faulty packing, or negligence of some other person.

16.3 Aspects of Carriage which are Important in Law

With Whom is the Carrier Dealing? Traditionally this has always been a point of difficulty. The consignor usually makes arrangements with the carrier but very often is not the owner of the goods, the property in them passing to the buyer (the consignee) at the moment that they are handed to the carrier for carriage. If loss, damage or delay occurs it is usually the consignee who suffers. With a common carrier there is no contract at all; the carrier carries by ancient custom of the realm – a practice which started long before contract law came into existence. Under ancient custom the carrier's liability was in tort to the owner of the goods.

When private carriers began to make contracts with their customers the question arose: who is the other contracting party? The answer is in every case a question of fact. If the consignor unambiguously contracts with the carrier he will be the principal, but more often he contracts as the agent of the owner (*Dawes v. Peck* (*1799*) and S.32 of the *Sale of Goods Act, 1979*). The problem is frequently resolved by the carrier covering the point in his conditions of carriage, so as to prevent any difficulty. A typical clause reads:

2 (1) The Trader warrants that he is either the owner of the goods in any consignment or is authorised by such owner to accept these Conditions on such owner's behalf.

(*Road Haulage Association Conditions of Carriage*)

In any difficulty the carrier will thus be able to deal with the owner of the goods, and if the owner is able to reject liability (for freight, for example) the carrier will be able to turn to the consignor for breach of warranty of authority, since he purported to be the owner's agent.

Delay in Carriage. Both common carriers and private carriers have a duty to deliver goods within a reasonable time, and what is reasonable depends upon the facts of every case. If the time taken is unreasonable then there has been a delay, and if this can be proved to be due to the carrier's negligence he will be liable. If delay is caused by deviation from the route the carrier will almost certainly be liable.

Deviation from the Route. Deviation is departure from the route the carrier has expressly or implicitly agreed to follow. It is also deviation to go past a destination, or to take a vessel in tow at sea. Where no express agreement is entered into about deviation the carrier must carry by his normal route, even if it is not the shortest route. A carrier by sea may depart from his route to avoid imminent peril and to save life, and presumably this would also apply to carriage by land.

The rules about deviation have always been strict. A carrier who deviates is taken to have repudiated the contract *ab initio* and consequently cannot rely upon any clauses in the contract limiting his liability. He is also deemed to be a wrongful possessor of goods, liable for every loss that occurs to them. This is an even more onerous liability than that borne by the common carrier, for to escape liability he must show that the loss was caused by one of the common law exceptions *and also* that it would have occurred even if he had not deviated. In *Morrison v. Shaw, Savill and Albion Co. Ltd* (*1916*) a ship deviated into a French port and was torpedoed as she came out again to resume her voyage. The carriers claimed it was an Act of the King's enemies, but it was held that they must also prove that the ship would still have been torpedoed had she not deviated. This they could not prove, and were held liable for the losses suffered.

Because of the onerous nature of the rules about deviation it is usual in conditions of carriage to have an express term such as the following:

The carrier shall be entitled to enter into contracts for the carriage of goods by any route, or by any means.

Misdelivery. The duty of the carrier is to deliver the goods to the consignee, and if he delivers them to any other person it is a misdelivery. If the carrier has to deliver to a given address it is a misdelivery if he delivers them anywhere else. If he delivers them to the correct address to someone who appears to be entitled to accept delivery he has performed his duty and cannot be held liable if the party who accepted them was not in fact entitled to do so.

If a carrier tries to deliver in normal working hours at the correct address, and is unable to do so for any reason, he is discharged from his duty to deliver and now holds the goods as a warehouseman. In this position he is liable only for negligence. In *Stephenson v. Hart (1828)* a carrier was instructed to deliver goods to a named address. When he arrived there it was clear the premises were deserted. He nevertheless left a card saying that the goods could be claimed at his depot. A person purporting to be the consignee presented the card, collected the goods and could not later be found. It was held to be a negligent misdelivery.

Stoppage in Transit. SS.44–6 of the *Sale of Goods Act, 1979*, re–enacting the *Sale of Goods Act, 1893*, permit an unpaid seller who hears that his customer has become insolvent to stop the goods in transit, and retain them until payment or tender of the price. This naturally raises the question of when goods are in transit – and the Act lays down clear rules for deciding when the goods are in transit. This is from the moment they are given to a carrier or other bailee for the purpose of transit to the buyer until one of the following times:

(*a*) The moment when the buyer or his agent takes delivery at destination, or

(*b*) The buyer obtains delivery at some other place before the ultimate destination is reached, or

(*c*) The carrier acknowledges at the destination end of the journey that he holds them on behalf of the buyer – perhaps for delivery to some further destination, or

(*d*) The carrier wrongfully refuses to deliver them to the buyer. In this case the transit is at an end and the carrier will be liable to the buyer if he 'stops' them in transit.

The transit is not at an end – i.e. the goods may be stopped and returned to the seller – if the buyer refuses the goods. When goods are delivered to a ship chartered by the buyer it is a question of fact whether they are held on behalf of the buyer or on behalf of the master of the ship acting as carrier. When a part delivery has been made the balance of goods may still be stopped unless the delivery of the first part was made on the clear understanding that the possession of the whole would be surrendered.

The unpaid seller exercises his right of stoppage in transit by giving notice to the carrier, or to the person actually possessing the goods – usually the driver of a vehicle. If the notice is given to the carrier it must be in time for him to contact the servant or agent in actual possession. The carrier must then redeliver the goods to – or to the order of – the seller, who must pay the costs of redelivery.

The Carrier's Lien. A lien is a carrier's right to retain the goods in his possession until such time as the charges connected with them are paid. At common law the carrier's lien is a **particular, passive, possessory lien.** In most conditions of carriage the carrier specifies a **general, active lien.** The differences are as follows:

(*a*) A *particular lien* entitles the carrier to retain goods only as long as the charges due on that particular package are not paid. If the customer pays the carriage on the package it must be surrendered, irrespective of *what other sums are owing to the carrier* (*Prenty v. Midland Great Western Railway Company* (*1866*)). By specifying a *general lien* the private carrier claims the right to retain goods in his possession until *all* sums owing to him are paid.

(*b*) A *passive, possessory lien* confers upon the carrier only the passive right to retain possession of the goods. An active lien entitles him to sell the goods – after due notice to the owner – so that an opportunity is afforded to pay the freight due. When sold, the freight payable may be deducted and the payment of any balance to the owner is full settlement of any claim by him, provided that the goods have been sold at the best price obtainable in the circumstances.

A typical lien clause in a set of conditions reads as follows:

The Carrier shall have a general lien against the owner of the goods for any moneys whatever due from the Trader or such owner to the Carrier. If any such lien is not satisfied within a reasonable time the Carrier may at his absolute discretion, sell the goods, or part thereof, as agent for the owner and apply the proceeds towards the moneys due and the expenses of the retention, insurance and sale of the goods and shall, upon accounting to the Trader for any balance remaining, be discharged from all liability in respect of the goods.

(*Road Haulage Association Conditions of Carriage*)

Dangerous Goods. At common law the consignor of dangerous goods who does not declare their dangerous nature to the carrier is liable for every loss that occurs to persons, goods or the vehicle. If the carrier has a statutory duty to carry, the consignor of dangerous goods is liable whether or not he knew of the danger, or could reasonably have been expected to know of it. With private carriers it is usual for the conditions of carriage to include a clause about dangerous goods, making it perfectly clear that if the carrier agrees to carry them the consignor is responsible for a full and frank declaration of their nature. They must be packed and documented according to law, and the trader must indemnify the carrier against all loss or damage arising out of their carriage. The ADR Convention (*Accord Dangereux Routiers*) is a European convention adopted by the UK which governs the packing, marking and carriage of dangerous goods. It runs to 500 pages and full text is available from Her Majesty's Stationery Office.

Carriage by Two or More Carriers. In common law the duty of the carrier is to deliver the goods to the consignee. If he hands the goods over to another carrier and there is a misdelivery or any other loss or damage he will be liable to the owner even though it was the fault of the other carrier. To avoid this liability it is usual to include a clause reading

2 (2) The Carrier and any other carrier employed by the Carrier may employ the services of any other carrier for the purpose of fulfilling the Contract in whole or in part and the name of every such other carrier shall be provided to the Trader on request.

(*Road Haulage Association Conditions of Carriage*)

The Measure of Damages. The measure of damages at common law is the same as for any ordinary contract, and was laid down in the case of *Hadley v. Baxendale* (see page 161). The damages are limited to those that follow naturally from the breach of duty, or breach of contract, unless the parties noted in advance that special damages would result from any breach by declaring the value of the goods or explaining the consequences of any breach. The parties may of course agree on any sum of liquidated damages they feel is appropriate to offset any loss that may occur, but if this sum is excessive it will be void as constituting a penalty.

In most sets of conditions of carriage the carrier's liability is limited by a special clause to some standard amount. It will never exceed the value of the goods themselves. In most international conventions the difficulties of stating values in money terms have now led to the limitations being expressed in Special Drawing Rights units (SDRs). This is a unit whose value is relatively stable because it is made up of a currency basket. The composition of 1 SDR unit is as follows:

0.45	$US
0.46	Deutschemarks
0.071	£ Sterling
0.74	French Francs
34.00	Japanese Yen

Its actual value in a real settlement currency is recalculated daily by the International Monetary Fund and published in the major financial journals.

Where SDRs are not yet in use and national currencies are used, the limits of liability have traditionally been fixed at £800 per ton. This still applies to road haulage, but British Rail currently quotes £2000 per metric tonne – a figure which appears to take fair account of inflation in the value of goods in recent years.

Himalaya Clauses. A celebrated legal case concerning the SS *Himalaya* led to a completely new clause being inserted in contracts of carriage. They were called by the popular name of **Himalaya Clauses.** The facts of the case were as follows:

Adler v. Dickson (1954). The plaintiff was a passenger on the SS *Himalaya* who was injured by a fall which she alleged was due to the negligence of the master and boatswain of the ship. Her ticket bore a clause saying that passengers were carried at their own risk and the company could not be held liable in any circumstances whatsoever, etc. **Held:** the company were protected by their contract, but the master and boatswain were not protected by the contract and the plaintiff's action against them must be allowed to proceed. Considerable damages were received by the plaintiff as a result.

The effect has been for nearly all sets of conditions of carriage to carry a Himalaya Clause which carries the benefit of the contract over to the servants and agents of the carrier. A typical wording is:

2 (3) The Carrier contracts for itself and as agent of and trustee for its servants and agents and all other carriers referred to in (2) above and such other carrier's servants and agents and every reference in Conditions 3–17 inclusive hereof to 'The Carrier' shall be deemed to include every such other carrier, servant and agent with the intention that they shall have the benefit of the Contract and collectively and together with the Carrier be under no greater liability to the Trader or any other party than is the Carrier hereunder.

(*Road Haulage Association Conditions of Carriage*)

16.4 Statutory Modifications to the Law of Carriage

Before considering the actual laws applicable to each mode of transport it is necessary to make a few points clear. These relate to:

(*a*) The development of the law of carriage in various fields.
(*b*) The international influences bearing upon the law of carriage.

Development of the Law of Carriage. Traditionally the law was divided into two parts: inland carriage (which meant carriage by road) and carriage by sea (in ships). However, the Industrial Revolution led to the growth of canals, a new form of inland carriage by inland waterways, which was akin to sea carriage because vessels (barges) were used. Then the railways networks provided a third kind of inland transport. Both of these new networks were open to abuse because they were **natural monopolies,** and the carriers could abuse their monopoly positions by discriminating against particular customers by excessive charges, etc. The result was that Parliament felt it necessary to interfere to ensure fair play, and in particular to see that a proper range of facilities was available to the public and that discrimination was not practised.

Meanwhile, in sea transport, problems had arisen over the bill of lading, a document used throughout the world, which in some cases was not worth the paper on which it was printed. International trade began to suffer and international agreement was called for. The solution found was to agree an international convention document, the **Hague Rules,** which member states could ratify and enact into their 'national' laws. When a sufficient number of nations had enacted the convention the law in all their countries became the same, and confidence in bills of lading returned. Similar problems arose in air transport, where the need to overfly territory and land anywhere in an emergency called for an international agreement in other ways too. An international convention document, the **Warsaw Rules**, was agreed and implemented in the same way by enactment in Parliament. We see therefore that statutory modifications of the law of carriage became increasingly important. When the movement of goods internationally by road and rail also began, with railway wagons and heavy goods vehicles rumbling across whole continents, even inland carriage became part of an international network. The enactment of conventions for road and rail movements followed.

These statutory modifications of the law of carriage will be explained in each section below at appropriate points.

16.5 Carriage by Road

Inland carriage by road is the traditional mode of carriage, and originally all carriers were common carriers subject to the strict rules already described. An early piece of legislation, the *Carriers Act, 1830*, gave statutory recognition to the common carrier's common law right to demand an extra freight for the carriage of valuable goods. It also contained provisions exempting the common carrier from all liability in respect of valuables which were not declared by the consignor. The Act provided that where goods in the valuable class (defined as gold and silver coins, gold and silver in a manufactured or non-manufactured state, precious stones, jewellery, watches, clocks, trinkets, bills of exchange, banknotes, stamps, maps, writings, title deeds, paintings, engravings, pictures, gold-plated or silver-plated articles, china, glass, silks, furs or lace – but later machine made lace was excluded – worth more than £10) were included in a package, the carrier shall not be liable for loss, except by the felony of his servants, unless the consignor has declared the value and paid an additional sum over and above the freight as insurance money, if the carrier demands it. The meanings of the words are to be interpreted in the popular use of the word and not strictly. Thus 'valuable paintings' refer to works of art, and not painted patterns belonging to a commercial traveller (*Woodward v. London and North-Western Rly* (*1878*)). The value is the value to the consignor on sending the goods. The Act is not of great importance now as there are so few common carriers, and the railways are not affected as they have been statutorily declared to be private carriers.

For inland road transport the vast majority of carriers stipulate that they are private carriers, carrying under conditions of carriage which are available on request. Often these are drawn up for them by a trade association, such as the Road Haulage Association.

The *Carriage of Goods by Road Act, 1965*, and the *Carriage by Air and Road Act, 1979*. When international road haulage began to develop in the post-war years, it soon became clear that some internationally agreed rules of law were required. The conditions of carriage used by many UK carriers excluded liability, even for negligence, which seemed manifestly unfair to foreign buyers of goods. They were not used to the old figment of English law which held that all the parties to a contract were equally powerful in the eyes of the law. Since in many cases they had not been party to the negotiations when the contract of carriage was concluded it all seemed very nonsensical to them.

The result was an international convention at Geneva, the *Convention de Marchandises par Route* (CMR), which may be freely translated as the convention on merchandise carried by road hauliers. It held that all international carriage except the mails, funeral consignments and furniture removals should be controlled by the provisions of the CMR Convention and be documented by a CMR consignment note. However, Ireland has not ratified the Convention, and Northern Ireland is treated as part of the UK so internal transits to Northern Ireland would not be covered by the Convention. The Convention was embodied in English law by the *Carriage of Goods by Road Act, 1965*. The *Carriage by Air and Road Act, 1979*, changes the basis on which compensation is offered to take account of the use of SDR as the monetary unit in any calculations. The important points of the Convention, which may be read in full in the Acts referred to, are as follows:

Basis of legal relationship between the parties. This is a statutory relationship, based upon the acts mentioned. The Convention over-rides what the parties have agreed in their private contracts if it differs from the Convention.

The definition of international carriage This is defined as 'carriage of goods by road in vehicles for reward, when the place of taking over the goods and the place designated for delivery as specified in the contract, are situated in two different countries, of which at least one is a contracting country (i.e. has ratified the CMR Convention) irrespective of the place of residence and the nationality of the parties.

Extent of the carrier's liability. The hauler is liable for total or partial loss or damage to goods between take-over and delivery, unless he can show fault of the plaintiff, inherent vice or circumstances beyond his own control. He is also liable for delay and failure to collect COD charges (if requested).

Official document. This is the CMR consignment note, which must bear a large sign 'CMR' and the words 'International Consignment Note'.

Limitation of liability. This is limited to 8.33 SDR units of account per kilogram of gross weight, or the full value, whichever is less.

Jurisdiction of the courts. Action may be brought (*a*) in any place mutually agreed, or (*b*) where the defendant is resident or has his principal place of business or an establishment where the contract was made, or (*c*) where the goods were taken over by the carrier, or (*d*) in the country of delivery. This virtually means that any aggrieved party can have the case tried in his own country, and his courts will have jurisdiction.

Time limit on actions. Action must be brought within one year, but this is extended to three years if wilful misconduct is alleged.

16.6 Carriage by Rail

Railways were originally common carriers, and liable to the full extent as common carriers for every loss that occurred except those caused by the common law exceptions listed earlier (see Section 16.1). During the nineteenth century a running battle between Parliament and the monopolist railway companies led to almost annual Railway Acts, with Parliament attempting to load responsibilities onto the companies which they proceeded to evade by clever legal advice. A notable legal rule developed in this period was the **'doctrine of the fair alternative'**, which held that railway companies could exclude their liability for negligence in their conditions of carriage if they offered customers a fair alternative. This was carriage at company risk for a slightly higher charge, which amounted to an insurance premium payable by the customer.

Unfortunately, by the time Parliament had really gained control of the railway companies (the actual date was January 1, 1893) the internal combustion engine had arrived to destroy their monopoly, and they had become a high-cost enterprise at just the wrong moment. It has been truthfully said that it takes 60 years for any major development to work its way through the economy; it took 60 years to rivet chains on the railways and make them behave properly, and another 60 years to remove the chains so that they could survive as a transport system. This happened in 1962 when the *Transport Act, 1962*, made them private carriers, carrying by virtue of private contracts with their customers, and relieving them at last of the onerous liabilities of the common carrier.

The carriage of goods by rail is now regulated by five sets of conditions of carriage. These are:

(*a*) The general conditions of carriage.
(*b*) Carriage by water.
(*c*) Carriage of livestock.
(*d*) Carriage of coal, coke and patent fuel.
(*e*) Warehousing.

They may be obtained on request from the Board of British Rail.

Before considering these conditions of carriage it is necessary to take into account the impact of international rail travel on carriage by rail. As an island the UK has not been notably concerned with international rail carriage. Continental countries naturally have much greater scope for international rail haulage. The very first international convention on carriage was a rail convention introduced in 1914, and still in use today, called the **CIM convention**. CIM stands for the Convention on International Merchandise, a name which reflects the fact that road haulage has not yet developed to challenge the monopoly of transport enjoyed by the railways. The Convention did not include the word 'railway' in the title, because it was the only mode of international transport available at that time, apart from shipping.

Later the CIM Convention was adopted into British Rail contracts, not by the usual process of Parliamentary ratification of the Convention, but by the contractual adoption of a clause in the contract of carriage adopting the Convention as part of the contract. The thinking behind the Convention also modified the general conditions of carriage because the conclusions arrived at by the international meeting about what was 'fair' in conditions of carriage appeared to the Board of British Rail, in today's modern climate of consumer-orientated business, to be appropriate for home trade as well. The general background to these conclusions was that railway companies should be liable for their own and their servants' negligence, but not for the negligence of others. So for the first time in 150 years conditions of carriage began to say 'The Board shall be liable for . . .' instead of always saying it would not be liable for anything.

General Conditions of Carriage BR 18793/1. Space does not permit the reproduction in full of these conditions or a detailed discussion of them. The student is referred to the book already mentioned – Ridley, J., *The Law of Carriage of Goods by Land, Sea and Air* – where they are reproduced in full and commented upon.

The CIM Convention and the CIV Convention. There are two current conventions on international carriage by rail: the CIM convention already referred to and the CIV convention (*Convention Internationale de Voyageurs*) which is about passenger travel. They both came into effect in 1975, but earlier versions were available before that date.

The *Carriage by Railway, Act 1972*, gives statutory force to some parts of both conventions which have never been fully enacted into English law. It provides:

(*a*) That no action of any kind relating to a liability in respect of which provision is made by the Railway Passenger Convention or the Railway

Freight Convention may be brought against a railway undertaking or its servants or agents except in accordance with that convention (S.6).

(*b*) That the rights and obligations of the consignee of goods carried under the CIM convention shall be regulated by that convention.

(*c*) Both surcharges levied by the railway company and compensation paid by the railway company under both conventions shall be recoverable, and the railway company has a lien on the goods carried for the surcharges due.

Apart from these statutory rules the conventions have the force of law by virtue of their contractual adoption. Details, for example, from the CIM convention are as follows:

The consignment note. This bears the symbol CIM and is written in three languages: English, French and German. Goods carried under this symbol are regarded as contractually adopting the Convention and actions may only be brought in accordance with it as required by the 1972 Act.

Definition of international carriage. Carriage of goods under a through-consignment note for carriage by rail over the territories of at least two contracting states and exclusively over lines listed in S.59 of the Convention.

Speed of transit. This decides whether delay has occurred. There are two speeds – fast carriage and slow carriage – and within these speeds full wagons are expected to travel faster than part-wagon loads. Full wagon loads at fast carriage must leave within 12 hours and then travel 300 km in the first 24 hours and 400 km in each subsequent 24 hours. Part-wagon loads must leave within 12 hours and then travel 300 km in each subsequent 24 hours. For slow carriage the goods must leave within 24 hours and travel 200 km in the next 24 hours and 300 km per day thereafter. Less than full wagon loads at slow carriage leave within 24 hours and then travel 200 km per day. A red-bordered consignment note is for fast travel, a green note is for slow carriage.

The Route. This may be specified by the consignor. If it is not the railway must send the goods by the most favourable route *for the customer*.

Customs. The railway acts as the agent of the sender in clearing the goods through customs. The sender is responsible for the documentation necessary, and a **Simplified Customs Procedure** is available.

The carrier's liability. The carrier is liable for total or partial loss or damage to the goods unless it can prove fault of the claimant, inherent vice or circumstances beyond its own control. Delay is failure to achieve the speeds of transit prescribed above. The carrier may also be held liable for failure to collect COD charges.

Limitation of liability. Liability is limited to 17 European Units of Account per kilogram converted to currency on the date payment is due. The value of EUA (ECU) is recalculated daily by the European Commission.

Jurisdiction. The plaintiff selects the railway he wishes to sue and brings an action in the courts of the state where the railway is. Thus a consignee could sue his own railway company even if it never received the goods, to enable the consignee to sue in his country. Claims for delay must be made within 30 days of arrival. One year is allowed for all other claims unless wilful misconduct is alleged, when the time limit is three years.

16.7 Carriage by Inland Waterways

Canals and inland waterways are not regarded as 'seas' and consequently carriers who use them are treated in law as if they were carriers by road, except that they do use craft which are a form of ship. A ship is defined in the *Merchant Shipping Act, 1894,* as a vessel which is not propelled by oars, so it is incorrect to use the word 'boat' for barges and other river craft. A carrier by inland waterway warrants that his craft is seaworthy – in other words, fit for the purpose for which it is to be used. They are common carriers, but the *Carriers Act, 1830*, does not apply to inland waterways. They may, like all common carriers, make a special contract, and they may hold themselves out as only private carriers if they wish to do so. However, there is a point of difficulty here which concerns the existence of a third type of carrier, which Lord Esher called 'public carriers'.

In *Liver Alkali Company v. Johnson (1874)* Lord Esher took the view that in carriage by sea and inland waterway all those who carry as professional carriers are either **common carriers** or **public carriers**. Common carriers carry under the same rules as common carriers by road, but public carriers are special in that they are not under a duty to carry, and may always refuse to carry if they wish to do so, but if goods are carried the public carrier is liable – like the common carrier – for every loss that occurs, unless it was caused by one of the *six* common law exceptions (for at sea there is a sixth exception – jettison).

Who then is a private carrier by sea or inland waterway? The answer is a person who does not carry on the profession of carrier, but only carries as an ancillary activity to his main business. Thus in *Consolidated Tea and Lands Co. v. Oliver's Wharf (1910)*, where the wharfingers had agreed to warehouse items for the company, but only carried in so far as this was necessary to bring the goods to the warehouse, they were held not to be carriers, but only warehousemen, and only carried as an incidental activity to their main business. They were therefore private carriers. Similarly, those who carry for one consignor only are not common carriers or public carriers, for they do not carry for the public at large. Lord Esher's view has been upheld in several cases, so it appears that all who carry as professional carriers are liable as insurers of the goods (unless they have made a special contract to avoid this) but public carriers are not liable in tort for refusal to carry.

16.8 Carriage of Goods by Sea

A contract for the carriage of goods by sea (a contract of affreightment) may be made in two ways, and there are several bodies of law which apply – most notably the Hague-Visby rules (see below). The two methods are:

(*a*) A contract for the carriage of goods in a general ship, the contractual document being a bill of lading.

(*b*) A charterparty, which provides for the hiring of the ship itself. A charterer may then carry goods for other people on bills of lading, or may find cargo himself and issue bills of lading referring to these goods, but the charterparty will be the main contractual document between the charterer and the shipowner.

The bodies of law affecting these contracts are as follows:

(*a*) In some cases the carrier is a common carrier and the law that applies is the common law.

(*b*) In many cases where bills of lading are in use the law that will apply is the *Carriage of Goods by Sea Act, 1971,* which embodies the Hague-Visby rules into English law. This will be explained later.

(*c*) Certain statutes have important legal consequences, notably the *Merchant Shipping Acts 1894, 1958 and 1981.*

(*d*) The law relating to charterparties.

Once again it is possible in the present text to give only a brief outline – those with a particular interest should read Ridley, J., *The Law of Carriage of Goods by Land, Sea and Air.*

Historical Development of Carriage by Sea. The reason the law is so involved, as explained in (*a*)–(*d*) above, is that until 1925 it was based upon the common law, and sea carriers were common carriers liable for every loss that occurred, unless the common law exceptions applied. There were six common law exceptions in carriage by sea, **jettison** being added to Act of God, act of the Queen's enemies, inherent vice, fault of the consignor and fraud of the consignor.

Jettison is the deliberate sacrifice of cargo to save a vessel, and the carrier is not liable. Instead the law of general average applies. This has been explained already (see pages 224–5).

Warranty of seaworthiness. A carrier warrants that his vessel is seaworthy, and if it is not he is liable (unless the contract expressly excludes this liability). The warranty is that the ship is *reasonably* fit for the *stage* of the voyage that is about to commence. The warranty extends beyond the actual ship's condition to include such things as the adequacy of the crew, illness or drunkenness of the officers, provisions and medicines for the voyage, security of the portholes, etc.

As is usual in such situations, shipowners began to protect themselves from such harsh rules applicable to common carriers by excluding liability in the conditions of carriage written on the back of bills of lading. This had a disastrous effect on the value of bills of lading. Let us stop here to consider the legal aspects of bills of lading.

Bills of lading. A bill of lading is a document given by a shipowner (or a charterer) to a consignor of goods as a receipt for the goods. It is not essential that a bill of lading be issued, but the master of a vessel as the agent of the shipowner will always supply one if requested. It is usual to demand a *shipped* bill of lading, since it confirms that the goods have crossed the ship's rail. A *received for shipment* bill of lading is not so satisfactory, except where the carrier is a multi-modal operator assuming the role of **combined transport operator (CTO)** liable for every stage of the journey. Even he will hold back the received for shipment bills of lading he normally issues so that they can be stamped **shipped** after the goods are actually on board, if he is requested to do so.

We can list the functions of the bill of lading as follows:

(*a*) It is a receipt for the goods shipped.

(*b*) It is a document of title, which may be transferred to another person by assignment.

(*c*) It is evidence of the contract of carriage.

With regard to (*b*) above this is the chief use of the bill of lading. Since sea journeys take a long time and prices of cargoes fluctuate, the owner of a cargo may wish to sell goods while they are on the high seas. He does this by assigning the bill of lading to the party prepared to buy it, who can then claim the goods by presenting the bill of lading to the master of the vessel on arrival at the destination port. The bill of lading is often said to be quasi-negotiable, which means almost negotiable (quasi = almost). It is not fully negotiable – like a bill of exchange – because the assignee does not get a better title than the giver had, but only the same title as the giver had. The assignee always takes subject to the equities, i.e. the equitable rights of others.

With regard to (*c*) the bill of lading is only strong evidence of the contract of carriage, but it is permissible to introduce evidence that in fact the contract was made earlier. Since space has to be booked on ships well in advance in many cases it is likely that the discussions at that time will make a binding contract before the bill of lading has even been completed. In the 'Ardennes' case the facts were as follows:

The Ardennes (*owners of cargo*) *v. The Ardennes* (*owners*) (*1951*). In the negotiations leading up to the loading of the cargo the shipowner said that the ship would proceed direct to London. The bill of lading contained a deviation clause which permitted the owner to proceed to ports in any order he chose. By going to Antwerp the vessel was delayed and when it did arrive in London the owners of cargo were charged a higher rate of duty than would have been the case if the vessel had proceeded direct. **Held:** The contract was made earlier than the bill of lading and the safeguarding clause could not protect the shipowner, who was liable for the extra duty charged to the cargo owners.

Returning to the historical aspects, when bills of lading were assigned from one person to another the property in the goods (which were on the high seas) passed to the assignee, but the original contract of affreightment was still between the shipper and the shipowner. This meant, by the strict rules of privity of contract, that the new owners of the goods could not sue the carrier if anything was wrong with the goods on arrival, since they were not a party to the original contract. Also, if clauses were inserted by the shipowners in their bills of lading which denied liability in any circumstances it meant that those who took bills of lading in good faith for value found that when cargoes arrived – if they were damaged or had suffered losses – no redress was available against the carrier. This led to a serious loss of confidence in bills of lading.

Parliament took action by passing the *Bills of Lading Act, 1855*. Although a very short Act, this did something to remedy the problems.

Bills of Lading Act, 1855. S.1 of the Act, which is reproduced below, gave the assignees of a bill of lading the right to sue upon the original contract, which travelled with the bill, giving the assignee the same rights (and the same duties) under the contract of affreightment as were available to the original shipper. The Section reads:

1. Consignees and endorsees of bill of lading empowered to sue. – Every consignee of goods named in a bill of lading, and every endorsee of a bill of lading, to whom the property in the goods therein mentioned shall pass upon or by reason of such consignment or endorsement, shall have transferred to and vested in him all rights of suit, and be subject to the same liabilities in respect of such goods as if the contract contained in the bill of lading had been made with himself.

S.2 made it clear that this new right did not affect the right of stoppage in transit, or the right of the carrier to claim freight against the original shipper.

S.3, the most important clause, reads as follows:

Every bill of lading in the hands of a consignee or endorsee for valuable consideration representing goods to have been shipped on board a vessel shall be conclusive evidence of such shipment as against the master or other person signing the same, notwithstanding that such goods or some part thereof may not have been so shipped, unless such holder of the bill of lading shall have had actual notice at the time of receiving the same that the goods had not been in fact laden on board: Provided that the master or other person so signing may exonerate himself in respect of such misrepresentation by showing that it was caused without any default on his part and wholly by the fraud of the shipper or of the holder or some person under whom the holder claims.

This has the effect of making the master (or other signatory of a clean bill of lading) liable for goods which are lost or arrive damaged, unless it is possible to falsify the bill of lading by clear proof that the bill misrepresents what was actually loaded without any default on the master's part, but solely because of the fraud of the shipper, or holder, or some person under whom the holder claims.

Although the *Bills of Lading Act, 1855,* did solve some of the problems in carriage by sea it did not say anything about exemption clauses entered into bills of lading and these clauses excluding liability continued to be a cause of trouble. Eventually an international conference held at Brussels in 1922 produced a set of rules which came to be known as the **Hague Rules**. Later these were modified to become the **Hague-Visby Rules**. These are explained below, but first we must look at *Merchant Shipping Acts 1894, 1958 and 1981.*

The *Merchant Shipping Acts 1894, 1958 and 1981.* There are many matters to regulate about the safety of merchant shipping and only one or two affect the law of carriage, but these sections are important.

SS.492–501 of the *Merchant Shipping Act, 1894*, extend the right of lien of the carrier with regard to warehoused goods. A valuable ship cannot wait around in port for someone to collect his cargo, and the Act permitted a carrier who is delayed for more than three days in this way to unload the goods into the care of a warehouseman empowered to release the goods on payment of the sum the carrier had declared to be due. Exact arrangements for the release of the goods and the payment of the money to the carrier are then laid down.

S.502 is a re-enactment of a section of an earlier act about fire at sea. Fire at sea is a devastating event and the Section says that no British shipowner shall be liable for losses at sea caused by fire unless it can be shown that the fire was actually caused by his 'actual fault and privity'. This means that he is not vicariously liable for the faults of servants or employees, but only liable for his own actual acts or faults.

The *Merchant Shipping Act, 1894*, also introduced a protection for shipowners where valuables had been brought on board undeclared, and were subsequently stolen or made away with secretly. The shipowner is not liable in these circumstances under S.502 of the Act.

S.503 of the Act limited the liability of the shipowner for loss of life, injury or damage to goods or other vessels, to an aggregate amount of 3100 gold francs per ton of the ship's tonnage for loss of life or injury, and 1000 gold francs per ton of the ship's tonnage for damage or loss of goods. The use of the gold franc later gave rise to difficulties and this was eventually decided to be the gold franc of 65½ milligrams of gold of millesimal fineness 900. The value of this was published in orders called Sterling Equivalent Orders from time to time but, as we shall see below, the *Merchant Shipping Act, 1981,* has resolved the difficulty.

The *Merchant Shipping Act, 1958.* After the case of *Adler v. Dickson* (*1955*) referred to earlier, it was resolved to introduce what was virtually a 'Himalaya Clause' into the Merchant Shipping Acts to protect the masters and other servants of the shipowner from personal actions brought by aggrieved parties unable to sue the shipowner or carrier because of exclusionary clauses in their contracts. The Act provides that they cannot be held liable except in cases of their 'actual fault and privity'. Therefore, while they will always be liable for robbery, theft or secretly making away with valuables, they will not be liable for personal injuries or loss of or damage to goods unless they can be shown to have been personally at fault. The clauses about limitation of liability were also extended to them on the same terms as limitations of the liability of shipowners.

The *Merchant Shipping Act, 1981.* This Act resolved the old difficulty about the value of the gold franc by replacing it with a designation in SDR units. The Special Drawing Rights unit is a currency basket, made up of a selection of currencies. Its value is more stable than gold, and consequently the problems due to the changing value of gold do not arise. The 3100 gold francs per ton is changed to 206.67 SDRs, and the 1000 gold francs per ton is changed to 66.67 SDRs. For the *Carriage of Goods by Sea Act, 1971,* the figure of 10,000 gold francs per package is changed to 666.67 SDRs, and the figure of 30 gold francs per kilogram is changed to 2 SDRs per kilogram.

Conventions on the Carriage of Goods by Sea. The Convention on the Carriage of Goods by Sea, which came to be known as the **Hague Rules**, was embodied in English law by the *Carriage of Goods by Sea Act, 1924.* Its later revised version, known as the **Hague-Visby Rules**, was embodied in English law by the *Carriage of Goods by Sea Act, 1971*. Like all such Acts it could not commence until the required number of states had ratified it, and the effective date proved to be June 1977. This is now the effective Act, but a new set of rules, the **Hamburg Rules**, have been drawn up by the United Nations. These are slightly more favourable to cargo owners and unfavourable to the carriers, but at present they await ratification.

The essence of the Hague-Visby rules is that bills of lading for the international carriage of goods shall have such validity that those who wish to buy goods which are on the high seas will not hesitate to buy the bill of lading that represents the goods. To establish this validity the Convention makes it clear what are the duties of the shipowner, what faults he can be held liable for, what is the limitation of that liability, etc.

The definition of international carriage is given in Article X as follows:

'The provisions of these rules shall apply to every bill of lading relating to the carriage of goods between ports in two different states if:

(*a*) the bill of lading is issued in a contracting state, or

(*b*) the carriage is from a port in a contracting state, or

(*c*) the contract includes a clause that the Rules, or the laws of a country which has ratified the Rules, are to apply to the contract evidenced in the bill of lading, whatever may be the nationality of the ship, the carrier, the shipper, the consignee or any other interested person.'

Because this is a rather restrictive definition Parliament enacted in the Act that the rules as far as English law was concerned should also apply to coastal traffic and to the carriage of goods to such places as Northern Ireland, Gibraltar and a few other dependent territories not covered by the definition of 'two different states.' The essential features of the Hague-Visby rules reproduced in the 1971 Act in full are as follows:

Legal relationships between the parties. The contractual terms of the bill of lading forming the legal relationship between the parties are superseded by the statutory rules now enacted by the inclusion of the Convention Document as a Schedule of the Act. No **clause paramount** (a clause in the bill of lading formally recognising the existence of the Convention rules) is required under the 1971 Act (but the new Hamburg Rules do call for such a clause). As far as the 1971 Act is concerned the rules apply to every bill of lading issued by the master of a British ship under the definitions given in the Act.

The liability of the carrier. The shipowner must exercise due diligence in providing a seaworthy and cargo-worthy ship. The absolute warranty of seaworthiness under the common law is therefore reduced to a duty to exercise 'due diligence'. This means that the carrier will be responsible if he is negligent in any way in performing his duty as carrier – and this liability will extend to his servants or agents who perform duties for him *as a carrier*. It does not extend as far as agents who act wrongly outside their terms of reference. In *Leesh River Tea Company Ltd v. British Indian Steam Navigation Co. Ltd (1967)* the action against the shipowner failed because the damage complained of was the result of a theft of a cover from a storm valve by independent stevedores, who in doing so were outside the scope of their employment.

The shipowner must 'properly load, handle, stow, carry, keep, care and discharge the cargo'. He is not liable for errors in navigation or the management of the ship, nor for fire, perils of the sea and a long list of exceptions which include all the common law exceptions. Notably it is permitted under the rules to save not only life, but also property, at sea. The exclusions are comprehensive because they include 'any other course arising without the **actual fault and privity** of the carrier, his servants and agents'. This makes it clear that the carrier *is* liable for those losses that do arise because of his actual fault or privity (and even more, the Rules make it clear that anyone claiming these exceptions has to prove that the actual fault of the shipowner or his servants *did not contribute to the loss or damage*).

Limitation of liability. The limitation of liability is set under the Rules at 10,000 gold francs per package or 30 gold francs per kilogram, whichever is higher. These figures were agreed in 1968, when the use of currency baskets had not been developed. The *Merchant Shipping Act, 1981*, which still awaits a Commencement Order, will change them to 666.67 SDR units and 2 SDR units respectively. (Note that the Hamburg Rules call for 835 SDR units and 2.5 SDR units respectively.)

Jurisdiction of the courts. The Convention is silent about jurisdiction of the courts, which leaves the courts of every country free to decide whether they have jurisdiction in any dispute that arises. Naturally the rules vary from nation to nation, but in England, Wales and Northern Ireland the rules are:

(*a*) Original jurisdiction exists in any action where the defendant is present in the country and can be served with a writ.

(*b*) Jurisdiction will be assumed where:

(i) A contract is governed by English law, or concluded or broken in the English jurisdiction.

(ii) Where the contract specifies that the English courts shall have jurisdiction.

(iii) Where an international convention specifies circumstances which bring the case within English jurisdiction (but of course the Hague-Visby rules are silent on this point).

(iv) Where a foreign partnership or limited company operates within the English jurisdiction. Such an organisation must nominate a person on whom writs may be served.

In any of the above circumstances the courts will give permission for a writ to be served outside the jurisdiction, but reserves the right to refuse this if to do so would be unfair to the defendant by reason of undue difficulty or expense.

Time limit on actions. This is fixed at one year, but may be extended by mutual consent.

16.9 Charterparties

A charterparty is a contract between a shipowner and a person wishing to use his ship – the charterer. This use may be for a single voyage or a series of voyages (a **voyage charterparty**) or a period of time (a **time charterparty**). There is also a **lump sum charterparty** where a ship is chartered for a particular event, possibly of quite short duration, and the sum payable is decided and paid at once and not based on the time the ship is in use by the charterer. All these are charterparties not by way of demise. With a **demise charterparty** the shipowner surrenders the vessel to become virtually a part of the charterer's own fleet and the master and crew become the servants of the charterer and not the shipowner. In this case the master signing bills of lading signs them on behalf of the charterer, not the shipowner, and the charterer is the carrier of the goods. Where the bill of lading covers the charterer's own goods he is carrying his own goods. In voyage, time and lump sum charters the shipowner is the carrier, the master and crew are his servants and the shipowner is carrying both for the charterer and any other parties who are given bills of lading.

Stipulations in the charterparty. The following stipulations are usually made in a charterparty:

(*a*) The name of the ship.

(*b*) The nationality of the ship. This is a warranty, and if the shipowner transfers the ship during the lifetime of the charterparty in such a way that its nationality is changed, damages may be claimed.

(*c*) The class of the ship, i.e. sailing ship, steamship, etc. This is again a warranty, and may be a condition precedent – though firm legal decision on this is not yet available. (A condition precedent is one which must be met before the contract can commence.)

(*d*) The carrying capacity and registered tonnage. These may be conditions precedent, as when the charterparty calls for the charterer to load a full cargo and he needs to know what constitutes a full cargo for the vessel. At other times they may be irrelevant and of no importance.

(*e*) The position of the ship at the date of the charterparty. This is a condition precedent. In *Behn v. Burness* (*1863*) a ship was 62 miles from the place stated and it was held that the charterer was entitled to refuse to load, and could treat the contract as repudiated.

(*f*) The date at which the ship will be ready to load at the port of loading. Where there is an express stipulation of this sort it is a condition precedent and if it is not met the charterer may treat the contract as repudiated. If the stipulation is only that she will proceed without delay to the port of loading, and she does delay, there is a breach of warranty only and damages will be awarded.

(*g*) A cesser clause. A cesser clause is one which relieves the carrier from the need to pay demurrage (a charge for delaying the vessel longer than the stipulated 'lay days' when she will be available for loading) once he has completed loading. It is a question of construction in every case as to the exact meaning of a cesser clause.

Liability to load. The shipowner wishes to earn a living by carrying goods for others. It is therefore necessary to keep the ship on the move and be perfectly clear what the arrangements are with the charterer as to loading. The master of the vessel must give notice to the charterer that the vessel is actually ready to load; intention to load at a future time is not good enough. In *Christensen v. Hindustan Steel* (*1971*) it was held that a master who had given notice that a ship would be ready to load on the following day had not given notice that she was ready to load, but only that she was *not* yet ready to load at the time he gave the notice. The notice was one of anticipated readiness.

The charterparty usually contains a stipulation that the charterer will load a full cargo. He will only be excused if it is a fault of the shipowner, or the charterparty has been frustrated, or if the charterparty permits only a partial load in certain circumstances. 'Fault of the shipowner' refers to breaches of a condition precedent. Breach of a mere warranty does not entitle the charterer to refuse to load, it only entitles him to damages.

Usually certain exceptions from liability for failure to load are included in the charterparty at the charterer's request, and as such are interpreted strictly against him as the one who drew them up. They include strikes, lockouts, labour disputes, riots, civil commotions, accidents for which the charterer is not responsible and ice, frost, fog, snow and storm. To illustrate the strictness of the interpretation, it is usual to apply these exceptions only to the actual loading of cargo. If the accident or bad weather prevents goods reaching the port that is not covered by the exceptions unless expressly included in the terms of the charterparty. Similarly, the terms are taken to give excuse only if the events occur during the lay days. If a strike occurs in the demurrage days the carrier will escape liability only if his clause expressly extended the exception from liability into the demurrage days.

Usually the charterer is bound to load a full cargo, and if he does not must pay **dead freight** (an agreed freight for that part of the ship's stowage space which he has failed to utilise). This agreed freight rate must be reasonable, since the shipowner's right is to damages for breach of contract, and if the rate specified was excessive it would be void as constituting a penalty.

Lay days and demurrage. Both loading and discharge are usually required to be carried out within a specified period of time – the lay days. If no lay days are specified the duty of the charterer is to load or discharge in a reasonable time. If the charterer fails to load or discharge within the lay days it is a breach of contract, unless the charterparty also specifies 'demurrage' days. Demurrage days are a further period, after the end of the lay days, in which loading or discharging may be completed on payment of demurrage – an agreed sum for delaying the ship, payable for each day of delay.

The lay days, and consequently the demurrage days as well, run from the time the ship is declared ready for loading or unloading. This does not necessarily mean she has reached a berth and can be unloaded, but that she is an '**arrived ship**', having arrived within the commercial area of the port. This has led to a great deal of dispute, and is frequently crucial in legal cases about demurrage. In *Stag Line Ltd. v. Board of Trade* (*1950*) the charterparty gave the charterer the right to name a particular berth, and it was held that the ship had not arrived until she actually lay at that berth. No demurrage was payable for the six days she was waiting for a berth. By contrast, in *Shipping Developments Corporation SA v. v/o Sojuzneftenport: The Delian Spirit* (*1971*) the vessel reached Tuapse on February 19 and her master gave notice of readiness to load. She was directed to her berth on February 24 and began to load shortly after arrival. She was held to have arrived on February 19, and the lay days began to run from that time. The charterer was not liable for delaying the vessel until the lay days had expired, but could use his lay days to lie conveniently close until a berth was available. The test of whether a ship is an arrived ship is one of whether she is at the charterer's complete disposal for unloading. If she is, then she has arrived. In the Johanna Oldendorff case, *Oldendorff (E.L.) and Co. v. Trader Export SA (1973)*, it was held that if a ship was lying where the port authorities told her to lie, and was available to be called up for loading directly a berth was available, she had arrived. The test is: 'Had the ship reached a position within the port where she was at the immediate and effective disposition of the charterers?'

The charterparty, or the customs of the port concerned, may determine what 'days' are to be counted as 'days' for the purpose of the contract – whether they are running days, working days or weather working days.

The loading and discharge of the goods. The concept of safe arrival is an important one in transport, and the concept of a 'safe port' is crucial to the relationship between a shipowner and a charterer. It is an implied condition of the contract that the charterer will only use safe ports. If he names an unsafe port he will be liable to the shipowner for any damage caused to the ship, unless the master was at fault in not recognising the danger. In such circumstances the master's duty is to take the cargo to the nearest safe port and unload it there (*The Teutonia (1872)*). If a port cannot be entered without lightening the vessel in the roads, it is not a safe port (*The Alhambra (1881)*).

The Hamburg Rules: the UN Convention on the Carriage of Goods by Sea, 1978. The problem with international trade has always been that 'the strong take what they want, and the weak yield what they must'. Thus the carriers have always been powerful enough to insert clauses restricting their liabilities for losses, etc., and the relatively disorganised owners of cargo have been less well placed to resist such measures. However, the Hague Rules, and today the Hague-Visby Rules, have done a great deal to reduce the severity of such clauses in bills of lading. The United Nations feels that further modifications are required and has proposed the Hamburg Rules. These will strengthen the position of weaker nations, particularly the developing nations. The chief points of interest are:

(*a*) The Hamburg Rules will apply to all contracts whether bills of lading are issued or not.

(*b*) The courts will be expected to regard foreign decisions as very persuasive (if not binding) precedents.

(*c*) The carrier's responsibility is extended to cover all times when the goods are in his care, and not just the time from loading until discharge.

(*d*) The carrier's liabilities are clearly stated, and the list of exclusionary clauses is much reduced – in particular he is liable for defects in the management and navigation of the ship.

(*e*) The Hamburg Rules call for a paramount clause, specifically stating that the Hamburg Rules apply.

(*f*) The limits of liability are expressed in SDRs: 835 SDRs per package or 2.5 SDRs per kilogram of gross weight.

(*g*) Unlike the Hague-Visby Rules, which are silent about jurisdiction, the Hamburg Rules (in Article 21) are very clear about the matter.

The adoption of the Hamburg Rules appears as yet to be some distance in the future. The full text cannot be reproduced here, but is given in the textbook referred to earlier, Ridley's *Law of Carriage of Goods by Land, Sea and Air*.

16.10 Carriage by Air: the Warsaw Rules

Carriage of goods by air began in the years following the First World War, and was soon the subject of an international convention which became known as the Warsaw Rules. These rules have been revised from time to time, and the latest version (the Montreal Version) awaits ratification at present. The original Warsaw Rules were embodied into English law by the *Carriage by Air Act, 1932*. A later version was enacted in the *Carriage by Air Act, 1961*. This became effective in 1967 under the *Carriage by Air Acts* (*application of provisions*) *Order, 1967* (SI 1967, No. 480). This order also included a set of Non-International Carriage Rules, which effectively applied many of the international rules to domestic flights. Finally, the *Carriage by Air and Road Act, 1979*, has embodied the Montreal Version of the Rules into law, but this Act still awaits a commencement order. From past experience it is usually several years before a quorum of nations ratifies such an international convention.

The situation as regards carriage by air is therefore rather complex and the following list may help the reader:

(*a*) When enough nations ratify the Montreal Version this new set of Warsaw Rules will apply to all contracts of carriage by air between the citizens of nations which are high contracting parties.

(*b*) Until then the vast majority of contracts for international carriage are covered by the amended convention signed at Guadalajara in 1955, which is embodied in the 1961 Act.

(*c*) For the few nations that have not ratified the 1955 Convention, the 1932 Act and the original Warsaw Rules apply.

(*d*) For the very few nations that have not ratified any convention, and for domestic flights, the Non-International Carriage Rules, 1967, apply.

(*e*) Common law does not apply at all to carriage by air.

In the outline of the law which follows, the Montreal Version, which is likely to be implemented very shortly, has been used as the basis for the statements made, since it best reflects the current position of air carriage. The vast volumes of passenger and freight traffic now moving by air have called for some streamlining of procedures, since aircraft worth millions of pounds cannot be held up by petty bureaucracy, and the increasing use of computerised data instead of documents makes earlier conventions somewhat obsolete. Where necessary a note pointing out differences between earlier conventions and the Montreal Version is included.

International Carriage. The definition of international carriage is as follows:

'For the purposes of this Convention, the expression international carriage means any carriage in which, according to the agreement between the parties, the place of departure and the place of destination, whether or not there be a break in the carriage or a transhipment, are situated either within the territories of two High Contracting Parties or within the territory of a single High Contracting Party if there is an agreed stopping place within the territory of another state, even if that state is not a High Contracting Party. Carriage between two points within the territory of a single High Contracting Party without an agreed stopping place within the territory of another State is not international carriage for the purposes of this Convention.'

Under this definition a flight from London to New York is international carriage, governed by the amended convention of 1955 since both the UK and the USA have ratified the amended convention. A flight between London and Zaïre, which has not ratified the amended convention, is governed by the original convention and the *Carriage by Air Act, 1932*. A flight between London and Gibraltar is not international carriage, since Gibraltar is not an independent state. It is therefore governed by the Non-International Carriage Rules.

The air waybill. Article V of the amended convention provides that an air waybill shall be delivered to the carrier by the consignor with at least three copies (but in practice there are 12 copies). The carrier's copy must be signed by the consignor; the consignor's copy must be signed by the carrier; and the consignee's copy must be signed by both the carrier and the consignor. The air waybill must include an indication of the places of departure and destination; the place of an intermediate stopping place if departure and destination airports are both in the same country; and an indication of the weight of the consignment.

The earlier conventions held that unless the air waybill complied exactly with the convention the carrier could not rely on the clauses in the convention limiting his liability. This has now been dropped, for it is generally agreed that a mere slip of the typewriter should not disqualify a carrier from receiving the benefits conferred upon him by the convention. The Montreal Version also permits the air waybill to be replaced by electronic data, provided it permits the identification and tracing of a consignment in the electronic records. In general, an air waybill is not negotiable, but there has never been any objection to the issue of negotiable air waybills and they are still possible under the Montreal Version. There is little point in negotiable air waybills as the transit times are so short that the need to sell goods in transit rarely arises.

Stoppage in transit. A consignor who has sent goods by air has a copy of the air waybill to prove it. Under Article 12 on production of this copy he may stop the goods in transit and redirect them in any way he likes, up to the moment when they reach the destination airport.

The rights of the consignee. These rights start on arrival of the goods at the destination airport. The carrier must notify the consignee of their arrival, and release them on payment of any charges due. If the carrier admits the loss of goods, or if they have not arrived within seven days of the estimated time of arrival, an action may be commenced.

The liability of the carrier. The new Rules state quite explicitly that the carrier *is* liable for loss or damage to cargo sustained during the carriage by air, provided the loss was not attributable to inherent vice, defective packing, act of war or act of public authority. The duty of care extends for the whole period of the carriage by air – whether in an airport, on board an aircraft or in an emergency landing in any place whatsoever. It does not cover carriage by land, sea or inland waterway, unless by the nature of the carriage by air such transhipment was essential for loading or delivery and therefore part of the carriage by air.

The limitations of liability. This version of the Rules has adopted SDRs as the basis of compensation, and will thus avoid (when implemented) all the problems arising from the use of the gold franc in the original convention. The limits of liability are:

(*a*) For destruction, loss or damage to passengers' baggage, 1000 SDRs per passenger. Courts may also award legal costs.

(*b*) For loss, damage or delay to cargo, 17 SDRs per kilogram, unless the consignor declared a value to be covered and paid an extra sum by the way of premium.

Under the Amended Convention the limits are 5000 gold francs per passenger and 250 gold francs per kilogram.

Any attempt to reduce the carrier's liability by a clause in the contract is declared null and void, without damaging the remainder of the contract.

There is a 'Himalaya Clause' (Article 25A) in the convention to protect servants and agents of the carrier sued personally, provided they have acted within the scope of their employment. They are given the protection of the Convention as to the limitation of liability. Article 24 makes it perfectly clear that however a legal action is brought, whether in contract or tort, any compensation payable is subject to the limitations given above.

Jurisdiction and the time limit for actions. Actions for damages may be brought at the option of the **plaintiff** in the territory of one of the High Contracting Parties, before a court having jurisdiction in the place where the carrier is ordinarily resident, or has his principal place of business, or has an establishment by which the contract was made, or before the court having jurisdiction at the place of destination. It is also possible to bring the case in the country where the plaintiff is ordinarily resident if the carrier has an establishment there.

An action can be brought only if the carrier was given notice of the damage or loss within 14 days of receipt of the cargo, or within seven days of receipt of the baggage. If delay is alleged there are 21 days to notify a complaint.

There is a time limit of two years on the commencement of a legal action, reckoned from the time of arrival, or the time when the aircraft ought to have arrived, or from the date when the carriage stopped.

16.11 Comparison of Conventions on International Carriage

To assist the reader in comparing the various conventions on international carriage, Tables 16.1 and 16.2 have been reproduced by courtesy of Woodhead Faulker Ltd, from *Elements of Export Law*.

Table 16.1. Comparative tables on the international carriage of goods

Basic concepts

Aspect of law.	*CMR* (International road haulage).	*CIM* (International rail carriage).
Basis of legal relationship between the parties.	Statutory – by the *Carriage of Goods by Road Act, 1965*, which enacts the CMR convention. Later amended by the *Carriage by Air and Road Act, 1979*.	Contractual – the CIM convention is adopted by a 'paramount clause' on the rail consignment note.
The definition used for 'international' carriage.	The convention applies to every contract for the carriage of goods for reward by road haulage where the place of taking over the goods and the place of delivery are in two different countries of which one at least is a country which has adopted the convention.	The carriage of goods consigned under a through consignment note for carriage by rail over the territories of at least two contracting states and exclusively over lines listed in Article 59 of the convention.
Extent of carrier's liability.	The haulier is liable for total or partial loss or damage to goods between takeover and delivery, but not where he can prove fault of the plaintiff, inherent vice, or circumstances beyond his own control. He is also liable for unreasonable delay, and for failure to collect COD charges.	The railway is liable for total or partial loss of the goods and for damage thereto between takeover and delivery unless it can prove fault of the claimant, inherent vice or circumstances beyond its own control. The time of transit is calculated on one of four formulae. Exceeding this time of transit leads to liability for delay. (See text for details.)

Hague–Visby Rules, Carriage of Goods by Sea Act 1971, also *Hamburg Rules* awaiting ratification.	*Warsaw Rules* (Carriage by Air) Montreal Version awaiting commencement order.	*ICC 298* (Uniform Rules for a Combined Transport Document).
Statutory – a clause paramount is not required under the Hague–Visby Rules but will be required under the Hamburg Rules.	Statutory – by the *Carriage by Air Act, 1961*. The Montreal Version of the rules is enacted in the *Carriage by Air and Road Act, 1979*, but awaits a commencement order.	Contractual – the Uniform Rules are adopted contractually whenever a combined transport document is issued.
The carriage of goods by sea in ships from any port in Great Britain or Northern Ireland to any other port whether in or outside Great Britain or Northern Ireland, provided a bill of lading is issued and goods are not live animals or deck cargo.	Carriage between a place of departure and a place of arrival which are in the territories of two different high contracting parties (states which have ratified the convention), or carriage between two places in the same state if there was an intermediate stop in any other state whether a high contracting party or not.	The carriage of goods by at least two different modes of transport from a place situated in one country to a place designated for delivery situated in a different country.
The shipowner must exercise due diligence in providing a seaworthy and cargoworthy ship. He must properly load, handle, stow, carry, keep, care for and discharge the cargo. He is not liable for errors in navigation or management of the ship, nor for fire, perils of the sea, and a long list of exceptions. See the text for major changes in the Hamburg Rules awaiting ratification.	The operator is liable for loss, destruction or damage to cargo during the carriage by air (whether in an aircraft, or an aerodrome or in the event of a forced landing anywhere else). Not liable if he can prove that he took all necessary measures, or that it was not possible to take such measures. Not liable if he can prove fault of the claimant. (Montreal version increases these immunities.) Liable for delay.	The CTO (combined transport operator) is liable for loss or damage to the goods from time of takeover to time of delivery caused by his own, his servants' or his sub-contractors' acts. Liable for delay.

Table 16.2. Comparative tables on the international carriage of goods

Comparison of rules

Aspect of law.	*CMR* (International road haulage).	*CIM* (International rail carriage).
Official document.	CMR consignment note.	CIM consignment note.
Does it have a 'paramount clause'?	The consignment note bears a large sign 'CMR' and the words 'International Consignment Note'?	Consignment note bears the sign 'CIM International carriage by rail' – in English, French, and German, and a clause adopting the Convention.
Limitation of liability. (*a*) Liability never exceeds the total value. (*b*) Gold franc consists of 65.5 mg of gold of millesimal fineness 900. (*c*) SDR unit recalculated daily by IMF.	8.33 SDR units of account per kg of gross weight.	17 European Units of Account per kg converted to currency at the rate prevailing on the date that payment is made.
Jurisdiction of the courts.	Action may be brought: (*a*) anywhere that is agreed, or (*b*) where the defendant is resident, or has his principal place of business or an establishment where the contract was made, or (*c*) the place where the goods were taken over by the carrier, or (*d*) in the place of delivery.	The plaintiff must select the railway he wishes to sue, under the rules of Article 43, and must bring his action in the courts of the state to which the railway belongs.
Time limit on legal action.	One year, extended to three years if wilful misconduct is alleged.	One year, extended to three years if wilful misconduct is alleged against the railway.

Hague–Visby Rules, Carriage of Goods by Sea Act, 1971, also *Hamburg Rules* awaiting ratification.	*Warsaw Rules* (Carriage by Air) Montreal Version awaiting commencement order.	*ICC 298* (Uniform Rules for a Combined Transport Document).
Bill of lading.	Air waybill (1961 Act), Air consignment note (1932 Act).	Combined Transport Document.
The 1971 Act makes no mention of a paramount clause. The Hamburg Rules, when implemented, do require a paramount clause.	It bears a warning that if the carriage is international carriage, the convention will apply and limit the carrier's liability.	The Uniform Rules say it must bear the heading 'Negotiable combined transport document' issued subject to Uniform Rules for a Combined Transport Document (ICC Publication 298) or 'Non-negotiable combined, etc.'.
666.67 SDRs per package or 2 SDR's per kg, whichever is higher. The Hamburg Rules will change these limits to 835 SDR units per package or 2.5 SDR units per kg of gross weight.	250 gold francs per kg unless a higher value has been declared and a supplementary charge paid. The Montreal version will change this to 17 SDR units per kg and for baggage 1000 SDR units per passenger.	30 gold francs per kg unless a higher value has been declared by the consignor.
The convention does not mention jurisdiction – so the court would decide whether it was competent to hear a case and which law should be applied. The Hamburg Rules give very clear instructions about jurisdiction.	Action must be brought, at the option of the plaintiff in the territory of one of the high contracting parties where the carrier: (*a*) is ordinarily resident, or (*b*) has his principal place of business, or (*c*) has an establishment where the contract was made, or (*d*) at the place of destination.	The Uniform Rules are silent about jurisdiction and therefore it will be for the courts to decide whether they have jurisdiction in a particular case.
One year normally, but by mutual consent this may be extended.	Two years.	Nine months after (*a*) delivery, or (*b*) date when the goods should have been delivered, or (*c*) date decided by Rule 15 (which says goods are deemed lost 90 days after a reasonable time for delivery has elapsed).

16.12 Revision Test

Answers	*Questions*
–	**1.** What is a common carrier?
1. A person who holds himself out as ready to carry for the public at large.	**2.** What is the extent of the common carrier's liability?
2. He is liable as an insurer for every loss that occurs unless he can show that one of the common law exceptions applies.	**3.** What are the common law exceptions?
3. (*a*) Act of God; (*b*) act of the Queen's enemies; (*c*) fault of the consignor; (*d*) fraud of the consignor; (*e*) inherent vice.	**4.** What is a private carrier?
4. One who holds himself out as a carrier, but reserves the right to choose for whom he will carry – making a private contract with each customer.	**5.** What form does the private contract take?
5. It incorporates a set of standard *conditions of carriage* into the contract, covering all the points where difficulties usually arise.	**6.** List these points of difficulty.
6. (*a*) With whom was the contract made; (*b*) delay; (*c*) deviation; (*d*) stoppage in transit; (*e*) lien; (*f*) dangerous goods; (*g*) carriage by two or more carriers; (*h*) the measure of damages.	**7.** What is the *Carriers Act, 1830*, about?
7. Carriage of valuables by common carriers. As it only now applies to road carriage and many carriers make it quite clear they are not common carriers, it is of limited application today.	**8.** What is the *Carriage of Goods by Road Act, 1965*, about?

Answers	*Questions*
8. It implemented the CMR Convention and makes international carriage subject to the CMR rules.	**9.** How does an international convention work?
9. (*a*) Matters of dispute are discussed at an international meeting and fair rules are agreed. (*b*) These rules are clearly stated in a Convention document. (*c*) The delegates go back to their own countries and get their own legislatures to ratify the convention and enact it into national law. (*d*) When enough countries have ratified it a commencement date is agreed, and from that time the convention over-rides unfair terms in private contracts.	**10.** What are the chief international conventions on the law of carriage of goods?
10. (*a*) The CIM Convention (on rail carriage); (*b*) the CMR Convention (on road carriage); (*c*) the Hague–Visby Rules (on carriage by sea); (*d*) the Warsaw Rules (on carriage by air).	**11.** What are the Hamburg Rules?
11. A United Nations sponsored convention to replace the Hague–Visby Rules on carriage by sea. It is awaiting ratification.	**12.** List the chief matters requiring harmonisation in such conventions.
12. (*a*) The basis of legal relationships between the parties. (*b*) The definition of international carriage. (*c*) The extent of the carrier's liability. (*d*) Which courts shall have jurisdiction. (*e*) What is the time limit on legal actions. (*f*) What currency, or what basket of currencies, is to be used in settling disputes resolved by arbitration or legal decisions in the courts.	**13.** In this sort of test it is only possible to ask general questions. Students might like to make up their own test on each of the Conventions listed in **10** above, asking questions about each of the points mentioned in **12** above. Then try some of the questions in Appendix 1.

17
Negotiable Instruments

17.1 The Concept of Negotiability

A negotiable instrument is one which passes from hand to hand without notice being given to the party who is liable on it, and without the recipient having to take it 'subject to the equities' (see S.11.6). Consider an ordinary Bank of England £10 note: on it the Bank of England declares that it promises to pay the bearer on demand the sum of £10. If I transfer this to a shopkeeper to make a small purchase, I do not need to notify the Bank that in future they should pay the shopkeeper and not me (as I would have to do if I transferred an ordinary debt by a legal assignment under S.136 of the *Law of Property Act, 1925*). Nor is the shopkeeper put upon enquiry as to whether I am the *bona fide* owner of the £10 note. He does not take 'subject to the equities'. So long as the shopkeeper takes the note in good faith, for value, he gets a perfect title to the note, even if I have stolen it. It would be a different matter of course if he took the proceeds of a bank robbery, say 100 000 £10 notes, for 20 pence each. That is not 'in good faith', or 'for value'.

This use of certain documents – particularly bills of exchange and promissory notes – as negotiable instruments arose out of the law merchant. Merchants found that the best way to get round difficulties about notifying the parties liable on such documents, and the risks that a document might have been stolen, was to disregard the difficulty. By custom, or usage, it became generally understood that such documents were freely transferable, the one liable to pay simply honouring the document, whoever presented it, for payment on the due date, provided everything appeared to be in order. The person who took such a document in good faith for value acquired a good title to the document, even if the giver of it had no title. Later this behaviour was recognised in the common law courts as valid behaviour – under the general rule that the courts will always uphold the reasonable expectations of businessmen. Finally, as we shall see, a statutory enactment – the *Bills of Exchange Act, 1882* – put the seal of Parliamentary approval on these arrangements.

The most common negotiable instruments are listed below:

(*a*) Bill of exchange (including cheques: a cheque is defined as 'a bill of exchange, drawn on a banker, payable on demand' – *Bills of Exchange Act, 1882*, S.73).

(*b*) Promissory notes (including bank notes).
(*c*) Treasury bills.
(*d*) Dividend warrants.
(*e*) Bankers' drafts.
(*f*) Certificates of deposit.
(*g*) Bearer bonds of various sorts.

The law is best explained by considering bills of exchange as the typical representative of negotiable instruments, and studying the *Bills of Exchange Act, 1882*.

17.2 Definition of a Bill of Exchange

The definition which is given below should be learned by heart, since it is one of the most succinct legal definitions ever drafted. There is not a superfluous word in it, and although it sounds complicated it can easily be committed to memory in five minutes, and clarifies a great many ideas about bills of exchange if it is fully comprehended.

S.3 of the Act reads:

(1) A bill of exchange is an unconditional order in writing addressed by one person to another, signed by the person giving it, requiring the person to whom it is addressed to pay on demand or at a fixed or determinable future time a sum certain in money to or to the order of a specified person, or to bearer.

Considering this definition in relation to the bill of exchange shown in Fig. 17.1 we have the following points to note:

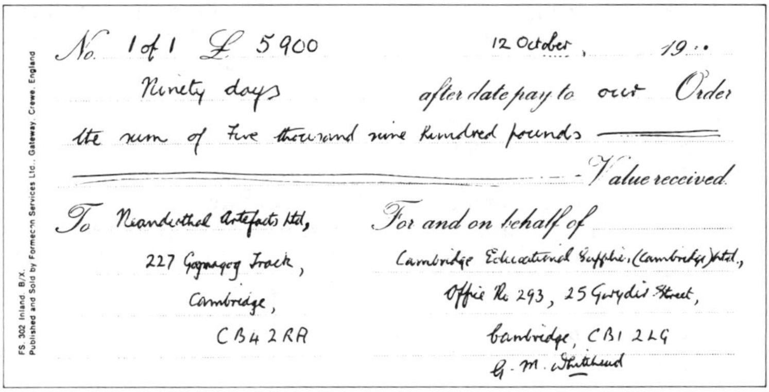
No. 1 of 1 £ 5900 12 October, 19..
Ninety days after date pay to our Order
the sum of Five thousand nine hundred pounds
Value received
To Neanderthal Artefacts Ltd,
227 Gogmagog Track,
Cambridge,
CB4 2RR
For and on behalf of
Cambridge Educational Supplies (Cambridge) Ltd.,
Office No 293, 25 Gwydir Street,
Cambridge, CB1 2LG
G. M. Whitehead
FS. 302 Inland B/X.
Published and Sold by Formecon Services Ltd., Gateway, Crewe, England

Fig. 17.1. An inland bill of exchange

(*a*) *The bill is an unconditional order in writing*. It says quite clearly 'pay'. It does not say 'provided the good ship *Peerless* arrives safely from Bombay' or put in any other condition about payment; it says 'pay to our order' without any conditions at all.

(*b*) *It is 'addressed by one person to another'.* The person who writes the order out is called the **drawer** of the bill because he draws it up. In this case G. M. Whitehead, of Cambridge Educational Supplies (Cambridge) Ltd, is the drawer, and the bill is addressed to another firm, Neanderthal Artefacts Ltd. This company is the **drawee** (the one drawn upon). It is possible to have the drawee a completely fictitious character like 'Robinson Crusoe', but in the vast majority of cases it is a real firm. This is explained below.

(*c*) *It is 'signed by the person giving it'.* In this case G. M. Whitehead has signed the bill as the representative of Cambridge Educational Supplies (Cambridge) Ltd. When the drawer signs in this way he immediately becomes liable on the bill (indeed everyone who signs his name on the bill becomes liable on it) and will be obliged to honour it on the due date. The fairness of this arrangement is explained below. Certainly Neanderthal Artefacts are not liable on it yet, for they have not yet signed the bill, and if it had been made out in the name of a fictitious character like Robinson Crusoe we could not have expected him to honour it on the due date.

(*d*) *It is for 'a sum certain'.* Note that the Act does not say 'a certain sum', it says 'a sum certain'. The implication is that a clear amount must be stated – in this case £5900. It would not be a bill of exchange if the bill called for 'the amount my house fetches at auction', for this is an uncertain sum and those handling the bill later, who perhaps do not even know the drawer, would not be able to guess what the value of the bill might be.

(*e*) *It is not 'on demand' but it is 'at a fixed or determinable future time'.* The bill reads 'Ninety days after date pay . . .' and the date is October 12, 19 . . (The authors apologise for the use of 19 . . here but this avoids the need to redraw the artwork every year or so; regard this as the year in which you are reading the book.) Ninety days after October 12 is easily determinable; it is January 10. At one time three days of grace were allowed for the bad conditions of British roads, and such a bill would have been payable on January 13. This practice has been discontinued, but it may still apply in some countries which have followed British practice and have not discontinued the arrangement.

(*f*) *The bill is an 'order' bill.* The definition says that a bill of exchange must order the drawee to pay a sum certain to – or to the order of – a 'specified person, or to bearer'. This bill is not a bearer bill, but it does say 'pay to our order', which means that we will tell them whom to pay, at some time in the future. We shall do this by endorsing the bill. This is also explained later.

This concludes the consideration of how the bill of exchange fits in with the definition of a bill given in the Act. There is still, however, much to say. This is best explained by considering the uses of a bill of exchange.

17.3 The Use of Bills of Exchange

Consider the situation shown diagrammatically in Fig. 17.2. Read it carefully now.

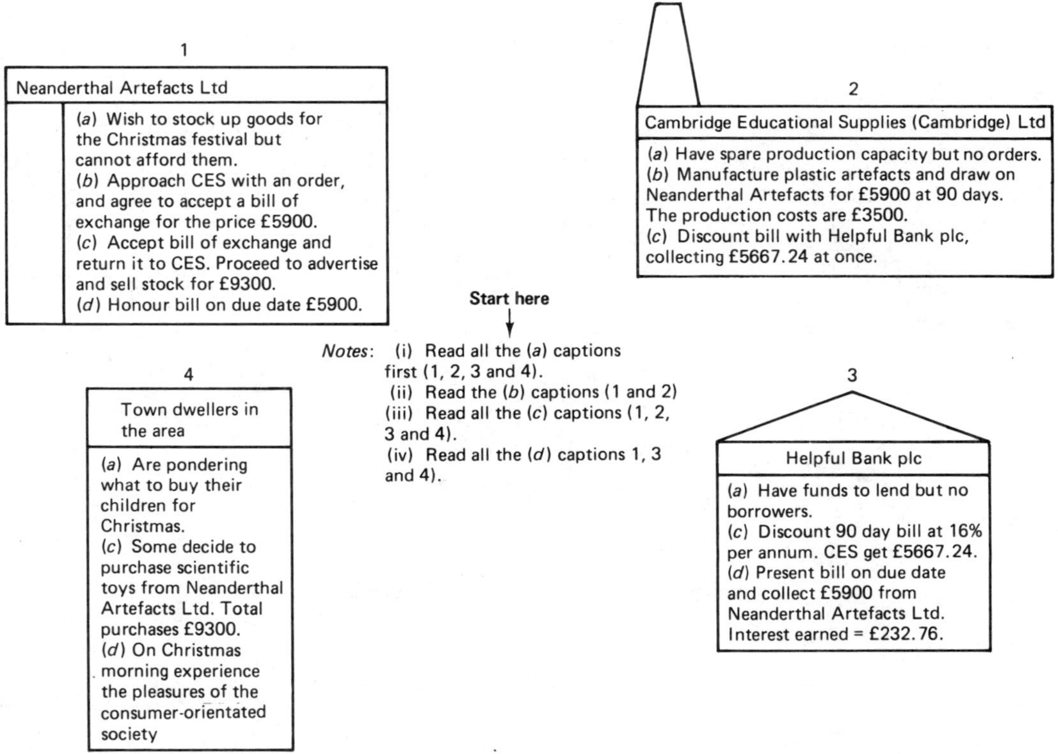

Fig. 17.2. The use of a bill of exchange

This diagram is largely self-explanatory, and illustrates the chief use of bills of exchange as a means of financing business, giving all the parties involved a chance to engage in their particular business activities. All bills should be self-liquidating, which means that by the time the due date arrives the business activity which they fostered has provided the funds to honour the bill. In Fig. 17.2 the following situations have been arrived at by the due date:

(i) Cambridge Educational Supplies have kept their factory going by manufacturing goods which cost them £3500. They have been paid £5667.24, and have thus made a profit of £2167.24.

(ii) Neanderthal Artefacts have obtained supplies three months before Christmas, which they sold for £9300. They have been able to honour the bill for £5900 on January 10 and have £3400 left towards their overheads, and of course their profits.

(iii) The Helpful Bank lent £5667.24 and were repaid £5900, giving interest earned of £232.76. This is an effective rate of 16.66 per cent.

(iv) The ordinary consumers have experienced the satisfactions of the consumer society.

The legal points that need stressing are as follows:

(*a*) *Acceptance of the bill.* When the drawer of the bill presents it to the drawee for acceptance he expects the drawer to give his assent to the order it contains by writing *accepted* on it, and signing it. Even just the signature will do. The drawee is now the 'acceptor' and is legally bound to honour the bill on the due date. The drawer is now the holder of the bill (but not a holder in due course – see below). Cambridge Educational Supplies can now do one of the following things:

(*ai*) *They can keep the bill until maturity, i.e. the due date, and present it for payment.* If they do this they will collect the face value of the bill, £5900, but they will of course have to wait 90 days before they have the use of their money.

(*aii*) *They can discount the bill with a bank.* If they do this, as in the example given above, they only collect the discounted value of the bill, which at 16 per cent for 90 days is £5667.24. The bank now owns the bill, it having been endorsed to them. When a holder of a bill endorses it to someone else he writes an order on the back of the bill (*in dorso* (Italian) – on the back). (Note that 'endorse' and 'indorse' have the same meaning.) The order might read 'Pay Helpful Bank Plc' and this order would be signed by the drawer – in this case CES Ltd. The drawer has now become the **first endorser**, and the bank has become a 'holder in due course'.

The bank may keep the bill to maturity, or may re-discount it at any time for the number of days it has to run. There is a whole market, the London Discount Market, for such bills. One of the chief functions of the discount houses is to take from the banks such trade bills as they do not wish to retain in their own portfolios. If they do take such a bill from a bank it will be endorsed over to them, and the bank adds its name to the bill as second endorser. The more names a bill collects in this way the safer it is, for every name on the bill is liable to honour it. Sometimes a bill is completely full on the back, and a piece of paper called an **allonge** has to be stuck on it to take any extra negotiations of the bill to further parties. The word 'negotiation' implies the transfer of a bill of exchange or other negotiable instrument from one party to another, free of the equities.

(*aiii*) *They can negotiate the bill to other third parties for value received.* A third party taking a bill in this way becomes a holder in due course.

(*b*) *Holder in due course.* A holder in due course, as defined in S.29 of the 1882 Act is anyone who holds a bill of exchange under the following conditions:

(i) That he obtained it before it was overdue and without notice of any dishonour.
(ii) That he took it in good faith, for value, and without notice of any defect in title of the person who gave it to him.
(iii) That the bill is complete and regular on the face of it.

To follow this situation consider what happens if Cambridge Educational Supplies wish to buy raw materials from S for their factory. If S is agreeable, W, for CES Ltd, can endorse the bill to him on some fair basis, taking account of the period before payment is due. S could in turn negotiate it to T, who could negotiate it to X. We can now see why it is fair for the bill to be honoured by the drawer should the acceptor dishonour it. The acceptor's undertaking to honour the bill was made to the drawer, CES Ltd, who subsequently became the first endorser. S became the second endorser, T the third endorser and X the holder of the bill. If X presents the bill to the acceptor on the due date and it is dishonoured, that is no reason why T should not pay X for the value he received from X. Similarly, S must pay T and W must pay S. Ultimately W must honour the bill, because he is the drawer and it is his customer, the acceptor, who has failed to pay. If W honours the bill everyone else is satisfied and W must pursue the acceptor to obtain payment for the goods originally supplied 90 days earlier. The holder of a bill which has been dishonoured may approach anyone higher up on the bill than himself and demand payment, but the most logical person to approach is the drawer, for he must honour the bill in the end. In practice the bill often moves 'backwards to the drawer', each person seeing the person who negotiated the bill to him and demanding payment.

Inland Bills and Foreign Bills. An inland bill is one which is either both drawn and payable within the British Isles, or drawn within the British Isles on some person resident therein. Any other bill is a foreign bill. An important distinction between them is their **treatment on dishonour**. When an inland bill is dishonoured the holder's rights against the drawer and endorsers of the bill are effective at once, but if desired a more formal procedure may establish the fact of dishonour. The bill is taken to a notary public who presents it again, establishes that it is in fact dishonoured and attaches a slip of paper to the bill stating the answer received when presenting the bill, the date and his signature. This is called **noting** and must be done either on the day of dishonour or the next day. Such a 'note' can be turned into a formal protest at any time thereafter (S. 93, 1882 Act).

With foreign bills, and with inland bills where insolvency or bankruptcy of the acceptor takes place before maturity, a more formal **protest** is required. This is a certificate containing a copy of the bill, certifying that the notary presented it for payment and that payment was refused. Such a protest is recognised in international law as proof of dishonour, and binds the drawer and endorsers to honour the bill. Without it they are discharged from liability, and the holder's only recourse is against the acceptor of the bill. A notary public is a solicitor empowered by the courts to act in such matters; not every solicitor is a notary public. In the absence of a notary public any householder or substantial resident may protest a bill, in a form given in Schedule 1 of the 1882 Act.

Sets of Bills. In foreign trade bills are sometimes issued in sets, though the practice is reducing as communications improve. The idea is that all the bills in a set constitute *one* bill, and each refers to the existence of the others. The drawee only accepts one of them (if he accepts more he is liable on each one he accepts). The bills could then be sent off by different mails and the first to arrive would be honoured. The others at once become void, but if the copy honoured was not the accepted copy the acceptor could still be liable upon it. If a set of bills is improperly used, and the different copies are negotiated (sold) to different parties, the individual endorsers of them are liable upon them. Fig. 17.3 explains the position.

Copy	Drawer	Other holders of the bill				Position on presentation
1	A	A	A	A	A	A – paid by acceptor
2	A	B	D	E	G	J – refused on presentation
3	A	C	C	F	H	K – refused on presentation

Fig. 17.3. Improper negotiation of a set of bills

Notes

(i) At the beginning all three copies are in A's possession. Copy No. 1 has been accepted.

(ii) A negotiates (sells) the other copies to B and C, who negotiate them to other parties as shown.

(iii) A presents the accepted copy to the acceptor who honours it. The other bills are now void as far as the acceptor is concerned, and he refuses to honour them.

(iv) J may now look to G, E, D, B and A to honour Copy No. 2 and A has the eventual liability on this bill.

(v) K may look to H, F, C and A to honour Copy No. 3, with A having the ultimate liability on it.

Inchoate Instruments. If a bill or cheque is incomplete, with the amount or the name of the payee or some other detail left out, it is said to be inchoate. A person signing such a paper implies authority to the receiver to complete it in the manner agreed between them. If A gives his son B a cheque with no amount filled in to purchase a second-hand car, for example, the son has *prima facie* authority to fill in the amount when he finds a suitable car. The son cannot – even if he completes the document – have the rights of a holder in due course, for he did not take it 'complete and regular on the face of it', but if he negotiates it to someone else for value that person will be a holder in due course and can sue on the bill, since at the time he took it for value it was complete, and not an inchoate instrument.

17.4 The Parties to a Bill of Exchange

These have been referred to above, but to recapitulate they are:

(*a*) **The Drawer** – the person who writes the bill out in the first place and signs it.

(*b*) **The Drawee** – the person drawn upon. If the drawee is the same person as the drawer or if the drawee is a fictitious person, the holder may treat it either as a bill of exchange or as a promissory note. The point is that the person liable on such a bill is the drawer, and therefore he has effectively promised to pay the money to anyone who presents it on the due date. If the drawee is a real person who has been drawn upon in the normal course of business he will usually become in due course the acceptor of the bill.

(*c*) **The Acceptor** – the drawee who assents to the order in the bill accepts it as already explained, and by accepting it engages that he will honour it on the due date according to the **tenor** of the bill (the period for which it is to run). In doing so he is precluded from denying to any future holder in due course the existence of the drawer, or the genuineness of his signature, or his capacity or authority to draw the bill. If the bill is an order bill, either to the drawer's order or a payee's order, since these parties may endorse the bill to other parties the acceptor cannot deny their right to do so (though he cannot guarantee the genuineness or the validity of their signatures – S.54).

(*d*) **The Payee** – the person to be paid. It is quite usual for this to be the drawer, since the bill may read 'pay me . . .' or 'pay to our order . . .', but it may be a third person who is to have the benefit of the bill. The Act says that if a bill is made payable to a payee, it must name the payee so that there is reasonable certainty who is intended to benefit on the due date.

(*e*) **Holders** – are defined in the Act as 'payees or indorsees of a bill or note who are in possession of it, or the bearers thereof'. It follows that a person could hold a bill – because he had been given it, for example – and yet not be a 'holder in due course'. A holder for value is a person who holds a bill for which value has been given at some previous time, even if not by him. Such a holder for value may look to the acceptor and all prior parties to honour the bill.

(*f*) **Holders in due course** – explained above. Their legal position is that they may sue upon the bills in their own names, and may defeat any defences depending on defects of title or depending on the relations between the various parties prior to the bills coming into their possession.

(*g*) **Endorsers** – any endorser of a bill undertakes that it will be honoured on the due date and that if dishonoured he will reimburse the person to whom he endorsed it, or any subsequent endorser who has been obliged to pay it. He is precluded from denying to any holder in due course the validity of the drawer's signature or the signature of any endorser prior to himself.

(*h*) **Bearers** – a person bearing a bearer bill of exchange (i.e. having it in his possession). A **bearer bill** is one expressed to be payable to bearer, or one which is endorsed 'in blank' by the last endorser. An endorsement is 'in blank' when it consists of the endorser's signature and nothing else. Thus a bill endorsed 'Pay T. Jones, signed J. Blenkinsop', is not endorsed in blank, but a bill endorsed 'J. Blenkinsop' is endorsed in blank, and becomes a bearer bill. Any bearer of this bill may present it for payment on the due date.

(*i*) **Transferor by Delivery** – where a bill is a bearer bill the person who transfers it is called the transferor by delivery, and the party to whom it is transferred is the transferee by delivery. Since a bearer bill does not need to be endorsed, the transferor does not sign the bill, and is not liable on it, but he does warrant to the transferee that the bill is what it purports to be, that he has a right to transfer it and that he knows of no defect in it rendering it valueless. The immediate transferee therefore does have a recourse against the transferor should the bill prove defective.

(*j*) **Accommodation parties.** An accommodation party is someone who adds his signature to a bill to make it a first-class bill, because he is eminently credit-worthy, to accommodate a friend who is less credit-worthy. He may sign as drawer, acceptor or endorsee. Thus if A, a wealthy businessman, accommodates B, who is in need of funds, by accepting a bill of exchange for £1000 drawn on him at 90 days, he does not receive any value for the bill. He hopes that by the time 90 days has passed B will have funds available to honour the bill. In the meantime A is liable on the bill to the holder of it on the due date, since his intention in accepting it was to give it validity, but he is not liable to the drawer for its value, since he had no benefit from the bill. On the due date, if B is in funds, a holder who presents it to A may be referred to B for settlement. If B is not in funds A must honour it and pursue the settlement of the debt with B.

17.5 The Acceptance of a Bill

The drawer draws upon the drawee in unconditional terms. Acceptance of these terms unconditionally is called a **general acceptance**. A holder of a bill who presents it for acceptance is entitled to expect a general acceptance and if the drawee offers anything less the holder may treat the bill as dishonoured by non-acceptance. (See dishonour of bills below.) A general acceptance may be given in the following ways by the drawee:

(*a*) By merely signing the bill.

(*b*) By signing the bill and writing *accepted.*

(*c*) As in (*b*) but also giving the date. The date is essential on any bill expressed to be payable at a certain period 'after sight' for the time cannot begin to run until the bill has been presented for acceptance and the date the drawee sighted the bill has been fixed.

(*d*) It is permissible to insert the place where payment will be made, and this is still a general acceptance – but if it is specified that this is the only place where the bill will be honoured the bill is said to be a **'local' bill** and it is not a general acceptance.

Qualified Acceptance. A qualified acceptance is one where some qualification is introduced. Examples are:

(*a*) *Partial acceptance*, where the drawee undertakes to honour only part of the sum ordered to be paid.
(*b*) *Local acceptance*, which is explained above.
(*c*) *Qualifications as to time*, where the drawee attempts to extend the time available for payment.
(*d*) *Conditional acceptance*, where the drawee inserts some condition about the charges, costs, etc., in connection with the bill.
(*e*) *Failure of one drawee to sign.* Where two or more drawees are named, it is possible some will refuse to sign. If the holder agrees to accept the signature of the others it is a qualified acceptance.

S.44 has some important rules regarding qualified acceptances. If the presenter accepts a qualified acceptance the drawers and endorsers who are not a party to the acceptance and have not given authority for it to be taken are discharged from liability on the bill. If they have been given notice, or if they receive notice and do not express their dissent, they are deemed to have assented to it. If a foreign bill is the subject of a partial acceptance it must be protested for the balance of the value (see *Dishonour by non-acceptance* below).

Rules about Presentation for Acceptance. A bill must be presented for acceptance in the following circumstances:

(*a*) Where it is payable after sight and must be presented so that the date of sight can be fixed, and hence the date of maturity of the bill can be determined.
(*b*) Where it is not payable at the drawee's home, or place of business and consequently the drawee must know what his obligation is and how it is to be fulfilled at the date of maturity.
(*c*) Where it is a requirement of the bill.

Apart from these cases a bill need not be presented for acceptance, and the drawer and other endorsers will be liable upon it even if it is not accepted by the drawee.

Presentment must be made in normal business hours, before the bill is overdue. If the bill is addressed to more than one drawee it must be presented to them all, unless one is authorised to accept for all. If the drawee is dead or bankrupt, presentment must be made to the personal representative or the trustee in bankruptcy but the bill may also be treated as dishonoured by non-acceptance, since presentment is excused in these cases. It is also excused where due diligence has been shown in attempting to find the drawee without success, or where the drawee appears to be a fictitious person, or to lack capacity (for example, a minor). Just because you suspect a bill will be dishonoured on presentment is no excuse for not presenting it.

Dishonour by non-acceptance. The holder of a bill which has been dishonoured by non-acceptance, either because the drawee refuses to accept it or because presentment is excused for one of the reasons given above, has an immediate right of recourse against the endorsers or the drawer. The bill may be dealt with in a formal legal manner, by notice or protest, but this is not necessary for an inland bill and the holder's right of recourse is immediate (S.43, 1882 Act). For a foreign bill protest is essential to establish a proper legal basis for future action. Notice and protest have already been described above.

17.6 Negotiation of a Bill

Negotiation is the transfer of a bill in such a way as to constitute the transferee the holder of the bill. Thus a bearer bill may be negotiated by mere delivery; an order bill is negotiated by endorsement and delivery to the transferee. If an order bill is transferred for value without endorsement the transferee has the right to demand endorsement by the transferor.

To be a valid negotiation an endorsement must:

(*a*) Be written on the bill, or on an allonge, and be signed by the endorser. Even the signature alone is enough.

(*b*) It must be an endorsement of the entire bill. A partial endorsement, or one transferring the whole bill to two or more endorsees severally is not a valid negotiation.

(*c*) If there are several payees all must endorse the bill, unless one has authority to act for the rest (as with a partnership).

(*d*) If a name is misspelt the endorser should sign with the misspelt name but may add his proper signature if desired.

(*e*) An agent may endorse in such a way as to deny any personal liability, e.g. 'T. Green *per pro* Robinson and Co.'.

(*f*) A restrictive endorsement is permissible, e.g. 'Pay T. Green only'.

(*g*) A conditional endorsement is permissible, i.e. *sans recours* (without recourse to this particular indorser).

17.7 The Payment of a Bill

A bill must be presented for payment on the due date, and if it is not the drawer and endorsers are discharged. The rules about presentment are as follows:

(*a*) If the bill is payable on demand it may be presented at any time, but if the drawer or endorsers are to be held liable on it presentment must be made within a reasonable time. What is reasonable depends upon the facts of every case.

(*b*) If it is not payable on demand it must be presented on the due date.

(*c*) It must be presented at a reasonable hour on a business day at the specified place, or if no place is specified at the usual business address or the known residence. If these places are not known then it may be presented wherever the acceptor or drawee can be found, or at his last place of address.

(*d*) If two or more drawees are named the bill must be presented to both, or all, and the rules already mentioned about death or bankruptcy on presentment apply again.

(*e*) If agreement or usage authorises it presentment may be made through the post.

Presentment is excused where the drawee is a fictitious person, and also where reasonable diligence has failed to find the drawee. It is not excused just because the holder feels it is unlikely to be honoured.

Dishonour occurs when it is presented for payment and payment is refused, or when presentment is excused and the bill is overdue and unpaid. In all these cases the holder has an immediate right of recourse against the drawers and endorsers.

17.8 Dishonour of a Bill

Upon dishonour the holder has the right of recourse against all those who have endorsed the bill. He must give notice to the drawer and all endorsers, and any drawer or endorser who is not given notice is discharged from liability on the bill. The notice must be given by or on behalf of the holder, or an endorser who is liable on the bill, and may be given in any form, orally or in writing, or by the return of the bill itself to any person who is liable on it. When this is done the notice given constitutes proper notice for all parties subsequent to the party to whom the notice is given. For example, consider Fig. 17.4. In each case the holder is the last person shown, and the party featured in a box is the one to whom notice is given. AC is the accepter who has dishonoured the bill and Dr is the drawer of the bill. The other parties are all endorsers of the bill.

Case 1	AC,	Dr,	A	B	C	D	E	F	G	H
Case 2	AC,	Dr,	A	B	C	D	E	F	G	H
Case 3	AC,	Dr,	A	B	C	D	E	F	G	H

Fig. 17.4. Notice of dishonour

Notes

(i) In Case 1, H is the holder who presents it to AC for payment. On payment being refused, he immediately gives notice to G, the person who transferred it to him, and G is obliged to honour it. G will then have a right of immediate recourse against all the other parties, i.e. Dr, A, B, C, D, E and F.

(ii) In Case 2, H, who knows C, gives him notice of the dishonour. This notice is valid for all endorsers subsequent to C, so D, E, F and G are released from any obligation on the bill as soon as C pays H. C must now look to Dr, A or B for recourse.

(iii) In Case 3, H goes direct to the drawer, who has the primary responsibility on the bill. If Dr pays H all the other endorsers are discharged from liability and Dr is left to bring an action against AC to recover the money due to him.

(iv) Whoever honours a bill is entitled to receive it at once, and may then take such action as he wishes on it.

The Measure of Damages on Dishonour. The measure of damages in any action on a dishonoured bill of exchange is (*a*) the value of the bill, plus (*b*) interest from the time the bill was presented (if a demand bill) or the due date, plus (*c*) the expenses of noting or protest. If the bill is a foreign bill expressed in a foreign currency the damages is the amount of the re-exchange at the time of dishonour. Thus if a bill for 24 000 Deutschemarks had been discounted at DM4 = £1 (i.e. £6000), but on dishonour the bank sought recourse against the endorser at a time when the rate had hardened to DM3.5 = £1, the bank would require £6857.14, plus interest from the due date, and expenses. The Act does not prescribe a rate of interest but it does say that the court may exercise its discretion to reduce the interest payable if it is deemed fair to do so. A Practice Direction of the Queen's Bench Division dated February 24, 1983, states that the plaintiff may properly ask for a reasonable rate around, or somewhat above base rate – the Short Term Investment Account rate is a safe guide.

17.9 The Discharge of Bills

The discharge of a bill is the cessation of all obligations on the bill and the extinguishment of all rights of action on it.

A bill is discharged normally by payment on the due date by the acceptor to the *bona fide* holder, in good faith without notice of any defect in his title to the bill.

If a bill payable to a third party is honoured by the drawer it is not discharged but the drawer may not reissue it; he may only use it to enforce payment against the acceptor. Similarly, payment by any endorser is not discharge of the bill, since a right of recourse against earlier parties exists.

A bill may also be discharged by the acceptor becoming the holder at maturity, or renunciation of the holder's rights against the acceptor, or cancellation of the bill by the holder. This involves writing on the bill that it is cancelled, or striking out the acceptor's signature – an action which would automatically discharge all parties to the bill. Similarly, any endorser may be discharged from the bill by striking out his name on the bill, and this will discharge all subsequent endorsers, but it will not discharge the bill itself because all earlier endorsers and the acceptor would still be liable on it.

Material alteration of a bill discharges all parties except the one making the alteration and subsequent endorsers. Material alteration is alteration of the date, the sum payable, the time of payment or the place of payment. Where an alteration is not apparent the innocent holder can also hold endorsers prior to the alteration liable for the *original* sum, so that they are not discharged entirely from the bill.

17.10 Forgeries

Forgery is the act of falsely making or altering any document with the intention of defrauding anyone who takes the document. The forgery of a signature is a special case of forgery. An unauthorised signature, as where an unauthorised director signs on behalf of a company may, or may not, amount to a forgery. The difference is that an unauthorised signature which does not amount to a forgery may be ratified to make it valid.

The effect of both forged and unauthorised signatures is that they are totally inoperative (S.24, 1882 Act) and no right to retain a bill or enforce payment on it can follow from such a forgery. On a normal bill which has been negotiated via a series of endorsers to an ultimate holder there is an unbroken chain of parties, as shown below:

Acceptor A, Drawer D, Endorsers M, N, O, P, Q, R, S (the holder)

If a forgery appears at any point the effects will be as follows:

(i) *Forgery of the acceptor's signature.* The only effect is that the bill has not been accepted. When the drawee (who has not signed as acceptor) declares the signature to be a forgery and states that he knows nothing of the bill the holder S may apply to D or any of M, N, O, P, Q and R. There is no break in the chain of responsibility right back to the drawer, who is, as usual, the primary person responsible on an unaccepted bill.

(ii) *Forgery of the drawer's signature.* If it is the drawer's signature that has been forged the document is not a bill at all, because it has not been 'signed by the person giving it'. Forgery of the drawer's signature usually occurs when cheque-books are stolen; there would therefore be no acceptor and the person who takes the forged cheque is the loser. No claim, says S.24, can follow from a forged signature and the only redress is against the thief, who can usually not be found.

(iii) *Forgery of an endorser's signature.* In this case there is a break in the chain. Suppose O lost the bill, and his signature was forged by the finder in negotiating the bill to P. There is a break in the chain at P and S; the holder can only claim from P, Q and R. P, the victim of the forger's deception, must be the loser, and his only claim is against the forger. Q, R and S, although they have no valid title to the bill, can rely on S.55 of the Act to help them, since in each case the person negotiating the bill to them is estopped from denying the validity of the bill. This leaves P as the loser by the forgery.

Estoppel. Estoppel is a legal maxim which prevents a person denying the genuineness of some activity or event because of his earlier failure to do what he should have done. Thus if A, knowing that B regularly writes out cheques in his name in such a way that the paying banker is misled into believing they are genuine signatures, he cannot later claim that they are forgeries and sue the bank for conversion. There are five cases where estoppel may affect bills of exchange:

(*a*) Where a person has positively asserted a signature to be genuine or regular (*Bank of England v. Vagliano Bros.* (*1891*)).

(*b*) By failure to fulfil a legal duty. In *Greenwood v. Martins Bank* (*1933*) Greenwood failed to tell the bank that his wife had forged cheques, and was held to be estopped from denying the validity of her signatures.

(*c*) In the case of inchoate instruments, where the bill has been left to be completed by another person. If that person is deceitful the drawer cannot deny the genuineness of the bill.

(*d*) Where the drawer or other party complaining has been negligent.

(*e*) Under SS.54 and 55 of the 1882 Act, which hold that the accepter is precluded from denying the genuineness of the drawer's signature, and the drawer is precluded from denying the identity of the payee and his power to endorse the bill.

17.11 Cheques

A cheque is a bill of exchange, drawn on a banker, payable on demand. Today banks are organisations recognised by the Bank of England, and listed on a register of banks published periodically by the Bank of England, by authority conferred on it by the *Banking Act, 1979*.

SS.73–82 of the *Bills of Exchange Act, 1882,* deal with cheques, and a later act, the *Cheques Act, 1957*, revises the earlier rules and extends the protection given to paying bankers and collecting bankers.

There is no need for the words 'on demand' to appear on a cheque since by S.10 of the 1882 Act any bill of exchange is payable on demand if no time for payment is expressed on it. Cheques can be protected by **crossings**. A crossing is an instruction to the banker to pay the cheque only into a bank account, not over the counter. A general crossing permits payment into any account; a special crossing includes the name of a particular bank and the cheque should be cleared into an account of that particular bank. The cheque may be crossed by the drawer, with or without the words '& Co.' in the transverse lines, or it may be crossed by the holder. The addition of the words 'not negotiable' does not mean it may not be assigned, but only that it cannot transfer a better title to the assignee than the holder had from whom he took it. The crossing 'a/c payee' is not a statutory crossing, but is sanctioned by usage. Its effect is not to restrict the cheque to the actual account of the payee, but to put the collecting bank upon enquiry to ensure that if it is paid elsewhere a proper authority has been given for the money to be collected on behalf of that other person.

Where a cheque appears on the face of it to have been in circulation for an unreasonable length of time it is said to be **overdue** (S. 36, 1882 Act). What is 'unreasonable' is a question of fact in every case. The onus of proving a cheque is overdue rests with the person seeking to avoid paying it. A **stale cheque** is one that has been in circulation for more than six months, and the return of a stale cheque implies that the paying banker prefers not to pay it until it has been confirmed by the drawer as a valid cheque. A **post-dated cheque** is one that has a date on it later than the date it was made out. Post-dating does not make a cheque invalid, but postpones the payment of the cheque until that date. A creditor who has been paid with a post-dated cheque has a valid bill of exchange which is better than nothing at all, but it is obviously less satisfactory than a cheque payable on demand.

The banker has a duty to pay his customer's cheques: the order in the cheque – 'pay . . .' – gives authority to pay. However, the authority to pay may be countermanded by an express instruction to 'stop' a cheque. It may also be terminated in several other circumstances, as follows:

(*a*) By notice of the customer's death or unsoundness of mind.

(*b*) By notice that a bankruptcy petition has been presented against him or that a Receiving Order (an order winding up a company) has been made; or in the case of a company that winding-up proceedings have commenced.

(*c*) By service of a **garnishee order** attaching the customer's funds for use in the manner directed by the court.

(*d*) By injunction.

Where a bank wrongfully dishonours a customer's cheque it is liable in damages for breach of contract and, if the customer's reputation is damaged thereby, for libel. Proof of special damage is not required, damages being assessed without reference to pecuniary loss.

Where a cheque is fraudulently increased the bank will not be liable for paying it if the drawer has negligently left space to permit the alteration (*London Joint Stock Bank Ltd v. MacMillan and Arthur (1918)*).

The *Cheques Act, 1957.* This Act recognised that over the years since 1882, when the *Bills of Exchange Act* defined a cheque as 'a bill of exchange, drawn on a banker, payable on demand', subtle changes in the use of cheques had occurred. Cheques were no longer used as transferable documents, but simply as a ready method of payment, the payee paying them in for collection by a collecting banker. Therefore the Act sought to abolish the need for endorsement of cheques by payees who were merely paying in the cheques for collection. It also gave some additional protection to paying bankers and collecting bankers in various respects described below.

Protection of the paying banker. A banker who is drawn on in a cheque is required to pay the payee. He is protected as far as this payment is concerned in the following ways:

(*a*) *Where an endorsement is forged.* Provided payment is made in good faith, and in the normal course of business, the bank is not liable (S.60, 1882 Act).

(*b*) *Where there is no endorsement or an irregular endorsement*. An irregular endorsement is one where the signature is genuine, but is not in exactly the same style as the designation on the face of the cheque (e.g. where a cheque payable to J. J. Hilbride is endorsed 'James Hilbride') (*Cheques Act, 1957,* S.1).

(*c*) *Where the cheque is crossed and is correctly paid according to the crossing*. S.80 of the 1882 Act protects a banker who pays a crossed cheque in a proper manner to the true owner.

Protection of the collecting banker. A collecting banker who collects payment on behalf of a customer is liable to be sued for conversion if the customer proves to have had no title to the cheque he paid in for collection. Therefore S.4 of the *Cheques Act, 1957,* protects the collecting banker who collects in good faith, and without negligence, for a customer. The word 'customer' is important, since the bank may be held negligent if they have accepted a customer without making proper enquiries (*Hampstead Guardians v. Barclays Bank Ltd* (*1923*)). It may also be negligent if it accepts from a customer cheques made out to his employer, or made out in his official capacity, or as agent for someone else, and does not institute enquiries about them. In Marfani's case (*Marfani and Co. v. Midland Bank Ltd* (*1968*)), the bank was held to be protected by S.4 even though its enquiries were not, according to the evidence, particularly careful.

17.12 Revision Test

Answers	*Questions*
–	**1.** What is a negotiable instrument?
1. A document which passes from hand to hand without notice having to be given to the party who is liable on it, and without the recipient having to take it 'subject to the equities'.	**2.** What are the common negotiable instruments?
2. (*a*) Bills of exchange; (*b*) cheques; (*c*) promissory notes; (*d*) Treasury bills; (*e*) bankers' drafts; (*f*) certificates of deposit; (*g*) dividend warrants; (*h*) various types of bearer bonds.	**3.** Define a bill of exchange?
3. See the definition on page 262.	**4.** How is a bill of exchange used?
4. As a means of financing business activity in the time interval between production and consumption.	**5.** What is meant by the phrase 'bills should be self-liquidating'?
5. By the time the bill comes to maturity the business activity which brought it into existence should have provided the funds to honour it.	**6.** Who are the parties to a bill of exchange?
6. (*a*) The drawer; (*b*) the drawee – who becomes the acceptor; (*c*) the payee; (*d*) the endorsers; (*e*) the holder; (*f*) the holder in due course; (*g*) accommodation parties; (*h*) bearers; (*i*) transferors by delivery.	**7.** What is acceptance of a bill of exchange?
7. The assent of the drawee to the order in the bill. On signing the 'drawee' becomes the 'acceptor', and is the primary person liable on the bill.	**8.** What are the types of acceptance?

Answers	*Questions*
8. (*a*) General acceptances; (*b*) qualified acceptances, which may be: (i) partial; (ii) local; (iii) qualified as to time; (iv) conditional; (v) qualified as to parties.	**9.** What is negotiation of a bill of exchange?
9. The transfer of a bill in such a way as to constitute the transferee the *holder* of the bill.	**10.** How is a bill negotiated?
10. A bearer bill is negotiated by mere delivery. An order bill is negotiated by endorsement and delivery.	**11.** What is a holder of a bill?
11. The payee or endorsee in possession of it, or the bearer of a bearer bill.	**12.** What is the holder in due course?
12. A holder who takes a bill, complete and regular on the face of it, before it was overdue, and without notice of any previous dishonour, in good faith, for value and without notice of any defect in title of the person who negotiated it to him.	**13.** What are the rights of a holder in due course?
13. (*a*) He may sue on the bill in his own name; (*b*) he can defeat any defences based upon defects of title, or relations between earlier parties to the bill, before it came into his possession.	**14.** Go over the questions again until you are sure of all the answers. Then try some of the questions in Appendix 1.

18
Arbitration

18.1 The Nature of Arbitration

Where a dispute arises in a matter of contract the expenses of a court may be very great, and the law's delay may be tiresome. There are no special arrangements for hearing disputes out of business hours and litigants are often kept waiting around for a previous case to conclude so that the court's time shall not be wasted. Witnesses may need to be brought from around the world, when a simple affidavit would be perfectly satisfactory and infinitely cheaper. A cheaper alternative is arbitration.

Arbitration is the voluntary submission of a dispute to a person qualified to settle it, with an agreement that the arbitrator's decision shall be final and binding.

In many disputes the argument is not a legal matter, but a question of quality, price, delivery, custom of the trade, etc. Judges are experts in law, not in the quality of coffee, etc., and there may be better people to 'judge' the matter in a dispute at the coffee exchange than in the courts of justice. Many contracts consequently provide that any dispute that arises shall be settled by arbitration. An arbitrator may be named, but more usually a method of choosing an arbitrator will be specified, such as 'a senior member from the Board of the relevant Trade Association'.

18.2 The Advantages and Disadvantages of Arbitration

The advantages of arbitration may be listed as follows:

(*a*) The arbitrator can be an acknowledged authority on the subject concerned. Thus he may be a technical specialist, a scientist, a financial expert, a transport specialist, etc.

(*b*) The evidence can be submitted in writing beforehand, so that all viewpoints have been formally (and thoughtfully) expressed and witnesses' oral evidence is not required. The arbitrator comes to the meeting fully knowledgeable about the dispute, and only needing to hear the personal attitudes of the chief parties concerned.

(*c*) The hearing can be at a time and place convenient for the various parties, often after working hours. The hearing is informal and friendly, a resolution of a difficulty rather than a trial.

(*d*) Arbitration is private; the press are not entitled to be present as they are in a legal trial, and public attention is not called to the attitudes or behaviour of the parties.

(*e*) Foreigners prefer arbitration, which avoids conflicts of law. Decisions of arbitration proceedings are more easily enforced abroad and the enforcement is largely voluntary – to preserve goodwill between trading partners – rather than imposed by an 'external' authority.

(*f*) Appeal is possible to the courts on any legal point, and the court does exercise supervision over arbitration proceedings. This is explained in S.18.3 below.

Against these advantages we may enumerate the following disadvantages:

(*a*) There is no judicial precedent created by arbitration decisions, so that every case is said to be 'thrown away'. There is also the possibility that conflicting decisions will be arrived at on the basis of identical sets of facts. Arbitration proceedings are therefore unnecessarily numerous, and there is no certainty about the decisions.

(*b*) Although technically a matter of choice between equals, in many standard form contracts the arbitration clause is inserted by a stronger party (for instance, the insurance company) against a weaker party (the assured). Since in many contracts we are statutorily required to take certain actions (for example, to insure) we may in fact be statutorily compelled to contract on another person's terms and thus be forced to accept arbitration when appeal to the Courts is a citizen's true birthright.

(*c*) Where the matter in dispute involves a legal point we may have to go to the courts for a ruling anyway.

(*d*) Arbitration is not all that cheap, especially when every case is 'thrown away' and the point in dispute may need to be settled many times. An interesting case is:

International Sea Tankers of Liberia Inc. v. Hemisphere Shipping Co. of Hong Kong (*1981*). During the war between Iraq and Iran certain ships were trapped in the Shatt al Arab. The plaintiffs sought leave to appeal against the decision of an arbitrator who had ruled that the time charterparty had been frustrated. In granting leave to appeal it was held that 'events in this war were likely to give rise to many frustration cases, and the courts ought to give a definitive ruling in order to avoid inconsistent rulings in different arbitrations'.

This illustrates the point that a simple decision on a matter of frustration might be heard many times by countless arbitrators, when one single piece of judicial precedent would resolve them all, and save enormous effort in collecting depositions, writing accounts of events, etc. At the same time certainty would be introduced into the proceedings.

18.3 The *Arbitration Acts 1950, 1975* and *1979*

The *Arbitration Act, 1950*, is the major statute and controls the general conduct of arbitration proceedings. The 1975 Act gives effect to the New York Convention on Recognition and Enforcement of Foreign Arbitral Awards. The 1979 Act reduces the courts' influence over arbitration proceedings other than by appeal. These Acts will be looked at in reasonable detail below.

Reference to an Arbitrator. Matters may come before an arbitrator in three possible ways:

(*a*) *By agreement between the parties.* This is the commonest procedure, it having been agreed in the contract that disputes will be settled by arbitration. It is possible that oral agreement is enough but the Acts apply only to written agreements to submit present or future difficulties to arbitration, whether an arbitrator is named therein or not.

(*b*) *By order of the court.* The court may refer any matter to an arbitrator, and will tend to do so if the documents under dispute are detailed and need expert investigation – for example, by scientists, accountants, etc. – or if they need local examination. The court may call for a report, or may delegate the trial of the matter to an official or referee.

(*c*) *By Statute.* Many statutes provide for difficulties that may arise to be settled by arbitration and will usually specify how the arbitration is to be conducted, but if not the Acts of 1950, 1975 and 1979 apply.

Arbitration Arrangements. To clarify difficulties that may arise the Act provides that unless the arbitration agreement makes it clear otherwise, the reference to an arbitrator is taken to mean a single individual. If the reference is to two arbitrators, one appointed by either party, there is an implied provision that the arbitrators shall appoint an umpire immediately they have been appointed, and on informing him that they cannot agree the umpire may forthwith enter on the reference in lieu of the arbitrators.

If the reference to arbitration calls for three arbitrators, the award of any two of them shall be binding. If one of them is to be appointed by each party, and the third by the other two, he is treated as an umpire as described above.

All parties to an arbitration must, by the 1950 Act, be prepared to submit to examination under oath, and be prepared to bring before the arbitrator all documents and other evidence as required. The arbitrator is empowered to administer oaths.

The arbitrator must use all reasonable dispatch in making an award, and may make an interim award unless this is specifically excluded by the reference to arbitration in the contract. The arbitrator has the same power as the High Court to order specific performance of the contract (except where an interest in land is concerned). The award is final and binding on both parties.

The Control of Arbitration by the Courts. The usual thing is for an arbitration agreement to exclude an appeal to the courts but the court may become involved in the following circumstances:

(*a*) Under the 1950 Act the court may appoint an arbitrator if:

(i) The arbitrator dies or the formula for his appointment proves for some reason to be inappropriate, or if the parties cannot agree upon an arbitrator (S.10).

(ii) Where an arbitrator acts improperly (S.23) the court may remove him and appoint another.

(*b*) Where a witness fails to appear at an arbitration proceedings any party to the reference may sue out a writ of subpoena and the High Court or judge thereof may order that a writ be issued to compel the attendance of the witness before the arbitrator or umpire.

(*c*) Where a party to a domestic arbitration agreement commences a legal action the other party may at once apply to the courts for a 'stay' of proceedings, provided that he is willing and ready to proceed at once with the arbitration. If the court is satisfied that this is so it will order a 'stay' pending resolution of the problem by arbitration (S.4, 1950 Act). The requirements for a stay are: (i) that the matter comes within the terms of reference of the arbitration clause; (ii) the applicant has taken no step in the legal proceedings, such as entering a defence to the claims made; (iii) the applicant must have been ready and willing from the start to proceed with all dispatch to arbitration.

The court will refuse a stay if it believes that the arbitrator will not be impartial or if the dispute alleges fraud, and it is desirable that this allegation is investigated.

The *Arbitration Act, 1975*, varies the rules about staying proceedings in non-domestic arbitrations (arbitrations held abroad, involving foreign citizens or foreign incorporations). This Act gives effect to the New York Convention on the Recognition and Enforcement of Foreign Arbitral Awards, dated February 25, 1975. Naturally an international convention should not lightly be displaced by national laws, and the Act therefore says that if a non-domestic arbitration agreement has been made the courts will stay any proceedings commenced by one party in the courts, if the other party requests a 'stay' and it is proved that the arbitration agreement is not null and void, inoperative or incapable of being performed, and that the dispute between the parties comes within the terms of reference of the agreement to arbitrate.

(*d*) The High Court may be called upon in numerous situations to make orders in respect of such matters as discovery of documents, giving of evidence by affidavit, examination on oath of witnesses, preservation and sale of goods which are the subject matter of dispute, securing money which is in dispute and bringing it into court, the issue of any interim injunction, or the appointment of a receiver.

(*e*) An interesting situation about judicial control of arbitration proceedings has been changed by the 1979 Act. Until that Act it was the case that under S.21 of the Act of 1950 an arbitrator or umpire might – or if directed to do so by the High Court must – state a case for consideration by the court on any point of law, or about the amount of any award. The court would then decide the point of law and this decision would be deemed to be a judgment of the court (so that an appeal could be lodged against it). The award could then be remitted to the arbitrator for reconsideration. The principle behind such a procedure was that there could not be any ouster of jurisdiction of the courts on questions of law (in other words, a private agreement to arbitrate could not deprive any citizen of his right to appeal to the courts on a question of law). By the 1979 Act this rule has changed and the stating of cases in this way has been discontinued. Instead, those who feel that an award has gone against them through the arbitrator's misreading of the law may appeal in the following circumstances:

(*i*) If all the parties to the arbitration agree to the appeal being made, or (*ii*) If the court gives leave to appeal (but the court will not do so if the parties have signed an agreement not to appeal).

If the appeal is allowed the court may confirm, vary or set aside the award, or remit the reward back to the arbitrator for reconsideration, and he shall make a new award within three months after the date of the order.

By S.2 of the 1979 Act, however, it is possible if the arbitrator, or the umpire, or *all* the parties ask it, for the High Court to give an early decision on any point of law arising, if the court is satisfied that to do so will considerably reduce the costs in any arbitration proceedings.

The rules about 'exclusion agreements' which exclude the right to appeal are complex. As regards non-domestic arbitrations governed by the international convention, the High Court will not exercise its powers under the 1950 Act (S.24) to take steps to allow the court to determine the matter. For domestic arbitrations the exclusion clause will only operate if it was made *after* the commencement of the arbitration, and for statutory arbitrations an exclusion agreement cannot operate to prevent an appeal on a matter of law, or an award made. There are also special rules about Admiralty matters, insurance and commodity contracts.

Finally, the chief point of the 1975 Act was to implement the New York Convention. S.3 of the Act says that where there is a Convention award made in a foreign country the award must be enforced in the UK Courts just as if it was a domestic award. This explains why those engaged in international trade prefer arbitration of disputes, since the awards can be enforced in any country which has ratified the Convention.

18.4 Revision Test

Answers	*Questions*
–	**1.** What is arbitration?
1. It is the voluntary submission of a dispute to a person qualified to settle it, with an agreement that the arbitrator's decision shall be final and binding.	**2.** What are the advantages of arbitration?
2. (*a*) Usually it is cheaper; (*b*) delays are reduced; (*c*) evidence can be submitted in writing; (*d*) the arbitrator can be a qualified person; (*e*) Hearings can be at a time convenient to the parties; (*f*) the hearing is private; (*g*) foreigners prefer arbitration.	**3.** What are the disadvantages?
3. No judicial precedent is created and hence every case is 'thrown away'; (*b*) conflicting decisions	

Answers	*Questions*
may be given on similar sets of facts; (*c*) often it is not a free choice – arbitration becomes compulsory in many standard form contracts; (*d*) if a legal point is involved we may have to go to law anyway.	**4.** How may cases be placed with an arbitrator?
4. (*a*) By agreement – a clause in the contract; (*b*) by order of the court – if detailed research or analytical study is required; (*c*) by statute – many statutes provide for arbitration of disputes arising from the statute.	**5.** How do the courts control arbitration?
5. They exercise general supervision in any circumstances where difficulties arise, such as the death of an arbitrator, refusal of a witness to appear, etc. They may 'stay' proceeding, in certain circumstances; they may determine points of law in certain circumstances, and aggrieved parties may seek leave to appeal to the High Court against awards made, or on points of law.	**6.** What is the main Act of Parliament on arbitration?
6. The *Arbitration Act, 1950.*	**7.** What did the *Arbitration Act, 1975,* do?
7. It implemented the New York Convention on the Recognition and Enforcement of Foreign Arbitral Awards.	**8.** What was the chief purpose of the *Arbitration Act, 1979?*
8. To end the arrangement whereby parties could require the arbitrator to state a case for the High Court, which could then set aside an award or remit it for reconsideration.	**9.** What must aggrieved parties do now?
9. Seek leave to appeal on a point of law.	**10.** Go over the questions again. Then try some of the written questions in Appendix 1.

Part 5: Public Law

19
Administrative Law

19.1 Introduction

Governments have always exercised power. Administrative law has grown up over the centuries to control and supervise the use of government powers. With the advent of the Welfare State and its subsequent development, the provision of state services has increased. The progressive development of the mixed economy has ensured that the state plays an important role in an individual's life. The body of administrative law has therefore developed at the same time to control and regulate this relationship between the state and the individual.

Administrative law is concerned with the settlement of disputes between individuals and the various organs of both central and local government engaged in administration. In addition to governing the relationship between various administrative agencies set up to implement public policies and those individuals or private bodies affected, administrative law also regulates and controls the relationship between these various agencies – for example, the relationship between a minister and a local authority.

It is not intended to list all the numerous and varied activities of the state that affect its citizens. Indeed, not all of these state activities are governed by administrative law. To give an idea of the areas that fall under this branch of the law we may list those concerned with the provision of social services, health and education, others with the running of public utilities such as water, gas, postal services, transport and, lastly, the state's involvement with individuals in areas such as immigration control, licensing, town planning, social security, housing, etc.

As far as businesses are concerned their environment is to some extent hemmed in by administrative controls: planning permission, regulations about pollution, noise, dangerous goods and materials, consumer regulations, labelling and similar requirements, health and safety regulations, etc. Whilst endeavouring to meet the requirements of countless laws of this sort, the business person may find that powers are being exceeded or abused. It is in this area that administrative law seeks to control officials acting outside their powers.

The presentation of this section is as follows:

(*a*) Controls by the ordinary courts over the activities of public authorities, i.e. the various grounds on which the courts can intervene to question decisions made by public officials.

(*b*) A look at the various administrative remedies that are available where a dispute arises which lacks a legal remedy in the ordinary courts. These include the use of administrative tribunals and public enquiries.

(*c*) The functions of the Parliamentary Commissioner for Administration (the Ombudsman).

19.2 Judicial Control of Administrative Powers

In the administering of public services, the actions of public authorities directly affect individuals. Their actions in regulating private activities through licensing and other controls confer rights and impose burdens on individuals. While political and administrative control over the actions of public authorities is no less important, judicial control is the most certain and effective way of ensuring that a public authority does not exceed its powers, and enables the rights and duties of an individual to be determined and enforced.

Although Parliament normally provides a right of appeal to an administrative tribunal against an administrative decision with a possible further right of appeal to a court, the courts can nevertheless intervene on various well established grounds to question a decision of a public authority. These grounds are in no way substitutes for other possible remedies available to an aggrieved citizen against the action of a public authority, i.e. an action under tort or contract law. For example, a hospital authority is vicariously liable for the negligence of its servants (nursing staff, physicians, surgeons, etc.) in the performance of their duties (*Cassidy v. Ministry of Health* (*1951*) and *Roe v. Minister of Health* (*1954*)). A contract made by a public authority is essentially subject to the same rules that govern contracts between individuals with the exception that where a public authority exceeds its authority in entering a contract, that contract is void and unenforceable (*Rhyl UDC v. Rhyl Amusements Ltd* (*1959*)).

All remedies are of course subject to whether or not Parliament has conferred immunity on the public authority from being sued or prosecuted. For example, under common law, a sheriff executing a court order is protected from personal liability. Similarly, persons closely involved in the compulsory detention of a mental patient do not incur civil or criminal liability (S.141, *Mental Health Act, 1959*). Therefore, when Parliament has authorised an action to be taken, that action cannot be wrongful and compensation for any harm that results is payable only if provision for compensation exists under the statute.

19.3 Grounds for Judicial Intervention

The action of public authorities may be ruled invalid for a variety of reasons. The courts have consistently upheld the following matters as justifying the control of officials: *ultra vires* actions (actions beyond the powers granted); incorrect procedure; improper purpose; irrelevant consideration;

error of law; lack of evidence; and abuse of discretionary powers. It has been suggested that these grounds of judicial intervention are not independent justifications for intervention but merely specialised applications of the *ultra vires* rule or doctrine. Each of these grounds will be considered individually below.

One aspect of administrative law which constantly arises is the **'test of standing'**. If a review of the use of administrative powers is to be held it ought not to be demanded at the whim of any citizen, whether he is affected or not, but should only be undertaken if the plaintiff has a sufficient standing to demand the relief claimed. To pass the 'test of standing' Webster J. in *Steeples v. Derbyshire County Council* (*1984*) held that if the decision made affected the plaintiff in a way that was over and above the effect on an ordinary member of the public, this would give him the requisite standing to entitle him to claim the relief sought.

(*a*) **The *Ultra Vires* Rule.** Where a public authority is given certain powers and it exceeds those powers then the acts in excess are considered *ultra vires* and invalid. For example, where a public authority is authorised to establish a wash-house where people can wash their own clothes, the installation of a modern laundry to be run as a business is clearly *ultra vires* and a ratepayer would succeed in preventing the public authority from this action (*Att.-Gen. v. Fulham Corporation* (*1921*)). A further example is:

R. v. Minister of Health, ex p. Davies (*1929*). The Minister had power to confirm improvement schemes submitted by local authorities under the *Housing Act, 1925*. A property owner brought an action to prevent the Minister approving a scheme submitted by a local authority which did not show how it proposed to develop its compulsorily acquired land. The scheme left the local authority complete freedom to develop, sell or lease the land for any purpose it saw fit. **Held:** since the provisions in the scheme were *ultra vires* the *Housing Act, 1925*, it would have been beyond the power of the Minister to confirm it. Hence a prohibition order was issued to prevent the Minister from considering the scheme.

In *R. v. GLC and Another* (*1984*) the right of the GLC to second seven full time members of staff to conduct a political campaign against a particular political proposal (the abolition of the GLC) was challenged. Gildwell J. stated that if the object of the decision was not to discharge local authority functions but to carry out some other purpose then the decision was *ultra vires*. The court was satisfied that the object was to conduct a political campaign which was an irrelevant consideration and outside the powers of the GLC.

The ultra vires rule, estoppel and the Crown. Since the Crown cannot, in theory, ever act in an ultra vires way, it has long been held that the doctrine of estoppel can only be used in a very limited way against the Crown. In a recent case *Gowa and Others v. Attorney General* (*1984*) the Court held that the Crown was estopped from denying assurances given 30 years earlier by British officials to certain persons that they were British Citizens and need not apply for citizenship. They had relied on the assurances given in error by a senior official and had therefore become statute-barred from making applications for citizenship, through no fault of their own. In order to clarify the position entirely the Appeal Court gave leave to the Attorney General to appeal to the House of Lords.

(*b*) **Incorrect Procedure.** Where an Act of Parliament lays down a procedure to be followed before arriving at a decision, failure to follow the procedure may render the decision invalid.

The exercise of power in such circumstances is declared a nullity. Thus, where an Act of Parliament (*Police Act, 1919*) provided that before the dismissal of a chief constable by the police committee, a formal inquiry was required into the charges against him, the failure of the Brighton police committee to hold an inquiry meant that the dismissal was void and ineffective (*Ridge v. Baldwin* (*1964*)). It must be noted, however, that not every non-compliance with the procedure would render a decision invalid. For a decision to be declared void and invalid there must have been a substantial non-compliance with the procedure and not merely a minor procedural error.

For example, in *Coney v. Choyce and others* (*1975*) information concerning the proposals to reorganise the Roman Catholic schools in a number of towns was widely circulated in the surrounding areas as required by the *Education Act, 1944*. However, in the case of two schools these requirements were not fully complied with as no notice was posted or displayed at or near the entrances to these schools. An action was brought by the parents of a child to prevent the defendants from implementing the proposals and for a declaration that the Secretary of State's approval of the proposals was invalid on grounds of non-compliance. The court held that there was substantial conformity with the requirements of the 1944 Act and no substantial prejudice was suffered by those for whose benefit the requirements had been introduced. The action of the parents was dismissed. However, in *Bradbury v. London Borough of Enfield* (*1967*) the decision made by the local authority was affected when in introducing a comprehensive education system for its secondary schools it failed to give public notice in advance of the proposed changes as required by the *Education Act, 1944*. Local ratepayers succeeded in preventing the authority from introducing a comprehensive system in its schools until the procedure was followed.

(*c*) **Improper Purpose.** If power has been conferred for a particular purpose it must be utilised for that purpose only. The exercise of the power for a different or improper purpose is invalid:

Sydney Municipal Council v. Campbell (*1925*). The Corporation was given powers to acquire land compulsorily in order to improve the infrastructure of the city. The Corporation, however, acquired development land with the intention of making profit when its value increased. **Held:** the Corporation could not exercise powers given for one purpose for another.

In *Congreve v. Home Office* (*1976*) the Court of Appeal held that there would have been an improper exercise of the Home Secretary's powers of revoking television licences when the Home Secretary threatened to revoke the licences of certain television users if they did not pay the extra £6 (the increase in the licence fee). The court held that the power to revoke licences must be exercised in accordance with the law and it would have been an unlawful exercise of the Home Secretary's discretionary powers of revocation to threaten revocation 'as a means of extracting money'.

(*d*) **Irrelevant Consideration.** When arriving at a decision public bodies must take into account all the relevant matters. If irrelevant considerations are taken into account in arriving at a decision, that decision is likely to be rendered invalid by the courts. In *R. v. West London Supplementary Benefits Tribunal, ex p. Clarke* (*1975*) a supplementary benefits tribunal were taking into account irrelevant considerations when assessing the financial resources of a claimant – namely, the financial means of a relative of the claimant who was not legally bound to support the claimant. Similarly, in *R. v. Birmingham Licensing Planning Committee, ex p. Kennedy* (*1972*) the Birmingham Licensing Planning Committee, as a prerequisite to a hotel company receiving a new licence for a hotel, required the hotel company to make a payment of some £14,500 as a price for obtaining a licence, the sum that would be used to relieve the Birmingham Corporation of the liability to pay compensation to holders of licences in suspense. The court held that the licensing planning committee had taken into account extraneous and irrelevant considerations in arriving at its decision. The committee was accordingly directed to consider the application for a licence on proper grounds.

In *Roberts v. Hopwood* (*1925*) the House of Lords held that the Poplar Borough Council was guided by irrelevant considerations when it decided to pay its servants minimum wages far in excess of the national average wage for similar workers. The Council was primarily concerned to set an example as a model employer paying generous wages having regard to the efficiency of the work people, the purchasing power of the wages and its duty to both its employees and rate payers. The court was of the opinion that the Council should take into account considerations such as the cost of living, awards of joint industrial councils and wages paid by other similar employers both local and national.

(*e*) **Error of Law.** If a decision has been arrived at through a misinterpretation of the law or an error of law has been made, the decision can be rendered invalid in a court of law. In *Perilly v. Tower Hamlets Borough Council* (*1973*) the Borough Council was under a misapprehension that when applications for licences to trade in the Petticoat Lane market were received they were to be dealt with in the strict order of receipt, so that if a market stall became vacant the first person on the waiting list would automatically be entitled to that stall. Perilly's mother had a stall where she had been trading for 30 years, and on her death the Council refused a licence to Perilly, the licence being granted to a newcomer to the market. The court ordered that the licence should be issued to Perilly after quashing the licence issued to the newcomer.

(*f*) **Lack of Evidence.** If a decision arrived at is based on insufficient or lack of evidence, the decision can be quashed in a court of law. In *Coleen Properties Ltd. v. Minister of Housing and Local Government* (*1971*) the Minister had agreed to a proposal by a local authority to purchase compulsorily two rows of houses in bad condition. However, the proposal to acquire also related to a first-class modern property at the junction of the houses. The Council took its decision and the Minister agreed despite the local inspector's recommendation that it was not necessary to purchase the modern house and hence it should be excused from the order. The owner of the modern property now sought to quash the compulsory purchase order relating to his property only. The Court of Appeal, in complying, held that the Council had not produced satisfactory evidence to show why the modern property should also be compulsorily acquired and hence the Minister lacked material evidence to overrule the inspector's recommendation and therefore his decision in relation to the modern property was wrong.

(*g*) **Abuse of Discretionary Powers.** Where a public body is given discretionary powers, these must be exercised properly and all relevant considerations must be taken into account before arriving at a decision. Where a discretion is exercised for an improper purpose contrary to law, the decision arrived at can be questioned in the courts.

In *Padfield v. Minister of Agriculture* (*1968*), under the *Agricultural Marketing Act, 1958*, a complaints procedure was laid down under which farmers could complain to a committee of investigation about the workings of the statutory marketing schemes if the Minister in any case so directed. The Minister refused to refer a complaint made by Padfield, who was a farmer in south-east England, alleging that the 1958 Act had given him unfettered discretion whether or not to refer complaints to the committee of investigation. The House of Lords held that in refusing to refer the complaint, the Minister was frustrating the intention and objects of the 1958 Act and hence an order of mandamus lay to compel him to appoint a committee. Lord Reid had the following to say:

'. . . The policy and objects of the Act must be determined by construing the Act as a whole. . . . If a Minister having misconstrued the Act or for any other reason, so uses his discretion as to thwart or run counter to the policy and objects of the Act, then our law would be very defective if persons aggrieved were not entitled to the protection of the court.'

The court found that the intention of the Act was to provide a machinery by which complaints of farmers could be investigated by a committee which was independent of the Milk Marketing Board. Hence, in refusing to appoint a committee to which complaints could be referred, where it was obvious that people had a grievance, the Minister was frustrating the intention of the Act.

Other variations on this theme are instances when a discretion is fettered or surrendered, or where there is an unreasonable exercise of a discretionary power or a complete failure to exercise a discretion. In *Stringer v. Minister of Housing and Local Government* (*1970*), an agreement between Cheshire County Council and Manchester University, under which the Council were to exercise its planning powers to discourage development in the neighbourhood of the Jodrell Bank telescope, was held to be *ultra vires*. The agreement prevented the Council from taking into account other relevant considerations and dealing with future planning applications on merit. The Council had basically fettered its discretion.

In *Lavender & Son Ltd v. Minister of Housing & Local Government* (*1913*) it was held that the Minister had failed in the proper exercise of his discretion in acting solely in accordance with his policy of refusing planning permission to extract minerals from any agricultural land where the Minister for Agriculture, Fisheries and Food objected to the proposed use. This was an improper delegation of his duties to another government department. Hence the law of agency *nemo dat quod non habet* applies, i.e. where power is delegated to a body or a person that power cannot be subsequently redelegated. In *Barnard v. National Dock Labour Board* (*1953*) the suspension of Barnard from work was declared void since the disciplinary powers of suspension delegated to the London Dock Board had unlawfully been delegated to the port manager who had suspended Barnard from work.

The grounds of judicial intervention mentioned above are not the only grounds on which courts may intervene and it was not intended at the outset to list all of them. Besides, there are no constraints on the courts from inventing or adding to the existing list of recognised categories of judicial intervention whenever a situation so demands. It must be stressed that these grounds are not absolutely independent or autonomous categories and hence they may overlap each other and a case may encompass more than one of these grounds. For example, in *Ridge v. Baldwin* (*1964*) the court found that not only was there a breach of the principle of natural justice but the correct procedure for the dismissal of the Chief Constable was also not followed. One judge or writer may describe a ground as *ultra vires* whereas another may describe it as abuse or excess of power. In one textbook a ground may be described as improper purpose whereas another calls it excess of power. A ground may be described as frustrating the policy of the statute, as in *Padfield v. Minister of Agriculture* (*1968*), or as an abuse of discretionary power. It is obvious that there are no hard or fast rules for categorising the various grounds of judicial intervention and describing a particular ground in a particular manner is therefore merely a matter of convenience.

In concluding judicial intervention, a recent case having significant bearing on this area is the decision of the House of Lords in *R. v. Greater London Council ex parte Bromley London Borough Council* (*1981*). The House of Lords was considering an appeal by the Greater London Council (GLC) against the decision of the Court of Appeal. The issue before the Court of Appeal was that the GLC had made a supplementary rate demand on its ratepayers in order to cover the costs of reduced fares on London Transport's buses and tubes. The Court of Appeal, while allowing an appeal, held that the action of the GLC in requiring the London Transport Executive (LTE) to reduce bus and tube fares by 25 per cent was an abuse of power by the GLC under the *Transport* (*London*) *Act, 1969* and therefore *ultra vires*. The Court of Appeal issued an order of *certiorari* to quash the supplementary precept of 6.1p in the pound on the ratepayers. The House of Lords dismissed the appeal, holding that the actions of the Greater London Council and of the LTE were indeed *ultra vires* the 1969 Act. In the opinion of Lord Wilberforce, the GLC had a duty firstly to meet the needs of Greater London transport users and secondly the GLC 'owed a duty of a fiduciary character' to its ratepayers. Therefore in making a grant to support the fares reduction the GLC had acted in breach of its fiduciary duty. Lord Diplock mentioned another ground on which he believed the supplementary precept to be void: namely, that in exercising the collective discretion under S.11 of the 1969 Act, the members of the majority party had acted 'on an erroneous view of the applicable law' in that 'they regarded the GLC as irrevocably committed to carry out the reduction whatever might be the additional cost to the ratepayers. . . .'

Lord Keith was of the opinion that 'it was contrary to the LTE's duties under the Act to submit proposals which involved an arbitrary reduction' of that scale (25 per cent). Lord Scarman was of the opinion that the 'Act required that fares be charged at a level which would, so far as practicable, avoid deficit' and in yielding to policy preference rather than business principles, the GLC was in 'breach of duty owed to the ratepayers and wrong in law'. Lord Brandon said that under the Act it was a matter of administrative discretion as to what extent the passenger services for Greater London was financed by fares paid by passengers and by grants from the GLC. In this case the GLC had not exercised its 'administrative discretion lawfully' in approving a 25 per cent overall reduction in fares.

19.4 Rules of Natural Justice

A public body, whether exercising judicial, quasi-judicial, administrative or executive functions, is required to act fairly. Hence an underlying and important principle of all judicial review is that all powers given to public officials must be exercised in accordance with the principles or rules of natural justice. Compliance with the rules of natural justice is essential for the interests of justice to prevail and the courts will intervene whenever these rules are not complied with. Two main rules of natural justice are:

(*a*) The rule against bias: no man to be a judge in his own cause (*nemo iudex in causa sua*), and
(*b*) The right to be heard (*audi alteram partem*).

These rules will now be considered individually.

(*a*) **Impartiality, or the Rule against Bias.** For a decision of a court of law or a tribunal to be just, the judge or any other person presiding must be impartial and fair. In *R. v. Rand* (*1866*) it was laid down that this rule of impartiality is breached (i) where a judge has any pecuniary interest, no matter how small, in the case before him and (ii) where there is a real likelihood of the judge being partial towards one of the parties to the case. As Lord Chief Justice Hewart said in *R. v. Sussex Justices, ex parte McCarthy* (*1924*): 'Justice should not only be done, but should manifestly and undoubtedly be seen to be done.'

The case concerned an applicant who had applied for a decree of *certiorari* to quash a decision of magistrates in a case when he was successfully prosecuted and convicted of a motoring offence. It was alleged that at the time of his court proceedings, the acting clerk to the court was a member of a firm of solicitors who were to represent the other party involved in the accident. Despite the fact that the clerk had not taken any part in the decision-making process, nor had he given advice or opinion to the justices, the decision of the magistrates to convict the applicant was quashed on grounds of bias. The court was saying that the question of whether there was a bias depends not on what was actually done but upon what might appear to be done. 'Nothing is to be done which creates even a suspicion that there has been an improper interference with the course of justice.'

Similarly, in *Metropolitan Properties Ltd v. Lannon* (*1969*), a decision of a rent assessment committee was quashed on the grounds that the chairman of the committee was a solicitor who was living with his father in a block of flats owned by the plaintiff and he was already negotiating rents with the landlords on behalf of all the tenants in the block.

(*b*) **The Right to a Hearing.** This is the second rule of natural justice and embraces the following aspects:

(i) A right to know the case against oneself.
(ii) A right to fairness in any proceedings.
(iii) A right to be heard.
(iv) A right to know in advance the case one has to meet.
(v) A right to know the reasons for a decision.

In *Ridge v. Baldwin* (*1964*) (see page 298), where the Chief Constable of Brighton was dismissed by the Watch Committee, the House of Lords quashed this decision on the grounds that (i) the correct procedure as laid down in the *Police Act, 1919*, was not followed and (ii) the rules of natural justice required that the Chief Constable should have been given a hearing by the Watch Committee before being dismissed from the force.

In *Cooper v. Wandsworth Board of Works* (*1863*) damages were awarded to the plaintiff when the Board demolished his partly-built house because he had failed to notify the Board of his intention to build the house. Although this gave the Board a statutory right to demolish the house, the court held that the Board should have given a hearing to the plaintiff before exercising the right to demolish his house. Accordingly, damages awarded against the Board.

In *R. v. Aston University Senate, ex parte Roffey* (*1962*) two students were dismissed from the University on failing their examinations. The court held that this decision was contrary to natural justice and the students should have been given an opportunity to be heard before the final decision was made by the examiners. The decision is in line with another case where a Minister, empowered by a statute, dissolved a municipal council without giving the council a hearing. The Judicial Committee of the Privy Council held that the council was entitled to a hearing and the decision made was of no effect (*Durayappah v. Fernando* (*1967*)).

Rules of natural justice apply to numerous factual situations and it is not proposed to mention all the cases covering these situations. Some of the situations where the courts have insisted on adherence to the rules of natural justice concern, for example, the expulsion of a member from a union, expulsion of students from educational institutions, granting of licences to gaming establishments and the trade unions at GCHQ, Cheltenham, where failure to consult staff rendered the Minister's ban 'invalid and of no effect'.

19.5 Methods of Judicial Review

Apart from the ordinary civil remedies of damages, injunction and specific performance that are normally available and have been mentioned elsewhere in this book, the following remedies are available under judicial review:

(*a*) **Mandamus.** This is a peremptory order issued by the Queen's Bench Division of the High Court against a public body or person requiring performance of a public duty imposed by common law or statute. The order is available at the discretion of the Court and does not lie against the Crown or its servants except in case of a duty owed to a member of the public, e.g. a statutory duty imposed on a minister or a department as in Padfield's case (see page 300).

(*b*) **Certiorari and Prohibition.** *Certiorari* and *prohibition* are normally sought in the same proceedings. Both are issued by the Queen's Bench Division of the High Court, the latter being an order preventing an inferior court from exceeding its jurisdiction or acting contrary to natural justice and the former intended to transfer a case from an inferior court or tribunal to the Queen's Bench Division.

Although they cover broadly the same ground, the main difference between them is that whereas *certiorari* is a means of quashing a decision already arrived at, prohibition is intended to prevent a decision from being made. Originally, both remedies were a means of preventing inferior courts and tribunals from exceeding their jurisdiction. Over the years they have become available against public bodies exercising administrative functions. In the words of Atkin, L.J., in *R. v. Electricity Commissioners, ex parte London Electricity Joint Committee* (*1924*), *certiorari* and prohibition will lie 'wherever any body or persons, having legal authority and having the duty to act judicially, acts in excess of their legal authority . . .' Any decision which affects the rights of an individual is a judicial decision for the purposes of issuing *certiorari*. Therefore, a decision made by a legal aid committee is a judicial decision for the purposes of *certiorari* (*R. v. Manchester Legal Aid Committee, ex parte Brand & Co. Ltd* (*1952*)).

(*c*) **Injunction.** Under private law this remedy is intended to restrain a breach of a contract or the commission of a tort. Under administrative law it is intended to restrain a public body or person from doing a particular act. For example, in *A.G. v. Fulham Corporation* (*1921*) a ratepayer obtained an injunction restraining the Council from acting *ultra vires*. The remedy is available at the court's discretion and is not available against the Crown or its servants. Since a private individual cannot normally sue for an injunction, the action is commenced by the Attorney-General where public interest is involved. The exception when a private individual may sue is when there is both an interference with a public right as well as the right of the individual concerned – for example, an obstruction placed on a highway affects the rights of the general public as well as in particular the right of the individual in front of whose house the obstruction lies preventing him free access to the house.

(*d*) **Declaration.** This is an order of the court which declares the legal rights of the parties concerned. A declaration will normally prevent a public body or official from acting illegally. Apart from other instances, a declaratory order would be particularly convenient in a dispute between a ratepayer and his local authority or between two public authorities. This is a particularly useful remedy for those who are not certain of the legal position and wish to clarify this before embarking on a certain course of action. Once a declaratory judgment is made, any action taken contrary to the declaration is almost certain to be declared null and void in subsequent proceedings.

19.6 Administrative Justice

Administrative justice refers to the justice that is the prime concern of those administrative bodies which have been specifically set up to adjudicate disputes between the citizen and the administration; these disputes are specialist in character and cannot normally be settled in the ordinary courts due to lack of jurisdiction. There are four distinct areas of administrative justice. These are:

(*a*) Administrative tribunals.
(*b*) Public inquiries.
(*c*) Tribunals of inquiry.
(*d*) The 'Ombudsman' office and the Commissioners for the National Health Service and Local Government.

(*a*) **Administrative Tribunals.** These could be regarded as specialised courts permanently set up to adjudicate matters which cannot be settled in the ordinary courts (although there may be an ultimate right of appeal to a court of law).

They are administrative bodies set up to deal with disputes involving the rights and duties of citizens and the state. They can also be viewed as specialised courts which stand apart and as an addition to the ordinary machinery of justice provided by the courts.

The Government today plays an important role in all aspects of an individual's life due to its increased involvement with the economic and social life of the community. This relationship is bound to give rise to all kinds of disputes which simply cannot be settled in the ordinary courts of law. The courts are already burdened with their existing legal work and could not possibly take on additional jurisdiction without the risk of a complete breakdown. The court procedure is slow, formal, detailed and costly and may not attract a person seeking quick, cheap and informal settlement of his claim. He may find a tribunal more attractive and, above all, accessible as the legal profession does not have a monopoly of representation. He may prefer his case to be presented by an accountant, a doctor, a trade union official or a social worker rather than a lawyer. Certain matters are more appropriate for a tribunal than a court. For example, a dispute between a citizen concerned with his rights and a minister, Government department, local authority or public official can be settled without recourse to a court. Besides, certain disputes involve specialist knowledge and the courts cannot be expected to provide this. For example, the determination of the extent of disability or injury is a task performed by a doctor on a Pensions Tribunal and this task could not be adequately discharged in a court presided over by a judge.

In comparing tribunals with the courts, the following differences emerge:

(i) No formal rules of evidence or procedure apply to a tribunal.

(ii) Appointment and dismissal of members is the responsibility of the minister of the department concerned.

(iii) Members need not have legal qualifications and, with the exception of certain tribunals, there is no right of appeal to the ordinary law courts. Nevertheless, the ordinary courts do exercise their supervisory jurisdiction over tribunals and may intervene where there is a clear breach of the rules of natural justice (see page 301) or where one of the grounds (mentioned on pages 296–301) for judicial intervention applies.

There is a Council on Tribunals originally set up by the *Tribunals and Enquiries Act, 1958*; this Act is now re-enacted in the *Tribunals and Inquiries Act, 1971*. The Council is an advisory body which keeps under review the constitution and workings of a large number of tribunals. Some of the listed tribunals under the supervision of the Council which appear in its annual report are the Agricultural Land Tribunals, National Insurance Tribunals, Betting Levy Appeal Tribunal, Commissioners of Income Tax, Industrial Tribunals, Mental Health Review Tribunals, War Pensions Appeal Tribunals, Rent Tribunals, Value-Added Tax Tribunals, Rate Valuation Courts, Civil Aviation Authority (in its licensing function), Supplementary Benefits Appeal Tribunals and the National Health Service Family Practitioner Committees.

There are bodies which may be regarded as tribunals but which do not fall under the supervisory jurisdiction of the Council on Tribunals. In this category comes the Criminal Injuries Compensation Board, the Gaming Board, the Parole Board, the Legal Aid Committees and many professional disciplinary bodies – for example, the Solicitors' Disciplinary Tribunal and the General Medical Council.

A look into the structure of some of the leading tribunals will convey a better understanding of matters such as their composition, functions, powers and jurisdiction and, lastly, the procedure followed by the tribunal.

(i) *National Insurance Tribunals.* Various schemes providing insurance against sickness, unemployment, widows' benefits, retirement and industrial injuries have been in existence since the beginning of this century. New schemes for national insurance and industrial injuries were introduced in 1948 to provide a unified scheme of insurance. Today, the important Acts concerning this area are the *National Insurance Act, 1965*, and the *National Insurance (Industrial Injuries) Act, 1965*. Although the *Social Security Acts, 1975–80*, replaced the scheme of contributions and benefits of the two Acts, the tribunal system contained in the Acts has been retained with minor modifications.

Under the *Social Security Acts, 1975–80*, the following procedure applies for claiming benefits. Initially a claim for benefit is submitted to an insurance officer for his decision. Insurance officers are full-time civil servants employed at the local offices of the Department of Health and Social Security. If a claimant disagrees with the decision of an insurance officer, a right of appeal exists to a local tribunal. An insurance officer can, if he so wishes, refer a question to an insurance tribunal for its decision instead of deciding it himself. There are now over 150 local tribunals in England and Wales.

A tribunal consists of a chairman and two members. The chairman is a lawyer appointed by the Secretary of State from a panel drawn up by the Lord Chancellor. The two members are each drawn from two representative panels, one representing employers and insured persons other than those in employment and the other representing employed persons. Members of the tribunal work on a part-time basis and receive allowances for travelling, subsistence and loss of earnings.

From the decision of a local tribunal there is a right of appeal to National Insurance Commissioners. The Commissioners are appointed by the Crown and are barristers or advocates. An appeal is heard by a single commissioner and in exceptional circumstances by three. An appeal can be lodged by the claimant or the insurance officer, or in some cases by an association like a trade union. Although no right of appeal exists from a Commissioner's decision, a decision can be reviewed by the courts.

Hearings before the tribunal and the commissioner are in public except where public security or intimate personal or financial circumstances are involved. An appeal is heard orally, legal representation is allowed and witnesses can be called for questioning. Reasons for a decision are required to be given and, in the interest of consistency, a system of precedent is observed. Once a decision is made it binds all insurance officers and local tribunals. Leading decisions of the commissioners are published and are available to the public.

Although industrial injuries are dealt with by the National Insurance Tribunals, the questions such as the extent of disablement on account of industrial injury are matters for medical boards and medical appeal tribunals. Medical boards consist of two doctors and medical appeal tribunals consist of two doctors and a lawyer who is the chairman. An appeal, on a point of law, lies from a medical appeal tribunal to a national insurance commissioner.

(ii) *Lands Tribunal*. The Lands Tribunal is the creation of the *Lands Tribunal Act, 1949*. The Tribunal consists of a president and other members appointed by the Lord Chancellor. The president is a person who either has held a judicial office under the Crown or a barrister of at least seven years' standing. The other members, whose number is determined by the Lord Chancellor according to the circumstances of a particular case, are barristers, solicitors or persons qualified and experienced in valuation work.

The jurisdiction of the Tribunal can be enlarged by an Order in Council and at the moment it covers matters such as appeals on rating matters from the local valuation courts. The Tribunal's procedures provide for public sitting except in certain circumstances, e.g. cases arising under the *Atomic Energy Act, 1946*. Parties are allowed to appear in person or be represented by a lawyer, a friend or any other person. The Tribunal has power to administer an oath and it can also award costs. Its decision is required to be put in writing along with a statement of reasons. There is a right of appeal to the Court of Appeal on a point of law by way of case stated and subsequently to the House of Lords.

(iii) *The Commissioners of Income Tax*. Anyone disputing a decision of the Inland Revenue officials concerning income tax liability can appeal to either the General Commissioners or the Special Commissioners of Income Tax. The General Commissioners are usually local businessmen, magistrates or professional people appointed by the Lord Chancellor and hold office at his pleasure. The Commissioners are not required to possess special knowledge of tax law as they are assisted in their work by a qualified clerk. The jurisdiction of the General Commissioners is local and there are approximately 431 such tribunals with about 4000 General Commissioners.

The Special Commissioners, unlike the General Commissioners, are full-time Crown servants appointed by the Treasury from officials of the Inland Revenue Department or from amongst barristers specialising in taxation work. Once appointed their whole time is devoted to the appellate work and hence they do not perform any administrative duties.

The sittings of both the General and the Special Commissioners are in private. Their main function is to apply revenue law to the facts of individual cases before them. Both can be required to state a case on a point of law for the opinion of the High Court.

(iv) *Solicitors' Disciplinary Tribunal.* The *Solicitors Act, 1974*, set up a Disciplinary Tribunal exercising disciplinary powers over solicitors. Its purpose is to hear applications against solicitors where allegations are made by clients. Being officers of the court, solicitors are required to conform to a public disciplinary code of conduct, any breach of which may result in an action before the Tribunal. The Tribunal is appointed by the Master of the Rolls and when hearing applications a board is convened consisting of two practising solicitors and one layman. The Tribunal acts as a judicial body and the legal procedure of a court of law is followed during a hearing. The powers of the Tribunal are extensive. It can order suspension from practice, strike a solicitor off the roll, impose a fine and order payment of costs. The hearing before the Tribunal is in private although its decisions are made public. There is a right of appeal to the High Court or to the Master of the Rolls.

(*b*) **Public Inquiries.** These are set up to give the citizen affected by a Government proposal a right to be heard before a final decision is made. They are especially important in relation to the use and development of land. Since Britain is a densely populated country, it is important that all use and development of land is centrally planned and controlled. Although the ultimate decision on use and development of land lies with one of the central Government departments, the members of the public affected by such a decision are given a say in the decision-making process. This is achieved by holding public inquiries where those affected can raise reasoned objections before a final decision is made. There are numerous circumstances where a public inquiry becomes an essential prerequisite before a decision is made. An inquiry might be held, for example, when a motorway, a power station or an airport is planned. An inquiry may be held when land is compulsorily acquired, when the use of land has environmental consequences, or following proposed developments under the *Town and Country Planning Act, 1971*, or the *New Towns Act, 1946*.

Public inquiries are an important aspect of the administrative process in addition to the tribunals and both therefore come under the jurisdiction of the Council on Tribunals. According to the Franks Committee, set up to look at the whole area of administrative justice, which reported in 1957, the twofold objects of an inquiry are to protect the interests of the citizens most directly affected by a Government proposal by granting them a statutory right to be heard in support of their objections and to ensure that thereby the minister is better informed of the whole facts of the case before the final decision is made.

Under S.11 of the *Tribunals and Inquiries Act, 1971*, the Lord Chancellor, after consulting the Council on Tribunals, can make procedural rules for statutory inquiries. These procedural rules provide that:

(i) Persons affected by an administrative decision must know reasonably in advance of the inquiry the case to be met.

(ii) Departmental representatives must attend such inquiries and disclose the policy of the department concerned.

(iii) On the question of the subject-matter of the inquiry, the inspector in charge of the inquiry is under the control of the Lord Chancellor and not the Government department.

(iv) Reasons for decisions must be given.

(v) Persons appearing before an inquiry have a right to legal representation or to be represented by any other person.

(vi) Procedures at an inquiry are the concern of the inspector and the degree of formality depends on the circumstances of an inquiry.

(vii) A decision can be challenged in the courts on grounds of jurisdiction and procedure.

(viii) An individual who is dissatisfied with an aspect of a public inquiry can also complain to the Council on Tribunals, which has powers to consider and report on the conduct of public inquiries.

(*c*) **Tribunals of Inquiry.** A tribunal of inquiry can be set up to inquire into any matter of urgent public importance on the resolution of both the Houses of Parliament (*Tribunals of Inquiry* (*Evidence*) *Act, 1921*). Tribunals of inquiry are set up in two circumstances. First, where serious allegations of corruption or improper conduct are made against those in public service – for example, in 1957 a tribunal was appointed to investigate the premature disclosure of information relating to the pending increase in the Bank Rate. In 1971 a Tribunal enquired into the collapse of the Vehicle and General Insurance Company. Secondly, tribunals may be set up to investigate a matter of public concern which may not be adequately dealt with before the ordinary courts. Examples are the inquiries into the Aberfan coal-tip disaster in 1966 and the 'Bloody Sunday' shootings in Londonderry in 1972. The Scarman Inquiry into the Brixton riots was essentially a judicial inquiry under the *Police Act, 1964*, although arguably it assumed tribunal of inquiry proportions.

The overall purpose of a tribunal is to produce an authoritative and impartial account of the facts and attribute responsibility or blame as necessary. The tribunal of inquiry is presided over by a chairman, normally a senior judge, and two members who are often lawyers. In exceptional circumstances an inquiry can be conducted by a single judge. Thus Lord Chief Justice Widgery sat alone on the 'Bloody Sunday' inquiry.

A tribunal has all the powers of a High Court and hence it can compel attendance of a witness or the production of a document. Its proceedings are inquisitorial and, apart from cross-examination of witnesses by a counsel, witnesses may also be questioned by members of the tribunal. Being an inquiry, it cannot impose any penalty or order payment of damages. Any serious breaches before a tribunal may be reported to the High Court for inquiry and punishment. Immunity from criminal prosecution may be granted to a witness by the Attorney-General in respect of matters arising out of his evidence. In addition, witnesses enjoy the same immunities and privileges as in the High Court and hence they cannot be sued for slander for anything said in evidence. Legal representation can be allowed, the cost of which may be met from public funds. Although tribunals sit in public, where public interest requires a tribunal may sit in private.

(*d*) **The Parliamentary Commissioner for Administration.** Prior to 1967 the various means of obtaining administrative redress against oppressive or faulty government were the courts, the tribunals, the holding of public enquiries and representation to an MP with a view to obtaining a solution through Parliament. All these approaches were found to be inadequate as they all had limitations, and to give further protection to the citizen in administrative matters, the *Parliamentary Commissioner Act, 1967*, was passed. This Act set up the Office of the Parliamentary Commissioner for Administration (the ombudsman). Although the idea of an ombudsman first developed in Sweden, where it was set up at the beginning of the nineteenth century, and in New Zealand, where it was set up in 1962, the British model is different from these and is essentially based on our existing political institutions.

The Commissioner is appointed by the Crown on the Prime Minister's advice; the first appointment was Sir Edmund Compton, the then retiring Comptroller and Auditor-General. The Commissioner holds office during good behaviour and can be dismissed following addresses by both Houses of Parliament. He is paid out of the Consolidated Fund and his status resembles that of the Comptroller and Auditor-General. He appoints his own staff subject to Treasury approval, almost all of whom are experienced civil servants like the Commissioner himself.

Functions and jurisdiction. The Commissioner's prime function is to investigate complaints from members of the public who claim to have sustained injustice as a result of maladministration by Government departments. The Act does not define maladministration but the term probably means corruption, bias, incompetence, unfair discrimination, neglect, delay or other related administrative sins. His jurisdiction extends to consideration of complaints against nearly all Government departments, a list of which appears under Schedule 2 of the Act.

Excluded from his jurisdiction are the local authorities, the police, the courts, the Post Office, the nationalised industries and tribunals. Certain types of action by departments are excluded from investigation and these appear at Schedule 3 of the Act. Some of the excluded matters are those affecting international relations, diplomatic relations, security of the state and the administration of dependent territories. Others are those under the *Extradition Act, 1870*, and the *Fugitive Offenders Act, 1967*, and appointments, discipline and personnel matters concerning the civil service and the armed forces.

Further limitations on his jurisdiction are that first he cannot investigate a matter in respect of which the complainant has a right of recourse to a court of law or a tribunal and, secondly, he cannot investigate matters in respect of which the complainant allowed 12 months to elapse before making a complaint to an MP.

Powers. The Commissioner has full investigative powers on matters within his jurisdiction. It is for him to determine whether a complaint falls within his jurisdiction and he has complete discretion whether or not to investigate a complaint. He has full access to Government departments and can require any minister, officer or member of a department or any other person to furnish any relevant document or information. After completing his investigation he reports the results to the MP through whom the complaint was made. The Commissioner makes an annual report or interim reports, if he thinks fit, to Parliament on his performance in office. He may also make special reports to Parliament upon cases of maladministration where it appears that the injustice complained of has not been or will not be remedied. For the purposes of the law of defamation, anything the Commissioner says in his reports to Parliament or to individual MPs is absolutely privileged.

Although the Commissioner has no executive powers as he cannot alter a departmental decision or award compensation to a citizen, nevertheless ministers are normally under strong pressure to accept his findings to avoid prejudicial political implications. A Select Committee of the House of Commons exists to examine the reports he lays before Parliament and to support the Commissioner in his work.

It is up to the Commissioner to allow legal representation and he may reimburse any legal costs incurred or any other expenses properly incurred as a result of his investigation.

Procedure. A complaint must be made by an individual or any body of persons (corporate or incorporate) in writing to a member of the House of Commons. It is for the MP to decide whether to refer the complaint to the Commissioner. If the MP chooses to refer the complaint, it should include a statement of approval by the complainant for the MP to refer the complaint to the Commissioner; the name and address of the complainant; the identity of the department against which the complaint is made; and, lastly, a statement of the circumstances in which the alleged injustice occurred. The complaint received is examined by the Commissioner to decide whether it falls within his jurisdiction. An investigation is then carried out and the Act requires all the proceedings to be held in private. Finally, a report is sent to the member from whom the complaint was received.

The commissioner's case-work. One of the cases, of which there are many, which supports and justifies the continuing work of the Commissioner was the Sachsenhausen Case in late 1967. The case concerned the question of payment of compensation to victims of Nazi persecution. The Foreign Office had withheld compensation from 12 claimants because in its opinion they did not fall within the criteria laid down for dispensing compensation, since they were detained not in a concentration camp but outside the perimeter of the camp in a special block and hence received better treatment compared to prisoners in the main camp. An independent inquiry was refused and the complaint was referred to the Commissioner. The Commissioner's investigation revealed defects in the administrative procedure by which the Foreign Office reached its decision. His report was debated in the House of Commons and the Foreign Office reviewed the cases and paid normal compensation without at the same time admitting any default or maladministration.

(*e*) **Commissioners for the National Health Service and Local Government.** The Health Service Commissioner holds an independent office established under the *National Health Service Reorganization Act, 1973*. His function is to investigate complaints of injustice or hardship from members of the public against the Regional Health Authorities, Area Health Authorities and other bodies under the National Health Service. The Commissioner cannot investigate matters which are solely a consequence of clinical judgements, e.g. the diagnosis of an illness or the treatment of a patient. A special procedure for dealing with such complaints operates from September 1, 1981. This involves a review of the case by two independent consultants in active practice in the appropriate speciality.

Many of the aspects of the Parliamentary Commissioner for Administration apply both to the Health Service Commissioner and the Commissioner for Local Administration, which was set up by the *Local Government Act, 1973*. Statutory provisions encourage various commissioners to co-operate with each other. Complaints of maladministration against local authorities, joint boards, police authorities (other than the Home Secretary) and water authorities can be made by affected individuals to the Commissioner for Local Administration.

19.7 Revision Test

Answers	*Questions*
—	**1.** What is administrative law?
1. It is the branch of law which deals with the control of government power.	**2.** Why is Government power so omnipresent today?
2. Because of the huge part played by the state in the national economy, in particular (*a*) traditional state functions of defence, law and order, justice, etc., (*b*) social matters, such as education, health and welfare, (*c*) nationalisation of industries in a wide variety of fields, (*d*) planning, ecological and economic activities.	**3.** What are the grounds for judicial intervention when an abuse of power may have occurred?

Answers	*Questions*
3. (*a*) The *ultra vires* rule; (*b*) incorrectness of procedure; (*c*) improper purpose not sanctioned by Parliament; (*d*) weight being given to irrelevant considerations; (*e*) error of law; (*f*) lack of evidence; (*g*) abuse of discretionary powers; (*h*) abuse of natural justice.	**4.** What are the chief types of abuse of natural justice?
4. (*a*) Bias – administrators must be impartial; (*b*) the right to be heard.	**5.** What are the methods of judicial review?
5. (*a*) *Mandamus* – a peremptory order from the court requiring a public body to do what it is supposed to do. (*b*) *Certiorari* – an order preventing an inferior court from acting outside its jurisdiction or against natural justice, and quashing its decision. (*c*) Prohibition – an order preventing an inferior court from making a decision outside its jurisdiction, or against natural justice. (*d*) Injunction – in administrative law this restrains an official body from acting unlawfully. (*e*) Declaration – an order of the court declaring the rights of individuals in a particular matter.	**6.** How is administrative justice secured?
6. By (*a*) administrative tribunals, (*b*) public inquiries, (*c*) tribunals of inquiry and (*d*) the 'ombudsman' office, and similar commissioners.	**7.** What is the correct title for the ombudsman?
7. The Parliamentary Commissioner for Administration.	**8.** Go over the page again until you are sure of all the answers. Then try some of the questions in Appendix 1.

Part 6: The Businessman and the Law of Tort

20
Introduction to the Law of Tort

20.1 The Nature of the Law of Tort

A tort is a civil wrong which gives rise to a private, civil action commenced by one party (the **plaintiff**) against another (the **defendant**). The party alleging the wrong normally claims monetary compensation (**damages**) for the harm or loss suffered. The harm alleged may take the form of physical injury, injury to one's character or reputation, financial loss or interference with an individual's right to enjoy his property. Apart from damages other remedies may be appropriate in a particular case – for example, an injunction is more suitable to prevent or restrain someone from committing a tort like nuisance. There is a large number of recognised and listed torts and these will be looked at individually in the following order:

(*a*) Negligence.
(*b*) Liability of occupiers of premises.
(*c*) Strict liability.
(*d*) Trespass to property.
(*e*) Nuisance.
(*f*) Defamation.
(*g*) Miscellaneous torts of conspiracy, deceit and injurious falsehood.

Before these we must consider several matters which have a common bearing or application to the whole area of tort.

20.2 Definition of Tort

Defining tort is not an easy matter and one has to be careful not to define it too broadly so as to encompass matters other than torts or to define it too narrowly so as to exclude some torts. Two contrasting definitions of tort are offered; one by Salmond, the other by Professor Winfield. They represent different schools of thought.

Salmond defines a tort as *'a civil wrong for which the remedy is a common law action for unliquidated damages, and which is not exclusively the breach of a contract or a breach of trust or other merely equitable obligation'.*

The late Professor Winfield contended that *'all tortious liability arises from the breach of a duty primarily fixed by law; such duty is towards persons generally, and its breach is redressable by an action for unliquidated damages'.*

Both these definitions refer to unliquidated damages. Damages are unliquidated when they are not predetermined or pre-estimated (as they are, for example, in an action in contract to recover a debt) but are determined at the absolute discretion of the court.

One school maintains that there is a 'law of torts' which consists of a number of specific torts and to succeed in an action you must show that the alleged wrong falls within the scope of one or more of these torts. The other school maintains that there is a 'law of tort' (not torts) based on a general principle of liability and all harm is actionable *per se* unless the defendant can show a just cause or excuse. There are no inherent contradictions between the two schools of thought as both accept that new categories of torts may be created and the existing law can be expanded to bring new wrongs within its confines. As Professor Glanville Williams puts it: 'To say that the law can be collected into pigeon-holes does not mean that those pigeon-holes may not be capacious, nor does it mean that they are incapable of being added to.'

Damnum sine injuria and *injuria sine damno.* Although normally any harm or damage suffered is actionable as a tort, there can be instances when a harm can be done by an individual against another for which the law does not provide a remedy. This is called *damnum sine injuria* (damage without legal wrong). For example, if you suffer bankruptcy as a result of the undercutting of prices by your competitor(s), then you have no legal remedy although your family may suffer as a result:

Ajello v. Worsley (1898). The defendant had advertised in newspapers the sale of the plaintiff's pianos below their wholesale price. **Held:** no wrong was committed as the defendant was within his legal right to sell at whatever price he wished and to advertise despite the fact that he did not have any of the plaintiff's pianos in stock.

Similarly, there can be instances when although no real damage or harm has resulted to a plaintiff, yet a defendant's acts or omissions may be actionable *per se* (by itself). When you trespass on someone's land this can give rise to an action in tort, although the land owner has not suffered any particular harm or loss. Similarly, a libel is actionable without proof of the fact that the plaintiff has suffered any real loss. The situation where a legal wrong has taken place although no harm or loss is suffered is termed *injuria sine damno* (legal wrong without injury). It must be pointed out, however, that not all torts are actionable *per se* as most require proof of the actual damage or harm suffered by a plaintiff.

Mental element in tort. Injurious conduct is normally actionable as a tort and as a general rule the intention or motive of the defendant is not important. For example:

Bradford Corporation v. Pickles (1895). The appellants owned a waterworks and the respondent owned adjoining land from which a valuable supply of water flowed into the appellants' reservoir. It was alleged by the appellants that in order to coerce them into buying the respondent's land at a high price, the respondent commenced harmful activities on his land which resulted in a reduction of the water flow and pollution. The appellants sought an injunction to prevent these activities which it was contended were actuated by malice. The court refused to grant an injunction, holding that the action of the respondent was lawful as he was merely exercising a right over his own property. Hence his motive or intention were irrelevant.

Comparing tort, crime and contract. When comparing a tort to a crime or a breach of a contract, the following distinctions emerge:

Tort	*Crime*	*Contract*
1. The rights and duties are the result of the application of civil law made up of statute law and common law.	The rights and duties are the result of the criminal law.	The rights and duties depend on the obligations undertaken under the contract.
2. A civil action is normally commenced by one individual against another. A typical tort case would be cited as *Smith* v. *Brown* (*1980*).	The action is brought by the police as agents of the state against another person. A typical criminal case would be cited thus *R.* v. *Brown* (*1980*).	The action is brought by the party alleging breach of the contract against the other party to the contract. A contract case would have a similar citation to a tort case.
3. The successful party is awarded damages or other remedies where applicable, such as an injunction.	The guilty party is punished by way of imprisonment, or by fine or other non-custodial sentence.	Apart from damages, other remedies like specific performance, injunction, payment on *quantum meruit* and rescission may be available.
4. A tort arises as a result of the operation of the civil law of the country.	A crime is a result of the operation of criminal law of the country.	A breach of a contract results exclusively from a breach of agreement between the parties.
5. A duty is owed towards persons generally.	Criminal conduct is prescribed by the criminal law and a duty is owed to the general public.	A duty is owed to a specific person who is a party to a contract. (There may, of course, be more than one person.)

Having mentioned some differences between the three, one can come across instances when there may be an overlap between them. For example, if you were travelling in a taxi which, due to the negligent driving of the taxi driver, collides with a lamp-post, this may result in the following actions: a criminal action by the police against the taxi driver for dangerous driving; if you have suffered physical harm, an action by you for negligence against the driver; a breach of contract of hire between the taxi driver and the cab owner or between the taxi driver and the passenger. The tort of negligence and the contractual duty to drive carefully overlap. There is also an overlap between the negligent driving of the driver and the crime of dangerous driving or other road traffic offences. So it is apparent that the three are not absolutely exclusive and the same wrong may give rise to all three.

20.3 General Defences in Tort

In addition to special defences peculiar to particular torts, the following general defences are available, wherever appropriate, to a defendant in an action for any type of tort:

(*a*) ***Volenti non fit injuria.*** Translated this Latin phrase means that in law no wrong is done to a person who voluntarily consents to undergo it. In sports, if you are injured as a result of normal sporting activities, whether you are a player or a spectator, you have no cause of complaint. For example, if, as a boxer, you are punched and injured, no tort is committed; similarly, if you are injured as a spectator as a result of the sporting activity, there is no cause of action:

Hall v. Brooklands Auto Racing Club (*1933*). Two spectators died as a result of a racing car colliding, leaving the race track and hitting the spectators. **Held:** in the absence of negligence, the defendants were not liable as the spectators had impliedly consented to the risk inherent in such a sport.

It is important that the consent of the plaintiff to the risks involved must be either written, oral or be able to be implied from the circumstances. The consent must be genuine, obtained without any force or compulsion. Mere knowledge of the risks involved is not enough to constitute consent. In *Smith v. Baker* (*Charles*) *& Sons* (*1891*), the plaintiff was a workman employed by the defendants on a construction project. While working in a quarry he was aware of the danger from a crane working overhead and had in fact complained along with other workers about this danger. On one occasion he was injured as a result of some stones falling on him because of the activity of the crane. He successfully sued his employers in negligence as the defence of *volenti non fit injuria* did not apply. His awareness of the danger did not make him a volunteer and true consent on his part was lacking.

In *Dann v. Hamilton* (*1939*), a girl who was aware of the potential danger posed by a driver's drunkenness, accepted a lift and was subsequently injured as a result of a collision. In an action for negligence against the estate of the deceased driver, the defence of *volenti non fit injuria* failed as she was not a volunteer who had assented to the negligent driving. Today, in such a case since the plaintiff is aware of the driver's state she is considered as having contributed to the negligence and the damages awarded eventually are reduced in proportion to the extent of her own negligence (*Owens v. Brimmell* (*1976*)).

An employee obeying his employer's instructions will rarely be a volunteer injured in the performance of his duties unless the risk he ran was not connected with his ordinary duties:

Bowater v. Rowley Regis Corporation (*1944*). The plaintiff, who was employed as a carter, was injured because the horse he was provided with bolted and ran away. He had on previous occasions complained to his employers about the vicious propensity of the animal, but continued to work under protest. **Held:** He would succeed in an action for damages as the Corporation had been negligent and the defence of *volenti non fit injuria* did not apply as the employee had not truly consented to the risk involved.

We look finally at the defence of *volenti non fit injuria* and its application to a particular set of circumstances commonly known as the **rescue cases**. A dangerous situation is created by the defendant's negligent act and the plaintiff decides to act to save or protect lives or injury to others from the danger created and in doing so is thereby injured. If the plaintiff brings an action for negligence against the defendant, can the latter plead the defence of *volenti non fit injuria*? The law is that where there is an imminent danger to others and a plaintiff who is motivated by a moral and/or legal duty in protecting life or property, acts to protect others, the defence of *volenti non fit injuria* will fail to protect a defendant who claims that the plaintiff acted voluntarily. In these circumstances the knowledge on the part of the plaintiff of the risks involved does not make the plaintiff a *volens* (a party acting willingly).

Haynes v. Harwood (1935). A two-horse van was left unattended on a crowded street. Due to this negligent action on the part of the defendant's servant, the horses bolted and were brought under control by the courageous action of a police constable on duty who had perceived the danger created. The constable was, however, injured due to this action and sued the defendant successfully in negligence. The defence of *volenti non fit injuria* did not apply as mere knowledge of the risk involved did not make the constable a volunteer who acted willingly.

Baker v. T. E. Hopkins & Son Ltd. (1959). A doctor died when he went down a well in order to rescue two servants of the defendant company who were engaged in a cleaning operation using a petrol-driven pump. The servants were overcome by the fumes created by a concentration of carbon monoxide and so was the doctor when he went to rescue them. All three lost their lives. The doctor's executors succeeded in claiming damages for the defendants' negligence in creating the dangerous situation. The doctor had acted under a moral compulsion and hence the defence of *volenti non fit injuria* would fail.

In contrast, in situations where no real emergency exists as there is no imminent danger to anyone, then any action of a person is considered gratuitous and voluntary and the defence of *volenti non fit injuria* will succeed.

Cutler v. United Dairies (London) Ltd (1933). The plaintiff was injured when he tried to stop a bolting horse drawing a milk cart down a quiet country road. There was no danger or urgency demanded by the circumstances and therefore the plaintiff was considered to have acted freely and voluntarily and the defence of *volenti non fit injuria* provided a complete defence.

Sylvester v. Chapman Ltd (1935). The plaintiff, who was mauled by a leopard when he crossed a barrier to put out a lighted cigarette end, was not entitled to damages as he was considered to be a volunteer; there were keepers available to do the job without risk.

(*b*) **Necessity.** This defence is pleaded when a tortious act is done intentionally to avoid a greater harm being done to the defendant himself, to a third party or to the Realm. The defence will succeed if the harm or damage done is reasonably justifiable having regard to the circumstances.

Cope v. Sharpe (1912). The defendant gamekeeper, in order to prevent fire spreading from the adjoining land and engulfing his master's sitting pheasants, went to the plaintiff's land and set fire to some patches of heather. In an action for trespass, the defence of necessity succeeded as the gamekeeper's action was reasonable in the circumstances.

Esso Petroleum Co. Ltd v. Southport Corporation (1955). A vessel had run aground in a narrow and shallow channel and in order to save the vessel and the crew from grave danger, the master of the ship discharged considerable quantities of oil which polluted the respondent's beaches. The Southport Corporation, who brought an action to recover the costs of clearing the beaches, failed as necessity was a complete defence to any claim based on trespass or nuisance. The action of the master was reasonable in the circumstances and therefore, he was not guilty of negligence.

In the case of *The King's Prerogative in Saltpetre* (*1606*) necessity was a good defence to an action for trespass in circumstances where it is necessary for the Crown or its subject to trespass onto the land of another in order to erect fortifications for the defence of the Realm.

(*c*) **Mistake.** As with contract law, ignorance of the law is not accepted as an excuse. The law does not accept either a mistake of law or of fact as a defence in tort. A trespass is actionable even if the trespasser acted in the mistaken belief that the land was his or that he had a right of entry (*Basely v. Clarkson* (*1682*)). Similarly, an auctioneer is liable for conversion to the true owners of the goods if he auctions goods for a customer in good faith without any negligence (*Consolidated Co. v. Curtis & Son* (*1892*)).

In certain circumstances, like malicious prosecution or false imprisonment, mistake may provide a defence. For example, where a crime has been committed and an ordinary citizen or a policeman mistakenly arrest an innocent person because there exist reasonable grounds for suspicion that the person arrested has committed the offence, then mistake may provide a defence to an action for false imprisonment (*Beckwith v. Philby* (*1827*)). Powers of arrest by a citizen or a policeman are covered by S.2 of the *Criminal Law Act, 1967*, and in certain circumstances statutory protection may be claimed under this section.

(*d*) **Inevitable Accident.** This is a good defence in circumstances where it can be shown that an accident could not have been prevented by any reasonable precaution, care or foresight:

Stanley v. Powell (*1891*). The plaintiff and defendant were both members of a pheasant-shooting party. The plaintiff received injuries from a pellet fired in a proper manner by the defendant when it glanced off a tree and struck the plaintiff. **Held:** the defendant was not negligent. The plaintiff's injury was accidental and the action for damages for trespass to the person must fail.

(*e*) **Statutory Authority**. Parliament sometimes confers authority on public bodies to act in a manner which may otherwise be considered tortious. The authority, which may be either absolute or conditional, is normally conferred on local councils by an Act of Parliament or subordinate legislation. An **absolute authority** imposes a duty on the public authority to act even if this may cause harm to others, provided it acts reasonably. A **conditional authority** is a power to act provided no harm results to other persons. Whether or not an authority is absolute or conditional is strictly a matter of construction of the relevant statute.

The House of Lords laid down in *Geddis v. Proprietors of Bann Reservoir* (*1878*) that it was 'thoroughly well established' that 'no action will lie for doing that which the legislature has authorised, if it be done without negligence . . . but an action does lie for doing that which the legislature has authorised, if it be done negligently' (*per* Lord Blackburn).

Vaughan v. Taff Vale Railway Co. (*1860*). A railway company was authorised by Parliament to operate a railway which ran through the plaintiff's land. Despite all the care taken by the company, a spark from one of their locomotives caused fire which destroyed eight acres of the plaintiff's wood. **Held:** In the absence of any negligence, the railway company was not liable as it had statutory authority.

Metropolitan District Asylum Board v. Hill (*1881*). A hospital authority had conditional authority to erect a smallpox hospital. It erected such a hospital in a residential district of Hampstead where it caused danger of infection in the neighbourhood. **Held:** the hospital constituted a nuisance and an injunction was granted restraining the use of the building as a smallpox hospital. The obligation imposed by the statute on the hospital authority was permissive and not imperative.

(*f*) **Self-Defence.** Where a person commits tort in defence of himself, his family, his property or in defence of persons generally then self-defence may provide a good defence provided the force used is in proportion to the harm or danger threatened. For example, a blow is not proportionate to verbal provocation (*Lane v. Holloway* (*1967*)). Similarly, to shoot at trespassers or to set up traps or spring-guns to injure them is a disproportionate use of force to the likely harm threatened or done.

Dale v. Wood (*1822*). In answer to a claim for assault, the defendant proved that the plaintiff had approached him menacingly on horseback, dismounted, held up a stick at him and provoked him. **Held:** The defendant's action was justified in the circumstances.

Similarly, if a neighbour's dog attacks your cattle or sheep, you are justified in shooting the dog if it is the only reasonable way of preventing harm: (*Cresswell v. Sirl* (*1948*)) – now replaced on a somewhat wider basis by S.9 of the *Animals Act, 1971*.

(*g*) **Act of God.** This defence applies to circumstances when injury or harm results to others which no human precaution or foresight can prevent.

Nichols v. Marsland (*1876*). Due to an exceptionally violent storm, artificial pools on the defendant's land which were well constructed and adequate for normal circumstances, were destroyed and the escaping water damaged bridges belonging to the plaintiff county council. **Held:** In the absence of negligence, the defendant was not liable as the accident was entirely due to an extraordinary act of nature.

(*h*) **Act of State.** The *Crown Proceedings Act, 1947*, places the Crown in the same position as a private person or employer for any tort committed by its servants, although the Queen continues to enjoy personal immunity from legal proceedings. However, neither the Crown nor the officials responsible can be sued in tort where the acts concerned are acts of state, i.e. they are official acts either authorised or subsequently ratified by the Crown, if these acts take place outside the territorial jurisdiction of the Crown (*Buron v. Denman* (*1848*)). This is because acts of state in foreign parts, such as warlike activities or annexation of territories, are not the concern of the English courts. However, the defence of act of state will fail in respect of damage or harm done to British subjects anywhere (*Nissan v. Attorney-General* (*1969*)), or done to a citizen of a friendly state when he is within the Crown territory (*Johnston v. Pedlar* (*1921*)). When this defence fails the affected party may be entitled to compensation.

20.4 Capacity of the Parties

Although as a general rule any person of full age can sue and be sued in tort, it is necessary to consider the following categories of persons whose capacity is limited.

(*a*) **The Crown.** The *Crown Proceedings Act, 1947* (S.2), places the Crown in the same position as a private citizen for any tort committed by its servants or agents. A servant or an agent of the Crown is one who is directly or indirectly appointed by the Crown and would include Ministers of State, their subordinates and all other persons employed in Government departments. The following are excluded:

(i) *The police.* Although the police are employed by the local authority they are not considered servants of the local authority (*Fisher v. Oldham Corporation* (*1930*)). The *Police Act, 1964* (S.48), makes the chief police officer for the area vicariously liable for any tort committed by his officers in the course of their employment. Any damages and costs due are paid out of the police fund.

(ii) *Local authorities.*

(iii) *Hospital authorities.* Both the above have a legal personality of their own, and may be held vicariously liable for any tort committed by their servants.

(iv) *Public corporations.* Although basically they are not Crown servants it does depend on the Act which created them. If the Act provides that a corporation acts for the Crown then it will probably be a crown servant. Otherwise it acts on its own behalf although it may be controlled by a Government department (*Tamlin v. Hannaford* (*1950*)).

(v) *The Post Office.* Although no longer a Government department, it continues to enjoy immunity for any tort arising from any loss or damage resulting from loss or delay in the post, unless the packet has been registered (*Post Office Act, 1969*).

(*b*) **Infants and Minors.** A minor (a person under 18 years of age) is normally responsible in tort and infancy is not a defence. However, the standard of care expected from a minor is not that expected from an adult, but one that is commensurate with the minor's age. Besides, in torts which require malice or intention an infant defendant may be considered unlikely to have formed the necessary intent.

If an act complained of is a tort as well as a breach of contract, a plaintiff would not be allowed to frame his action in tort to escape the immunity that a minor enjoys under contract law. (For contractual capacity of minors see pages 87–9).

Jennings v. Rundall (*1798*). The infant defendant hired a horse for riding and was sued in tort for injuries received to the animal through excessive riding. **Held:** there was no liability for negligence as this was essentially a breach of contract.

However, in contrast, where an alleged act goes beyond the bounds of a contract, as when a child kills a mare by jumping her against express instructions, this conduct may be considered independent of the contract and hence a minor will be liable in tort (*Burnard v. Haggis* (*1863*)).

Although a parent is not liable for a child's tort, if he or she affords the child an opportunity to commit the tort, there may be liability in negligence. In *Bebee v. Sales* (*1916*), despite previous damage done and despite complaints made, a father allowed his son to keep an air-gun with which he caused injury to another boy's eye. The father was held liable in negligence.

Although minors have full legal capacity to sue in tort, they require to be represented by an adult acting as 'next friend'. In principle, an infant can sue his parent (*Deziel v. Deziel* (*1953*)). The *Congenital Disabilities* (*Civil Liability*) *Act, 1976*, gives a child a right to sue those whose intentional act, negligence or breach of a statutory duty results in prenatal injuries to that child. Although a mother cannot be held liable for negligently causing injuries to the unborn child, a father's liability is not excluded.

(*c*) **Judicial Immunity.** A judge discharging his judicial function enjoys absolute immunity from any action in tort and so do justices of the peace when acting within their jurisdiction (*Law v. Llewellyn* (*1906*)). Similar immunity also extends to counsels and witnesses concerning matters relating to a judicial proceeding.

(*d*) **Foreign Sovereigns and Diplomats.** A foreign sovereign is not liable in tort since he is not subject to an English court's jurisdiction unless he waives this immunity and submits to it. Similarly, foreign ambassadors, other diplomats, members of their families and certain categories of employees at foreign embassies enjoy diplomatic immunity and cannot be sued in tort during their terms of office. They become liable immediately after finishing their terms of office, although the alleged tort may have been committed when they enjoyed diplomatic immunity. They can also voluntarily submit to a local court's jurisdiction.

(*e*) **Corporations.** A corporation is a legal person and hence it can sue in its corporate name for any tort committed against it. It is also vicariously liable and can therefore be sued for any tort committed by its agents or servants when acting within the scope of their authority. The Companies Act, 1985, is silent about tortious activities and hence a corporation is not liable for a tort committed when a servant or an agent was engaged in an *ultra vires* activity without express authority, whereas it is liable under S.35 for contractual activities engaged on by staff with third parties unaware of the *ultra vires* nature.

(*f*) **Trade Unions.** Trade unions are unincorporated associations and they enjoy certain immunities from actions in tort. A trade union cannot be held liable for torts committed by its members or officials in furtherance of a trade dispute unless the acts involve 'unlawful act', such as illegal picketing, etc.

(*g*) **Persons of Unsound Mind.** Although, in general, a person suffering from mental disorder is liable for his torts, the state of mind of a person is important in torts requiring a mental ingredient, e.g. malicious prosecution or deceit. A person of unsound mind is considered incapable of forming the necessary intent or malice for committing such torts. Similarly, if it is proved that a person is so insane that his actions cannot be considered to be voluntary, then he may escape liability in tort. It must be shown that he neither knew of the nature and quality of his act nor that what he was doing was wrong (*Morris v. Marsden (1952)*).

(*h*) **Aliens.** There are two categories of aliens – namely, enemy aliens and other aliens. The latter are in the same position as ordinary citizens and hence do not suffer any disability or enjoy any immunity. As regards enemy aliens, these are nationals of a state which is at war with the UK. They also include British subjects who voluntarily reside or carry on business in such a state. Enemy aliens have no right to bring an action in tort although they may defend one, if sued.

(*i*) **Partners, Principals and Agents.** All partners are jointly and severally liable for a tort committed by one of them in the ordinary course of business. A principal is only liable for the tort of his agent as long as it was committed by the agent when acting within the scope of his authority.

(*j*) **Husband and Wife.** The *Law Reform (Husband and Wife) Act, 1962*, provides that 'each of the parties to a marriage shall have the like right of action in tort against the other as if they were not married'. Thus a wife may bring an action for assault and battery against a husband or vice versa. A court may stay such proceedings if it appears:

(i) That no substantial benefit would accrue to either party from the continuation of the proceedings; or

(ii) That the question or questions in issue could more conveniently be disposed of under S.17 of the *Married Women's Property Act, 1882*. This provides a summary procedure for determining questions between spouses concerning title to or possession of property.

Since the *Law Reform (Married Women and Tortfeasors) Act, 1935*, a wife is fully liable for her torts unless there exists an employer/employee or principal/agent relationship, in which case the husband may be vicariously liable for the wife's tort.

20.5 Remedies for Torts

Apart from extra-judicial remedies such as abating nuisances or ejecting trespassers, which are mentioned under specific torts, the judicial remedies that are available to a plaintiff are damages, the granting of an injunction and in some cases restitution of property.

(*a*) **Damages.** This is monetary compensation awarded to the party that has suffered a wrong and the underlying principle is one of restitution *in integrum*, i.e. to restore a plaintiff as far as possible to the position he would have been if no wrong had been committed against him. Damages are classified in a number of ways:

(i) *General and special damages*. General damages are awarded for the mere fact that a tort has been committed and the law presumes that loss or injury automatically follows from the tort. General damages are awarded at the discretion of the court and are also termed **unliquidated damages**. Unlike general damages, for the award of special damages a plaintiff must prove the loss or injury resulting from a tort. Special damages are pleaded specially and the pleading sets out the exact amount being claimed. Special damages are awarded for losses which are exactly calculable, e.g. loss of earnings up to the date of the trial, medical expenses, etc. Damages which cannot be calculated precisely, e.g. damages for loss of future earnings, damages for pain and suffering and damages for loss of expectation of life, are termed general damages.

(ii) *Nominal and substantial damages.* Nominal damages consist of a small sum of money which is awarded, not as compensation, but in mere recognition of the fact that a plaintiff's rights have been infringed. Nominal damages apply to torts actionable *per se*, e.g. trespass to land that involves no physical damage to the land or any other loss to the plaintiff. Substantial damages are normally unliquidated damages awarded for the actual loss or injury suffered by a plaintiff. They are compensatory in nature and are intended to restore a plaintiff to the position he was in before the commission of the tort.

(iii) *Exemplary damages.* These damages are awarded as a means of punishing a defendant rather than compensating a plaintiff. Hence they are also called **vindictive** or **punitive damages**. The House of Lords, in *Rookes v. Barnard* (*1964*), mentioned the circumstances in which these damages are awarded. These are:

1. Where a plaintiff is harmed as a result of oppressive, arbitrary or unconstitutional action of a Government servant.
2. Where a defendant's conduct was calculated to make a profit which might exceed the compensation payable to the plaintiff.
3. Where a statute authorises exemplary damages.

(iv) *Aggravated damages.* These are awarded in circumstances where a defendant's conduct is wilful and malicious – for example, slapping someone in a public place may cause greater injury to his feelings and the damages awarded would be larger than the sum that would normally be awarded for such an act.

Remoteness of damage. To succeed in obtaining damages it is essential that the plaintiff's act or omission and the consequence suffered by the defendant are not too remote. We are really concerned with the consequences of tortious conduct. Should the defendant be liable for all the consequences that follow his act or omission or should he be answerable only for the immediate consequences? In order to determine this, the rule before 1961 – as established in *Re Polemis & Furness, Withy & Co. Ltd* (*1921*) – was that a defendant was liable in negligence for all the direct consequences of his act irrespective of the fact that he could not have reasonably foreseen them.

However, as a result of the decision by the Judicial Committee of the Privy Council in *Overseas Tankship* (*UK*) *Ltd v. Morts Dock & Engineering Co. Ltd* (*1961*), a case also known as *The 'Wagon Mound'* (*No. 1*), the test that has been established is that a defendant is liable for the consequences of his negligent act or omission only if he could have reasonably foreseen that his tortious conduct would result in those consequences. The test depends on the foresight of a reasonable man. The facts were as follows:

The 'Wagon Mound' (*No. 1*) (*1961*). Through the carelessness of the appellants' servants, a large quantity of bunkering oil was spilt into a bay while a vessel was discharging gasoline products and taking in oil. It was found as a fact that the appellants did not know, and could not reasonably have been expected to know, that the oil was capable of being set alight when spread on water. Molten metal falling from the respondents' wharf set fire to some cotton waste floating in the oil, which in turn ignited the oil itself and caused a serious fire. Considerable damage was done to the respondents' wharf and equipment. **Held:** the appellants were not liable in negligence for the damage because they could not reasonably have foreseen it.

'The authority of *Polemis* has been severely shaken, though lip service has from time to time been paid to it. In their lordships' opinion, it should no longer be regarded as good law . . . It is a principle of civil liability, subject only to qualifications which have no present relevance, that a man must be considered to be responsible for the probable consequences of his act. To demand more of him is too harsh a rule . . . Thus foreseeability becomes the effective test. In reasserting this principle, their lordships conceive that they do not depart from, but follow and develop the law of negligence as laid down by Alderson, B., in *Blyth v. Birmingham Waterworks Co.*' (*per* Viscount Simonds).

Although the decision of the Privy Council in the 'Wagon Mound' is of persuasive authority and consequently does not bind an English court, the decision seems to have been accepted by the House of Lords in *Hughes v. Lord Advocate* (*1963*) and specifically by the Court of Appeal in *Doughty v. Turner Manufacturing Co. Ltd* (*1964*).

Damages that are too remote cannot normally be recovered unless the harm or loss was actually intended by the defendant. Harm or loss are presumed intentional when they are the natural and inevitable consequences of a tortious conduct. For example, if A strikes a blow at B intentionally and B suffers a greater harm than an ordinary person because of a previous illness, A nevertheless is fully responsible for the consequences of his act and B's illness cannot be put forward as a defence.

Smith v. Leech Braine & Co. Ltd (*1962*). As a consequence of the defendant's negligence, molten zinc hit the lip of the plaintiff's husband and caused a burn. The husband was a galvaniser employed by the defendants. Three years later the husband died as a result of cancer which developed in the burn. **Held:** the defendants were liable for damages to the wife although the death of the husband could not have been reasonably foreseen. (See also *Meah v. McCreamer* (*1986*)).

Novus actus interveniens (a new act intervening). Sometimes a loss resulting from an act or omission of a defendant may be too remote (not foreseeable) and therefore may not be recoverable because of the intervention of an extraneous act. This intervention may have broken the chain of causation resulting from the original act or omission. For example:

Cobb v. Great Western Railway (*1894*). The plaintiff passenger was hustled and robbed of £89 because the defendants had negligently allowed a railway carriage to become overcrowded. **Held:** plaintiff could not succeed in recovering the loss as the robbery was a *novus actus interveniens* which broke the chain of causation caused by the defendant's negligence.

Where the intervening act does not break the chain of causation caused by the original act or omission, then the defendant is liable for the consequences:

Scott v. Shepherd (1773). The defendant threw a lighted squib into a crowded market. The squib fell on a stall belonging to Yates whereupon a bystander called Willis in order to protect himself and Yates' stall seized the squib and threw it across where it fell on the stall belonging to Ryal, who in order to protect his goods, threw the squib to another part of the market where it exploded and caused injury to the plaintiff. **Held:** the defendant was liable as there was no *novus actus interveniens*. The chain of causation resulting from the defendant's action was not broken by the intervening actions of either Willis or Ryal.

(*b*) **Injunction.** This is an equitable remedy and is available at the discretion of the court. An injunction will be refused where damages would be an appropriate remedy and the High Court has power to award damages in lieu of an injunction. An injunction may be granted by any division of the High Court and also by the county courts. It may be granted to forbid the commission of a tort (**prohibitory injunction**) or it may be granted to compel the defendant to do something, e.g. to abate a nuisance (a **mandatory injunction**). An **interlocutory injunction** is granted by the court on the basis of a plaintiff's affidavit to prohibit or restrain the activities of the defendant and maintain the status quo, pending a court hearing. **Perpetual injunction** is granted after the case has been tried and is intended either to compel the defendant to do something or to prohibit him from some act.

The courts may suspend the operation of an injunction for a time to enable the defendant to comply with it. For example, in *Pride of Derby and Derbyshire Angling Association Ltd v. British Celanese Ltd (1953)* the court issued an injunction to prevent the activities of the defendant company which resulted in pollution of a river. However, the company was given time to carry out the necessary alterations to its sewage plant in order to comply with the injunction.

(*c*) **Restitution of Property.** The courts have discretion to order specific restitution of land or goods in cases where a plaintiff has been tortiously deprived of property by a defendant. In addition, a defendant may be called to give an account of the profits made as a result of his wrongful act, i.e. the deception. For example, if you carry on business activities under a business name of an existing and reputable company, you commit the tort of passing off and you can be compelled to refrain from doing so; you can also be called to account for the profits received by you as a result of the deception.

20.6 Limitation of Actions

The law on the limitation of actions was consolidated in the second *Limitation Act, 1980*, which now contains the law concerning the period within which an action in tort must commence. The rules are:

(i) As a general rule, action in tort must commence within six years of the date on which the right of action accrued. In torts actionable *per se*, this time runs from the date on which the tort was committed. In torts actionable only on proof of damage, the time runs from the moment damage takes place.

(ii) In case of a tort, like nuisance, which consists of a continuing wrong, a new cause of action arises every day.

(iii) If a tort is committed against a party under a disability (e.g. a person of unsound mind or a minor), the actionable period runs from either the time of the cessation of disability or of his death. Where disabilities are successive, time begins to run from the *last* one.

(iv) Where an alleged wrong consists of a fraud or mistake, the beginning of the period of limitation does not begin until the plaintiff discovers the fraud or mistake.

Other Statutory Limitations. The 1980 Act re-enacts certain earlier measures about the periods during which action must commence from the date of accrual of the cause of action:

(*a*) For personal injuries due to nuisance, negligence or breach of duty (statutory, contractual or independent of either) the period is three years. For personal injuries, the limitation period can also run from the date a plaintiff learns that his injury was significant.

(*b*) *Fatal Accidents Act, 1976*. Three years.

(*c*) *Maritime Conventions Act, 1911*, S.8. Two years in respect of life or personal injury to persons on board a vessel or damage to a vessel or her cargo.

(*d*) *Carriage by Air Act, 1961*. Two years for carriers subject to the Act.

(*e*) *Carriage by Sea Act, 1971*. One year, but the time limit may be extended by mutual agreement.

(*f*) *Limitation Act, 1980* (S.10). Two years from the date of a judgement for a tortfeasor seeking contribution from a joint tortfeasor.

(*g*) *Nuclear Installations Act, 1965* (S.15). Thirty years in respect of damage arising from nuclear incidents.

(*h*) *Proceedings Against Estates Act, 1970*. Actions in tort against the estate of a deceased person must commence within the normal six-year period or three years in respect of personal injuries.

The Survival of Actions. The *Law Reform* (*Miscellaneous Provisions*) *Act, 1934*, provides that a right of action in tort survives in favour of the estate of a deceased plaintiff and against the estate of a deceased defendant. Two exceptions to the rule are: (*a*) no action in respect of defamation survives after death unless damage is done to the deceased's property; and (*b*) exemplary damages are not awarded to the estate of a deceased plaintiff. Damages can be recovered in respect of pain and suffering, loss of earnings before death, medical expenses, loss of expectation of life and funeral or mourning expenses.

The *Fatal Accidents Act, 1976*, allows the personal representative of a deceased person to bring an action for damages on behalf of the deceased's dependants if death accrued as a result of a tortious act on the part of the defendant. Action must commence within three years of the death. A plaintiff must show that pecuniary loss (probably loss of financial benefit) has been suffered by the dependants and that the deceased was a breadwinner; damages for mere mental suffering will not be awarded. Dependants include the deceased's wife or husband, parent, child, grandparent, grandchild, step-parent, stepchild, brother, sister, uncle and aunt; also the issue of the latter four and illegitimate and adopted children.

Although claims for the same fatal accident may be brought under both the 1934 Act (for cause of action arising before the death) and the *Fatal Accidents Act, 1976*, a court will ensure that double benefits are not awarded to a defendant. For example, if an award is made to a surviving wife as a result of her husband's death (under the 1934 Act), any benefit she receives under the *Fatal Accidents Act, 1976*, would be reduced accordingly.

20.7 Vicarious Liability

This term refers to a situation where a person who has not himself committed a tort is held responsible for the commission of a tort by another. Vicarious liability will be looked at under the following headings: (*a*) principal and agent; (*b*) master and servant; (*c*) liability for the acts of an independent contractor.

(*a*) **Principal and Agent** (see Chapter 13). A principal is vicariously liable for all the acts of an agent which he has either authorised originally or ratified subsequently. To incur liability, the agent must have acted on behalf of the principal and either the principal must be aware of the agent's acts or the agent must have complete authority to act.

In *Ormrod v. Crosville Motor Services Ltd* (*1953*), it was held that a friend of an owner of a car who drove the car for the owner's purposes, and with his consent, was an agent of the owner, who was therefore vicariously liable for the friend's negligence. However, in *Morgans v. Launchbury* (*1972*), the House of Lords held that where a car owner had authorised his or her spouse to drive and the spouse delegated the driving to another person, the owner would not be vicariously liable for the acts of the latter.

(*b*) **Master and Servant.** The general rule is that a master is vicariously liable for the torts of his servant committed in the course of his or her employment. The court in *Hewitt v. Bonvir* (*1940*) approved Salmond's definition of a servant as 'any person employed by another to do work for him on terms that he, the servant, is to be subject to the control and direction of his employer in respect of the manner in which his work is to be done'. A servant is one who works under a contract of service, unlike an independent contractor who works under a contract for services. The relationship must be a voluntary one and the following is considered as evidence of this relationship: the power of an employer to select or appoint; the power to dismiss; and the payment of salary or wages. The various guidelines laid down by the courts for deciding whether a person is a servant or not are not principles of law and neither are they conclusive; the courts will therefore reserve their right to decide this question on the merit of the facts of each individual case.

Some of the cases in this area are mentioned below to give an idea of the circumstances where a vicarious liability may or may not be incurred:

Collins v. Hertfordshire County Council (*1947*). A hospital authority was held vicariously liable for the negligence of a student and a pharmacist who were both employed by the Council, but not for the negligence of a consultant surgeon as the authority had no control over the way in which the latter carried out his duties.

Roe v. Ministry of Health (1954). Where the question concerned the vicarious liability of the defendants in respect of acts committed by a visiting specialist anaesthetist, Denning, L.J., had the following to say on the liability of hospital authorities:

'They are responsible for the whole of their staff, not only for the nurses and doctors but also for the anaesthetists and the surgeons. It does not matter whether they are permanent or temporary, resident or visiting, whole-time or part-time . . . The only exception is the case of consultants or anaesthetists selected and employed by the patient himself.'

Mersey Docks & Harbour Board v. Coggins & Griffiths (Liverpool) Ltd (1947). The question concerned the vicarious liability of the Harbour Board who had lent a crane and a driver to the stevedores (Coggins & Griffiths Ltd). A third person was injured due to the crane driver's negligence. The crane driver was paid by the Harbour Board who also had the power to dismiss him. **Held:** the Harbour Board was vicariously liable as employers since they had control over how the work was to be done.

Watkins v. Birmingham City Council (1975). The Education Authority was not vicariously liable for the negligence of a pupil who helped in the distribution of milk at the school. The boy was not the Authority's servant.

Beard v. London General Omnibus Co. (1900). The defendants were not vicariously liable for the negligence of a bus conductor who, in the absence of the driver, drove a bus and injured the plaintiff. **Held:** the conductor had not acted within the scope of his employment.

Limpus v. London General Omnibus Co. (1862). The defendant's driver deliberately obstructed one of the plaintiff's omnibuses, despite specific instructions to the contrary, causing injury and damage to the plaintiff's horses and omnibus. **Held:** The defendants were vicariously liable for all reckless or improper conduct of the driver occurring within the scope of his employment.

Century Insurance Co. Ltd v. Northern Ireland Road Transport Board (1942). Petrol was being delivered to a garage. When the petrol was being transferred from a lorry to a tank, the respondent's driver threw away a lighted match after lighting a cigarette. This resulted in an explosion and subsequent damage. **Held**: the driver's employers were liable since he was acting within the course of his employment.

For fraud committed by a servant, see Section 13.8 (*Lloyd v. Grace, Smith & Co. (1912)*).

Warren v. Henlys Ltd (1948). The defendants were not vicariously liable for the assault committed by their petrol pump attendant on a customer. **Held:** The attendant's assault was an act of personal vengeance and therefore not within the scope of his employment.

Poland v. John Parr & Sons (1927). A servant of the defendants, with a view to protecting his employer's property from theft, struck a boy who then fell off the back of the cart and injured himself. **Held:** Since the servant was acting within the scope of his implied authority, the employers were liable.

It must be noted that in principle both the master and the servant are liable jointly for a wrong committed by a servant, but usually the master is sued since he happens to be the wealthier of the two, and therefore more worthy. If a master is sued he may recover a contribution or indemnity from the servant for the amount paid in damages to a third party.

Lister v. Romford Ice & Cold Storage Co. Ltd (*1957*). Both the father and son were employed by the respondent company. Due to the negligent driving of the son, the father was injured. The father obtained damages against the company who were held vicariously liable for the actions of the son. The insurers of the company then sued the son and obtained an indemnity of the amount for which the company had been made liable to the father. **Held:** The appellant was in breach of his duty to the company to take reasonable care in the performance of his duties.

(*c*) **Independent Contractors.** Unlike a servant who works under the supervision and direction of his master, an independent contractor is more or less his own master. An independent contractor works under a contract for services and has discretion concerning the manner in which the work is to be done and the time of doing it. The general rule is that an employer is not vicariously liable for the torts committed by an independent contractor. However, there are certain exceptions to the rule which are based not on vicarious liability but on a breach by the master of a non-delegable duty of care binding on himself. Some of these exceptions are:

(i) Where an employer owes a primary duty to a plaintiff, he will be held responsible personally for any tort committed. In *Ellis v. Sheffield Gas Consumers Co.* (*1853*), a duty arose because of the employer's wrongful behaviour. A company employed a contractor to dig trenches in a street without proper authority. The company was held liable to the plaintiff who fell and injured himself as a result of the contractor's servants leaving a heap of stones on the road.

(ii) Where a statute imposes an absolute duty upon an individual, he will be liable since the performance of this duty cannot be delegated to an independent contractor, e.g. the duties to fence dangerous machinery and to provide safe means of access imposed on an employer under the *Factories Act, 1961*.

(iii) Where the work concerned involves hazardous operations the employer will be liable and he cannot delegate the responsibility by employing independent contractors. In *Honeywell and Stein Ltd v. Larkin Bros.* (*1934*), the plaintiffs were liable to the owners of a cinema for a fire caused by the defendants who were employed by the plaintiffs to take flash-light photographs in the cinema.

(iv) There is liability on an individual under the rule in *Rylands v. Fletcher* (*1868*) (see page 348) for the acts of an independent contractor.

(v) Where a master owes his servants a duty concerning their safety, he will not escape liability by delegating its performance to a contractor, e.g. the duty of an employer under the *Employers' Liability* (*Defective Equipment*) *Act, 1969*. An employer having to pay damages for the torts of an independent contractor may claim an indemnity from the contractor if an indemnity clause exists in the contract between them (*Hosking v. De Havilland Aircraft Co. Ltd* (*1949*)). An employer is not liable for the collateral negligence of a contractor, e.g. wrongs committed by servants in the course of the contractor's employment. In *Padbury v. Holliday & Greenwood* (*1912*), a hammer left on a window-sill injured a passer-by when a gust of wind blew it down; the defendant employer was not liable.

20.8 Joint Tortfeasors

Where A and B commit a tort against C, A and B are said to be joint tortfeasors whose liability to C is joint and several. C has a choice of suing both of them or only one of them. Where C chooses to sue A alone, under the *Civil Liability (Contribution) Act, 1978*, A can claim contribution from B for any damages he pays to C. The amount that A recovers from B is dependent on the discretion of a court and on the extent of B's responsibility in the commission of the tort.

Under the *Law Reform (Husband and Wife) Act, 1962*, since both husband and wife are treated as independent parties for an action in tort, were a third party to sue a husband alone for the negligence of both the husband can now claim a contribution from the wife for any damages he pays to the third party.

20.9 Revision Test

Answers	*Questions*
–	**1.** Define a tort.
1. A tort is a civil wrong, actionable at the suit of the aggrieved party, which is not either a breach of contract, or a breach of trust or other merely equitable obligation (Salmond).	**2.** What are the chief torts?
2. (*a*) Negligence; (*b*) nuisance; (*c*) trespass; (*d*) defamation.	**3.** What is the chief remedy in tort?
3. Unliquidated damages, i.e. damages which are not predetermined, but are at the absolute discretion of the court.	**4.** What is the meaning of 'actionable *per se*'?
4. It means the tort is actionable merely because the rights of the plaintiff have been interfered with, even though no damage has actually been suffered.	**5.** Distinguish a tort from a crime.
5. (*a*) Tort is civil law, crime is criminal law. (*b*) In tort the plaintiff sues the defendant, but in crime the police prosecute the offender. (*c*) The unsuccessful defendant in tort must pay	

Answers	*Questions*
damages or observe an equitable remedy such as injunction. The guilty party in a crime is fined, or imprisoned, or some other penalty is imposed. (*d*) In tort a duty is owed to persons generally and action is at the suit of anyone who is aggrieved. In crime the duty is prescribed by the criminal law and the state will prosecute the offender.	**6.** What are the defences in tort?
6. (*a*) *Volenti non fit injuria*; (*b*) necessity; (*c*) certain types of mistake; (*d*) inevitable accident; (*e*) statutory authority; (*f*) self-defence; (*g*) act of God; (*h*) act of state.	**7.** Are infants liable in tort?
7. In general yes, but the standard of care may be less than for adults.	**8.** What are the remedies for torts?
8. (*a*) Damages, either nominal, substantial, exemplary or aggravated; (*b*) injunction, either prohibitory, mandatory or interlocutory; (*c*) restitution of property.	**9.** What is vicarious liability?
9. It is the liability of one person to offer himself as the target for a legal action by another, because the tort was performed by someone acting as his agent, or his servant.	**10.** What is the test to distinguish a servant from an independent contractor liable for his own torts?
10. Is the person concerned controlled both as to what is being done, and the manner in which the work shall be performed?	**11.** Go over the questions until you are sure of all the answers. Then try the written questions in Appendix 1.

21
Negligence

21.1 The Meaning of 'Negligence'

Negligence may be either a mode of committing other torts (e.g. trespass or nuisance) or an independent tort in its own right. Negligence is considered in this chapter in the latter sense.

Negligence is committed whenever any person owing a legal duty of care breaches this duty with the result that damage (physical, mental or financial) is caused to some other person or persons. Negligence has been defined as 'the omission to do something which a reasonable man . . . would do, or doing something which a prudent and reasonable man would not do' (per Alderson, B., in *Blyth v. Birmingham Waterworks Co.* (*1856*)).

On the meaning of negligence, Lord Wright in *Lochgelly Iron and Coal Co. v. McMullan* (*1934*) had the following to say: 'In strict legal analysis, negligence means more than heedless or careless conduct, whether in omission or commission: it properly connotes the complex concept of duty, breach and damage thereby suffered by the person to whom the duty was owing.' Hence to succeed in an action for negligence, a plaintiff is required to prove (*a*) the existence of a legal duty of care, (*b*) a breach of this legal duty of care and (*c*) the damage suffered in consequence of the breach.

21.2 The Duty of Care

Before liability for negligence arises it must be shown by the plaintiff that the defendant owed him a duty of care. There is no legal definition of the term duty of care and we may all be as careless as we wish, providing such carelessness does not cause harm, loss, injury or damage to those around us or to those with whom we have business or other dealings. Whether or not a duty of care arises in a particular circumstance is a question of law, to be decided by a judge. In *Donoghue v. Stevenson*, the House of Lords formulated a general principle known as the 'neighbour principle' for determining whether a duty of care was owed. The facts were as follows:

M'Alister (*Donoghue*) *v. Stevenson* (*1932*). A shop assistant, the appellant, drank some ginger-beer which had been manufactured by the respondents. The ginger-beer, which was in a dark opaque glass bottle, had been sold by the respondents to a retailer who in turn sold the drink for consumption by the appellant. As a second glassful was being poured out for her the appellant noticed a decomposed snail float out of the bottle. She became seriously ill and claimed damages for negligence. **Held:** the respondents owed the appellant a legal duty to take care that the bottle did not contain noxious matter and they would be liable to her if that legal duty was broken as the manufacturer of an article of food, medicine or the like, sold by him to a distributor in circumstances which prevent the distributor or the ultimate purchaser or consumer from discovering by inspection any defect, is under a legal duty to the ultimate purchaser or consumer to take reasonable care that the article is free from defect likely to cause injury to health. 'You must take reasonable care to avoid acts or omissions which you can reasonably foresee would be likely to injure your neighbour. Who, then, in law is my neighbour? The answer seems to be – persons who are so closely and directly affected by my act that I ought reasonably to have them in contemplation as being so affected when I am directing my mind to the acts or omissions which are called in question' (*per* Lord Atkin). (Courtesy of *Cracknell's Law Students' Companion*)

The case established a new category of duty, a duty between manufacturer and consumer. The lack of privity of contract between the two (see Section 7.7) does not prevent a liability in tort. A consumer suffering physical injury because of a defective product will succeed on proof of negligence. Apart from this category, other recognised duties in law exist in respect of the following situations. It must be emphasised that these categories are not exhaustive and, as Lord Macmillan noted in Donoghue v. Stevenson, '*the categories of negligence are never closed*'.

(*a*) **Employers.** An employer owes his employees a duty of care. He must provide competent staff, ensure a reasonably safe system of work and provide adequate plant and equipment; the employer is liable for any injury received due to defective equipment, supplied by a third party (*Employers' Liability* (*Defective Equipment*) *Act, 1969*).

Cases: General Cleaning Contractors Ltd v. Christmas (*1953*) and *Bux v. Slough Metals* (*1973*). The *Employers' Liability* (*Compulsory Insurance*) *Act, 1969*, requires an employer to insure against physical injury received or disease contracted by employees at work.

(*b*) **Highway Users and Adjacent Occupiers.** A road user owes a duty of care to other road users. Similarly, occupiers and landlords owe a duty of care to other road users in respect of man-made structures adjoining the highways.

(*c*) **Professional People.** All professional persons (e.g. doctors, dentists, solicitors, bankers, etc.) owe a duty of care to persons having a professional relationship with them.

(*d*) **Occupiers of Premises** (see Chapter 22).

(*e*) **Carriers.** Carriers of persons or freight, bus companies, railway companies and other transport authorities owe a duty of care to their passengers, and for the goods carried. This duty of care is independent of any contractual liability that may arise as a result of a contract between the carrier and his customer.

(*f*) **Bailees.** A duty of care is owed to the bailer of goods independent of the contract of bailment.

(*g*) **The Local Authority.** In exercising its statutory powers e.g. of inspecting building foundations, a local authority owes a duty of care to all future owners or occupiers of the premises whose safety or health is likely to be affected by any defects in the building. (*Anns v. Merton London Borough Council* (*1978*) *A.C.728; Dutton's Case* (*1972*) *1 Q.B. 373*)

21.3 Breach of Duty and the Standard of Care

Having established a duty of care, the second question that must be proved by a plaintiff is that there has been a breach of this duty of care. This is a question of fact to be decided by a judge and it is difficult to lay down rules for deciding whether or not a breach of duty has occurred. In deciding this matter a court may consider a range of factors such as the nature of the activity in question, the feasibility of precautions, the conduct of the plaintiff, the status of the defendant, the level of knowledge at the time of the accident, the personal state of the plaintiff and so on.

In discharging the duty of care, the standard of care that is demanded of a defendant is an objective one, i.e. the standard of care of an ordinary reasonable man. The reasonable man is a fictitious character (the man on the Clapham omnibus) who is considered neither over-confident nor unduly apprehensive. The standard of care required from a person possessing special skill or knowledge is that which is reasonable having regard to the particular profession or occupation that person is engaged in.

For example, in *Roe v. Ministry of Health* (*1954*), a specialist anaesthetist administered contaminated nupercaine to a patient who became paralysed as a result. The anaesthetist was not negligent as he had displayed normal competence and the contamination could not have been reasonably foreseen or discovered (see also *Bolam v. Friern Barnet Hospital Management Committee* (*1957*)).

A selection of cases will illustrate both the existence of a duty of care and breach of that duty.

Cases in which a duty of care existed:

Carmarthenshire C.C. v. Lewis (*1955*) 1All ER 565. A mistress in charge of a nursery school was preparing to take children out. While she was dressing one child, another four-year-old child escaped from the school premises via an unlocked gate. He ran down a side lane into a busy highway, and into the path of a moving lorry. The driver swerved in order to avoid the child. In doing so he collided with a telegraph pole and was killed. The widow of the driver brought an action for damages in negligence. **Held:** the defendants were liable for not taking reasonable care to prevent the escape of the child from the school premises; they ought to have foreseen this eventuality and taken precautions against it.

McLoughlin v. O'Brien and Others (*1982*). Here the House of Lords was considering an appeal by Mrs Rosin McLoughlin. The facts were that Mrs McLoughlin's family was travelling in a car that was involved in an accident attributed to the negligence of two lorry drivers. Mrs M who was at home at the time, was informed of the tragedy. The family home was two miles away from the scene of the accident. Mrs M later visited the family in hospital and saw the family members in varying degrees of distress and injury. All this caused her shock and she became ill as a result. She sued the drivers for damages in negligence for the harm resulting from the nervous shock. **Held:** Mrs M would succeed in claiming damages as what happened to her was a reasonably foreseeable consequence.

Wilkinson v. Downton (*1897*). Here the defendant, as a practical joke, told the plaintiff that her husband had met with a serious accident and lay injured in a public house in Leytonstone. She was to go at once by taxi with two pillows and fetch him home. This caused the plaintiff nervous shock which resulted in severe and permanent physical injury. **Held:** the defendant was liable in damages for the consequences as they could have been reasonably foreseen.

Cases in which no duty of care existed:

Bolton v. Stone (*1951*). The plaintiff, who was standing outside a cricket ground where a match was in progress, was hit and injured by a cricket ball. The ball had travelled approximately 100 yards and traversed a 17-foot-high fence. Evidence showed that similar hits out of the ground had occurred on some six occasions in the previous 30 years. **Held:** the defendant was not liable in negligence as the probability of such an occurrence could not have been anticipated by a reasonable man.

Latimer v. AEC Ltd (*1953*). Due to exceptionally heavy rain, a factory floor became flooded. The rainwater combined with oil on the floor and caused slippery conditions. The occupier of the factory spread sawdust as far as possible until supplies ran out and some parts of the floor remained uncovered. The plaintiff who slipped and injured himself sued the defendants in negligence. **Held:** since the plaintiff had taken all reasonable steps to prevent injury or harm in the circumstances, they were not liable. It would not have been reasonable to expect them to shut the factory and send the employees home.

King v. Phillips (*1953*). A taxi-driver, when reversing his taxi without exercising proper care, ran into a child on a tricycle and injured the child slightly. At the time the mother of the child was in her house some 70 or 80 yards away. She heard a scream and glanced out of the window. She saw the child's tricycle under the cab but not the child. This caused her tremendous nervous shock and she became ill as a result. She sued the taxi-driver for damages in negligence. **Held:** the driver was not liable. He did not owe the mother a duty of care since he could not have reasonably foreseen that his actions would cause her injury.

21.4 Liability for Negligent Misstatements

Apart from liability for misleading statements that may arise under a contract (see Misrepresentation, Chapter 10), there may be liability in tort for misleading statements. The House of Lords in an important case decided in *Hedley Byrne & Co. Ltd v. Heller & Partners Ltd* (*1963*) that liability arises not only in respect of negligent acts but also negligent words. The facts of the case were as follows:

Hedley Byrne and Co Ltd v. Heller and Partners Ltd (*1963*). The appellants, becoming doubtful about the financial position of Easipower Ltd asked their bank to communicate with Easipower's bankers, the respondents. This they did by telephone, asking the repondents 'in confidence, and without liability (on the respondents' part) whether Easipower would be good for a contract of £8000 to £9000. The respondents replied that they believed Easipower 'to be respectably constituted and considered good for its normal business engagements'. Six months later the appellants' bank wrote to the respondents to ask whether they considered Easipower trustworthy, in the way of business, to the extent of a £100,000 per annum contract and the respondents replied: 'Respectably constituted company, considered good for its ordinary business engagements.' The appellants relied upon the respondents' statements and as a result lost over £17,000 when Easipower Ltd went into liquidation. The appellants sought to recover this loss from the respondents as damages on the ground that the respondents' replies were given negligently and in breach of the respondents' duty to exercise care in giving them. **Held:** while bankers are under a duty to give honest answers and, perhaps, owe enquirers (such as the appellants) a duty of care, in this case the respondents never undertook any duty to exercise care in giving their replies and it followed that there was no liability on their part. 'The appellants' bank, who were their agents in making the enquiry, began by saying "they wanted to know in confidence and without responsibility on your part", i.e. on the part of the respondents. So I cannot see how the appellants can now be entitled to disregard that and maintain that the respondents did incur a responsibility to them.' (*per* Lord Reid). (Courtesy of *Cracknell's Law Students' Companion*)

Note: Under the *Unfair Contract Terms Act, 1977*, cases of tortious liability are caught by S.2, which holds that a person cannot disclaim responsibility (as in the case just quoted) unless it is reasonable to do so. A disclaimer of this type will only be effective if it satisfies the requirement of reasonableness.

In *Esso Petroleum Co. Ltd v. Mardon* (*1976*) Lord Denning, M.R., explains the rule established in Hedley Byrne & Co. as follows: 'If a man, who has or professes to have special knowledge or skill, makes a representation by virtue thereof to another – be it advice, information or opinion – with the intention of inducing him to enter into a contract with him, he is under a duty to use reasonable care to see that the representation is correct, and that the advice, information or opinion is reliable. If he negligently gives unsound advice or misleading information or expresses an erroneous opinion, and thereby induces the other side to enter into a contract with him, he is liable.'

For other cases on this area of tort, see *Sutcliffe v. Thackrah* (*1975*); *Mutual Life & Citizens Assurance Co. Ltd v. Evatt* (*1971*); *Rondell v. Worsley* (*1967*); and *Saif Ali v. Sydney Mitchell & Co.* (*1978*).

21.5 *Res Ipsa Loquitur* (The thing speaks for itself)

Normally the burden of proving negligence is on the plaintiff, who has to prove the existence of a legal duty of care, the breach of that duty of care and the subsequent damage resulting from the breach. However, where the principle ***res ipsa loquitur*** (the thing speaks for itself) applies, a court will infer negligence from the facts proved in the absence of any explanation by the defendant. *Res ipsa loquitur* is a rule of evidence under which negligence is presumed and hence a plaintiff is entitled to have his case put to the jury. The burden of proof shifts from the plaintiff to the defendant, who must now prove that he was not negligent, but that the events that occurred were caused by some force outside his control.

Scott v. London & St Katherine Docks Co. (*1865*). Six bags of sugar fell on the defendant as he was passing in front of the plaintiff's warehouse. **Held:** 'There must be reasonable evidence of negligence, but where the thing is shown to be under the management of the defendant or his servants, and the accident is such as in the ordinary cause of things does not happen if those who have the management use proper care, it affords reasonable evidence in the absence of explanation by the defendant, that the accident arose from want of care.' (*per* Erle, C.J.). See also *Byrne v. Boadle* (*1863*).

Where the facts disclosed do not raise a presumption of negligence or the thing causing the accident is not under the defendant's control (*Wilks v. Cheltenham Home Guard Motor Cycle and Light Car Club* (*1971*)), or where there is an explanation for the accident (*Barkway v. South Wales Transport Co. Ltd.* (*1950*)), *res ipsa loquitur* will not apply.

21.6 Contributory Negligence

Where a defendant who is negligent shows that the plaintiff was also partly responsible for the injury that resulted to him, the damages awarded to the plaintiff will be reduced to take account of the plaintiff's own negligence. This principle; which applies to collisions of ships at sea, is now contained in S.1(1) of the *Law Reform (Contributory Negligence) Act, 1945*. The section provides that 'where any person suffers damage as a result of his own fault and partly of the fault of any other person or persons, a claim in respect of that damage shall not be defeated by reason of the fault of the person suffering the damage, but the damage recoverable in respect thereof shall be reduced to such extent as the court thinks just and equitable having regard to the claimant's share in the responsibility for damage.'

The adjustment for contributory negligence is usually some simple fraction of the total, for example $\frac{1}{2}$, $\frac{1}{3}$, $\frac{1}{4}$ or $\frac{1}{10}$th of the total damages payable. To take a simple example, suppose a motorcycle rider X who is not wearing a crash helmet collides with a car driven negligently by Z. X sues Z for damages. The court decides that in the circumstances X is entitled to damages of £9000 against Z. However, the court also finds that the extent of the injury received by X could have been reduced had he worn a crash helmet and accordingly he is one third to blame for the consequences. The court will therefore reduce the damages awarded to X by £3000.

In *O'Connell v. Jackson (1971)* a plaintiff moped-rider not wearing a crash helmet was held to have contributed to the consequences caused by the defendant's negligent act and the plaintiff's damages were reduced accordingly.

Similarly, in *Froom v. Butcher (1975)* failure to wear a seat belt constituted contributory negligence and the damages awarded were reduced proportionately to the extent of injury caused through not wearing a seat belt.

In the case of a child plaintiff, the contributory negligence depends on his age and capacity. For example, in *Yachuk v. Oliver Blaise and Co. Ltd (1949)* a child aged nine was held not to have contributed negligence since he was not sufficiently capable of taking care of himself.

The Doctrine of Alternative Danger (the 'Dilemma Principle'). An act done in the heat of the moment to protect oneself may not be considered contributory negligence. For example, imagine you are a passenger in a bus and are put in a perilous situation due to the negligent conduct of the bus driver. Anticipating an accident, you take evasive action to protect yourself and are injured. Will you succeed in obtaining damages against the driver if it transpires that the crash you anticipated did not materialise and had you remained in your seat you would have been quite safe? The court in *Jones v. Boyce (1816)* held that a plaintiff in a similar situation will succeed if his action is considered reasonable in the circumstances.

21.7 Revision Test

Answers	*Questions*
–	**1.** What is negligence?
1. A breach of a duty of care owed by one person to another, so that the person suffers some damage.	**2.** What must the plaintiff normally prove to the satisfaction of the court?
2. (*a*) The existence of a legal duty of care; (*b*) breach of that duty; (*c*) damage suffered as a result of the breach.	**3.** What was the case of *Donoghue v. Stevenson* about?
3. It was the 'snail in the ginger-beer bottle' case. It established the 'neighbour principle'.	**4.** What is the 'neighbour principle'?
4. The principle that established that 'anyone is my neighbour who is so closely and directly affected by my act that I ought reasonably to have them in my contemplation when I direct my mind to acts or omissions which may be called in question'.	**5.** What is the standard of care required?
5. It is a reasonable one – bearing in mind the profession or occupation concerned.	**6.** What does *res ipsa loquitur* mean?
6. The facts speak for themselves.	**7.** What is the effect of *res ipsa loquitur*?
7. The facts speak for themselves so the plaintiff need not prove that the defendant was negligent. The burden of proof shifts to the defendant, who must show that he was *not* negligent.	**8.** What is 'contributory negligence'?
8. It is where the damage suffered by the plaintiff is aggravated by his, or her, own negligence. The damages awarded are reduced by some simple fraction to allow for the contributory negligence of the plaintiff.	**9.** What is the 'dilemma principle'?

Answers	*Questions*
9. It is a principle which holds that a person who is placed in a situation of stress by the negligent act of another, and who takes evasive action which results in injury, may claim damages even though the feared event was in fact avoided.	**10.** Go over the page again until you are sure of all the answers. Then try some of the questions in Appendix 1.

22
The Liability of Occupiers of Premises

22.1 The *Occupiers' Liability Act, 1957*

The law concerning the duty of an occupier of premises towards his lawful visitors is contained in the *Occupiers' Liability Act, 1957*. An '**occupier**' is not necessarily the owner of a premises but he can be a person with a degree of control over the premises; there can be more than one occupier. '**Premises**' include land, buildings, fixed or movable structures, vehicles, ships and aeroplanes. '**Visitors**' are those to whom the occupier has either given permission to use the premises or those who are deemed to have this permission. Whether or not a visitor has implied permission to enter premises is a question of fact depending on the circumstances of each case and the burden of proof rests on the person claiming such permission. Visitors can include persons who enter by right of law (e.g. factory inspectors, gas and electricity meter readers, postmen, refuse collectors, etc.), those lawfully on the premises such as customers in shops or those who have implied permission to enter although their presence may be objectionable to the occupier, e.g. door-to-door salesmen.

Under the Act an occupier of premises owes a 'common duty of care to all his visitors, except in so far as he is free to and does extend, restrict, modify or exclude his duty to any visitor or visitors by agreement or otherwise' (S.2.1).

The extent of the duty is laid down in S.2.2 of the Act: 'A duty to take such care as in all the circumstances of the case is reasonable to see that the visitor will be reasonably safe in using the premises for the purpose for which he is permitted by the occupier to be there.'

Although the Act permits an occupier to exclude his liability towards a visitor by framing a suitable notice, the power and extent of excluding liability depend on judicial and legislative restrictions in force. Judicial restriction means whether or not the courts consider an exclusion of liability reasonable in the circumstances. A major legislative restriction on excluding liability is the *Unfair Contract Terms Act, 1977*. According to S.2 of the Act any liability arising from death or personal injury resulting from negligence cannot be excluded; an exclusion or restriction for other loss or damage will depend on whether or not the courts consider it reasonable. The Act only applies to 'business liability', i.e. liability that arises from the occupation of premises by an occupier who uses the premises for business purposes. Hence trespassers and non-business visitors are excluded from the scope of the Act.

Liability to Children. S.2(3) of the 1957 Act provides that 'an occupier must be prepared for children to be less careful than adults'. An occupier is compelled to ensure that precaution is taken to prevent harm resulting to children from things which conceal danger but which appear attractive or are alluring to children.

Cooke v. Midland G.W. Rly of Ireland (1909). The defendants kept a turntable close to a public road. A boy aged four was injured while playing along with other children on the turntable. Although the defendants' servants were aware of the fact that children habitually came on to the land to play with the turntable, the defendants took no action to prevent this. **Held:** they were liable to the child. Because of the defendants' acquiescence in the trespass, the child trespasser was in the position of a lawful visitor.

Glasgow Corporation v. Taylor (1922). A child aged seven died, having eaten poisonous berries picked from a shrub growing in a public park belonging to the Glasgow Corporation. It was alleged that despite the fact that the Corporation was aware that these berries were poisonous and children frequented the park, no precaution was taken to warn children of the danger. **Held:** the Corporation was liable to the deceased child's parents since the berries constituted an allurement.

Liability to Trespassers. The tort of trespass is dealt with more fully in Chapter 23. Since the *Occupiers' Liability Act, 1957*, applies to lawful visitors only, the rules of common law continue to apply to trespassers.

In *Addie & Sons v. Dumbreck (1929)*, a trespasser was defined as 'one who goes on to the land without any invitation of any sort and whose presence is either unknown to the proprietor, or, if known, is practically objected to'. The general rule is that no active duty of care is owed to a trespasser; a trespasser enters at his own risk and takes the premises as he found them. However, if a trespasser's presence is known to an occupier, he is under a duty to refrain from intentionally or recklessly inflicting damage on the trespasser. For example, an occupier cannot set up spring-guns to cause physical injury to a trespasser (*Bird v. Holbrook (1828)*). However, reasonable defensive measures in protection of one's property are permitted, e.g. laying broken glass on the top of high walls.

When it comes to child trespassers a much higher duty of care is required of an occupier. The general rules are that an occupier must be prepared for children to be less careful than adults.

In *British Railways Board v. Herrington (1972)*, the plaintiff was a boy aged six. He was playing with his two brothers in a park through which ran an electrified railway. Although there was a fence on both sides of the railway, the fence was in a dilapidated condition. The Board were aware that people (including children) were quite regularly taking 'short cuts' through the broken fence. The plaintiff was seriously injured when after having crossed the fence he came into contact with a live rail. The House of Lords held the Board liable for breaking its duty of care to the child trespasser. The decision also established that the old rules relating to liability towards trespassers no longer applied. Lord Reid laid down the following twofold test on liability towards trespassers:

(*a*) Did the occupier know that there was a 'substantial probability' of the presence of trespassers?

(*b*) Could a 'conscientious humane man' with that knowledge, and with the skill and resources which the occupier in fact had, be reasonably expected to have done or refrained from doing before the accident something that would have avoided it?

22.2 The *Defective Premises Act, 1972*

The Act imposes on a landlord a wider duty of care and he cannot restrict or exclude any of the duties imposed by the Act.

S.4 of the *Occupiers' Liability Act, 1957*, has been repealed and under the *Defective Premises Act, 1972*, a landlord is liable to all persons who it is reasonable to expect will be affected by defects in the premises. These will include, in addition to the tenant, his family and his visitors, also neighbours, passers-by and possibly trespassers. Under the *Defective Premises Act, 1972*, a builder, any specialist subcontractor, the developer and professional people involved with the construction of new houses owe a statutory duty of care to purchasers and their successors.

Defences to an Action. An action may be defended by proving that:

(*a*) The visitor has been warned of a danger (S.2.4). This does not in all the circumstances absolve the occupier from liability; it all depends whether in the circumstances the warning was adequate to enable the visitor to be reasonably safe.

(*b*) Where damage is caused to a visitor through the faulty workmanship of an independent contractor employed by the occupier, the contractor will be held liable (*O'Connor v. Swan & Edgar and Carmichael Contractors* (*1963*)).

(*c*) S.2(5) encompasses the principle of *volenti non fit injuria* (see page 320), i.e. risks willingly accepted by a visitor.

22.3 Strict Liability

Strict liability is a liability which would arise irrespective of whether a person was at fault or not. There are two types of torts falling under this category – namely, *breach of statutory duty* and *the rule in Rylands v. Fletcher* (*1866*).

(*a*) **Breach of Statutory Duty.** An injured party can sue in tort for a breach of a duty imposed by a statute. Most claims in this area concern industrial injuries arising under the *Mines and Quarries Act, 1954*, the *Factories Act, 1961*, and the *Health and Safety at Work Act, 1974*. Whether or not an injured party will succeed in his action depends on the construction of the statute in the context of the circumstances surrounding the case.

Where on construction a statute imposes an absolute duty, then no proof of negligence or wrongful intent is required. In *Groves v. Lord Wimborne* (*1898*) the plaintiff was injured because of a breach of the defendant's statutory duty to fence dangerous machinery. The defendant was liable because the statute imposed an absolute duty.

If, on the other hand, a statute does not impose an absolute duty, negligence will have to be proved. In *Hammond v. Vestry of St Pancras* (*1874*), because the defendants were in breach of their statutory duty to repair sewers, the plaintiff was injured. The defendants were not liable in the absence of proof of negligence.

For a plaintiff to succeed in his action he must prove the following:

(i) That a statute was broken and the breach was the direct cause of the injury or damage.

Bonnington Castings Ltd v. Wardlaw (*1956*). A plaintiff was injured as a result of inhaling silica dust because of the defendant's breach of the Factories Acts. The House of Lords held: for a plaintiff to succeed, it is not enough to prove that there was a breach of a statutory duty; it must be proved in addition that this breach was the direct or material cause of the injury. In the words of Lord Reid: 'The employee must, in all cases, prove his case by the ordinary standard of proof in civil actions; he must make it appear at least that, on a balance of probabilities, the breach of duty caused, or materially contributed to, his injury.'

(ii) The plaintiff was a person or from a class the statute intended to protect:

Hartley v. Mayoh & Co. (*1954*). The plaintiff, a fireman, was electrocuted while fighting an outbreak of fire at the defendant's factory because the defendant was in breach of statutory regulations. **Held:** Since the regulations were expressly for the benefit of the factory employees only and as the fireman did not fall within this category, the plaintiff's action failed.

(iii) The injury complained of is one the statute intended to prevent:

Gorris v. Scott (*1874*). The plaintiff's sheep were washed overboard because the defendant shipowner, in breach of his statutory duty, had not provided pens on the ship's deck. **Held:** the plaintiff would not succeed in his action for breach of statutory duty since the object of the statute was to protect animals from the spread of contagious disease and not to provide protection against sea hazards.

Defences to an Action

(*a*) *Volenti non fit injuria*. On grounds of public policy this defence is not available to an employer when he is being sued by his employees. However, where an employer is being sued on grounds of vicarious liability for breach of a statutory duty committed by his workmen, this defence is available. In *ICI Ltd v. Shatwell* (*1964*) two qualified shot-firers were injured when they tried to test a circuit without taking shelter. Both knew the practice to be dangerous and contrary to the company's policy and statutory regulations. When one of the injured sued the company on grounds of its vicarious liability, it was held that *volenti non fit injuria* was a complete defence.

(*b*) *Contributory negligence*. This defence is available and the damages may be apportioned under the *Law Reform* (*Contributory Negligence*) *Act, 1945*. (*Caswell v. Powell Duffryn Associated Collieries Ltd* (*1939*)) (see page 341.)

(*c*) *Delegation of statutory duty.* Where a statute imposes an absolute duty on an employer it is not a defence to say that it was delegated to a reasonably competent person. However, a workman would be prevented from recovering damages in circumstances where the fault is entirely his.

Ginty v. Belmont Building Supplies Ltd (1959). The plaintiff workman failed to use a crawling-board when working on a roof. This was breach of statutory regulations binding on both his employers and himself. When injured he sued his employers for breach of statutory duty. **Held:** the workman's action failed since he had failed to show that his employers had committed any breach of statutory duty other than the one committed by the workman himself.

In cases where a statutory duty has been delegated but in performance of that statutory duty both the employer and the employee are at fault, damages will be apportioned between them. In *Ross v. Associated Portland Cement Manufacturers Ltd (1964)*, the employers were held two thirds liable for the plaintiff workman's injuries since in delegating their statutory duty to the workman, they had not given him proper instructions in the performance of his task and besides the workman was not qualified to perform the task.

(*b*) **The Rule in *Rylands v. Fletcher*.** The rule as stated by Blackburn, J., in the Court of Exchequer is as follows:

'The person who for his own purposes brings on his lands and collects and keeps there anything likely to do mischief if it escapes, must keep it in at his peril, and, if he does not do so, is *prima facie* answerable for all the damage which is the natural consequence of its escape.'

The facts of *Rylands v. Fletcher (1866)* were that the defendant mill owner had employed independent contractors to construct a reservoir on his land. The reservoir was to be used for supplying water for the defendant's mill. During the construction work the contractors had found some disused mine shafts. These the contractors had failed to seal as it was not known to them or the defendant that the shafts connected with the adjoining land where the plaintiff had a mine. When the reservoir was filled with water the plaintiff's adjoining coal mine was flooded through the underground mine shafts. The facts did not disclose the defendants to be liable in negligence and for various reasons action could not be brought in trespass or nuisance. The only way the defendant could be held liable was for the plaintiff to establish that the defendant's liability in the circumstances was strict or absolute. This proposition was accepted by the Court of Exchequer and the defendant was held liable. On appeal, the House of Lords upheld the rule, thus establishing an independent form of tortious liability.

The rule can be summarised as follows:

(*a*) There must be an escape from the defendant's land of a thing 'likely to do mischief'. If there is no escape beyond the boundaries of the defendant's land the plaintiff will fail under the rule (*Read v. J. Lyons (1947)*).

(*b*) The damage arising must be the result of a non-natural use of the defendant's land.

(*c*) The rule is a strict liability one and hence no question of intent or negligence arises.

(*d*) Although the tort is actionable *per se*, at least some damage must be proved.

(*e*) The fact that the defendant employed a competent independent contractor to do the job cannot excuse him from incurring liability.

Although in *Rylands v. Fletcher* the 'thing' escaping was water, since then the following objects have been held by courts to be covered by the rule:

(*a*) Electricity – *Eastern & South African Telegraph Co. v. Cape Town Tramways Co.* (*1902*).

(*b*) Gas – *North Western Utilities Ltd v. London. Guarantee & Accident Co.* (*1936*).

(*c*) Wire fencing – *Firth v. Bowling Iron Co.* (*1878*).

(*d*) Sewage – *Jones v. Llanrwst UDC* (*1911*).

(*e*) Vibration – *Hoare & Co. v. McAlpine* (*1923*).

(*f*) Explosives – *Rainham Chemical Works v. Belvedere Fish Co.* (*1921*).

(*g*) Projecting trees – *Crowhurst v. Amersham Burial Board* (*1878*).

(*h*) Fire – *Musgrove v. Pandelis* (*1919*) – but the rule does not apply to accidental fires.

Defences. The following defences may be available to an action under the rule in *Rylands v. Fletcher:*

(*a*) *Act of God.* If the escape is due to natural causes, such as exceptionally heavy rainfall which could not have been reasonably anticipated, the defendant may escape liability (*Nichols v. Marsland* (*1876*)).

(*b*) *Statutory authority.* In *Green v. Chelsea Waterworks Co.* (*1894*) the defendants escaped liability arising from a burst main which flooded plaintiff's premises. **Held:** since defendants were under statutory duty to lay the main and to supply water and since they were not negligent, they were not liable.

(*c*) *Consent of the plaintiff.* Where a plaintiff expressly or impliedly consents to the presence of the 'thing' on the defendant's land or premises, the defendant will escape liability for any subsequent escape that causes harm or damage to the plaintiff, e.g. the escape of water from the upper floor in a building to lower floors; in the absence of negligence the occupier of the upper floor is not liable. In *Peters v. Prince of Wales Theatre Ltd* (*1943*), the plaintiff's shop was flooded because the sprinkler system which the defendant had installed in their theatre to prevent fire had frozen up. **Held:** defendant not liable to the plaintiff tenant.

(*d*) *Act of a stranger.* Where an escape is caused by the unforeseeable act of a third party (not the occupier's servants, independent contractors, family members or possibly guests), the defendant may escape liability. In *Rickards v. Lothian* (*1913*), due to the malicious act of an unknown person a tap in a top floor lavatory of a building leased by the defendant was turned on. The water had overflowed and damaged plaintiff's stock on the bottom floor. **Held:** the plaintiff could not recover, as the defendants were not negligent and the rule in *Rylands v. Fletcher* could not apply.

(*e*) *Default of the plaintiff.* Where the escape was due to the plaintiff's own fault, he cannot recover for the subsequent injury. Where a plaintiff is partly to blame, under the *Law Reform* (*Contributory Negligence*) *Act, 1945*, damages can be apportioned between the plaintiff and a defendant.

22.4 Liability for Animals

A person may incur liability for any damage done by animals either under the *Animals Act, 1971*, or under general principles in trespass, nuisance or negligence. In addition to retaining the common law rule of strict liability for keepers of dangerous animals, S.4 of the Act imposes a strict liability on a person in possession (not necessarily the owner) of livestock, which includes bulls, cows, sheep, goats, horses and poultry. Liability may arise under the Act for any livestock trespass that causes damage to a plaintiff's chattels or land. A plaintiff cannot recover for any personal injuries.

Although there is still a strict liability for cattle trespass, i.e. no fault need be proved by a plaintiff, it is no longer actionable *per se* and hence damage or loss resulting subsequent to entry must be proved.

A plaintiff must be either in possession of the affected land or he must be an owner not in possession. There is no longer any liability for damage caused by trespassing cattle to the chattels of a person not in occupation of the land (S.4). A plaintiff is entitled to claim the expenses of detaining and housing the straying livestock until such time as compensation is paid and the livestock can be returned to the owner. The occupier is also given the right to sell the detained animals after 14 days unless proceedings are pending for the return of the animals.

Under S.8 a duty of care is imposed on occupiers of land in respect of non-dangerous animals straying onto the highway. The rule in *Searle v. Wallbank (1947)* that an occupier was under no duty to fence his land in order to keep his animals off the highway has been abolished.

The various defences available under the Act are:

(*a*) The plaintiff was at fault (5.5.1).

(*b*) The animal had strayed accidentally from an adjoining highway (5.5.5).

(*c*) Trespass was the result of the failure of the plaintiff to fence his land adequately (5.5.6).

S.3 is concerned with damage done by dogs. It provides that 'where a dog causes damage by killing or injuring livestock, any person who is a keeper of the dog is liable for the damage, except as otherwise provided by this Act'. Two exceptions are: (i) damage is done wholly due to the fault of the person suffering it; and (ii) where trespassing livestock is killed or injured by a dog belonging to the occupier or authorised to be there by the occupier.

22.5 Revision Test

Answers	*Questions*
—	**1.** Which Act controls the liability of occupiers of premises?
1. The *Occupiers' Liability Act, 1957.*	**2.** What is the extent of the occupier's duty?

Answers	*Questions*
2. A duty to take such care as is reasonable in all the circumstances of the case to see that the visitor will be reasonably safe in using the premises for the purposes for which he is permitted to be on the premises.	**3.** What is a visitor?
3. A person whom the occupier has permitted to be there, or who may be deemed to have this permission.	**4.** What is the extent of liability to children?
4. This is a greater liability than to adult visitors. The Act says the occupier must be prepared for children to be less careful than adults.	**5.** Where is particular care necessary?
5. Where anything constitutes an 'allurement' to children.	**6.** What is the liability to trespassers?
6. In general there is no duty to trespassers, but there is now a twofold test: (*a*) does the occupier know there is a 'substantial probability' of trespass; (*b*) has he done all that a conscientious humane man would do to avoid harm to a trespasser?	**7.** What is meant by 'strict liability?'
7. It means that the occupier is liable for the loss even if he was not personally at fault because an absolute liability has been imposed on him by law.	**8.** What are the two cases of strict liability?
8. (*a*) Breach of statutory duty; (*b*) the rule in *Rylands v. Fletcher (1866)*.	**9.** What is the rule in *Rylands v. Fletcher (1866)?*
9. The person who brings onto his land and keeps there anything likely to do mischief if it escapes must keep it in at his peril, and if he does not do so is *prima facie* answerable for all the damage which is the consequence of its escape.	**10.** What are the defences to a *Rylands v. Fletcher* action?

Answers	*Questions*
10. (*a*) Act of God; (*b*) statutory authority; (*c*) consent of the plaintiff; (*d*) act of a stranger; (*e*) default of the plaintiff.	**11.** Go over the questions again until you are sure of all the answers. Then try some of the questions in Appendix 1.

23
Trespass to Property

23.1 Trespass to Land

The word 'trespass' means unlawful interference with the rights of another. Trespass to land consists essentially of any wrongful interference with land which is in another person's possession. 'Possession' means the right to exclude all others and it does not matter whether or not the possessor is physically present; possession can be exercised through servants or agents. It is important that the plaintiff is in possession of the land and it is not enough that he is the owner of the land. If land has been leased then the lessee is the person in possession. Mere use of the land – for example, as a lodger – is not possession. Since trespass is a wrong against possession, the defendant cannot raise the defence of *jus tertii*, i.e. that a third party has a better title to the land than the plaintiff.

A trespass to land can take various forms apart from unlawful physical entry upon the land or buildings in possession of another. Some of these forms of trespass are as follows:

(*a*) Placing objects on another's land (*Gregory v. Piper* (*1829*)).

(*b*) Discharging oil at sea so that it is subsequently carried onto the plaintiff's foreshore (*Esso Petroleum Co. Ltd v. Southport Corporation* (*1955*)).

(*c*) Blowing carbon monoxide or any other gas onto the property of another may constitute trespass (*McDonald v. Associated Fuels Ltd* (*1954*)).

(*d*) Entry below the surface (tunnelling or mining) is a trespass and so is entry into the airspace of another. In *Kelson v. Imperial Tobacco Co. Ltd* (*1957*) an advertising sign which projected a few inches above the plaintiff's airspace was held to be a trespass. By virtue of the *Civil Aviation Act, 1982* (S.76) civil aircraft flying at a reasonable height are exempted from incurring liability for trespass; strict liability is imposed on the owner of aircraft for any damage resulting from things falling from an aircraft. (The Act does not apply to aircraft on Her Majesty's Service.)

(*e*) If a right of lawful entry is abused subsequently then this may constitute a trespass (*Harrison v. The Duke of Rutland* (*1893*)).

(*f*) If an entry is authorised for one purpose and that purpose is exceeded on entry, this may constitute a trespass (*Hickman v. Maisey* (*1900*)).

(*g*) Where a person enters as a result of a common law or statutory right but subsequently abuses the right of entry by a wrongful act, he is deemed to be a trespasser *ab initio* (from the beginning), i.e. his trespass begins from his original 'lawful' entry.

The Six Carpenters Case (*1610*). Six carpenters, having entered an inn, consumed a quantity of wine and bread. They later refused to pay the price. **Held:** they were not trespassers *ab initio* since their act was a non-feasance (an omission) only. Had their act been a misfeasance then they would have been trespassers *ab initio*.

A trespass to land is actionable *per se* (in itself) and no proof of actual damage is required. Although trespass upon property is not a criminal offence, the *Criminal Law Act, 1977*, creates a criminal offence of using or threatening violence to gain entry to premises occupied by a person who opposes entry. Similarly, the law provides punishment for trespass on property for the purpose of committing a crime, e.g. theft or rape.

Remedies for Trespass. The following remedies for trespass to land are available to a plaintiff:

(*a*) *Damages*. This is normally the amount necessary to compensate for the diminution in the value of the land.

(*b*) *Injunction*. This is used to forbid the continuance or repetition of the trespass.

(*c*) *Forcible ejection*. The occupier of land may eject with reasonable force a trespasser after the latter has been requested to leave and a reasonable time has been given for him to leave:

Hemmings v. Stoke Poges Golf Club Ltd (*1920*). The plaintiffs, husband and wife, were employed by the defendant golf club. They were provided with a cottage by the defendant. After the termination of their employment, they were given notice to quit the cottage but they refused. The defendant, who forcibly ejected them, was sued in trespass. **Held:** their action must fail, since the defendant had used reasonable force in ejecting them.

(*d*) *Distress damage feasant*. Where straying animals have entered and have done damage, an occupier may exercise his right to seize the animals and retain them until such time as compensation is paid.

(*e*) *Re-entry*. A person dispossessed from his land by a trespasser may re-enter peaceably to repossess the land (*Hemmings v. Stoke Poges Golf Club Ltd* (*1920*)).

Defences to Trespass. The following defences to trespass exist:

(*a*) *Authority of law*. A police officer may enter to arrest or search premises under the *Criminal Law Act, 1967*. Similarly, he may enter to prevent a breach of the peace (*Thomas v. Sawkins* (*1935*)). A bailiff has a right of entry to distrain for rent or eject a tenant.

(*b*) *Entry by licence*. This applies to theatre guests, guests at any other place of public entertainment, and those with a licence – for example, to fell and remove timber from the land of another (*James & Sons Ltd. v. Tankerville* (*1909*)). When the licence expires the licensee must leave. If he does not leave he becomes a trespasser.

(*c*) *Retaking goods*. It is a good defence to show that the defendant entered plaintiff's land to repossess goods that had been wrongfully taken onto the plaintiff's land.

(*d*) *Necessity.* It is good defence to show that the defendant trespassed onto the plaintiff's land to avert danger to life (*Esso Petroleum Co. Ltd v. Southport Corporation* (*1956*), where it was held no trespass was committed when the defendants discharged oil from a tanker to save the crews' lives which were in danger; see also *Cope v. Sharpe* (*1912*), page 321).

23.2 Trespass to Chattels

Chattels are items of personal property. Trespass to chattels consists of unlawful interference (direct and forcible) with chattels in the possession of another. Trespass to chattels is actionable *per se* and hence no need arises to prove that damage resulted; mere proof of direct and unlawful interference suffices. The plaintiff is required to prove intention or negligence on the part of the defendant (*National Coal Board v. Evans* (*1951*)) and hence unintentional or accidental touching of another's goods is not actionable.

Unlawful interference with chattels in possession of another can take the form of trespass to goods, conversion of goods, negligence – so far as it results in damage to goods or to an interest in goods – and any other tort so far as it results in damage to goods or to an interest in goods (the *Torts* (*Interference With Goods*) *Act, 1977*). This Act has abolished the former tort of *detinue* (wrongful detention of goods), which is now treated as conversion. The Act has considerably simplified the law and procedure in this area of tort.

(*a*) **Trespass to Goods.** Trespass to goods, like trespass to land, is a wrong against possession and not ownership. Thus anyone in rightful possession of goods may sue. A bailee can sue during the term of his bailment, whereas a bailor cannot. Similarly, a hirer or a borrower in whose possession the goods are has the right to sue. So has a master who has given his servant the custody of the goods since legally the master is considered the custodian of the goods. A personal representative of a deceased person in possession of the deceased's goods can also sue. In *Armoury v. Delamirie* (*1721*), a goldsmith to whom a boy who had found a jewel took it to be valued, refused to return it. In an action in *trover*, it was held that the boy was entitled to recover by way of damages the full value of the jewel. (*Note:* S.8 of the *Torts* (*Interference with Goods*) *Act, 1977*, allows a defendant to plead that a third party had a better title than the plaintiff in all actions for wrongful interference.)

Defences to trespass to goods. The following defences are available to an action for trespass to goods.

(*i*) *Inevitable accident:*

National Coal Board v. J. E. Evans & Co. (*Cardiff*) *Ltd* (*1951*). The facts were that while digging Evans and Co. damaged an underground electricity cable belonging to the NCB. Neither the defendants nor the County Council on whose land the work was taking place were aware of the existence of the cable. **Held:** since the presence of the cable was not foreseeable the defence of inevitable accident would protect the defendants from any liability (*ii*) *Exercise of a legal right.* No trespass is committed when something is done in pursuance of any legal right or legal process, e.g. bailiffs exercising a legal right.

(*iii*) *Protection of persons or property.* It is not trespass when action is taken to avert impending danger to persons or property (*Cresswell v. Sirl* (*1947*) – see under Self-defence, page 323).

(*b*) **Conversion.** Salmond in his *Law of Torts* defines conversion as 'an act, or complex series of acts of wilful interference, without lawful justification, with the right of another, whereby the other is deprived of the use and possession of it'.

The definition consists of the following elements:

(i) Doing something to the chattel inconsistent with the rights of the rightful owner.

(ii) Intentionally denying a person's right to the chattel.

(iii) Preventing the rightful owner from asserting his right.

(iv) Wrongfully asserting ownership (*Douglas Valley Finance Co. Ltd v. S. Hughes* (*Hires*) *Ltd* (*1967*)).

Any interference that is not wilful and wrongful does not amount to conversion. In *Ashby v. Tolhurst* (*1937*) it was held that the defendant car-park attendant was not liable in conversion for negligently allowing a stranger to remove the plaintiff's car.

Who can sue in conversion? Any person who is in possession or entitled to be in possession of the converted goods can sue. It is not necessary for the plaintiff to be the owner of the goods. Possession is difficult to decide in cases where there are two or more claimants. In the absence of any general rule each case is treated on merit having regard to the circumstances. For example, in *Bridges v. Hawkesworth* (*1851*) it was held that the plaintiff, who found some bank notes on the floor of a shop, had a good title against everyone except the true owner.

In *Elwes v. Brigg Gas Co.* (*1886*) the lessor of the land where a prehistoric boat was found had a better title to it than the lessee with a 99-year lease. In *Hannah v. Peel* (*1945*) it was held that a soldier in a requisitioned house who found a valuable brooch had a better title than the owner of the house, who had never been in physical occupation of the house and did not know of the existence of the brooch, until the soldier found it. A recent case was:

Parker v. British Airways Board (*1982*). P found a gold bracelet at Heathrow Airport and handed it in to an official requesting that it be returned to him if not claimed. BAB sold it for £850 and refused to hand the money over to P. **Held:** The finder had a better title than the occupier, unless the occupier could show that it intended to exercise control over the object. The right to exercise control was not enough. £850 + £50 interest awarded to P. (All E.R. 834.)

Types of Conversion. Conversion may take the following forms:

(i) Where chattels are wrongfully taken from the possession of the rightful owner with the intention of exercising temporary or permanent dominion over them (*Fouldes v. Willoughby* (*1841*)).

(ii) Wrongful detention of goods with an intention to keep the goods from the person entitled to possess them.

(iii) Wrongful destruction of the goods, whereby the goods either cease to exist or change their identity, e.g. raw material converted into finished product.

(iv) Wrongfully disposing of the goods in such a way as to confer a good title on someone other than the original owner.

(v) Wrongfully delivering the goods to someone other than the person lawfully entitled to them (*Hollins v. Fowler* (*1875*)).

(vi) Under S.11(2) of the 1977 Act 'receipt of goods by way of pledge is conversion if the delivery of the goods is conversion'.

(vii) Although there can only be a conversion of chattels and not documents, e.g. the value on a cheque, the difficulty is overcome by treating the cheque as a chattel, i.e. a piece of paper, which can be converted (*Lloyds Bank v. Chartered Bank* (*1929*)). The principle can be extended to negotiable instruments, trading stamps, credit cards, book tokens, etc.

(For conversion of negotiable instruments, see page 281 and 283.)

Remedies for conversion of goods. The following remedies are available:

(*a*) Damages.
(*b*) Specific delivery of goods.
(*c*) Defendant given a choice of the above two.
(*b*) and (*c*) are discretionary remedies.

S.8 of the *Torts* (*Interference With Goods*) *Act, 1977*, abolishes the *jus tertii* rule and a defendant can successfully assert that a third party has a better title to the goods than the plaintiff. S.10 holds that co-ownership is no longer a defence to an action for both conversion and trespass to goods.

Defences to an action for conversion. These include:

(*i*) Where a defendant shows that he was merely in possession of the goods without title but he was not withholding possession from the rightful possessor.

(*ii*) Where a defendant shows that the plaintiff had either no possession or insufficient possession of the goods.

(*iii*) Contributory negligence was abolished as a defence by S.11(1) of the 1977 Act, but has been restored in relation to actions in conversion against a collecting banker by S.47 of the *Banking Act, 1979*.

(*iv*) A defendant (e.g. a warehouseman) who shows that goods had been merely deposited with him. Blackburn, J., in *Hollins v. Fowler* (*1875*) said: 'A warehouseman with whom goods have been deposited is guilty of no conversion by keeping them or restoring them to the person who deposited them with him, though that person turns out to have no authority from the true owner.'

Ineffectual defences. Mistake of law or fact is not a defence. It is no defence to claim that loss from the interference was not intended or that it was not the natural or probable result of the act of conversion (*Hiort v. Bott* (*1874*)). It is no defence to claim that the defendant was acting on behalf of another:

Consolidated Co. v. Curtis and Son (*1892*). A lady who had assigned certain of her furniture to the plaintiffs subsequently ordered the defendants to auction her property. They had no notice of the bill of sale and auctioned the items assigned. **Held:** Curtis and Son were liable for conversion.

Finally, it is no defence to claim that the loss or deprivation of possession by the plaintiff was only temporary.

23.3 Revision Test

Answers	*Questions*
–	**1.** What is trespass?
1. Unlawful interference with the rights of another.	**2.** Give some examples of the forms trespass to land can take?
2. (*a*) Physical entry on another's land; (*b*) placing objects on it; (*c*) discharging oil on it; (*d*) blowing gas over it; (*e*) entry below or above the land; (*f*) where the purpose of entry is exceeded or abused.	**3.** What are the remedies for trespass to land?
3. (*a*) Damages; (*b*) injunction; (*c*) forcible ejection; (*d*) distress damage feasant; (*e*) re-entry.	**4.** What defences can a defendant plead to an action for trespass?
4. (*a*) Authority of law; (*b*) entry by licence; (*c*) re-taking goods; (*d*) necessity.	**5.** What is trespass *ab initio*?
5. Trespass from the very beginning; as where a person who lawfully enters another's land then performs an unlawful act (a misfeasance) and becomes a trespasser *ab initio*.	**6.** Explain trespass to chattels.
6. This consists of any unlawful interference with the chattels in another's possession.	**7.** Give examples of trespass to chattels?
7. (*a*) Trespass to goods; (*b*) conversion of goods; (*c*) negligence.	**8.** What important changes has the *Torts* (*Interference with Goods*) *Act, 1977*, made in this area of the law?
8. (*a*) The Act has abolished the tort of detinue and treats it as conversion. (*b*) The Act has simplified the law and procedure.	**9.** Explain trespass to goods.

Answers	*Questions*
9. Any interference with the goods in lawful possession (not ownership) of another. For example, unlawful interference with goods in possession of a bailee, a hirer, a borrower or a personal representative of a deceased person.	**10.** What defences are available to trespass to goods?
10. (*a*) Inevitable accident; (*b*) exercising a legal right; (*c*) protection of persons or property.	**11.** Define conversion.
11. 'An act, or complex series of acts, of wilful interference, without lawful justification, with any chattel in a manner inconsistent with the right of another, whereby the other is deprived of the use and possession of it' (Salmond).	**12.** Give examples of conversion.
12. (*a*) Exercising temporary or permanent dominion over goods belonging to another person. (*b*) Wrongful detention of goods. (*c*) Wrongful destruction of goods. (*d*) Wrongful disposition of goods. (*e*) Wrongful delivery to another. (*f*) Under S.11 (2) of the 1977 Act. (*g*) There can be conversion of documents, e.g. negotiable instruments, stamps, credit cards, book tokens, etc.	**13.** What remedies are available for conversion?
13. (*a*) Damages; (*b*) specific delivery of goods.	**14.** What defences are available to an action for conversion?
14. (*a*) Where it is shown that the possessor did not withhold possession from the rightful possessor. (*b*) Where a plaintiff has either no possession or insufficient possession over the goods. (*c*) Contributory negligence (but only in actions against a collecting bank). (*d*) Where goods are properly deposited with a defendant, e.g. a warehouseman	**15.** Now try some of the written questions in Appendix 1.

24
Nuisance

24.1 Types of Nuisance

There are two kinds of nuisance: (*a*) private nuisance and (*b*) public nuisance. Private nuisance affects only a particular individual, or group, whereas public nuisance affects the general public. Public nuisance is generally a crime, and not a tort, but it may be a tort in certain circumstances, as explained in Section 24.3 below.

24.2 Private Nuisance

Private nuisance is an unlawful act or omission which interferes with a man's use of his property or affects his health, comfort or convenience. Any unreasonable interference with a person's use or enjoyment of his property or any unreasonable interference which causes injuries to one's servitudes or easements (e.g. right of way, rights to light, rights to support of walls, etc.) constitutes nuisance.

In the vast majority of cases private nuisances are interferences by owners or occupiers of property with the use and enjoyment of the property in the vicinity. The tort of nuisance is based on the principle of live and let live, i.e. one should use and enjoy one's property in such a way as not to cause harm to one's neighbours. Unlike trespass, nuisance is not actionable *per se* and hence to succeed a plaintiff must show that harm has resulted to him as a result of the nuisance.

The following points are relevant when considering a nuisance:

(i) There must be an unreasonable and substantial interference for an act or omission to constitute a nuisance.

Manchester Corporation v. Farnworth (1930). Poisonous fumes were emitted from the chimneys of a generating station which was erected by the Corporation. **Held:** Since all reasonable steps had not been taken to prevent the nuisance, the Corporation was liable.

Heath v. Brighton Corporation (1908). The incumbent and trustees of a church had alleged nuisance in the form of noise from the defendants' electricity works. The noise was not excessive. The congregation had not decreased and neither had the congregation complained. **Held:** in the absence of a sufficiently serious annoyance, the plaintiffs would be refused an injunction.

(ii) The standard of comfort is a variable one. Account is taken of the fact that life in Mayfair, for example, is quiet and peaceful whereas life in, say, Whitechapel may be noisy and bustling. So what may constitute nuisance in Mayfair may not necessarily be considered nuisance in Whitechapel. The only exception to this is interference caused to light. Where actual damage to property is caused as a result of nuisance the question of the area where the property is situated is immaterial.

(iii) It is not necessary to show direct injury to one's health; it is enough that one has been prevented from enjoying the ordinary comforts of life.

(iv) The abnormal sensitivity of a person or property is not taken into consideration in deciding whether an act or omission is a nuisance:

Robinson v. Kilvert (1889). The plaintiff's unusually sensitive paper was stored on the ground floor of the defendants' premises. The defendants were makers of paper boxes and they used a boiler for their purposes in the basement. This resulted in harm to the plaintiff's sensitive paper although in the circumstances no adverse effects would have resulted on any other kind of paper. **Held:** there was no nuisance. Lopes, L.J., said: 'A man who carries on an exceptionally delicate trade cannot complain because it is injured by his neighbour doing something lawful on his property, if it is something which would not injure anything but an exceptionally delicate trade.'

(v) Nuisance can take various forms and may include such things as fumes, smoke, dirt, damp, vibrations, noise, smell, a circus performance, church bell-ringing, use of radios, projecting tree roots or branches on neighbours' land, destructive animals and many others.

(vi) Some activities are necessary and useful for the community – e.g. pigsties, quarries, breweries, fried-fish shops – but these activities can still constitute a nuisance if they cause serious or appreciable discomfort to a plaintiff.

Adams v. Ursell (1913). The defendant's fried-fish shop allegedly caused odour and vapour to the plaintiff who had a house next to the shop. **Held:** an injunction would be granted to the plaintiff despite the fact that the shop served a working-class area.

This does not mean that a fried fish shop that is a nuisance in one place will be a nuisance in another. Each case is judged on its merits and account is taken of all the circumstances.

(vii) Sometimes malice (i.e. evil motive) may be important in showing whether or not the defendant was acting reasonably and lawfully:

Hollywood Silver Fox Farm Ltd v. Emmett (1936). The defendant deliberately and maliciously fired guns on his land to frighten the plaintiff's breeding vixen. **Held:** the defendant was liable in nuisance and damages plus an injunction were granted.

(viii) Where a nuisance is caused by the acts or omissions of several wrongdoers, a plaintiff may sue them either jointly or he may sue one of the wrongdoers. If the plaintiff sues one of them, the latter has a right to contribution from the other wrongdoers for any damages awarded to the plaintiff.

(ix) It is not necessary that the act complained of as nuisance be a continuous one. It may be an instantaneous one, e.g. an explosion (*British Celanese v. Hunt (1969)*). An isolated act cannot constitute nuisance (*Bolton v. Stone (1951)*). Where an act is a temporary one the court may not grant an injunction and award damages only.

(*x*) A person may acquire a right to commit a private nuisance, through **prescription**, i.e. through 20 years' continuous operation since the act complained of first began and first constituted a nuisance. This defence is not available in respect of an act or omission constituting a crime and no length of time can legitimise a crime.

Parties to an action for nuisance. Although usually it is the occupant of the property affected by a nuisance who has a right to sue (*Malone v. Laskey* (*1907*)), in some cases a landlord may sue where permanent injury to his property has been or will be caused. As regards the person to be sued, it is normally the person who has created the nuisance even if he has vacated the land. Other persons who may be sued, depending on the circumstances are:

(i) A person in possession may be sued unless the nuisance was caused by an independent contractor, a trespasser or where the nuisance existed before the occupier acquired the property. However, the person in possession may be sued despite the fact that the work has been given to an independent contractor if the work necessitates special precautions by the occupier (*Bower v. Peate* (*1876*)). Similarly, an occupier is liable if he adopts the nuisance committed by a trespasser (*Sedleigh-Denfield v. O'Callaghan* (*1940*)).

(ii) In a landlord/tenant relationship, the general rule is that the tenant as occupier is liable for any nuisance but the landlord will be liable where: (*a*) he knew or ought to have known of the nuisance before the tenancy; (*b*) he was covenanted to repair; (*c*) he has authorised the nuisance; (*d*) he has reserved the right to enter and repair.

(iii) An occupier is responsible for nuisance created by his servants, agents or anyone under his control, e.g. family and guests.

Defences to an action for nuisance. The defences are as follows:

(i) Absolute statutory authority (see page 322).

(ii) Inevitable accident (*Esso Petroleum Co. Ltd v. Southport Corporation* (*1956*) – see page 321).

(iii) Act of God (see page 323).

(iv) Contributory negligence (see page 341).

(v) Prescription: a private nuisance is legal after 20 years from the time when the plaintiff becomes aware of it.

(vi) Commission of a nuisance may be in the public interest. There are, however, two conflicting Court of Appeal decisions on this point. In *Miller v. Jackson* (*1977*), where cricket balls had hit the adjoining premises, it was held that an injunction would be refused and damages awarded. Public interest prevailed over the hardship of a few householders. However, in *Kennaway v. Thompson* (*1980*) the court refused to follow the above case, holding that it was wrong to allow continuance of a nuisance merely because the wrongdoer is able and willing to pay for any resulting harm.

Ineffectual defences. These may be listed as follows:

(i) If a nuisance injures a particular plaintiff it is no defence that the activity benefits the public generally (*Adams v. Ursell* (*1913*), see page 361).

(ii) It is no defence that the defendant used all reasonable care and skill to prevent harm to the plaintiff (*Rapier v. London Tramways* (*1893*)).

(iii) It is no defence that the plaintiff came to the nuisance:

Bliss v. Hall (*1838*). The defendant was a candle-maker and the plaintiff had moved into the adjoining premises. Plaintiff complained that the chandlery emitted noxious vapours and smells and brought an action in nuisance. In defence, the defendant contended that he had been carrying on his business for three years before the plaintiff's arrival. **Held:** in the absence of a right by prescription, defendants were liable.

(iv) It is no defence to say that one is making a reasonable use of one's property (*A.G. v. Cole* (*1901*)), nor is it a defence that the place which gives rise to a nuisance is a suitable one for carrying out the activities complained of.

Remedies. Apart from damages and injunction (see pages 326–9) abatement is an important remedy. Through a process of 'self-help' the cause of the nuisance may be removed, e.g. projecting roots and branches from a neighbour's tree may be cut off (*Lemmon v. Webb* (*1894*), but they remain at all times the property of the owner of the tree (*Mills v. Brooker* (*1919*)). Entry into another's land or infringement of another's rights are not permitted. Notice to the occupier of the land where the nuisance arises must be given except in cases of emergency or where it is possible to remove the nuisance without entry.

24.3 Public Nuisance

Public nuisance is an unlawful act or omission which interferes or endangers the lives, comfort, property or common rights of the public generally or 'any nuisance which materially affects the reasonable comfort and convenience of life of a class of Her Majesty's subjects . . .' (*per* Romer, L.J., in *Attorney General v. P.Y.A. Quarries Ltd* (*1957*)).

A nuisance is public only when the number of people affected is sufficiently large to constitute a class. This is a question of fact depending on the circumstances. In *R. v. Madden* (*1975*), where only the police, the telephonist and a few security guards were aware of a telephone call about a bomb at a local steel plant which turned out to be a hoax, it was held that the offence of public nuisance had not been committed since not enough persons were affected. By contrast, when dust, vibration, stones and splinters from a quarry had caused discomfort to the neighbours, it was held a public nuisance had been committed (*A.G. v. P.Y.A. Quarries Ltd* (*1957*).

A public nuisance is a crime and criminal proceedings can be taken by the Attorney-General on behalf of the public or by the police. A public nuisance may also be a tort and to prevent a multiplicity of actions, civil proceedings may be started only by a person who has suffered particular damage over and above that suffered by the public at large. In *Benjamin v. Storr* (*1874*), where the defendant's horses and vans waiting outside the plaintiff's coffee-house while obstructing the highway at the same time also obstructed light to the plaintiff's shop-window and generated smell, it was held that since the plaintiff had suffered special damage he would succeed in tort.

Acts or Omissions Constituting Public Nuisance. These can take various forms. Some of them are as follows:

(*a*) Obstruction of a highway (*A.G. v. Gastonia Coaches* (*1976*)).
(*b*) Dangerous premises (*Wringe v. Cohen* (*1940*)).
(*c*) Dangerous activities carried on or near the highway (*Castle v. St Augustine's Links* (*1922*)).
(*d*) Artificial projections on highways.
(*e*) Natural projections which obstruct a highway if the person responsible has known or ought to know that they are in dangerous condition (*Noble v. Harrison* (*1926*)).
(*f*) Keeping a brothel.
(*g*) Excessive emission of smoke, fumes or dirt from factories causing discomfort.
(*h*) S.44 of the *Highways Act, 1959*, imposes an absolute duty on the highway authorities to maintain highways, and the *Highways Act, 1961*, by removing any immunity that these authorities may have enjoyed, renders them open to an action for breach of their statutory duty.

Statutory Nuisances There are statutes which forbid nuisances. Some of these are the *Public Health Act, 1936*, the *Clean Air Act, 1956*, the *Noise Abatement Act, 1960*, the *Control of Pollution Act, 1974* and the *Deposit of Poisonous Wastes Act, 1972*.

24.4 Revision Test

Answers	*Questions*
–	**1.** What are the two types of nuisances?
1. Public nuisance and private nuisance.	**2.** What is a private nuisance?
2. Any unlawful act or omission that interferes with a person's use of his property or affects his health, comfort or convenience.	**3.** Outline the important factors when considering nuisance.
3. (*a*) There must be an unreasonable and substantial interference. (*b*) The standard of comfort varies from one locality to another. (*c*) Direct injury to one's health need not be shown. (*d*) Abnormal sensitivities of a	

Answers	*Questions*
person are not taken into consideration. (*e*) Essential activities for the community can constitute nuisance, e.g. quarries, breweries, fish-shops, etc. (*f*) The act constituting nuisance need not be a continuous one, e.g. an explosion. (*g*) Malice may be important in some cases. (*h*) A right to commit nuisance may be acquired through prescription.	**4.** What defences are available to an action for nuisance?
4. (*a*) Absolute statutory authority; (*b*) inevitable accident; (*c*) Act of God; (*d*) contributory negligence; (*e*) prescription; (*f*) public interest.	**5.** What remedies are available for nuisance?
5. (*a*) Damages; (*b*) injunction; (*c*) abatement.	**6.** What is abatement?
6. A person against whom nuisance is committed can remove the cause of the nuisance, e.g. any roots or branches projecting on to your land from a neighbour's land may be cut off.	**7.** What is a public nuisance?
7. An unlawful act or omission which interferes with or endangers the lives, comfort, property or common rights of the public generally or a class of Her Majesty's subjects.	**8.** What is the main difference between a private and a public nuisance?
8. A public nuisance is a crime and criminal proceedings can be commenced by the Attorney-General or the police.	**9.** Give examples of public nuisances.
9. (*a*) Obstructing a highway; (*b*) dangerous premises; (*c*) dangerous activities on or near a highway; (*d*) artificial or natural projections on highways; (*e*) keeping a brothel; (*f*) excessive emission of smoke, fumes or dirt from factories.	**10.** What statutes forbid nuisances?

Answers	*Questions*
10. (*a*) *Public Health Act, 1936*; (*b*) *Clean Air Act, 1956*; (*c*) *Noise Abatement Act, 1960*; (*d*) *Control of Pollution Act, 1974*; (*e*) *Deposit of Poisonous Wastes Act, 1972.*	**11.** Now try some of the written questions in Appendix 1.

25
Defamation

25.1 What is Defamation?

Defamation as a tort consists in the publication of a false statement made without lawful justification concerning a plaintiff's reputation.

According to Lord Atkins in *Sim v. Stretch* (*1936*), a statement is defamatory if the words in the statement 'tend to lower him in the estimation of right-thinking members of the society'. Hence a defamatory statement basically injures a plaintiff's reputation; it tends to make the right-thinking members of society shun or avoid the plaintiff. A statement capable of affecting a plaintiff's reputation would be one that imputed either criminality, dishonesty, immorality, insanity or certain diseases to the plaintiff; one that reflected adversely on the plaintiff's trade, business or profession; and, lastly, one that imputed that the plaintiff has been raped. Defamation is distinguished from mere vulgar abuse, which injures a man's dignity and not his reputation. In *Penfold v. Westcote* (*1806*) it was held that the words 'blackguard, rascal and scoundrel' were mere abuse.

25.2 Forms of Defamation

Defamation can take the form of libel or slander. The differences between the two forms are as follows:

Libel	*Slander*
(*a*) The defamatory statement is in permanent form, e.g. a written or printed statement, a film (*Yousoupoff v. MGM Pictures Ltd* (*1934*)), pictures, an effigy, a statue, a caricature, a record, or broadcasting on radio and television (*S.1, Defamation Act, 1952*). Under S.4 of the *Theatres Act, 1968*, publication of words (including pictures, visual images and gestures) in the public performance of a play is treated as libel.	(*a*) The statement lacks permanence and is in transitory form, e.g. speech or gesture (*note*: except for broadcast speech, and speech in the public performance of a play – see libel *opposite*).

(*b*) It is actionable *per se*, without proof of any damage.	(*b*) Proof of actual financial loss by the plaintiff is required except in cases where a plaintiff is imputed with any of the following: (i) Crime punishable by imprisonment; (ii) Contagious or infectious disease, e.g. venereal disease, plague or leprosy; (iii) Where the plaintiff is a female and unchastity or adultery are alleged (*Slander of Women Act 1891*) or lesbianism (*Kerr* v. *Kennedy* (*1942*)). (iv) Unfitness as regards 'any office, profession, calling, trade or business held or carried on by him at the time of the publication' (*Defamation Act, 1952*).
(*c*) Can be a crime as well as a tort if it is a breach of the peace, e.g. sedition or obscene libel.	(*c*) Can never be a crime.

25.3 The Standard of Proof Required

In a typical defamation case the function of the judge is to decide as a *matter of law* whether in the circumstances a reasonable man would take the view that the statement allegedly made by the defendant is capable of being defamatory. If a judge is not satisfied he can withhold the case from the jury, whose function is to decide, where a case is submitted to it, whether *on the facts disclosed* the statement is in fact defamatory (*Capital & Counties Bank Ltd* v. *George Henty & Sons* (*1882*)). For a successful claim in defamation a plaintiff must prove:

(*a*) *That the statement was defamatory*. In deciding this the intention of the defendant, although useful in mitigating damages, is not crucial, i.e. innocence is no defence. The test is: What meaning would be imputed by right-thinking members of society from the statement? It follows that a defamatory intention is not significant where others do not reasonably understand the defamatory meaning.

Byrne v. *Deane* (*1937*). The plaintiff had alleged that a typewritten poem on the notice-board of a golf club was defamatory since it showed that he had been disloyal to his fellow members. Earlier the plaintiff had reported to the police that gambling machines were kept on the premises and these had to be removed. **Held:** the statement was not defamatory for although it may lower the plaintiff in the estimation of his fellow-members, right-thinking members would not think less of him because he helped in the process of law enforcement.

Sometimes words are used in a statement which may not appear at first sight to be defamatory but may carry hidden meaning or implications harmful to the plaintiff. In such a case, if a plaintiff shows that the words defame him by implication (**innuendo**) and that this is also the implication drawn by reasonable persons from the words, he will succeed.

Tolley v. *Fry* (*1931*). The plaintiff, who was a leading amateur golfer, alleged that a published advertisement showing him playing golf with a bar of chocolate in his pocket carried the innuendo that for financial gains the plaintiff had prostituted his amateur golf status. **Held:** the defendants were liable and damages were awarded to the plaintiff.

Cassidy v. Daily Mirror (*1929*). The *Daily Mirror* had published a photograph of a couple with a caption that their engagement had been announced. The plaintiff, Mrs C, who was the wife of the man Mr C in the photograph, alleged that the caption by innuendo imputed that Mrs C was 'living in sin' with Mr C. **Held:** the defendants were liable in damages although they had acted quite innocently.

Today the defence of unintentional defamation may be available to a newspaper under S.4 of the *Defamation Act, 1952.*

(*b*) *That the statement referred to the plaintiff.* It must be shown that the plaintiff as an individual has been identified by reasonably-minded persons as being connected with the defamatory statement. It is no defence that the defendant never intended to refer to the plaintiff.

Hulton v. Jones (*1910*). There appeared in a newspaper a humorous article describing the immoral life of a fictitious character by the name of Artemus Jones. There was in real life a person by the same name who was a barrister. Evidence was shown that those who knew the real Artemus Jones thought that the article referred to him. **Held:** the newspaper was liable in damages.

Whereas in the above case it was no defence for the newspaper to say they had not intended to refer to the plaintiff, in *Newstead v. London Express Newspaper Ltd* (*1940*) it was no defence to say that the words were true and intended to refer to a third party and not the plaintiff. It is not necessary that the plaintiff be named or described. Any pointer or indicator to the plaintiff in the statement is sufficient (*Morgan v. Odhams Press Ltd* (*1971*)).

There cannot be defamation of a class of persons, e.g. lawyers, priests, politicians, etc. However, where a particular ethnic or racial group has been defamed a criminal action may arise under the *Race Relations Act, 1976.*

(*c*) *The defamatory statement was published by the defendant.* To constitute publication, the statement, whether oral or in writing, must be made known to at least one person other than the plaintiff. The following examples provide more information on published and unpublished statements:

(i) There is publication when an author of a letter reveals its contents to a secretary.

(ii) When a postcard is sent through the post or a telegram is despatched or a document is printed, it is presumed that there is publication.

(iii) The communication of a statement by a husband to his wife or vice versa about a third party does not constitute publication (*Wennhak v. Morgan* (*1888*)). However, a statement by a third party to a wife defaming her husband is a publication (*Wenman v. Ash* (*1853*)).

(iv) Where a servant wrongfully opens his master's letter there is no publication (*Huth v. Huth* (*1915*)).

(v) A statement may be published by dictation to a secretary unless the communication is privileged (*Osborn v. Boulter* (*1930*)).

(vi) There is no publication where a printer returns a defamatory manuscript which he has printed to its author (*Eglantine Inn Ltd v. Smith* (*1948*)).

(vii) There may be publication when defamatory matter is written or posted on one's premises unless it is almost impossible or very difficult to remove (*Byrne v. Deane* (*1937*)).

Repetition and Dissemination. Every repetition of a defamatory statement is a new and distinct publication and hence gives rise to a new cause of action. Where a newspaper or a book is published, the proprietor, editor, publisher and printer may all be sued. However newsagents, booksellers, distributors and libraries are not liable if they are unaware of the defamatory statement and could not have reasonably found out about it; if they are negligent in not discovering the defamatory statement, they are liable (*Vizetelly v. Mudie's Select Library Ltd* (*1900*)).

(*d*) *That the plaintiff suffered damage as a consequence of the publication of the defamatory material.* Proof of financial loss is required in respect of slander only, unless one of the four exceptions mentioned above applies.

25.4 Defences to Defamation

Apart from denying that the alleged matter is defamatory, or that there has been any publication, the following defences are available where appropriate:

(*a*) **Justification.** Where a statement is true both in substance and in fact, this is a good defence; small inaccuracies will not be allowed to defeat the defence. For example:

Alexander v. N.E. Railway Co. (*1865*). The plaintiff had been convicted of an offence of travelling without paying his rail fare and was sentenced to a fine or two weeks' imprisonment. The rail company had published a poster in which the alternative sentence was given as three weeks. **Held:** the defence of justification was good and the minor inaccuracy about the sentence did not defeat the defence.

Two statutory provisions affecting this area are:

(i) S.5 of the *Defamation Act, 1952*, provides that in an action for libel or slander concerning words which contain two or more distinct charges against the plaintiff, the defence of justification will not fail because the truth of every charge cannot be proved, if the charge that is found not to be true does not materially injure the plaintiff's reputation having regard to the true charges. For example, a person has been convicted of murder, or manslaughter, and he brings an action against someone who has called him a thief and a murderer. The action will not succeed since his reputation is hardly tarnished by being called a thief even if in reality he is not.

(ii) S.8 of the *Rehabilitation of Offenders Act, 1974*, provides that where a defendant maliciously publishes details of a 'spent conviction', the plaintiff may recover damages. Under the Act if a successful rehabilitation period of between five to ten years has elapsed since the conviction for a crime carrying a sentence of 30 months' maximum imprisonment, the convicted person is treated in law as if he had *not* been charged, prosecuted, convicted or sentenced.

(*b*) **Fair Comment.** This defence applies where the statement made is a fair comment, made in good faith and on a matter of public interest. The statement must be made without any malice or improper motive and the defendant must have honestly believed in its truthfulness. In addition, the statement must be a statement of opinion and not fact, and the facts relied on by the defendant must have existed at the time of the comment and not facts which may have occurred some time before (*Cohen v. Daily Telegraph* (*1968*)).

What constitutes matters of public importance or interest is decided by a judge. The following areas would be included: operations of central government and public authorities, conduct of persons in public life, trade unions, the police, matters concerning broadcasting, television, books, plays (*London Artists Ltd v. Littler* (*1969*)), writing, painting, sculpture, music, etc. However, the private lives of persons involved in the above mentioned areas are excluded.

(*c*) **Privileges.** On grounds of public policy and in order to preserve and protect the cherished right of freedom of speech, certain statements which may be defamatory are protected by the law. The public interest in free speech is allowed to override the private right or interest of a person whose reputation has been injured. The two classes of privileges are absolute privilege and qualified privilege:

Absolute privilege. This is a complete defence and it does not matter whether a statement was false or actuated by malice. The following statements would enjoy absolute privilege:

(i) Anything said in the Houses of Parliament (*Bill of Rights, 1689*).

(ii) Reports of parliamentary proceedings published by order of either House (e.g. Hansard) or any subsequent republication in full (*Parliamentary Papers Act, 1840*).

(iii) Statements made by judges, advocates, jurors, witnesses or parties in the course of judicial proceedings, i.e. civil, criminal or military but not administrative proceedings at a tribunal (*Royal Aquarium Society Ltd v. Parkinson* (*1892*)). The privilege extends to tribunals exercising a judicial function, e.g. the Disciplinary Committee of the Law Society (*Addis v. Crocker* (*1961*)).

(iv) A statement made by one officer of state to another in the course of their official duty (*Chatterton v. Secretary of State for India* (*1895*)). Officers of state would include ministers, secretaries of state, senior officials communicating with a minister, High Commissioners reporting to the Prime Minister, and a military officer reporting to his superiors, but it is uncertain whether and how far this privilege would extend to those in subordinate ranks.

(v) Statements between husband and wife.

(vi) Statements made between a client and his solicitor in the course of their professional relationship (*Watson v. McEwen* (*1905*)).

Qualified privilege. This defence will succeed provided the person making the defamatory statement is not actuated by malice and honestly believes in its truth. Qualified privilege would be available on the following occasions:

(i) The person making the statement is under a legal or moral duty to communicate it to a person having a similar legitimate interest, e.g. testimonials or references to employers (*Jackson v. Hopperton* (*1864*)).
(ii) Statements made as a consequence of protecting one's private interests (*Osborn v. Boulter* (*Thomas*) *and Sons* (*1930*)).
(iii) Statements made to public authorities and professional bodies, e.g. a complaint to a local authority or police.
(iv) Communication between a client and his solicitor in the course of their professional relationship. However, it seems that the relationship might also enjoy absolute privilege but this matter has not been absolutely settled (*Minter v. Priest* (*1930*)).
(v) Fair and accurate reporting of parliamentary or judicial proceedings. The privilege does not extend to tribunals where members of the public are not admitted, or to domestic tribunals.
(vi) S.7 of the *Defamation Act, 1952*, confers qualified privilege on fair and accurate reporting in newspapers (including monthly publications) or broadcasting of various matters of public interest and importance, e.g. reports of public meetings or meetings of public companies, public and local authorities, reports of public proceedings of colonial or dominion legislatures, the United Nations Organisation, the International Court of Justice and the British Courts-martial.

(*d*) **Unintentional Defamation.** S.4 of the *Defamation Act, 1952*, may be invoked by a defendant who alleges that the alleged statement was published innocently and makes an offer of amends. The following conditions of innocence must be satisfied:

(i) The defendant did not intend to publish the offending words and he was unaware of the circumstances whereby they might be taken to refer to the plaintiff.
(ii) The defendant was unaware of the circumstances by which *prima facie* innocent words might be understood to refer to the plaintiff.
(iii) The defendant exercised reasonable care in the publication.

A defendant relying on S.4 must plead his offer of amends, submit an affadavit to establish his innocence, offer to publish a suitable correction and lastly take reasonable steps to notify recipients of the offending matter. If the defendant's offer of amends is accepted there will be no further legal proceedings and the court may make an order for the payment of costs and expenses. If, however, the offer is rejected it will be a good defence to prove that the publication was made innocently and that an offer was made without delay.

(*e*) **Apology.** This defence is available under the *Libel Act, 1843*. A defendant can plead when sued for libel contained in a newspaper or other periodicals that:

(i) The publication was not actuated by malice or gross negligence.

(ii) An apology was published at the earliest opportunity.
(iii) A sum of money has been paid into the court.

25.5 Remedies for Defamation

The main remedies available to a plaintiff are damages and injunction. As regards damages, a defendant can mitigate these by apology, proof of provocation by the plaintiff and by producing evidence of the plaintiff's bad reputation prior to the publication.

25.6 Revision Test

Answers	*Questions*
–	**1.** What is defamation?
1. The publication of a false statement made without lawful justification about a plaintiff's reputation.	**2.** What forms can defamation take?
2. Libel or slander.	**3.** What is the essential difference between libel and slander?
3. Libel is in permanent form, e.g. written statement, while slander is in transitory form, e.g. speech or gesture.	**4.** What points must a plaintiff prove to succeed in an action for defamation?
4. (*a*) The statement is defamatory; (*b*) the statement refers to him; (*c*) the statement was published; (*d*) the plaintiff suffered damage as a consequence.	**5.** Who may be sued if defamatory material is contained in a book?
5. A right to sue arises against the proprietor, editor, publisher and printer of the book.	**6.** What defences are available when it is alleged that a published statement is defamatory?
6. (*a*) Justification; (*b*) fair comment; (*c*) absolute privilege; (*d*) qualified privilege; (*e*) S.4 of the *Defamation Act, 1952*, for unintentional defamation; (*f*) apology under *Libel Act, 1843*.	**7.** On what occasions would a statement enjoy absolute privilege?

Answers	*Questions*
7. (*a*) Statements in the Houses of Parliament. (*b*) Reports of parliamentary proceedings. (*c*) Statements by judges, and other parties during judicial proceedings. (*d*) Statements made by one officer of state to another in the course of official duties. (*e*) Statements between husband and wife. (*f*) Statements between a client and his solicitor in their professional relationship.	**8.** What do you understand by the defence of justification in defamation?
8. Where a published statement is true in substance and fact, justification offers a good defence (*Alexander* v. *N.E. Railway Co.* (*1865*)).	**9.** Why is S.8 of the *Rehabilitation of Offenders, 1974*, important?
9. If a defendant maliciously publishes details of a 'spent conviction', a plaintiff can recover damages.	**10.** What is meant by 'spent conviction' under S.8 of the Act?
10. A sentence is considered spent where a person has undergone a rehabilitation period of between 5 to 10 years since being convicted of a crime carrying a maximum sentence of 30 months.	**11.** Explain the defence of fair comment.
11. A fair comment, made in good faith and honestly on a matter of public interest without any malice or improper motive.	**12.** What remedies are available for defamation?
12. Damages and injunction.	**13.** Now try some of the questions in Appendix 1.

26
Miscellaneous Torts

26.1 Introduction

Besides the torts already dealt with there are one or two other torts which may be important to businessmen. They may be described as economic torts, in that their effect is to harm the plaintiff economically. They may be listed as:

(*a*) Conspiracy.
(*b*) Deceit, or fraud.
(*c*) Malicious or injurious falsehood.

26.2 Conspiracy

This tort is committed when two or more persons intentionally and without lawful justification combine together to injure the plaintiff, or do unlawful acts that result in injury to the plaintiff. To succeed in an action the plaintiff must prove that the predominant purpose of the defendants was to combine together unlawfully to cause him economic damage. If, however, the defendants had combined together to further their own interests, e.g. to defend the interests of union members, and economic damage was a consequence, no action for conspiracy will succeed. In *Crofter Hand-Woven Harris Tweed Co. Ltd v. Veitch* (*1942*) it was held that the action of the members of a union to refuse to load cheaper tweed made from mainland yarn in order to protect the members' interests was not a conspiracy to inflict damage on the plaintiffs. If the overall objective of a combination is to put forward or defend the trade of those who enter into it then no wrong results despite damage to the plaintiff (*Sorrell v. Smith* (*1925*)).

26.3 Deceit or Fraud (for Contractual Misrepresentation see page 141)

This tort is committed when a person acts to his detriment relying on a fraudulent misrepresentation of another. The essential requirements of deceit are as follows:

(i) A false representation is made. This must be a statement of fact.
(ii) The person making the representation knows it to be false or does

not believe it to be true or is reckless about it, not caring whether it is true or false.

(iii) The misrepresentation is intended to be acted upon.

(iv) The person to whom the misrepresentation is made has acted upon it.

This tort has reduced in importance since recognition by the House of Lords of a duty of care for negligent misstatements in *Hedley Byrne & Co. Ltd v. Heller and Partners Ltd* (*1963*) – see page 339. In addition to recovering for financial loss, a plaintiff may recover for physical injury (*Burrows v. Rhodes* (*1899*)). As regards what constitutes false misrepresentation, Lord Herschell's definition of fraud in *Derry v. Peek* (*1889*) is important: 'Fraud is proved when it is shown that a false representation has been made (1) knowingly, or (2) without belief in its truth, or (3) recklessly, careless whether it be true or false.' Hence it is not fraud if the person making the representation honestly believes it to be true.

The tort of deceit has sometimes been used to evade S.4 of the *Statute of Frauds* (which requires guarantees to be evidenced in writing). By alleging that an oral representation about credit was made fraudulently, and suing in tort for deceit, the requirement about written evidence was evaded. S.6 of Lord Tenterden's Act, the *Statute of Frauds Amendment Act, 1828*, prevents an action for deceit over a character reference designed to secure credit unless the fraudulent misrepresentation is in writing, signed by the person concerned.

26.4 Injurious Falsehood

Whereas in deceit and defamation damage is done to a plaintiff's reputation, in injurious falsehood a tort is committed against the plaintiff's business interests. An injurious falsehood is a false statement, made maliciously about a plaintiff's business interests whereby other persons are deceived, thereby causing damage to the plaintiff. Types of injurious falsehoods are as follows:

(*a*) *Slander of title and goods*. This arises when doubts are cast through the action of the defendant on the plaintiff's title to real or personal property, patents and copyrights, the quality of his goods or products (*Wren v. Weild* (*1869*)). According to S.3 of the *Defamation Act, 1952*, no special damage need be proved by a plaintiff in an action for malicious falsehood. Puffs and mere sales talk in general terms, although untrue, may not be injurious falsehood, i.e. to say that your products are of a superior quality to those of your competitors. The test is that if a reasonable man takes a statement seriously it is slanderous (*De Beers Abrasive Products Ltd v. International Electric Co. of New York Ltd* (*1975*)).

(*b*) *Slander of plaintiff's trade or business*. It is actionable to imply in a newspaper or other published material that a plaintiff has gone out of business with the result that the plaintiff's trade suffers (*Ratcliffe v. Evans* (*1892*)).

(*c*) *Passing off*. This consists of a deliberate act of the defendant to mislead others into believing that the defendant's goods are those of the plaintiff. In doing so the defendant takes on unfair advantage of the plaintiff's trade or business. The tort may take the form of:

(i) A statement that the business or merchandise of the plaintiff is the defendant's.
(ii) Marketing under the plaintiff's trade name (*Reddaway v. Banham* (*1896*)).
(iii) Using the plaintiff's trade mark – especially unregistered trade marks, since statutory protection is given to registered trade marks under the *Trade Marks Act, 1938* and the *Trade Marks* (*Amendment*) *Act, 1984*.
(iv) Imitating the presentation or appearance of the plaintiff's goods (*J. Bollinger v. Costa Brava Wine Co. Ltd* (*1960*)).

26.5 Revision Test

Answers	*Questions*
–	**1.** What is conspiracy?
1. It is where two parties conspire together to take actions which injure the plaintiff.	**2.** When is a combination of this sort not conspiracy?
2. When it is a combination to promote the interests of the combining parties rather than to injure the plaintiff.	**3.** What is a fraudulent misrepresentation?
3. A false representation knowingly or recklessly made by the defendant which the plaintiff was intended to act upon, and did act upon.	**4.** What is injurious falsehood?
4. A false statement, maliciously made, about a plaintiff's business interests which deceives others and consequently causes the plaintiff loss.	**5.** What are the chief types of injurious falsehood?
5. (*a*) Slander of title; (*b*) slander of goods; (*c*) slander of trade or business; (*d*) passing off.	**6.** Now try some of the questions in Appendix 1.

Part 7: Business Property

27
The Law of Property

27.1 Ownership and Possession

As far as English Law is concerned the concept of property is a relatively recent development, dating from the emergence of the capitalist system in the Industrial Revolution. Prior to that time (say, AD 1760) the rights of landowners were based on possession, and we commonly hear, even today, the expression 'Possession is nine tenths of the law'. The concept of ownership grew out of this earlier concept of possession and gradually extended to cover other types of property besides landed estates. Ownership has been defined as 'the entirety of the powers of use and disposal allowed by law (*Pollock: First Book of Jurisprudence*).

Property is anything that is capable of being privately owned by an individual (or other legal person). Such an owner has the legal right to deal with his property as he wishes, he may use it, alter it, sell it, give it away, destroy it, discard it or otherwise dispose of it subject only to such legal barriers as the law of nuisance, planning, litter, etc.

We may acquire ownership in three different ways: originally, derivatively or by succession.

Original Ownership may be ownership achieved by creating the thing in the first place, as where an artist paints a picture or a manufacturer produces a product. Original ownership may also be achieved by occupation; taking possession of land or goods not owned by anyone else, or abandoned by a previous owner. Finally original ownership can be achieved by accession, as where a mare has a foal, and the foal becomes the property of the mare's owner.

Derivative Ownership is ownership derived from the previous owner, either by purchase, or by gift or process of law – as where a bankrupt's property is sold, or where a prisoner's effects are forfeited and auctioned by order of the Court.

Ownership by Succession is ownership achieved as the result of the death of the former owner. The new owner may be a beneficiary under a will, or a person entitled to claim in an intestacy (a death where the deceased left no will).

While ownership involves all the powers of use and disposal, possession is based upon fact. If A owns a motor car and allows his son B to tour the Lake District in it, B has possession of the car and exercises temporary control over it. If C steals the car he has of course no rights to ownership, but he is in possession, and may exercise the rights of possession to the exclusion of everyone else except the true owner and his son. A finder of goods may retain them against the claims of everyone except the true owner.

When we say that 'possession is nine tenths of the law' we recognise that the law gives the person in possession considerable credibility as far as ownership is concerned. Possession is *prima facie* evidence of ownership (though not conclusive evidence). Even wrongful possession of goods for six years, or land for twelve years, may defeat the rights of the previous owner and constitute the possessor the lawful owner.

27.2 Types of Property

Property is of two kinds, real property and personal property. The term 'real' refers to land, and the two kinds of property are sometimes referred to as realty and personalty. The essential feature of real property is that in a dispute over it the law will restore the thing itself (in Latin *res*) to the true owner. This is true of landed property, but not of personal property where payment of a sufficient sum of money will almost always give sufficient satisfaction to the owner (though equity will sometimes order specific performance of a bargain). Real property is immovable; a particular part of the earth's surface or property actually fixed to a particular part of the earth's surface. Thus a piece of land or a house built upon a piece of land is real property. Today real property is called freehold property. Leasehold property, where the freeholder has granted a lease for a number of years to a leaseholder, is not real property in the true sense of the word, but a special type of chattel. Chattels are movable property, things that we own which are not fixed to a particular spot on the earth's surface. Leasehold property is a sort of halfway product – it is a right which can be exercised over a piece of land, but only for a short period (many leases are on a week-by-week basis). In classifying property leases are referred to as **chattels real**, to distinguish them from all other types of chattel, which are called **chattels personal**.

The chart shown in Fig. 27.1 shows the various types of property. Note that chattels personal are divided into two classes, **choses in possession** and

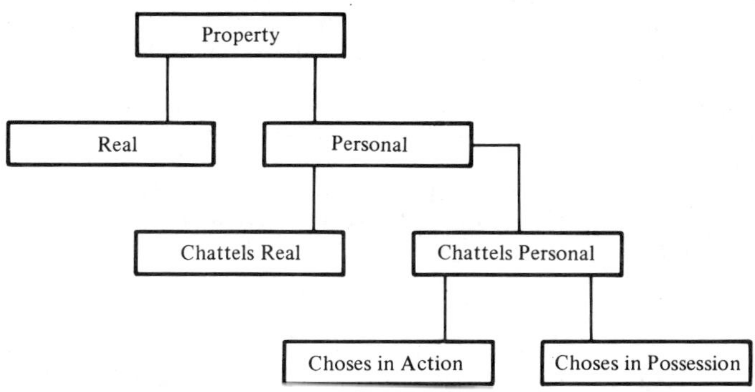

Fig. 27.1. Types of property.

choses in action. 'Choses' is just the old Norman French word for 'things'. Things in possession are items of personal property that we physically possess, such as a student's clothes, books, writing materials, personal transport, etc. Things in action are rights which we can exert by legal action in the courts (though the threat of such action is enough in most cases to persuade the parties concerned to recognise our rights). Thus debts, bills of exchange, cheques and patent rights will usually be honoured without legal enforcement being necessary.

27.3 Rights over Land

Land law in the United Kingdom developed from the feudal system imposed by William the Conqueror, in which he seized all the land and portioned it out to his nobles who held it as his vassals. They in turn subinfeudated it to lesser men who owed them loyalty in return. It gave a strong, centralised form of government which lasted for several centuries but was eventually eroded so that private ownership of land became possible. After 850 years land law had become so excessively complicated – with so many people having such a variety of interests in any particular piece of land that some pieces of landed property could never be transferred. It was essential to sort the muddle out, and five Acts (loosely called by the general term – the Property Acts) were passed in 1925. They were:

(*a*) The *Law of Property Act, 1925.*
(*b*) The *Settled Land Act, 1925.*
(*c*) The *Administration of Estates Act, 1925.*
(*d*) The *Land Charges Act, 1925.*
(*e*) The *Land Registration Act, 1925.*

There is no need in *Business Law Made Simple* to go into the many old wrongs which these five Acts put right, or to detail their many provisions for cutting the numerous Gordian knots that had been tied in almost a thousand years of legal and Chancery Court proceedings. The final result was this; the only two legal estates that could exist after 1925 were freehold estates and leasehold estates. An estate is a right in relation to land. It need not be extensive parkland like a stately home – a council tenant has only a small right in relation to land, but it is an 'estate' nevertheless.

A freehold estate is a 'fee simple absolute in possession'. The phrase means:

A *fee*: a right to the land which may be passed on to one's heirs.

Simple: it may be passed on to the general heirs and is not entailed – i.e. bound to pass to any particular person – like the eldest son.

Absolute: there is no time limit on the right – it continues forever.

In possession: the estate holder is entitled to immediate possession (though he may let someone else live there and just take the rents and profits to signify 'possession' of the property).

The freeholder is therefore the owner of the property – the rights extend down to the centre of the earth and up to the sky – though practical considerations mean that aircraft may fly over and occasionally an Act of Parliament will give authority to someone to tunnel under land or lay pipelines etc. Such matters aside, the freeholder is free to use his land as he likes subject to bye-laws, laws of nuisance, planning, etc.

A leasehold estate is called 'a term of years absolute'. It is a grant by a freeholder (the landlord) to a tenant (the leaseholder) of exclusive possession of the property leased for a stated period. The term of years includes fractions of a year, so that weekly, monthly and quarterly tenancies are possible (periodic tenancies) but long leases of 99 years and 999 years are also common. We can also have tenancies at will and tenancies at sufferance.

Besides these legal estates in land, freehold and leasehold, there are a number of interests or charges over land which can be created and conveyed at law. They are:

(*a*) An easement, right or privilege attaching to the land and enduring as long as the freehold (for ever) or the lease (the term of years agreed). Such an easement could be a right of way to one tenement (the dominant tenement) across another piece of land (the servient tenement). A right of support, and a right to light are similar easements. Similar to an easement are profits à prendre (the right to take something that is growing or a natural product of the land e.g. fishing rights, turf cutting, firewood, etc.).

(*b*) A rentcharge – a right entitling the owner to a sum of money payable periodically.

(*c*) A mortgage – which prevents the sale of the property until such time as a loan of money has been repaid.

(*d*) A land tax created by statute.

(*e*) A right of entry in respect of a lease (for the purpose of inspecting the upkeep of the property).

These are the only interests which the *law* will recognise – the only legal interests – but *equity* may recognise other interests (called equitable interests). Thus the deposit of deeds with a bank as security for a loan gives the bank an equitable interest in the property, but not a legal interest.

Business Premises. Although the purchase of business premises involves many problems, of site selection, suitability, change of use, etc., the legal problems associated with the property itself have special importance. They will either involve the purchase of a freehold property, or the purchase of a lease. These are difficult matters and require professional guidance and assistance not only in the actual purchase but in the general field of legal obligations.

27.4 The Purchase and Sale of Landed Property

There are two elements in the purchase of landed property, the contract of sale and the delivery of the land and the transfer of title to it. As far as the contract of sale is concerned the usual rules of contract apply. The parties must have capacity to contract, there must be an offer to sell, an agreement about the price, etc., and an unconditional acceptance of the offer. It is usual for a short time for the initial acceptance to be 'subject to contract', in other words a conditional acceptance, subject to a detailed contract being drawn up by the solicitors of the parties. There is no agreement at this stage, until the contracts are exchanged between the solicitors, when the contract becomes a binding contract. Under the *Law of Property Act, 1925*, contracts for the sale of land must be evidenced in writing, so that an oral agreement, while it may be binding, is unenforceable by legal action because it lacks the form required under the Act.

The stages of the purchase of landed property are therefore as follows:

(*a*) The agreement, subject to contract, after inspection of the property and a certain amount of haggling over price.

(*b*) The preparation of the contract by the parties' solicitors.

(*c*) The exchange of contracts between the solicitors, at which point the purchaser pays a deposit – usually 10 per cent.

(*d*) Delivery by the vendor's solicitors of an 'abstract of title'.

(*e*) Comparison of this abstract of title with the deeds to the property, by the purchaser's solicitor. This may require the purchaser's solicitor to deliver sets of questions to the vendor's solicitor on any points that are not clear.

(*f*) Searches by the purchaser's solicitor at the Land Registry and with the local authority to discover any encumbrances or restrictions on the use of the property which may affect the purchaser.

(*g*) Preparation of a conveyance and its completion by signature and delivery. This usually takes place at the vendor's solicitor's office, the purchaser's solicitor paying the balance of the price and receiving in exchange the conveyance and the deeds. The purchaser is then entitled to immediate possession of the property.

27.5 Acquiring Leasehold Premises

The procedure for acquiring leasehold premises is in many ways similar to the procedure already described if the lease is for more than three years and therefore has been created by deed. Once again professional advice is desirable since the terms of a lease can be onerous if not properly discussed by a knowledgable legal representative. There will usually be a number of express covenants about taking the premises in their existing state, undertaking to pay rent and service charges agreed, to pay the rates and taxes, to repair as necessary and permit inspection of the premises at reasonable hours, to insure against fire, etc. There is often a stipulation that the lessee may not assign or underlet without consent, and that the landlord's permission must be sought for any change of use.

In return the lessee gets quiet enjoyment of the premises, and the lessor must not derogate from his grant (i.e. he must not do anything which renders the property unsuitable for the purpose for which it was leased – for example use adjoining property in such a way as to spoil the lessee's quiet enjoyment of the property).

Where an existing lease is being assigned by an existing leaseholder it is essential to check that the business the purchaser proposes to engage in does not constitute a change of use, or that the landlord has given permission for any proposed change of use before the agreement goes beyond the 'subject to contract' stage. This 'change of use' must also be the subject of a planning application to the local authority. The assignee is bound to observe all the covenants binding on the assignor.

27.6 Restrictive Covenants

A restrictive covenant is one which restricts the use of freehold land by agreement with the original developer, but which can be enforced against future assignees even though they were not party to the original contract. The case for such enforcement is that a person who enters into an agreement knowing that an earlier party had rights under it ought not in equity, to disregard those rights but is in conscience bound to observe them. In *Tulk* v. *Moxhay* (*1848*) land sold by Tulk to a purchaser who agreed not to build on it was later sold to Moxhay at a cheap price because of the restrictive covenant, which he promptly disregarded; he started to use the land for building purposes. The site happened to be the centre of Leicester Square in London. Moxhay was held to be bound by the covenant. Under the *Land Charges Act, 1925*, all restrictive covenants entered into after 1 January 1926 are registerable as land charges. As such they become matters of public record of which everyone is deemed in law to have notice so that a purchaser cannot claim that he bought the property without notice of the restrictive covenant.

27.7 Mortgages

When money is borrowed it is usual to give some sort of security, as for example when a pawnbroker agrees to advance £20 against the 'pledge' of a gold watch. When the £20 is returned with interest the watch will be restored to its owner. When we wish to 'pledge' our landed property it is not so easy for we cannot physically deliver it to the pawnbroker nor move out of it with any convenience. The ancient solution was to provide a mortgage (a dead-pledge in Norman French) by which the property was conveyed to the mortgagee on a promise of re-conveyance when the loan was repaid with interest. Failure to repay meant that the land was forfeit and the loan was still repayable with interest. The resultant hardship can be imagined, and Chancery Court devised various equity rulings to reduce it.

Today there are two forms of mortgage, legal mortgages and equitable mortgages. In both cases the mortgagee (who is the person making the loan) acquires an interest in the property but not an estate. The legal mortgage gives a *legal* interest which the Courts will recognise; the equitable mortgage gives an equitable interest, which will be recognised by the Courts in equity. The usual remedy of the mortgagee in the event of non-payment is the sale of the property, out of which the loan with interest is redeemed, the expenses of the sale are paid and the balance (if any) is paid over to the mortgagor.

27.8 Revision Test

Answers	*Questions*
–	**1.** What is ownership?
1. It is the entirety of the powers of use and disposal allowed by law.	**2.** How may ownership be acquired?
2. Either originally, or it may be derived from a previous owner by gift, or purchase, or by succession on the death of the previous owner.	**3.** What is possession based upon?
3. It is based upon fact. The one in possession, and with the intention to exercise control over the property to the exclusion of others has a powerful right recognised by law.	**4.** What are the two types of property?
4. Realty and personalty. Realty is freehold property. Personalty is chattels, either chattels real or chattels personal.	**5.** What are chattels real?
5. Leases, which give control over land for a stated period of time.	**6.** What are chattels personal?
6. They may be *choses in possession* (personal belongings of all types) or *choses in action* (rights enforceable at law, such as patents, debts, bills of exchange and copyrights).	**7.** What are the two legal estates in land?
7. (*a*) Freehold and (*b*) leasehold	**8.** What is the full legal definition of these legal rights?
8. (*a*) Freehold land is a fee simple absolute in possession. (*b*) Leasehold land is 'a term of years absolute'.	**9.** Explain fee simple absolute in possession.
9. It is a legal right which may be passed on to one's general heirs, for ever, and gives the freeholder immediate rights to possession of the property.	**10.** Explain 'term of years absolute'.

Answers	*Questions*
10. It is a grant of rights by a freeholder (the landlord) to a leaseholder (the tenant) of exclusive possession and quiet enjoyment for the period of time stated in the lease.	**11.** What other legal interests are there? (Interests that will be recognised by common law rather than in equity.)
11. Easements, profits à prendre, rent charges, mortgages, land taxes imposed by statute and rights of entry.	**12.** How is ownership of freehold land transferred?
12. By conveyance; the deeds are transferred with a legal document (the conveyance) detailing the contractual arrangements.	**13.** What exactly is a mortgage?
13. The word means a 'dead pledge', and it is a way of pledging a property, either freehold or leasehold, as security for a loan. A variety of rights are secured by the mortgagee but the usual right to be exercised in the event of non-payment is the sale of the property, the balance of the loan being redeemed out of the proceeds.	**14.** Go over the page again until you are quite sure of all the answers. Then try the written questions in Appendix 1.

Appendix 1
Questions

Chapter 1. Elements of English Law

1. Define law. What are the essential institutions if laws are to be promulgated and the 'rule of law' sustained?

2. Distinguish between 'public law' and 'private law'. The ABCD Company Plc is in difficulties. First, its managing director after a business luncheon has driven the firm's car into a lamp-post, been breathalysed and told that action will certainly follow. Second, the company's most important customer has complained about serious defects in a recent contract and has informed ABCD that he is seeing a solicitor. What will be the effect of these two potential brushes with 'the law' upon ABCD?

3. What are the chief sources of law? Explain two of these sources in detail, with particular reference to the impact of law upon businesses.

4. Explain statute law, using as your example any statute with which you are familiar.

5. 'The Secretary of State, in exercise of the powers conferred by S.1(3) of the *Merchant Shipping* (*Liability of Shipowners and others*) *Act, 1958*, hereby makes the following order:

'For the purposes of S.1 of the Act named above £133.66 and £42.12 are hereby specified as the amounts which shall be taken as equivalent to 3100 and 1000 gold francs respectively.'

Explain the purpose of orders such as this.

Chapter 2. The Courts of Law

1. Describe the composition and jurisdiction of the County Courts. A plaintiff wishes to bring an action to recover £150 from a tenant for unpaid rent. How will this matter be dealt with?

2. An action for recovery of £175 000 allegedly lost as a result of a breach of contract is brought in the High Court. Explain the likely composition of the Court, and its general procedure.

3. Explain the doctrine of binding precedent. How is precedent effective in civil matters?

4. Explain the provisions of Article 177 of the Treaty of Rome with regard to preliminary rulings on the interpretation of the Treaty and Community Law.

5. Describe the composition and jurisdiction of *two* of the following courts: (*a*) Crown Courts; (*b*) Magistrates' Courts; (*c*) County Courts; (*d*) the High Court; (*e*) the Court of Appeal; (*f*) the House of Lords.

Chapter 3. The Legal Environment for Business Entities

1. Explain the concept of business entity. What is the position of a sole trader and a partner as far as business entity is concerned?
2. A sole trader uses the firm name 'Gimmicks Electronics'. How is this name brought to the attention of the public in compliance with the law?
3. Discuss the advantages and disadvantages of forming a partnership, with particular reference to the legal position of partners (*a*) *inter se* and (*b*) with regard to the world at large.
4. B, who is about to set up in partnership with A, has been told that a simple handshake is enough. Advise him.
5. What are the most important features of partnership law on the dissolution of a partnership? Y, who is a junior partner, feels he is unfairly treated by his senior partners who do not let him see the books and overrule his view on many matters he feels to be important. He wishes to know how to bring an end to the partnership and retrieve the capital he has contributed to it. Advise him.
6. Write notes on *two* of the following: (*a*) relation of partners with third parties; (*b*) the rights and duties between partners; (*c*) limited partnership; (*d*) dissolution of partnership; (*e*) advantages and disadvantages compared with other business entities.

Chapter 4. Business Entities: Unincorporated Associations

1. What is an unincorporated association? Who is in charge of such an association and what legal liabilities are faced by such persons?
2. A croquet club finds itself unable to attract members and proposes to sell its valuable land. How will this be arranged and how will the money provided be disposed of?
3. A is the secretary of a club. He asks B to redecorate the premises at a fee of £500. After the work has been completed it appears that the treasurer is unable to pay the bill, and claims that the work was not authorised by the committee. Advise B.
4. Why is the constitution (or rule book) of a club important? A, who has been banned from the club by S, the secretary, for rowdy behaviour, claims that he has been given no opportunity to explain his behaviour. Advise him.
5. What is the situation of (*a*) a club, (*b*) a trade union and (*c*) a partnership with regard to actions against them for tort. Who is likely to be held liable?
6. A, an innocent passer-by, has been seriously hurt by a missile thrown by B, a member of the Merry Revellers Wine Club. The Annual Club Dinner was in progress at the time, and the missile emerged from the club premises after breaking a window. Advise A.

Chapter 5. Business Entities: Limited Companies

1. What is the meaning of limited liability? Why is it such an important concept and how is it obtained by business persons?
2. Compare and contrast the different forms of business units, i.e. companies, partnerships and sole traders.
3. What are the formalities involved in registering a public company?
4. What are the basic differences between a public company and a private company under the *Companies Act, 1985*?
5. Explain the contents and purpose of: (*a*) a memorandum of association; (*b*) a set of articles of association.
6. Explain the *ultra vires* rule and the changes that have been effected in it by S.36 of the *Companies Act, 1985*.
7. What are the important legal consequences of incorporation of a company? Give cases where applicable.
8. What are the duties of directors of a company.
9. Explain the various forms of winding up a company.
10. Describe a typical structure for a public limited company. What is the relationship between the company and (*a*) its shareholders, (*b*) its directors and (*c*) its employees?
11. Discuss the proposition that 'worker' directors should be appointed to the boards of public companies. What conflicts of interest might a worker-director face?
12. Why are auditors appointed? What is their legal position relative to (*a*) the company and (*b*) the shareholders?
13. What is 'compulsory winding up'? In what way is it different from voluntary dissolution of the company?

Chapter 6. The Nature of Contracts

1. Define a contract. Who may make contracts? N, a school leaver aged 16, undertakes to work for B 'in the course of learning the trade of automobile mechanic' for a payment of £50 a week in the first three years, and £80 a week in the remaining two years. Discuss whether this contract is binding upon N.
2. What is a contract for necessaries? B, a student aged 17, is supplied with (*a*) groceries, (*b*) wines and spirits and (*c*) an optical telescope by Supermarkets Ltd, the account to be settled at the end of the month. B does not pay. Advise M, the supermarket manager.
3. What is the importance of the concept 'intention to create legal relations' in contract law? Refer in your answer to the following two cases:

(*a*) A asks B to redecorate his premises 'from top to bottom, inside and outside'. He is amazed at the size of the bill, which is completely documented and does not appear to contain any extravagant use of materials.

(*b*) C agrees with D to complete a football pool coupon regularly and hand it to him with the cash invested, after completing the coupon in the usual way, and signing his name on the part which reads. 'It is agreed that this coupon is binding in honour only'. D absconds with C's money each week, but this is not discovered until C 'wins' a large prize.

4. Balfour agrees with his wife that he will pay her £80 a week if she agrees to separate from him and live in rented accommodation. Some time later he is made redundant and is unable to keep up the payments. Advise Mrs Balfour of her legal rights in this matter.

5. Explain the term '*consensus ad idem*'. A agrees to buy B's camera, which B said was referred to in the Ornithological Society as being capable of taking long-distance colour photographs. He gives a £20 deposit, but when the camera is produced it proves to be quite a different model and not worth the price discussed earlier. Advise A (*a*) about the bargain made and (*b*) about the prospects of recovering his deposit.

Chapter 7. Offer, Acceptance and Valuable Consideration

1. Mrs A selects certain items in a supermarket, takes them to the check-out and offers to pay for them. The total bill is more than she has in her purse, and she regretfully has to leave two items behind. These are returned to the shelves by an assistant. Explain the following terms by reference to the above events: (*a*) invitation to treat; (*b*) offer; (*c*) acceptance; (*d*) valuable consideration; (*e*) revocation of offer.

2. A announces that an auction will be held in his sale rooms commencing at 2 p.m. on 14th November. B, who is interested in this type of sale, travels 50 miles to attend the sale, only to discover that it is cancelled because the items have been sold privately. Advise B.

3. X offers Y his horse for £900. Y telexes, 'Would you be prepared to take £600 and my stallion Pericles.' X replies 'No'. Y then telexes, 'Very well, accept your offer to sell at £900,' but X has already sold it to Z for £950. Advise Y.

4. Peter offers Paul an editorial post at 'a Mayfair salary'. Paul accepts this offer, but no starting date is arranged and Peter takes no further action. Advise Paul.

5. 'The rules about postal offers and acceptances can be very confusing.' What are these rules and what justification is there for them?

6. Discuss the concept of 'lapse of time' on offer and acceptance.

7. 'A smaller sum will not satisfy a larger sum.' Explain this principle, outlining the cases which illustrate it.

8. What is meant by 'quasi-estoppel', or the 'rule in the High Trees House case'? Explain in detail the facts and *ratio decidendi* of this case.

Chapter 8. Circumstances Affecting the Validity of Contracts

1. Distinguish between the various types of mistake.

2. In what ways might a contract be rendered illegal? What is the effect of illegality?

3. What are the 'presumptions' normally associated with undue influence?

4. M, the mother of S, who is over 18 years of age, persuades him to sell some shares and use the money to pay off her mortgage. Before S's stock-

broker can make the sale S contacts him to cancel the arrangement. M asks whether, in your opinion, she can force S to carry out his promise. Advise her.

5. Define duress. What is the effect of duress upon a contract?

6. A offers to sell his car to B for £4000. B has seen A driving an impressive modern vehicle which he considers well worth £4000, and accepts the offer. On delivery the vehicle proves to be a different vehicle altogether. B refuses to take delivery, or to pay the price. Advise A.

Chapter 9. The Terms of the Contract

1. (*a*) What are the main differences between representations and terms in relation to a contract? (*b*) B states early in the negotiations leading to the sale of a second-hand machine that it has been in regular use up to the time of sale. On delivery the machine is found to be rusted solid in one essential area and clearly has not been used for many years. Discuss the remedies available to A, the purchaser.

2. (*a*) Distinguish between express and implied terms in a contract. (*b*) B contracted to deliver goods to A, the contract expressly stating that the concrete posts required were essential for erection on May 5th, when contractors had agreed to do the job. They arrived on May 6th, due to a breakdown in B's vehicle, but by then the contractors had used their own supplies at a higher price per unit. Advise A.

3. The *effect* of a breach of contract is helpful to the courts in deciding whether a term in a contract is a condition or a warranty. Explain, referring in your answer to the case below.

P undertakes to deliver material to Z, the contract stating 'it is a condition of the contract that delivery be made by 3 p.m., Friday January 19'. The reason for this is that Z's religion forbids him to work after 5 p.m. on Friday, and a major contract is to start at his clothing factory on Monday. P's vehicle breaks down, but delivery is made early on Monday morning, the lorry being available at the opening of the factory and taking only half an hour to unload.

4. (*a*) What are 'standard trading conditions'? (*b*) B hires a machine from A, another plant-hire company, so that he can fulfil a contract made with C. The machine B hoped to hire to C had broken down, and could not be repaired in time. A's terms and conditions were sent on at a later date and contained a clause stating 'the cost of transport of machines hired is for the hirer's account'. B maintains that this was not part of the bargain. Discuss.

5. (*a*) A term in a set of standard trading conditions reads: 'If the customer sends any dangerous goods without notification to the carrier for carriage, and these goods cause damage to other goods or to the vehicle, the customer will indemnify the carrier and all claimants for the damage caused.' Is this term binding on the carrier's customers?

(*b*) A, who sends goods he believes to be harmless by the carrier mentioned in (*a*) above, does not know that when in contact with flour the product produces a dangerous effect. The carrier loads the goods next to a sack of wholemeal flour destined for a health-food shop. Three deaths occur and numerous other people are taken ill. No similar case has been recorded. Discuss the liability of A.

6. How have the courts mitigated the most onerous aspects of exclusion clauses used in contracts?

7. What have been the main effects of the *Unfair Contract Terms Act, 1977*?

Chapter 10. Misrepresentation

1. Why is it necessary for the law to draw up rules relating to misrepresentation?

2. What are the various types of misrepresentation, how do they differ and what remedies are available to injured parties?

3. What are the essential elements of a misrepresentation?

4. (*a*) Distinguish between a puff and a misrepresentation. (*b*) X says: 'This is the finest little car in England.' Y says: 'I will take it in part exchange for my own vehicle, which is a two-year-old Ford Sierra, and £800 to settle the rest.' X agrees. Both statements about the cars prove to be untrue. Advise X of his legal position.

5. 'Negligent misrepresentation is closer to fraudulent misrepresentation than it is to innocent misrepresentation.' Discuss this statement, referring in your answer to the following cases:

A, who is selling Tumbledown House, refers untruthfully to its 'complete freedom from woodworm or other pests'.

B, who is selling a similar property, replies to the question 'Is there any woodworm?' by saying 'I've never seen any.' Woodworm is found later to be present.

C, who is selling a similar property, warrants that it is free from woodworm, and produces a recent surveyor's report. Despite this, woodworm is found to be present.

6. 'Silence is not misrepresentation.' Discuss this statement. M completes an application form for life assurance which asks the question: 'Has any insurance company ever refused to cover you?' In fact, many years ago as a young motorcyclist who had bought a high-powered motorcycle, cover had been refused. M does not answer this question, leaving the space blank. Despite this a premium is agreed and paid for several years, when M is killed in a road accident. The insurance company refuses to pay, claiming misrepresentation. Advise M's wife, the beneficiary.

Chapter 11. The Discharge of Contracts

1. How is a contract normally discharged? A, an author, contracts with P, a publisher, to write a travel book. He goes to some expense to collect pictures and other material, only to be told that P is no longer able to proceed with publication. Advise A.

2. What is meant by the doctrine of substantial performance? J, a joiner, fulfills a contract to install guard rails around a staircase and landing, but fails to use a certain type of countersunk washer on the bolts concerned.

These were specified in the contract, but are no longer manufactured. A perfectly serviceable type of non-countersunk washer was used instead. P, the property owner, refuses to pay the price. Advise J.

3. Discuss the importance of valuable consideration in any contract to discontinue one bargain and replace it by another. Mrs A sues her doctor for negligence in prescribing a wrong dose of drugs and the court awards her £2000. She agrees with the doctor to accept £500 on the 1st January for the next four years. Later she asks for interest at 5 per cent on the outstanding balance to be added to each payment except the first. The doctor refuses. Advise Mrs A.

4. A contract to carry goods to India has just been concluded at a fair price when the Suez Canal is closed by military action. Discuss whether this frustrates the contract, which is much less lucrative if it is to be fulfilled by the long journey around southern Africa.

5. A contract between A and B for the construction of a major engineering works is affected by the outbreak of war, which requires A to divert his labour force to other projects in the national interest. The order requisitioning his men and plant is made under an Act entitled the Outbreak of Hostilities Act. Advise B, who feels that alternative labour is available, especially as a large exporter has discharged staff in the locality.

6. 'Breach of contract does not necessarily discharge the contract.' Explain this statement. In your answer refer to a breach of contract by a fashion designer, whose factories supply 12 000 garments to a major fashion house in four colours – cream, maroon, blue and grey. The contract called for cream, maroon, blue and green garments.

7. What is meant by a legal assignment of a contract? A, who has contracted to do work for B, is so busy that he cannot perform it. He asks B to allow C to take over the contract. Advise B of the legal position, and explain what will be the legal effect of any decision to assent to the proposal.

8. X, who is owed money by Z, agrees orally with Y to assign Z's debt to him. Y accordingly notifies Z that he must pay him (Y) and not X. Is this a legal assignment? If Z ignores the request, can Y sue Z, and will the Courts uphold it if he does?

Chapter 12. How the Law Enforces Contractual Obligations

1. What remedies are available (*a*) at common law, (*b*) in equity, to an aggrieved person disappointed by the failure of another person to perform a contract? C, who has agreed to lay a patio for D, is offered a more lucrative contract with E and tells D he is not able to perform the contract as arranged. What should D do, and what remedies are available to him for C's breach of contract?

2. What is 'repudiation of a contract?' X promises Y that he can get him a reconditioned engine within two days. Seven days later X is still waiting and is offered a similar engine for immediate delivery by Z. X badly needs his car. Advise him.

3. 'The case of *Hadley v. Baxendale* (*1854*) is one of the most important in contract law.' What was the case about and why is it important?

4. Distinguish between liquidated damages, unliquidated damages and a penalty. B agrees to build a turnstile for A at the entrance to his stately home, by a given date. Failure to do so will result in damages of £20 per day until completion. This is an estimate of the extra cost required in employing staff to supervise those seeking entry through an uncontrolled entrance area. B does not complete the work in time but refuses to pay damages. Advise A.

5. What is a *quantum meruit*? A starts to erect a house for B but gets into difficulties financially and B is forced to employ another builder to complete the work. X starts to erect a house for Y but after a while Y, who is disappointed with the quality of X's work, tells him to leave the house unfinished and he will seek a better workman. Discuss whether either, both or neither of these is entitled to be paid on a *quantum meruit*.

6. When will the courts grant a decree of specific performance? Why do they sometimes refuse to exercise discretion in this respect?

7. What is meant by the term 'statute-barred'? Why is it desirable that some time limit is set on legal action, particularly in such matters as the carriage of goods by sea and air?

Chapter 13. Agency

1. 'He who acts by another, acts for himself.' Explain this legal maxim, referring in your answer to common examples from business life where a businessman acts through another person.

2. 'Agency involves a tripartite arrangement.' Explain the tripartite arrangement and the legal relations of all these parties.

3. (*a*) Explain the term 'subsequent ratification of an unauthorised act'. (*b*) A who has been acting on behalf of B in the purchase of a vintage motorcar from C accepts C's offer to sell at £5000 although he knows he has only authority to go as far as £4500. C hears that A has exceeded his authority, and tells him that he is commencing an action against him for breach of warranty of authority. What is the position of A in these circumstances?

4. B appoints A to act as his agent in the purchase of a piece of property. What are A's duties to his principal, and what rights has he against the principal?

5. Define agency of necessity. A, the servant of Transporters (Wilbraham) Ltd, is the driver of a container lorry taking tomatoes from Southampton to Birmingham. He is involved in an accident and to preserve the fruit he sells them at a very low price to Chutney-makers Ltd. His travel documents include a 'case of need' address and telephone number for the South of England agents of the owners, B Ltd. Discuss the legal position of B Ltd, who have suffered considerably by the driver's action.

6. A is the agent for B in the sale of B's paintings, on a continuing basis. B dies, but before A has heard of this he disposes of an important painting to C. The executors refuse to ratify the agent's act, or to pay him commission on the sale. Discuss A's legal position with respect to C.

Chapter 14. Contracts for the Sale of Goods

1. (*a*) Define a contract for the sale of goods. (*b*) Explain whether each of the following is a sale of goods: (i) A transfers his motor vehicle to B for £1000, payable on the last day of the present month. (ii) A transfers his motor vehicle to B in exchange for shares in the General Electronic Ltd valued at £1000. (iii) A hires his motor vehicle to B for £65 per week during the long vacation. (iv) A agrees to leave his motor vehicle with B as security for a loan of £1000, repayable at the end of the long vacation.

2. (*a*) What is the special position of a minor under the *Sale of Goods Act, 1979*, with regard to the purchase of necessaries? (*b*) M, who is 17 years of age, lives in a rural area where there is no public transport. He is about to start a technical course at a college in a nearby town and 'buys' a motorcar for £485, payable when he receives his grant. A friend tells him the vehicle is not worth more than £130. Advise M.

3. (*a*) List the terms which are implied into a contract under SS.12–15 of the *Sale of Goods Act, 1979*. (*b*) Choose any one of these implied terms and explain in detail what the implications are.

4. (*a*) What is meant by the term 'merchantable quality'? (*b*) M, who is thinking of buying a large quantity of paint thinners from Cautious Ltd, asks for proof of its quality. Cautious Ltd states that they have never been asked for such proof before, and suggest that they will provide a single drum, randomly selected by M, for test purposes, free of charge. M asks his chemist D to select a specimen drum. He does so, but finds his own test facilities inadequate and does not test it other than superficially, by appearance, etc. A large order is placed, but it proves to be unsatisfactory. Advise M.

5. What are the rights of an unpaid seller? Basics Plc, who supply chemical raw materials to Doubtful Ltd, are anxious to write the contract in such a way as to ensure payment, even when the property passed to Doubtful Ltd has been mixed with other materials to produce quite different products. Advise Basics Plc.

6. M Ltd have placed an order for 5000 sacks of potting compost. What is the legal position in each of these cases: (*a*) a lorry arrives with 2000 sacks; (*b*) a lorry arrives with 6500 sacks; (*c*) a lorry arrives with 5000 sacks of a totally unsuitable mixture; (*d*) a lorry arrives with 5000 sacks of a different material, which will do at a pinch, but the price quoted for the original material is excessive for this material.

Chapter 15. Insurance

1. What is the nature of insurance? How would A, who wishes to obtain fire insurance cover for his factory, set about obtaining it? In the event that cover is arranged, what would be the procedure should a fire occur?

2. Explain the term 'insurable interest'. What persons might have an insurable interest in the safe arrival of a ship, loaded with containerised cargo, setting off from Southampton on a journey to Perth, Western Australia?

3. Why is a contract of insurance a contract *uberrima fides*? What statements would you expect to have to make in completing a proposal form for life assurance on your own life?

4. What is subrogation in insurance? A, who has insured goods sent by a carrier against all risks, hears that the carrier's driver has had an accident and is to be charged with drunken driving. The goods are seriously damaged and the insurance company agrees to pay full compensation. Where does subrogation enter into this scenario?

5. Explain each of the following terms: (*a*) indemnity; (*b*) measure of indemnity (in marine insurance); (*c*) benefit payable.

6. What are the 1.1.82 Policy Forms and Clauses? Why were they introduced, and to what extent are they an improvement on former practice?

7. A ship is in a dangerous situation and the master takes the following actions: (*a*) road haulage vehicles and containers on deck have shifted position – their restraining cables are severed and they fall overboard; (*b*) fuel in transit as deck cargo is used to feed the ship's engines; (*c*) damaged superstructure is hacked free and jettisoned. The ship and the rest of the cargo arrive safely. How will these losses be dealt with?

Chapter 16. Law of Carriage by Land, Sea and Air

1. (*a*) What is a common carrier? (*b*) What are the common law exceptions? (*c*) A, who is a lorry driver, set up in a business as a haulier without any special arrangements. He is carrying a load to the west country when a heavy storm sweeps away a bridge he is crossing, and he barely escapes with his life. Advise B, the owner of the goods, which are irretrievably lost.

2. (*a*) What is a private carrier? (*b*) How does a haulier usually make it clear that he is a private carrier, not a common carrier? (*c*) T, who is a private carrier, states that he will not be liable for losses sustained in transit, however caused. P's goods are stolen by T's driver, who is sent to prison. Advise P.

3. What is stoppage in transit? Why is it fair that the right of stoppage in transit should exist?

A has sent goods by B to C. B arrives with the goods and C asks him to hold them at his depot until next day, and to deliver them to D, who will pay B the extra freight charges. B agrees. On arriving back at his depot he receives a telephone call from A telling him to stop the goods in transit, as A has heard that C is insolvent and about to call in the receivers. Advise B.

4. What is a lien? Why does a haulier insert in his conditions of carriage a statement that he is entitled to a general, active lien on all goods carried?

5. What is the CMR convention? What difference would it make to A who has sent goods by B, a haulier, under a contract which says that B will not be liable for any loss, howsoever caused? B's vehicle is in poor repair, and due to handbrake failure on a French mountain road falls into a ravine where A's goods are a total loss.

6. What is the CIM Convention? How is it incorporated into English law? What does it say about: (*a*) contractual documents, (*b*) the liability of the carrier for loss, damage or delay?

7. What is a bill of lading? What functions does it serve and how is it affected by the Hague-Visby rules?

8. A carrier by sea is invited to carry hazardous cargo and agrees to do so – on deck. During a storm the container in which this cargo is packed begins to smoke. It is jettisoned. Advise A, the owner of the cargo disposed of.

9. Why is a definition of international carriage important in any international convention about the law of carriage? How is a sender of goods by air freight warned of the existence of clauses in the Warsaw Rules limiting the carrier's liability? What is the limit specified in the Rules?

10. ICC Publication No. 298 is about the carriage of goods by a combined transport operator under a Combined Transport Document. What is the purpose of this body of uniform rules, and how is it made effective in law?

Chapter 17. Negotiable Instruments

1. What is 'the concept of negotiability'? A takes a £5 note in a shop from B, a complete stranger, supplying goods and change to the full value. Later C enters, claiming that he lost the note, and that D, who has come along with C, saw B pick it up and make off with it in the direction of A's shop. D is a convincing witness. Advise C.

2. What is the definition of a bill of exchange? M orders P to sell his motorcar at auction, to keep 10 per cent for himself, pay 50 per cent to R and return any balance left. Discuss whether this order is a bill of exchange.

3. What is meant by the term 'acceptance' of a bill of exchange? What are the legal implications of acceptance and what are the consequences of failing to observe the legal requirements?

4. Write short explanations (5–8 lines) about each of the following: (*a*) the holder of a bill; (*b*) a holder in due course; (*c*) endorsement of a bill; (*d*) bearer bills.

5. What is the liability of the drawer upon a bill? M has drawn on N for £1000 for goods supplied. N accepted the bill; M discounted it with a bank B, who subsequently passed it to C. It then moved to E, F, G and H. H presented it on the due date but N regretted his inability to pay. H, who knows M as a business acquaintance, approaches M for payment. Explain why M should pay. If M cannot pay, who must pay H the value of the bill?

6. Define a holder in due course. What are his rights on a bill? R is the holder in due course of a bill of exchange, which on presentation proves to have been stolen earlier by T, a thief. T as a 'favour' endorsed it and gave it to S, who used it to buy goods from R. T has since disappeared and the acceptor has already honoured a substitute bill made out when the first bill disappeared. Who must pay R, and who stands the loss on the bill?

7. Write short explanations of the following terms: (*a*) open cheque; (*b*) crossed cheque; (*c*) bearer cheque; (*d*) special crossing; (*e*) 'not negotiable'; (*f*) account payee.

8. Define a cheque. What protection is given to bankers who pay cheques under the *Cheques Act, 1957*?

9. What protection is given to a collecting banker by the *Cheques Act, 1957*? When does a collecting banker lose protection?

Chapter 18. Arbitration

1. What is arbitration? What are its advantages? Are there any disadvantages?

2. Explain the terms 'arbitrator' and 'umpire' in arbitration proceedings. An arbitration clause says: 'In any dispute the matter shall be settled by the opinion of two arbitrators, one of whom – for the carriers – shall be a member of the sea freight trade association. The other shall be appointed by the cargo owners.' In such a situation who is the umpire?

3. 'In arbitration proceedings every case is thrown away, and of no legal effect whatsoever.' Appraise this statement using an imaginary situation in which a war closes both ends of the Suez Canal, trapping 18 vessels chartered by various charterers from various owners.

4. Under arbitration proceedings held in New York which included an agreement by the parties 'not to appeal to any court of law in any country, but to rely solely on the decisions of the arbitrators concerned', A must pay B 100 000 dollars. B, a British citizen, considers the award to have been unfair and the arbitrators biased. What will be the attitude of a British court?

5. What is the situation if X, a party who believes a point of law has been incorrectly viewed in domestic arbitration proceedings, wishes to bring the matter before the courts? Y, the other party, is not prepared to agree to the matter being referred to the courts, on the ground that the costs will be out of all proportion to any possible change in the award.

Chapter 19. Administrative Law

1. Explain briefly some of the grounds on which courts may intervene to set aside an administrative decision.

2. What do you understand by the concept of natural justice?

3. Write notes on at least *three* of the following methods of judicial control: (*a*) *mandamus*; (*b*) *certiorari*; (*c*) *prohibition*; (*d*) injunction; (*e*) declaration.

4. Explain what administrative justice is and discuss the workings of at least *two* administrative tribunals.

5. Compare and contrast public inquiries and tribunals of inquiry.

6. The office of the Parliamentary Commissioner for Administration (the Ombudsman) is an important means of redress against oppressive or faulty government. Discuss.

7. Explain fully, with case law examples, at least three grounds on which the courts may intervene to set aside an administrative decision.

Chapter 20. Introduction to the Law of Tort

1. What is tort and how does it differ from a crime or a breach of a contract?

2. Explain *three* of the following general defences available to an action for tort: (*a*) *volenti non fit injuria*; (*b*) necessity; (*c*) mistake; (*d*) inevitable accident; (*e*) statutory authority; (*f*) self-defence; (*g*) Act of God; (*h*) act of state.

3. What do you understand by vicarious liability in relation to the liability of: (*a*) principal and agent; (*b*) master and servant; and (*c*) an independent contractor?

4. Explain the various remedies available to an action for tort. M has attended an ice hockey match and been injured in the eye by a flying puck. He gained admission on a ticket bearing a warning: '*Note:* The management cannot accept responsibility for injury to members of the public attending this match.' Advise M.

5. T has been injured by a vehicle driven by X, the employee of Y. X was intoxicated, having spent his lunch-time in a bar. Y, who knows that X likes a drink, has specifically forbidden him to enter a bar during his lunch period. Advise T.

6. Distinguish between nominal, substantial and aggravated damages. Z has been injured in an accident due to the negligence of a crane driver in a port, who is the employee of the Port Authority. The injuries were made worse by Z's failure to wear a hard helmet provided to all visitors. Discuss what sort of damages are payable to Z.

Chapter 21. Negligence

1. Define negligence. It has been said that 'the categories of negligence are never closed'. Explain this statement, referring in your answer to a case in which people were made ill, and some died, because a carrier placed a sack of wholemeal flour alongside a sack of a new type of adhesive. Neither the manufacturer nor the carrier knew of the potentially dangerous nature of the new material. The baker, who is being sued by the relatives of deceased customers, seeks advice.

2. What do you understand by a 'duty of care'? To whom is a duty of care owed?

3. Explain the doctrine of *res ipsa loquitur*. A receives a crate of crockery which is smashed to pieces, although packed by professional packers. It was delivered by T Ltd, a multi-modal transport operator, whose conditions of carriage state that he will be liable for damage not attributable to fault of the consigner. Advise A (i) as to his need to provide proof of damage, (ii) as to any defences the carrier may raise to deny liability.

4. Why is the House of Lords' decision in *Hedley Byrne and Co. Ltd v. Heller and Partners Ltd* (*1963*) important?

5. What is contributory negligence? A was seriously injured while sitting in the front passenger seat of a car driven by B who has been found guilty of careless driving. A's seat belt was not in use at the time although it was available and in good condition. A does not believe people should be forced

to wear seat belts. B was not seriously injured in the crash, yet the impact the car sustained was on the driver's side. Discuss the 'negligence' implications in this case.

6. What is the 'neighbour principle'? Discuss whether A, who has a miscarriage when B's car collides with C's car in the street outside her house, is a neighbour of B or C.

Chapter 22. The Liability of Occupiers of Premises

1. What is the liability of an occupier of premises towards: (*a*) visitors; (*b*) children; (*c*) trespassers?

2. What are the main provisions of the *Occupiers Liability Act, 1957*, concerning the liability of an occupier of premises? Can an occupier exclude his liability?

3. What is meant by 'a breach of statutory duty'? To succeed in his action what must a plaintiff prove? Outline the defences available.

4. What is the rule in *Rylands v. Fletcher*? What defences are available?

5. Explain the important provisions of the *Animals Act, 1971*, concerning: (*a*) livestock; (*b*) animals straying on highways; (*c*) keepers of dogs.

Chapter 23. Trespass to Property

1. Explain what you understand by trespass to land, giving cases. Give examples of the forms trespass to property can take.

2. (*a*) What is trespass to land? (*b*) Explain some of the forms it takes. (*c*) What defences can be pleaded to an action for trespass to land?

3. Explain: (*a*) trespass to goods; (*b*) conversion.

4. Define conversion and explain the various types of conversion.

5. Write notes on *three* of the following: (*a*) trespass *ab initio*; (*b*) *Esso Petroleum Co. Ltd v. Southport Corporation* (*1955*); (*c*) remedies for trespass to land; (*d*) defences to trespass to goods; (*e*) ineffectual defences in conversion.

Chapter 24. Nuisance

1. Explain private nuisance and public nuisance.

2. What is a private nuisance and what factors are important when considering it?

3. What is meant by abatement of a nuisance? B uses a malodorous substance to manure his fields. At a public meeting he agrees to spray the substance on only once a month, but always chooses a day before a weekend. Advise A, who is unable to enjoy his garden.

4. Compare private and public nuisance. What defences are available to an action for private nuisance?

5. Write notes on *three* of the following: (*a*) the standard of comfort varies in private nuisance; (*b*) *Robinson v. Kilvert* (*1889*); (*c*) prescription;

(*d*) ineffectual defences in private nuisance; (*e*) *R. v. Maddox* (*1975*); (*f*) the forms public nuisance can take.

Chapter 25. Defamation

1. (*a*) Distinguish between a libel and a slander. (*b*) What defences are available when sued for defamation?

2. Explain, giving cases, what a plaintiff must prove to succeed in a claim for defamation.

3. Write notes on *two* of the following defences in defamation: (*a*) justification; (*b*) fair comment; (*c*) absolute privilege; (*d*) qualified privilege; (*e*) unintentional defamation; (*f*) apology.

4. Explain the differences between libel and slander. What is meant by innuendo?

5. What do you understand by the defences of absolute and qualified privilege in defamation?

Chapter 26. Miscellaneous Torts

1. Explain the tort of conspiracy. A and B, the employees of C, join a union to seek wage increases for themselves and their fellow employees. The resulting strike seriously affects C's business, not so much by the disruption it causes but by the publication of the wages paid to employees, which are abysmally low. Advise C.

2. A has been misled by B into purchasing shares in a company which subsequently collapsed. He has now discovered that A's statements were made the day after a crisis board meeting which A had attended in which the possible voluntary liquidation of the company was discussed. Before the discussion could be completed by a further meeting the company became insolvent. Advise A.

3. Distinguish between defamation and injurious falsehood. G, whose business has suffered by unfair adverse criticism in a magazine which confused his product with one with a similar name, is seeking damages for injurious falsehood. What would be the measure of damages in such a case?

4. J advertises a blend of synthetic alcohols and home-brewed wine as 'Scotch Heather Whisky'. A firm of Scottish whisky distillers markets a brand of Scotch whisky under the brand name 'Purple Heather'. What actions might they be able to bring against J?

Chapter 27. Property

1. What is property? What is ownership? What is possession?

2. List the different types of property and give three examples of each.

3. What is the difference between a legal interest in land and an equitable interest in land? In your answer refer to (*a*) rights of way; and (*b*) the deposit of deeds with a bank as security for a loan.

4. (*a*) What is a lease? (*b*) What is a covenant in a lease? (*c*) Tailor, who makes made-to-measure suits, buys the lease of shop premises with living accomodation above. A clause in the lease requires the lessee to live over the premises, and not to use the domestic part of the premises for trade purposes. Advise Tailor, whose wife does not like the arrangements and who would like to expand his business by employing several apprentices.

5. State the case for and against do-it-yourself conveyancing of business premises.

Appendix 2
Glossary of Terms

ab initio	from the beginning
actio personalis moritur cum persona	a personal action dies with the person
ad litem	with respect to a suit at law
administrator cum testamento annexo	administrator with the will annexed (which the court appoints him to administer)
administrator durante minor aetate	administrator during infancy (of the true appointee)
administrator pendente lite	administrator during the litigation (of a disputed will)
animus manendi	the intention to remain in that place or country
animus revocandi	the intention to revoke
audi alteram partem	hear the other side
bona fide	in good faith
bona vacantia	ownerless property
caveat emptor	let the buyer beware
certiorari	to be informed (an order of *certiorari* is explained on page 304)
cestui que trust	the person for whose benefit a trust is created; a beneficiary
chattels personal	personal goods
chattels real	a lease, forming part of personalty
chose in action	a thing in action; a personal right of property which can only be claimed or enforced by an action at law and not by taking physical possession
chose in possession	a thing that is the subject of physical possession (contrast with chose in action)
consensus ad idem	mutual agreement on the same point
cujus est solum ejus est usque ad coelum	the owner of land owns all the land below the surface and all the space above the land

cum testamento annexo	with the will attached
Curia Regis	the King's Court
cy-près	so near; as nearly as possible
damnum sine injuria	damage without legal wrong
de facto	existing in fact
del credere	in the belief that (the buyer is solvent)
delegatus non potest delegare	one to whom power has been delegated cannot delegate that power to another
de minimis non curat lex	'the law takes no notice of trifles'
de novo	anew
distress damage feasant	the right of an occupier of land to seize animals doing damage thereon
donatio mortis causa	a gift in anticipation of death
durante minore aetate	during infancy
ejusdem generis	of the same kind, or nature
equitas sequitur legem	equity follows the law
escrow	a sealed writing delivered conditionally, which condition being performed it operates immediately as a deed
estoppel	a rule of evidence whereby a party is precluded by some previous act to which he was party or privy from asserting or denying a fact. For example, a party cannot aver that a state of things is different from what he has led the other party to believe if the other party has acted upon such belief and changed his position to his detriment
ex gratia	as a matter of favour
ex nudo pacto non oritur actio	a bare promise (without consideration) does not give rise to any action
ex officio	arising from an official position, by virtue of his office
ex parte	on the application of. (An *ex parte* hearing is one at which only one side is represented.)
ex post facto	after the event
expressio unius est exclusio alterius	the express mention of one thing implies the exclusion of another
ex turpi causa non oritur actio	no action arises out of a base cause
ibid. = *ibidem*	in the same place
ignorantia juris haud excusat *ignorantia juris neminem excusat* *ignorantia juris non excusat*	ignorance of the law excuses no one
in consimili casu	in similar case to

in extremis	in imminent peril of death
in personam	against a person (as distinct from the whole world)
in pari delicto potior est conditio possidentis	where two parties are equally in the wrong, the condition of the possessor is the stronger
in pari delicto potior est conditio defendentis	of two wrongdoers it is better to be the defendant
in re	in the matter of
in rem	against a thing; a right *in rem* is a right in property such as land which is good against the whole world
in terrorem	as a threat, to cause fear
indenture	a deed to which there are two or more parties
injuria sine damno	legal wrong without damage
inter alia	among other matters
inter se	among themselves
inter vivos	during life
just accrescendi	right of survivorship
jus tertii	the right of a third party
laches	delay, e.g. in pursuing a remedy at law
lex loci contractus	the law of the place where the agreement was made
mandamus	we command (an order of *mandamus* is explained on page 304)
Magnum Concilium	the Great Council
mens rea	guilty mind
mesne	intermediate
nec per vim, nec clam, nec precario	peaceably, openly and as of right
nemo dat quod non habet	no one can give what he does not have
nemo iudex in causa sua	no one shall be a judge in his own case
non est factum	'not my act'
noscitur a sociis	the meaning of a word can be gathered from its context
novus actus interveniens	a new development intervening (to change the legal situation)
obiter dicta	sayings by the way
overt	open
pendente lite	during the litigation
per incuriam	by oversight (of a judge)
per se	by itself, by *or* through himself
per subsequens matrimonium	by subsequent marriage

per capita	by the number of individuals
prima facie	at a first view
puisne	lesser in importance
pur autre vie	for another's life
quantum meruit	as much as he has deserved
quasi	as if, as it were
quid pro quo	a mutual consideration; tit for tat
qui facit per alium facit per se	he who does a thing through another does it himself
ratio decidendi	the reason for the decision
res	thing
res extincta	the thing having ceased to exist
res ipsa loquitur	'the thing speaks for itself'
res sua	the thing being his own property
restitutio in integrum	restoration to the original position
sans recours	without recourse
sciens	knowing
scienti non fit injuria	one who knows cannot be harmed
seisin	effective possession of land by a freeholder
sic utere tuo ut alienum non laedas	so use your own property as not to injure your neighbour's
sine die	without fixing a day
stare decisis	to stand by past decisions
status quo	the state in which a thing exists
sue	to take proceedings in a civil action
sui juris	of full legal capacity
surrogate	deputy
tortfeasor	a person liable on a civil wrong other than a contractual or trust matter
trover	an early form of conversion in which a finding (*trover*) of the goods was alleged
uberrimae fidei	of the utmost good faith
ubi jus ibi remedium	where there is a right there is a remedy
ubi remedium ibi jus	where there is a remedy there is a right
ultra vires	beyond the powers of
viva voce	by word of mouth
volens	willing
volenti non fit injuria	no wrong can be done to one who consents to what is done

Appendix 3
Table of Cases

Appendix 4
Table of Statutes

Index